Interactive Whiteboards for Education:
Theory, Research and Practice

Michael Thomas
Nagoya University of Commerce & Business, Japan

Euline Cutrim Schmid
University of Education Heidelberg, Germany

INFORMATION SCIENCE REFERENCE

Hershey · New York

Director of Editorial Content:	Kristin Klinger
Director of Book Publications:	Julia Mosemann
Acquisitions Editor:	Lindsay Johnston
Development Editor:	Christine Bufton
Publishing Assistant:	Sean Woznicki
Typesetter:	Deanna Zombro
Quality control:	Jamie Snavely
Cover Design:	Lisa Tosheff
Printed at:	Yurchak Printing Inc.

Published in the United States of America by
Information Science Reference (an imprint of IGI Global)
701 E. Chocolate Avenue
Hershey PA 17033
Tel: 717-533-8845
Fax: 717-533-8661
E-mail: cust@igi-global.com
Web site: http://www.igi-global.com/reference

Library of Congress Cataloging-in-Publication Data

Interactive whiteboards for education : theory, research, and practice / Michael Thomas and Euline Cutrim Schmid, editors.
    p. cm.

 Includes bibliographical references and index.
 Summary: "This book contributed to the debate about the importance of research-based studies in the field of educational policy making in general and learning technologies, particularly the use of interactive whiteboards for education"--Provided by publisher.

 ISBN 978-1-61520-715-2 (hardcover) -- ISBN 978-1-61520-716-9 (ebook) 1. Interactive whiteboards. 2. Visual education. I. Thomas, Michael, 1969- II. Schmid, Euline Cutrim, 1969-
 LB1043.5.I645 2010
 371.33'466--dc22
                            2009046557

British Cataloguing in Publication Data
A Cataloguing in Publication record for this book is available from the British Library.

Editorial Advisory Board

Table of Contents

Section 1
Theory and Research

Part 1
Mapping the Field

Part 2
Classroom Research

Section 2
Practice

Part 3
Professional Development

Part 4
Teacher Perspectives

Afterword

Detailed Table of Contents

Section 1
Theory and Research

Part 1
Mapping the Field

Chapter 1

Dave Miller, Keele University, UK
Derek Glover, Keele University, UK

There has been considerable case study research into the installation and initial training for the use of IWB hardware and software. There now exists an extensive body of literature charting the gains from the use of this technology in presenting ideas and motivating students. Less has been written about the subsequent stage where pedagogy is modified as a result of the availability of higher levels of interactivity. This chapter provides a literature review that considers these major areas of research as well as reporting on studies of micro aspects such as gesture and the use of artifacts in a classroom context.

Chapter 2

Gemma Moss, University of London, UK
Carey Jewitt, University of London, UK

This paper explores why interactive whiteboards were rapidly adopted as an educational technology in England, and what lessons can be learnt from their early adoption. We draw attention to the different ways in which the technology adapts to existing practice in classrooms and argue that this is an inevitable consequence of the process. The pedagogic potential of the technology can in fact only emerge in this way. By reflecting on the history of interactive whiteboards in English schools, their emergence as a focus for policymakers' interests and their use in classrooms, this paper will consider to what extent the technology can lead to real pedagogic change.

This chapter discusses discourses commonly adopted within the literature in researching and referring to the presence and use of the interactive whiteboard in English primary classrooms. Four main forms of discourse are noticeable: transformation, affordance, orchestration and participation – with the latter two commonly occurring together. The adopted discourse can be seen to be influenced by the funding, curricular and policy context, as well as the theoretical context in which the research is framed. This chapter does not suggest that the discourses replace each other, but that the emphasis has shifted from focusing on the power of interactive whiteboard technology, to the power of the tool when in the hands of teachers and learners.

Intended for all those involved in producing and publishing resources for interactive whiteboards, this chapter is especially aimed at authors and editors working with educational publishers. It highlights the issues faced by all those involved in formulating digital publishing strategy and examines these from organizational, creative, production and commercial standpoints. The chapter also considers the emerging role of the teacher as a digital materials writer and the implications for educational publishing in the digital age.

Part 2
Classroom Research

This chapter contrasts the rhetoric of UK government policy driving the implementation of ICT in the compulsory education sector with teachers' working conditions within that sector. It refers to a small number of case studies of individual teachers to suggest that the popularity of the interactive whiteboard, particularly in Modern Foreign Language lessons, is mainly due to its potential for enhancing teacher control over lesson content and behaviour while reducing teacher/pupil conflict. These findings could well be seen to subvert government rhetoric about the power of ICT in education.

This chapter presents the findings from the first large-scale pilot project of the integration of interactive whiteboards in primary or elementary schools in the UK. The evaluation investigated the impact of IWBs on patterns of classroom interaction, teacher and student perceptions and on tested attainment in literacy and mathematics. Findings indicate that the use of the interactive whiteboards led to significant changes in teachers' practices in the use of technology and in aspects related to classroom interaction. Moreover, the perceptions of the participants were overwhelmingly positive vis-à-vis the technology. Nevertheless, the impact in terms of students' actual attainment on national tests was very small and short-lived.

This chapter presents an in-depth case study of one expert UK science teacher using the IWB to support "active learning" about the process of photosynthesis in secondary students over six lessons. Our focus is on the pedagogy underlying his practice and we document the strategies he used in exploiting the powerful functionality of the technology along with other digital resources. The methodology was one of collaborative video review and theory building undertaken by the practitioner, his colleague and two researchers. The study culminated in an interactive multimedia resource designed to support wider professional development.

This chapter offers a case study of the introduction of interactive whiteboard technology into the mathematics department of one school in the UK. It explores the context for successful introduction and accommodation of change. Moreover it highlights the importance of effective and available professional development that can help teachers to move from technical proficiency to pedagogic change as the effectiveness of interactivity is explored and put into practice.

Chapter 9

Karen Swan, University of Illinois at Springfield, USA
Annette Kratcoski, Kent State University, USA
Jason Schenker, Kent State University, USA
Mark van-'t Hooft, Kent State University, USA

This chapter reports on a study of the effects of the use of interactive whiteboards on student achievement in mathematics and language arts. The study compared achievement test scores between classes whose teachers used whiteboards and those whose teachers did not in grades three through eight in a small city school district in northern Ohio in the United States. Findings showed significant but meaningless effects for mathematics, and no significant difference for language arts. However, within group comparisons of the frequency and characteristics of use between whiteboard teachers whose students scored above the means on standardized tests and teachers whose students scored at or below the means revealed interesting differences. The results suggest that the use of interactive whiteboards can enhance student learning of mathematics and reading/language arts when teachers use them in a manner that takes advantage of their unique capabilities.

Chapter 10

Diana Bannister, University of Wolverhampton, UK
Andrew Hutchinson, University of Wolverhampton, UK
Helen Sargeant, University of Wolverhampton, UK

This chapter looks at the use of Learner Response Systems (LRS) and electronic voting devices within primary and secondary classrooms across the UK. The authors describe the development and research of the REVEAL Project (Review of Electronic Voting and an Evaluation of uses within Assessment and Learning). The chapter presents the Response Technology Pyramid, a model of implementation for both new and existing users of Learner Response Systems.

Section 2
Practice

Part 3
Professional Development

Chapter 11

Julie Cogill, King's College London, UK

This chapter is based on the IWB practice of 11 primary school teachers researched over the course of one year. The chapter first examines pedagogical theory, then, using empirical evidence from IWB practice a model for IWB pedagogy is proposed. Teaching behaviors which exemplify changes in pedagogical practice as a consequence of IWB use are set out across three levels: making practice more efficient, extending pedagogy, and transforming pedagogy. Finally, implications for teachers' professional development and further research are identified.

Chapter 12

This chapter argues that approaches to the design of training programs which may be valid in other contexts could prove inappropriate as a means of developing expertise in the use of digital IWB technology. By analyzing success factors identified from teacher and pupil interviews and video-recorded lessons observed during evaluations of implementations in the UK, the chapter suggests that the acquisition of technical skills and the adaptation of pedagogy are typically developed in tandem over a period of time. The term "Transformative Personal Development" (TPD) is used to describe a process whereby, following an induction that demonstrates the full repertoire of possibilities, participants with an initially limited grasp of the necessary technical skills, engage in work-based learning to develop their competence through a process of active experimentation, ideally working collaboratively with one or two colleagues in a "nuclear" Community of Practice.

Chapter 13

This chapter identifies competencies required by language teachers who want to exploit interactive whiteboards while utilizing a socio-cognitive approach to communicative language teaching. Moreover, it outlines a series of principles for the design and implementation of IWB technology training, which would best assist the teachers in achieving a successful outcome. The research data derive from a study conducted with English teachers using interactive whiteboards at a secondary school in Germany.

Part 4
Teacher Perspectives

A large number of UK secondary classrooms are now equipped with IWBs. This study considers the use of the IWB to support the teaching of Modern Foreign Languages. The impact of the IWB on learning is viewed from the pupils' perspectives. The study explores a range of features offered by the IWB and looks at how they can be used in the effective teaching of grammar. The findings suggest that IWB enhanced lessons have significant appeal to the pupils and a direct influence on their learning.

Chapter 15

Brenda Lim-Fong, University of British Columbia, Canada
Rebecca Robins, David Livingstone Elementary School, Canada

This chapter details a Canadian elementary school's journey using a "bottom-up" approach to implementing and integrating interactive whiteboards as part of its daily practice. Using an action research model, participants engaged in a process of inquiry to document their experiences of integrating interactive whiteboards in the classroom. Livingstone staff members have worked to create a more collaborative learning community that resulted in a shift from traditional pedagogy to a more co-constructed learning environment. The outcomes of this project have not only been a practical and meaningful form of professional development but have also strengthened the way students learn within a democratized classroom.

Chapter 16

Doris de Almeida Soares, Brazilian Naval Academy & Pontifical Catholic University
of Rio de Janeiro, Brazil

This case study describes the use of Promethean interactive whiteboard technology as a support for the development of two collaborative projects with a group of pre-adolescents in a language school in Rio de Janeiro, Brazil. The case focuses on the use of technology to enhance motivation and learner autonomy in a student-centered context. Findings indicate that the students view the use of IWBs as leading to increased levels of motivation in the classroom, especially in contexts where teachers adopt less of a centralized approach.

Chapter 17

Miriam Judge, Dublin City University, Ireland

This case study investigates the introduction of interactive whiteboards in Irish Schools based on a pilot project initiated by an innovative ICT Advisor. It is an example of a "bottom-up" initiative as the project received neither government funding nor support. The case study researched teacher and student reactions to IWBs and found that they were positively received by both parties. Despite the apparent success with IWBs in the pilot schools a policy vacuum still exists in Ireland in relation to the deployment of IWBs nationally. This situation could create a situation where schools are unequipped to deal with the challenges posed by the technology as IWB penetration increases. It could also have digital divide implications.

Afterword

Stephen Bax, University of Bedfordshire, UK

This chapter considers the possible role of the interactive whiteboard in education in the future. It summarizes the "normalization hypothesis" on sociotechnical change which suggests that only when a technology has become "normalized" so that we use it without even noticing it, as a natural part of our educational practice, has it reached its proper place. Reviewing what other contributors to this volume have suggested in terms of the place of the IWB in education, it concludes that although the technology is not yet fully normalized in our practice, if we take account of certain central factors, research others, and expect the technology perhaps to evolve over time, it appears likely that some modified form of IWB might become normalized in education in our future practice.

Foreword

What do Mexico and the UK have in common, at the time of writing, which is relevant to this book? The answer is that in both countries interactive whiteboards (IWBs) have become an integral part of classroom life. Although the situation is very different elsewhere, it seems likely that IWBs will become a familiar feature in schools across the world.

The large-scale implementation of IWBs in British schools began without a clear conception of what teachers would make of them and how their use could help good practice. In other words, the introduction of this expensive piece of equipment was "technology-led" (happening because the technology was available and politically attractive) rather than "education-led" (happening because it was known to meet the professional needs of teachers and the educational needs of students better than what was already available). Instead of evidence of their value, there was only political rhetoric about the wonders of new technology, with unsupported claims that IWBs would (and should) transform teaching. Research on the introduction of computers into schools tells us that a technology-led mode of introduction can create serious problems, especially regarding teachers' enthusiasm for using the technology.

However, there is something special about IWBs, which may explain why they have had quite a positive reception from teachers. The IWB is the only mainstream digital technology that has been developed with a classroom situation in mind (as compared with the hand-me-down technologies which schools have been given in the past). Even on first observing an IWB being used by an experienced teacher, it quickly becomes apparent that it is potentially a very useful tool for classroom education. It allows images, texts and sounds to be selected, saved, displayed, moved and modified in ways that conventional classroom display technologies cannot – and yet you can write on it too. It can be networked with other ICT equipment, such as web-linked computers, scanners and laptops operated by children in the class. In fact, the IWB is not really one educational tool, but rather a hub for the use of many.

There might therefore appear to be no problems with the introduction into schools of the IWB, because of its apparently good fit with the demands of classroom life. But like any tool, or toolkit, the IWB can be used well or badly. It has no powers of alchemy; it cannot transform poor pedagogy into good. We need to know more about how it can be used in a wide range of real-life situations, to pursue different educational goals. This book offers what we need in that respect. The chapters within it describe systematic studies of the IWB in use, in the context of practical, educational concerns. From across the continents, the authors explore the relationship between the affordances of IWB technology and the aims of education. I would encourage everyone involved in the introduction and use of IWBs to read this book. Only a good understanding of the use of this educational tool can ensure that teachers and their students gain the most benefit from it.

Neil Mercer
University of Cambridge, UK

Neil Mercer is Professor of Education and Fellow of Hughes Hall at the University of Cambridge, having previously been Professor of Language and Communications at the Open University, UK. He is a psychologist with particular interests in the development of children's language and reasoning, classroom dialogue and the use of digital technology in schools, who has worked closely with teachers and researchers in several countries. His most recent books are Words and Minds: How We Use Language to Think Together and (with Karen Littleton) Dialogue and the Development of Children's Thinking.

Preface

In a well-publicized speech in June 2009, the Governor of California outlined plans to replace commercially available textbooks with digital or eBooks. While Governor Schwarzenegger argued that this new policy reflected the importance of the digital revolution in education, namely that today's "digital native" (Prensky, 2001) learners should have new technologies in the classroom as much as in their social lives, his opponents interpreted it as a political stunt to cut much-needed expenditure from California's budget deficit. In this example, as in many others related to educational ICTs, reflection on the importance of developing teachers' awareness of how to use digital technologies is usually an afterthought rather than a structuring principle. Echoing the name of the education policy introduced in 2001 in the United States, "No Child Left Behind" (NCLB), it is equally important in today's digital age, where short-term fixes such as the one described above are often the norm, to underline the need for an education policy that is also aimed at continuing professional development for educators. Such a policy, we recommend, could be called "No Teacher Left Behind" (NTLB).

While the large-scale introduction of eBooks is still some way off, the interactive whiteboard has been perhaps the most significant learning technology to have received widespread attention and financial support over the last decade. This book is one of the first collections of research-based papers to consider the integration of interactive whiteboards in educational institutions around the world and includes chapters focusing on England, Wales, Germany, Canada, Brazil, the United States and Ireland. As such it responds to the increasing availability and recognition of digital technologies in the educational sphere (Beetham & Sharpe, 2007), while also emphasizing the importance of professional development, credible educational research and a dialogue between teachers, administrators, policymakers and learners to guide and inform the process of technology integration in education.

Typically fixed to a wall or mounted on a portable stand, interactive whiteboards provide a touch-sensitive digital display connected to a computer and data projector. The surface of the board can be written on with a special pen or finger and software applications from the attached computer can be displayed and manipulated by teachers and learners, either at the board or remotely with the aid of wireless devices such as voting pods or slates. The "interactivity" indicated by the name has given rise to two vastly different interpretations. Advocates suggest that the board establishes increased collaboration between teachers and learners underpinned by constructivist pedagogy. Detractors on the other hand, see the centrality of the board at the front of classrooms as re-establishing a transmission-based approach. This difference of perspective reinforces the point made by many of the contributors in this book, namely that it is teachers who are responsible for pedagogy rather than technologies.

Since the late 1990s the UK government has made substantial funding available for educational institutions across the age spectrum to improve their ICT infrastructure. It has also made ICT competence a necessary element in granting Qualified Teacher Status (QTS). One of the most visible signs of ICT funding in the UK has been the presence of interactive whiteboards in primary and secondary school classrooms, as well as to a far lesser extent in further and higher education, where they are mostly used in teacher training. Totaling approximately £330 million, the UK government's investment in ICT between 2002 and 2005 resulted in approximately 80% of primary schools having four or more IWBs, while 90% of secondary schools have almost 11 on average (Becta, 2006). Following the British lead, President Vincente Fox made a declaration to provide 145,000 IWBs and data projectors to state primary and secondary schools in Mexico in 2005. By 2006, the British Council had purchased approximately 350 IWBs for use in its English language teaching centers around the world (Wightman, 2006, p. 10). In addition to the UK and South America, numerous other national and international projects involving IWB technologies have emerged during this period, particularly in South Africa, China, the Middle East, Australia, and to a lesser extent, North America.

One characteristic many of the early IWB projects in the UK had in common was that the introduction of the technology preceded substantive research. Putting technology before pedagogy is not of course a new development, as anyone familiar with the history of educational technology from radio, through educational television to the microcomputer knows (Cuban, 2001). Interactive whiteboards have once again proven that far from being a solution to real pedagogical problems, educational ICTs have become a political football, promoted by a range of commercial and government interests, with teachers and learners left with the task of figuring out what to do with them long after they have been installed. One of the major problems with the "install first and understand later" philosophy is precisely the question of professional development, and that is why it is a major concern in this book.

Advocates of the technology have positioned IWBs in the history of learning technologies as the latest in a long line of devices aimed at transforming pedagogy. Swept along by their discourse of "transformation" and interactive whiteboard "magic" (Betcher & Lee, 2009), they have at times obscured any modest influence the technology has had or may have in the future. Critics, on the other hand, interpret IWBs as the latest example of an "oversold and underused" technology (Cuban, 2001), which does little to improve interactivity or enhance learning (Dudeney, 2006). These critics see it as an elitist tool that does more to widen the digital divide than close it. In this guise, IWBs reflect little more than the short term posturing of national governments that want to see an instant transformation in education without addressing the underlying problems of their own educational systems, such as large class sizes or meaningful professional development for teachers.

The integration of IWBs can also be situated in a much wider context, when we understand that the growing presence of ICTs in education over the last two decades has been the result of an increasing awareness by national and international policymakers of the need to prepare students for 21st century literacy skills (Lankshear & Knobel, 2007; Solomon & Schrum, 2007). Today's students and educators are living in the "information revolution" (Lankshear & Knobel, 2007) or "network society" (Castells, 2000) reflecting the transition to a globalized economy facilitated by digital technologies. The term ICT incorporates two aspects of the changing worldview associated with the network society. One is easy access to or an increasing overabundance of information. The second is the emphasis on communication. The investment by governments in digital technologies reflects the growing realization that students' ICT literacy skills have to develop in order for national economies to remain competitive in an increasingly interconnected world. Where once such a rationale was clear for more vocational disciplines and training purposes (mathematics and science), now it is equally applicable to a range of subjects in the humanities, including for example, language education, where IWBs have received a great deal of interest (Cutrim Schmid, 2007, 2008).

Since the early part of the twentieth century, numerous reasons have been advanced to establish a rationale to introduce new technologies into the classroom, many of which have been influential in relation to IWBs to date. Cuban's (1986) historical study of the classroom use of technology since 1920 in the United States identified a recurrent logic of "constancy and change" driving the process. Through this "fickle romance" between educators and technology, as he refers to it (Cuban, 1986, p. 4), educational institutions have also aligned themselves with the discourses of "social efficiency" and "social mobility" to provide a "rationale for [supporting] economic competitiveness" (Cuban, 2001, p. 10). The race to provide the latest technologies in the classroom goes well beyond the needs of "tech-savvy" teachers and reflects the importance of government policymaking and the prevailing market philosophy. A coalition of technology advocates, drawn from commercial providers of equipment to policymakers, to those seeking to bridge the digital divide of access, as well as classroom "missioners" (see Chapter 1, this volume), are driven by the "belief that if technology were introduced to the classroom, it would be used; and if it were used, it would transform schooling" (Cuban, 2001, p. 13). Davis and Karpatri (2005) have summarized these discourses, which have been active in shaping the reception of educational ICTs in general and IWBs in particular:

1. *ICT is strongly related to socio-economic competitiveness.* ICT promotes literacy skills essential for the 21st century and therefore has major implications for curriculum development in education.
2. *The use of ICT to enhance educational outcomes.* Research is often undertaken *after* the introduction of the ICT rather than before in a way which would have shaped its direction. While many studies exist, findings are mixed, and often unreliable in terms of more widely applicable conclusions.
3. *ICT can be used to improve access to education.* It can be used to provide access to educational materials and opportunities which would normally be denied to people with a range of physical, mental or learning difficulties.
4. *ICT is a driver of change.* It can be used to produce or initiate innovative changes in education and society.

During the initial stages of IWB integration in the UK context, they were seen as symbols of the transition to the global economy; they were considered essential to communicate with a new generation of learners; the technology was often aimed at technology schools in disadvantaged areas to address issues of social and technology equity in education; and they promised a new style of innovative classroom learning. Based on these framing discourses, and seen from the perspective of this book, it is possible to identify three stages in the reception of IWBs in the UK, a chronology that may be beneficial for educators from other countries to understand, as the technology becomes more international.

In its educational reforms, the New Labour government emphasized the need to increase the amount of whole class interaction, particularly in relation to young children with the aim of improving standards of attainment. In order to reach this aim, the National Literacy Strategy (NLS) was launched in 1998 and the National Numeracy Strategy (NNS) followed in 1999. Smith et al. (2004) and Kennewell and Morgan (2004) draw attention to the fact that a conflict was created between this drive for higher levels of attainment in literacy and numeracy and a more general focus on the development both of ICT skills and of greater autonomy in learning.

In the initial stages of integration as the technology emerged, there was a focus on small-scale case studies examining pupils' and teachers' perceptions, mostly conducted by practitioners whose predisposition was typically strongly in favor of the technology. Most of the research on the educational use of IWB technology in this phase was done in primary schools, as this was the context in which IWBs emerged (Burden 2002; Kennewell & Morgan, 2004; English et al., 2002; Burns & Myhill, 2004).

From approximately 2003 onwards a new phase can be dated in which reports funded by government agencies were published, and the focus shifted to the analysis of classroom use and more importantly the implications for pedagogical practice (Becta, 2003, 2004, 2006). During this stage the relationship between whole class teaching and higher levels of interactivity was widely questioned (English et al., 2002; Burns & Myhill, 2004; Smith et al., 2004; Hargreaves, 2003). Smith et al. (2004) for instance, pointed out that there was a lack of empirical evidence showing that whole class teaching was more interactive in the sense of promoting quality dialogue and discussion. Therefore, several authors (Smith et al., 2004; Hargreaves, 2003) set out to investigate patterns of whole class interaction in the literacy and numeracy lessons in order to find out if these lessons are genuinely "interactive". They argued that, although teachers have been obliged to use interactive whole class teaching, very little information on its meaning and almost no training programs on how to implement it have been provided for teachers.

Latterly, these research reports gave rise to the first wave of academic publications that culminated in the special edition on IWBs in the journal *Learning, Media and Technology* in 2007 edited by Kennewell and Higgins. This book continues this recent engagement with the subject, agreeing with Rudd (2007) who argues, it is now time to move the debate away from questions about whether IWBs are inherently "good" or "bad" technologies, and to engage with more appropriate questions concerned with "the optimum conditions for effective use; the factors that may support such use; the aspects that may influence future developments; as well as the types of evidence needed that will enable us to implement appropriate changes" (p. 1).

In addressing these issues, research on the use of IWBs during the third stage of reception still presents a mixed picture. On the one hand, it seems to support the technology's potential to improve and extend learning practices; provide better clarification and display facilities; model difficult concepts; increase attention spans and improve student focus; encourage greater tactile connection between learners and the learning environment; and develop "theatrical tension" by captivating learners (Kennewell & Beauchamp, 2007; Smith et al., 2005; Moss et al., 2007). Alternatively, other studies indicate that IWBs can be used to impede student control and reinforce the centrality of the teacher (e.g. Gray et al, 2007; Cutrim Schmid, 2008). Furthermore, the mere introduction of the technology does not guarantee an enhanced learning environment. The presence of IWBs can represent opportunities for teachers to use information in more effective ways, primarily in terms of organization and management, however this does not automatically suggest that the learning environment for students will be enhanced. The role of the teacher, his or her knowledge of the technology and how to use it, will be the most important factors in determining if successful progress can be identified and supported.

In the context of these differing viewpoints, Moss et al.'s (2007) assertion that, "the introduction of an IWB does not in and of itself transform existing pedagogies" (p. 5), is a warning that perhaps ought to be stamped on all new learning technologies rather like a government health warning. Such a more modest approach would emphasize the role of learning technologies like IWBs as tools to be used by teachers rather than vice versa and would not overemphasize their inherent "transformative" potential.

The integration of interactive whiteboards in classrooms around the world over the last decade provides a fascinating case study of the current state of pedagogy and increasingly interventionist role adopted by governments in directing education policies and national curricula. Unlike the previous books on interactive whiteboards which deal primarily with technical issues (Barber et al., 2007; Braham, 2006; Gage, 2004) or provide overly enthusiastic and uncritical accounts of the technology characterized by a missionary zeal (Betcher & Lee, 2009), this book attempts to consolidate the attempts to move discussion on the subject to a new stage. By including chapters from many of the most prominent researchers on the subject of IWBs to date, we hope that the book will make a contribution to the debate about the importance of research-based studies in the field of educational policy making in general and learning technologies in particular. Although much of the book deals with the UK provenance of IWBs, it is clear that over the last five years the technology has become increasingly international. The book should also be of value then to educators around the world who are looking for a context to understand where they are and where IWB technology can take them in the future.

AN OVERVIEW OF THE CHAPTERS

The book is divided into two main sections, "Theory and Research" and "Practice", each consisting of two parts. Part 1 - Mapping the Field, focuses on an overview of existing research in the field and begins with a detailed and wide-ranging literature review (Miller & Glover, Chapter 1). This focus is developed via a discussion of what can be learned from policy issues related to the early integration of IWBs in UK schools (Moss & Jewitt, Chapter 2), and the identification of a series of organizing discourses of "transformation, orchestration and participation" which mediated the integration process (Twiner, Chapter 3). Finally, a fascinating overview of the field of digital publishing is provided in Chapter 4 (Russell), which highlights the increasing importance of the role of teachers as writers of digital materials.

Part 2 - Classroom Research, consists of six chapters each examining influential research-based studies on classroom learning environments in the compulsory sector from leading IWB researchers. This section of the book responds to the need for research that investigates the impact of IWB on pedagogical practice and learning outcomes. Furthermore, many of the chapters provide detailed descriptions and analyses of lessons in which interactive whiteboards were used, and have a clear reference to the rationale underlying the pedagogical activities. Gray (Chapter 5) discusses the danger of IWB technology being used to support teacher-centered approaches to language teaching, while providing insights into the political and policy forces that helped shape the use of the technology in the English educational system. Higgins (Chapter 6) adds an interesting discussion on the challenges faced by research that investigates the impact of technology use on learning outcomes. The chapter points out, for instance, that although the findings obtained in the second year of the study indicated that the overall impact of technology use on standards was negligible, "it may also be that the introduction of the technology was beneficial for learning, but the indicators used to assess outcomes did not capture the changes that resulted". Hennessy et al. (Chapter 7) identified several pedagogical strategies that have been used by science teachers to harness the functionality of IWBs. Miller and Glover (Chapter 8) analysed changed pedagogy among maths teachers, highlighting the trajectory of IWBs from a presentational and motivational support tool to one which provides the basis for more effective conceptual and cognitive learning by students. Their findings are especially useful for informing teacher training in the area of mathematics teaching. Swan et al. (Chapter 9) investigated the impact of IWB use on learning outcomes in school-based research in the United States. In their conclusion, they highlight the importance of identifying indicators to assess the impact of technology on learning, an issue that needs to be discussed more thoroughly in the literature in the future. Bannister et al. (Chapter 10) provides the only full-length chapter focusing on the use of learner response systems (LRS) in connection with IWBs. Drawing on literature on LRS in education and data collected in a UK school to develop a model of teacher development, the authors answer some important questions about how LRS should and could be used in learning contexts.

The first part (Part 3) of Section 2 - Professional Development, considers the importance of developing training programs for teachers involved in the integration and development of IWBs. All authors in this section highlight the importance of investment in teacher training and professional development as a key element for supporting the integration of IWB into the curriculum in a way that enhances learning. All three chapters discuss the analytical frameworks for the evaluation of teachers' use of IWB technology and models of training and professional development. They emphasize the importance of a) the provision of continuous technological and pedagogical support and b) the establishment of communities of practice (or small group collaboration) in helping teachers to further their professional development in this area. A detailed model of pedagogical change is outlined by Cogill (Chapter 11), while Haldane (Chapter 12) articulates strategies for the process of professional development called Transformative Personal Development (TPD). Cutrim Schmid and Schimmack (Chapter 13) consider the concrete aspects of a model of IWB technology training for language teachers that may have more widespread appeal to teachers from all disciplines.

Part 4 - Teacher Perspectives, contains four chapters reporting on a series of international case studies and research projects from teacher practitioners. Since the introduction of the IWB in schools numerous action research projects have been conducted by teachers and many communities of practice have been created. While our collection provides only a few examples of these numerous projects, we would like to underline their importance and value to research in the area. In Chapter 14 Bettsworth focuses on the use of IWB in the Modern Foreign Languages classroom with a case study based on students' use of the technology at Lancaster Girls' School in the UK. Lim-Fong and Robins (Chapter 15) provide an insightful account of the "bottom up" integration of IWBs in Canadian schools where teachers took the initiative to develop a framework for teacher support and development using new technologies. Soares (Chapter 16) analyzes the use of IWBs to support the implementation of podcasting projects in language schools in Brazil. Judge (Chapter 17) discusses the first large-scale project to incorporate IWBs in schools in Ireland, describing how teacher-led initiatives that receive no government funding can be successful. Finally, in the Afterword to the collection, Stephen Bax reflects on the possible futures of IWBs by elaborating on his influential discussion of normalization in CALL (Bax, 2003) and considering new hybrid forms of the technology.

Michael Thomas
Nagoya University of Commerce & Business, Japan

Euline Cutrim Schmid
University of Education Heidelberg, Germany

REFERENCES

Barber, D., Cooper, L., & Meeson, G. (2007). *Learning and teaching with interactive whiteboards: Primary and early years*. Exeter, UK: Learning Matters.

Bax, S. (2003). CALL – past, present and future. *System, 31*(1), 13-28.

Becta (2003). *What the research says about interactive whiteboards*. Coventry, UK: Becta. Retrieved February 22, 2009, from http://partners.becta.org.uk/page_documents/research/wtrs_whiteboards.pdf

Becta (2004). *Getting the most from your interactive whiteboard: A guide for secondary schools.*Coventry, UK: Becta. Retrieved February 22, 2009, from http://foi.becta.org.uk/content_files/corporate/resources/foi/archived_publications/getting_most_whiteboard_secondary.pdf

Becta (2006). *The Becta review 2006: Evidence on the progress of ICT in education.* Coventry, UK: Becta. Retrieved June 10, 2009, from http://becta.org.uk/corporate/publications/documents/The_Becta_Review_2006.pdf

Beetham, H., & Sharpe, R. (2007). *Rethinking pedagogy for a digital age: Designing and delivering e-learning*. London & New York: Routledge.

Betcher, C., & Lee, M. (2009). *The interactive whiteboard revolution: Teaching with IWBs*. Victoria, Australia: Acer Press.

Braham, G. (2006). *How to survive and succeed with an interactive whiteboard*. Cambridge, MA: LDA.

Burden, K. (2002). *Learning from the bottom up the contribution of school based practice and research in the effective use of interactive whiteboards for the FE/HE sector. Learning and Skills Research*. Paper presented at the Making an Impact Regionally Conference, The Earth Centre, Doncaster, UK.

Burns, C., & Myhill, D. (2004). Interactive or inactive? A consideration of the nature of interaction in whole class teaching. *Cambridge Journal of Education, 34*, 35-49.

Castells, M. (2000). *The rise of the network society. The information age: Economy, society and culture, Vol. I.* Cambridge, MA & Oxford, UK: Blackwell.

Cuban, L. (1986). *Teachers and machines: The classroom use of technology since 1920*. New York & London: Teachers College, Columbia University.

Cuban, L. (2001). *Oversold and underused: Computers in the classroom*. Cambridge, MA & London: Harvard University Press.

Cutrim Schmid, E. (2007). Enhancing performance knowledge and self-esteem in classroom language learning: The potential of the ACTIVote system component of interactive whiteboard Technology. *System, 35*, 119-133.

Cutrim Schmid, E. (2008). Potential pedagogical benefits and drawbacks of multimedia use in the English language classroom equipped with interactive whiteboard technology. *Computers and Education, 51*(4), 1553-1568.

Davis, N., & Karpatri, A. (2005, July). *What works and what does not? ICT and education research revisited.* Paper presented at the Symposium at the World Conference on Computers and Education, Stellenbosch, South Africa.

Dudeney, G. (2006). Interactive, quite bored. *IATEFL CALL Review*, Summer, 8-10.

English, E., Hargreaves, L., & Hislam, J. (2002). Pedagogical dilemmas in the National Literacy Strategy: Primary teachers' perceptions, reflections and classroom behaviour. *Cambridge Journal of Education, 32*(1), 9–26.

Gage, J. (2004). *How to use an interactive whiteboard really effectively in your primary classroom*. David Fulton.

Gray, G., Hagger-Vaughan, L., Pilkington, R., & Tomkins, S. (2007). Integrating ICT into classroom practice in modern foreign language teaching in England: making room for teachers' voices. *European Journal of Teacher Education, 30*(4), 407-429.

Hargreaves, L. (2003). How do primary school teachers define and implement 'interactive teaching' in the National Literacy Strategy in England? *Research Pages in Education, 18* (3), 217-236.

Kennewell, S., & Beauchamp, G. (2007). The features of interactive whiteboards and their influence on learning. *Learning, Media and Technology, 32*(3), 227-241.

Kennewell, S., & Morgan, A. (2004). *Student teachers' experiences and attitudes towards using interactive whiteboards in the teaching and learning of young children.* Retrieved June 10, 2008, from http://crpit.com/confpapers/CRPITV34Kennewell1.pdf

Lankshear, C., & Knobel, M. (2007). *New literacies: Everyday practices and classroom learning.* Maidenhead, UK: Open University Press.

Moss, G., Carrey, J., Levaaic, R., Armstrong, V., Cardini, A., & Castle, F., (2007). *The interactive whiteboards pedagogy and pupil performance evaluation: An evaluation of the schools whiteboard expansion (SWE) project: London Challenge.* Institute of Education: University of London.

Prensky, M. (2001). Digital natives, digital immigrants. *On the Horizon, 9*(5), 1-6.

Rudd, T. (2007). *Interactive whiteboards in the classroom.* Retrieved October 24, 2007, from http://www.futurelab.org.uk/events/listing/whiteboards/report

Smith, F., Hardman, F., Wall, K., & Mroz, M. (2004). Interactive whole class teaching

in the national literacy and numeracy strategies. *British Educational Research Journal, 30*, 395-411.

Smith, H. J., Higgins, S., Wall, K., & Miller, J. (2005). Interactive whiteboards: Boon or bandwagon? A critical review of the literature. *Journal of Computer Assisted Learning, 21*(2), 91-101.

Solomon, G., & Schrum, L. (2007). *Web 2.0: New tools, new schools.* Eugene, OR: International Society for Technology in Education.

Wightman, B. (2006). The future of interactive whiteboards in ELT. *IATEFL CALL Review*, Winter, (pp. 8-12).

Section 1
Theory and Research

Part 1
Mapping the Field

Chapter 1
Interactive Whiteboards:
A Literature Survey

Dave Miller
Keele University, UK

Derek Glover
Keele University, UK

ABSTRACT

This chapter reviews the literature that has charted the progress of the use of interactive whiteboards within schools, predominantly within the UK. It is concerned, firstly, with the way in which change is introduced, managed and supported. The literature has also shown the progress from presentation and motivation issues to a consideration of the pedagogic possibilities of the integration of the interactive whiteboard in teaching situations. This involves an understanding of interactivity in educational contexts. This chapter also investigates the value for money issues implicit in the use of technology in pedagogic change and considers discussions related to technology and educational effectiveness.

INTRODUCTION

This is not a unique literature survey. Higgins et al. (2007), Cuthell (2007) and Glover et al. (2005), among others, have considered the emerging research literature into interactive whiteboard use and established typologies of introduction and use, developed the research rationale for classroom practice and pointed to the need for pedagogic change to accommodate the affordances offered by the technology. Smith et al. (2005) offer a more critical review of the literature pointing to the methodologi-

cal problems arising from considerable case-study research of a narrative nature which is frequently less than objective when undertaken by teachers who are convinced of the potential of IWBs. Slay et al. (2008) suggest that within developing countries there may be greater economy through the use of a data projector and screen than by using IWB technology. Our literature review makes no methodological judgments but draws on the growing body of published research in the various areas related to IWBs as a background to understanding trends in the practice and pedagogy of interactive learning. It follows the introduction of new technology into schools and colleges and looks at the way in

DOI: 10.4018/978-1-61520-715-2.ch001

which some teachers and researchers move from its use to enhance presentation and motivation to awareness of the need for changed pedagogic approaches.

Interactive whiteboard systems were developed experimentally in the 1980s largely in higher education law and medical faculties in the United States using an approach from the commercial world (Greiffenhagen, 2002; Murphy et al., 1995; Armstrong et al., 2005; Passey, 2006). Within two decades their use has spread throughout all sectors of education around the world. Most of the early commentators on IWBs (see for example, Greiffenhagen, 2000) begin with a description of the systems involved reflecting the need to inform readers of the technology. Later writers such as Hennessy et al. (2007) update this approach with an element of evaluation as follows:

Interactive whiteboard systems comprise a computer linked to a data projector and a large touch-sensitive board displaying the projected image; they allow direct input via finger or stylus so that objects can be easily moved around the board ('drag and drop') or transformed by teacher or students. They offer the significant advantage of one being able to annotate directly onto a projected display and to save the annotations for re-use or printing. The software can also instantly convert handwriting to more legible typed text and it allows users to hide and later reveal objects. Like the computer + data projector alone, it can be used with remote input and peripheral devices, including a visualiser or flexible camera (e.g. to display and annotate pupils' paper-based work or experimental results), slates or tablet PCs. (p. 2)

The technology may have become part of the information and communication technology armoury of schools but research into the way in which it has been introduced offers pointers for those seeking to introduce new technologies in general. Glover and Miller (2002) in consider-

ing the introduction of change within a local authority, a secondary school and five primary schools, identified three main types of user: "missioners", who were convinced of the potential of the technology; "tentatives", who were ready to consider change; and "luddites", who, for a variety of reasons, refused to accept or use the technology. At the same time Burden (2002) suggested an alternative process approach with three stages: "infusion", when a small number of teachers become interested in using the technology; "integration", when more become involved and attempt to extend its use; and "transformation", when the technology impacts on teaching. Cuthell (2006, 2007) extends this analysis by examining the process of changing practice working from an iterative stage where teachers do the same thing but in different ways, through the development of innovative materials and approaches, to changes in student and teacher collaborative working. As the use of the technology has been more widely accepted, associated research into effective use has moved from purchase and use, to pedagogy and classroom practice. This transition has been traced by Cuthell (2007), who notes the progression from the pioneer phase (Smith, 1999; Gerard et al., 1999; Levy, 2002; Goodison, 2002), through the larger scale studies of enhanced effectiveness (Beauchamp & Parkinson, 2005; Stein, 2005; Cuthell, 2005a, 2005b), to the development of enhanced interactivity and pedagogic change (Higgins et al., 2005; Miller & Glover, 2006a; Cuthell & Preston, 2007).

TECHNICAL ISSUES

The potential of IWB use - and hence the willingness of teachers to use it as classroom equipment - was based on a number of affordances, or more simply, tools of the technology (Kennewell, 2001). Kennewell and Beauchamp (2007), summarize research evidence and suggest that the benefits of IWBs spring from their suitability for whole class teaching, their use in demonstrations and displaying concepts, and their consequent value in meeting the needs of a wide range of students through the varied presentation of ideas and the use of multimedia approaches. The authors present a strong evidential case for IWB use as a means of capturing and sustaining student attention utilizing a wide variety of approaches, from written text to diagrams and the use of online websites.

The literature has also been concerned with the practicalities of use and this aspect of installation often appears to have been neglected at the purchase stage. Smith et al. (2005) have considered the problems inherent in the installation of IWB facilities for optimum use. Investigations by Tameside MBC (2003), Bell (2001), Miller et al. (2008) and Smith (2001), included the importance of establishing a clear line of sight, and the avoidance of direct sun on the board and hazardous wires in the room. Other concerns of this nature are related to board height, especially where primary age children are likely to be users, but this may be too low to allow teachers access to software menus (Canterbury, 2003). Practicalities include the size of the screen in relation to the room (Smith, 2001), the avoidance of dust on the projector lens (Levy, 2002) and problems where the IWB is moved from room to room or to different places within the room thus necessitating a need for re-calibration. Levy (2002) reported that where access to IWB facilities required pre-booking of either equipment or a teaching room, teachers would be less ready to explore their use. Glover and Miller (2001) and Greiffenhagen (2000) envisaged permanent access as a pre-requisite for effective pedagogic development.

That said, the installation of permanent boards in a greater proportion of rooms in schools minimizes such problems. Beyond this, however, users point to occasional but significant problems inherent in the equipment that can lead to malfunctions, which can only be remedied by access to adequate technical support (Miller et al., 2008), and which require a higher level of mentoring within a pattern

of continuing professional development (Selwood & Pilkington, 2005; Miller et al., 2008). These aspects of course also have extra costs involved. Although there may be initial costs in the time taken for teachers to prepare for IWB use (Glover & Miller, 2002), Starkman (2006) in a report on installations district wide in Ontario, Canada, showed that teachers were saving time through using laptops for lesson preparation thus making resources immediately available for IWB use.

Currently the cost of equipment and conversion is about £1,800 per room (a maximum cost that can be lower according to the specification of the equipment). Glover and Miller (2003, 2005) have shown how willingness to purchase and develop the technology within schools is related not only to attitudes to change but also to the comparative power of each group of participants. Where subject teachers, and headteachers responsible for school resourcing, are inclined to adopt a "missioner" position early, widespread purchase is more likely, and vice versa. The culture of the school with regard to ICT generally is a further factor in acceptance (Glover & Coleman, 2005). Passey (2002) suggests that IWBs can only be adopted where all stakeholders including governors and parents are aware of the rationale for their introduction and support a positive culture which recognizes a commitment for a long period of time. Nevertheless, Kent (2006) describes an unsatisfactory process of installation, such that teacher attitudes became negative during the developmental phase. It would seem that planned installation with strong emphasis on teacher motivation and competence development is an essential pre-requisite for the achievement of the pedagogic potential of the equipment.

ENHANCED PRESENTATION AND MOTIVATION

Initial gains in the classroom are related to the presentational and motivational qualities inherent in the technology. Research is essentially drawn from small-scale observation but shows the many factors that contribute to effective IWB use. In a review of the use of IWB resources by nearly 100 teachers, Cuthell (2003), comments on the opportunity for the use of a range of teaching styles:

> *There are consistent comments that have been made regarding changes in student learning: that students are able to participate in lessons more easily; that teaching in 2 and 3 dimensions facilitates understanding and that support for a wider range of learning styles is identified as an important contribution that the boards make to the classroom environment. The 'fun' element has returned to the classroom. (p. 6)*

A number of researchers, including Buckinghamshire (2002), Austin (2003), Jamerson (2002) and Ekhami (2002) through to Blanton (2008) and Branzburg (2008), comment on the gains in flexibility and versatility stemming from a whiteboard revolution and point to the motivational force when students are interested in their work. The ability to recall previous work saved as personal files and to use these for revision, reinforcement and subsequent time-saving development is seen as one of the more attractive features for the teacher despite time required in setting up materials (Walker, 2002; Miller et al., 2005; Dillenbourg & Traum, 2006). Kennewell and Beauchamp (2007) and Kennewell (2001) suggest that the benefits of IWBs spring from their suitability for whole class teaching, their use in demonstrations and displaying concepts, and their consequent value in meeting the needs of a wide range of students through the varied presentation of ideas and the use of multimedia approaches. The authors present a strong evidential case for IWB use as a means of capturing and sustaining student attention utilizing a wide variety of approaches, from written text to diagrams and the use of online websites.

Wall et al. (2005) and Smith et al. (2005) examined the ways in which students reacted to IWB presentations. Wall et al. (2005) do, however, report pupil frustration when there are technical difficulties and when the teacher is the sole IWB user. Graham (2003), Beastall (2006) and Bayliss and Collins (2007) show how lessons can be developed so that the interest of disaffected or "switched-off" children can be enhanced through the use of a range of visual devices, such as responding to invitations to use the board, and gains from stepped learning. Moss et al. (2007) also note these features as the possible basis of some improved attainment. Carr (1999) considers the whole class use of the IWB while Blane (2003) deals with motivation in the primary classroom; Clemens et al. (2001) describes the gains from the IWB when used in learning enhancement for slower learners, and Blanton and Helms-Breazeale (2000) describe attempts to enhance motivation through the use of technology to help those with special needs and literacy learning problems. All of this research points, however, to a seamless move from using presentational advantages through motivation to the development of resources to enhance the process of learning, though this does not always occur.

FROM PRESENTATION TO INTERACTIVITY

The emerging evidence from recent research into the use of interactive whiteboards in the United Kingdom highlights the need for a pedagogic change from a didactic to an interactive approach to learning and teaching, and from the use of the IWB as a visual support for lessons to the integration of the technology into lesson planning and delivery. This has been explored at length by, among others, Cuthell (2004), Miller et al. (2005a, 2005b), and Davison and Pratt (2003). Greiffenhagen (2000) has also shown that the use of the technology as an adjunct rather than as an integrated element in teaching minimizes interaction and matching of teaching to learning needs. McCormick and Scrimshaw (2001) developed this point further in their analysis of the contribution of ICT to pedagogic change in teaching mathematics and their contention is that teaching can only be enhanced if interactivity between pupils and teachers is understood and integrated into teaching approaches. There has been concurrent research into learning approaches and Jones and Tanner (2002) offer evidence to show that interactivity is most effectively sustained through effective questioning as well as a wider range of activity (see also Miller et al., 2008). Simpson et al. (1998), Cogill (2003), Robison (2000) and Damcott et al. (2000) demonstrate the use of interactive technology with diverse ability groups. They stress the need for changed approaches to teaching to optimize the teaching and learning value of the technology. But what are the necessary changes? Cuthell (2003) summarizes the situation where, despite some transformation of teaching approaches, outside observers still see students at desks. He continues:

The dichotomy, then, is between those teachers who feel that learning is interactive and has been transformed, and outside observers, who cannot see much transformation or interactivity. It may well be that teachers who report a transformation in the learning process, more involved and interactive students and more effective learning outcomes are using a previous pre-IWB base for their comparison. It should also be borne in mind that these teachers are making comparisons in the context of working with a prescriptive curriculum, and that the IWBs provide them with ways in which to be creative, make teaching more effective and learning more fun. (p. 12)

Interactivity as a concept is at the heart of change. Miller et al. (2008) note that even with the widespread use of IWBs in England in mathematics classrooms that presentational uses of the

IWB still dominate and cites the use of the IWB as a textbook rather than a learning tool and of teacher concern with presentation rather than the teaching potential. Other observers have raised concerns that the IWB could be an expensive piece of equipment which is then underused.

Kennewell (2001) argues that effective use is only possible if students themselves make regular use of the IWB or else they will revert to being passive learners. Overall the research literature indicates that effective learning is possible where teachers have been convinced of the value of the technology and fully understand the nature of interactivity and its pedagogic implications. Smith et al. (2005) summarize this mainly positive literature emanating from research with teacher and student users but caution that "such technology should be used in unique and creative ways above and beyond that which is possible when teaching with normal whiteboards or other projection methods" (p. 99).

In researching the introduction of IWBs in two secondary schools in Sheffield in the UK, Levy (2002) outlines the way in which activity based learning is adopted as a pedagogic approach and then developed as teachers become aware of the advantages of demonstration, a reduction in the time spent in preparing teaching materials, the use of a greater range of information resources and the possibility of independent learning through the use of internet links. She noted that teachers then move to recognize that time is freed for interaction and task-related activity, and for the presentation and discussion of a variety of ideas with more effective explanations and an enhancement of learning. Once these potential gains are recognized even the less competent teachers are attracted to the technology.

Cuthell (2003) has summarized a number of case studies of IWB use and argues that where the equipment has been introduced after staff consultation and discussion, effective basic training and sensible installation, teachers then work through gains in presentation and quickly move to integrate the resource in all their teaching. Competence leads to confidence. However, Reedy (2008) has investigated the use of PowerPoint programs as the basis of easily prepared materials for classroom use. He echoes the findings of Miller and Glover (2004) and of Higgins et al. (2005) that dependence on a single program which becomes a textbook on the board inhibits the optimum use of the IWB as both a presentational and pedagogic device.

THE NATURE OF INTERACTIVITY

As teachers become more fluent in their use of the technology and recognize the link to pedagogic change the IWB becomes the focus of changed approaches. The nature and implementation of interactivity are explored by many authors who seek methods of easing the transition from didactic to active approaches. These are illustrated in literature concerned with the development of generic or subject specific techniques. Damcott et al. (2000) measure the gains from a greater visualization of concepts, Murphy et al. (1995) analyze the methodology required for student use of IWB based data, Nonis and O'Bannon (2001) deal with the requirements of pupil questioning to maximize board use and involvement where the IWB becomes the focus of the lesson, and Olive (2002) outlines techniques to foster an active style of teaching and learning based upon constructivist principles so that conceptual learning contributes to cognitive understanding. Haldane and Somekh (2005) reflecting on IWB use in primary schools offer a progression from foundation, through formative and facility levels to fluency and flying as a description of the movement to a pedagogy of interactivity. Cuthell (2005a, 2005b) offers four elements in approaches to interactivity: ostensiveness, whereby learning is enhanced by imagery; ludic elements building on the elements of fun and games; visualization of concepts through the use of colors, movement and sequential development; and bricolage defined as the ability of teachers to think creatively about the way in which they

use resources. For Wood and Ashfield (2008) the teacher as mediator is shown in gains in the pace of lessons but they stress that this also depends on the way in which both teacher and students have technological competence and the ability to use resources in a creative way.

Such changes do, however, require marked changes of teacher attitude. For Davison and Pratt (2003) this involved an appreciation of learning styles and their use as the basis of lesson planning. Current evidence at both primary and secondary levels (Smith et al., 2006; Glover et al., 2004; Glover et al., 2005) points to a reluctance on the part of many teachers to do other than use the interactive whiteboard as a visual textbook in the same way lesson by lesson. As a result pupil boredom once again inhibits understanding and achievement and the potential for changed approaches is lost. To overcome this there is an awareness on the part of agencies and professional associations of the need for effective professional development to support enhanced use of the interactive whiteboard as shown by Becta (2004), Bayliss and Collins (2007) and Miller et al. (2008). Gibson (2001) posits that the interface between technology and pedagogy is marked by the "construction of knowledge", through activity and freedom of physical and intellectual movement (p. 42). This is expressed in collaborative enquiry and the critical review of ideas and concepts with the technology as a tool rather than tutor prompting "access to information, expert communications, opportunities for collaboration, and a medium for creative thought, expression and knowledge creation" (p. 42).

There is considerable evidence that as teachers gain confidence and competence in working with the new technology they also seek changes to the way in which they teach – so called "Eureka" moments (Becta, 2003, 2004; Beeland, 2002). But as Miller and Glover (2007) show the development phase has been longer for some staff than others and some staff will not necessarily move beyond this phase. Those who do achieve fluency in IWB use attempt to integrate concept and cognitive development in a way that exploits the interactive capacity of the technology.

This progression accords with the stages identified by McCormick and Scrimshaw (2001). They suggest that teachers move from the use of technology as an efficiency aid to an extension device and then finally as a transformative opportunity. Hennessy et al. (2007) also develop the idea of expert teachers working with an integrated approach by using the IWB to set challenges, build representations, prompt the evaluation of ideas, encourage speculation, and then turning students' ideas into formal presentations, thus encouraging student independence. But all of these new ideas require a high level of interaction. Jones and Tanner (2002) stress that there is a need to move beyond the representational use of the IWB, through questioning, to whole class interaction which requires much more flexible and responsive reaction by teachers so that student observation and discussion can be accommodated. Miller et al. (2008) extend this in mathematics with their notion of "at the board, on the desk, in the head" which they summarize as follows:

an interactive way of working with the IWB so that all lesson activities are integrated into an interactive (rather than a didactic or presentational) whole and orchestrated/facilitated using the IWB software as the means of storing and organising all the electronic resources for the lesson. ... A typical lesson will have pupils interacting with the teacher, the IWB and with each other. (p. 2)

They then recommend that in order to help this:

there is a need for a further range of IWB resources to be developed that reflect the nature of interactivity. These materials should be developed to offer, for example, practical activities together with a variety of 'interesting', 'enthusing' and/or inspirational starting points with indications of

the way in which they might be used, and include direct links to further internet sources and the New Mathematics Curriculum for 2008 onward. (p. 3)

These ideas can be seen as a development of the work of Ernest (1994) who, in developing increasingly interactive approaches in teaching, suggests an elementary typology to describe the role of the teacher. The teacher as "instructor" is concerned with the presentation of concepts as rules followed by practice, whereas the teacher as "facilitator" is concerned with approaches that enhance understanding. At the highest level is the teacher as "mediator" where, using the work of Tinzmann et al. (1990), there is a bridge between pupil understanding and subject development. Miller et al. (2005) have suggested that as competence improves, mathematics teachers, in particular, become more ready to develop and use manipulations (drag and drop; hide and reveal; the use of color, highlighting and shading etc.) as the basis of interaction. The effective use of these supports the role of teacher-as-mediator. It is also possible that some manipulations might lend themselves more easily to mathematical activities as defined by Watson and Mason (2002). Miller at al. (2005) point to the need for effective use of questioning to support the learning process and offer an approach based upon Bloom's (1956) taxonomy of learning so that students are led from recall to analysis, synthesis and evaluation of data. This has considerable implications for appropriate professional development activity.

Structured questioning as a feature of interactivity also requires willingness on the part of teachers and learners to indulge in dialogic approaches. Alexander (2008) defines this as "the power of talk to stimulate and extend childrens' thinking, learning and understanding" (p. 8). The IWB can be a powerful tool in this as recalled by Birmingham et al. (2002) who charted dialogic interaction, Bourne and Jewitt (2003) who examined the multi-modal nature of IWB associated discourse, and Armstrong et al. (2005) who noted the role of the teacher as mediator in this process. John and Sutherland (2005) summarize the potential for change thus:

The power of the IWB and its range of affordances clearly helped teachers improve the quality of their presentations, create more purposeful interactions, and increase the efficiency of knowledge transfer, all within a multi-modal environment. In fact, IWBs offered an adaptive solution to the tension between individual and common knowledge in a classroom and where they could counteract the emergence of too much 'idiosyncratic knowledge' (p. 411)

Such changes will involve the adaptation and integration of other associated technologies such as voting pads and slates but it is possible that we should pay greater attention to the way in which gesture is used by teacher and student at the board. The use of gesture is related to the "taken and shared ways in which a classroom community reasons, symbolises and argues" (Cobb & Yackel, 1996, p. 176). Multiple communication (Williamson, 2005), and the wide range of body language used in classroom interaction (Kendon, 2000; Miller and Glover, 2006b).

IMPACT

The impact of introducing new technology has been charted at both classroom and school level in case studies and wider surveys. Politicians have sought evidence that the use of scarce resources has been beneficial but the evidence is slow in coming and methodologically difficult. Recent work by Roythorne (2006) and Greenfield (2006) has stressed the importance of the use of IWB techniques including electronic flipcharts, software programs and internet access as factors in enhancing pupil motivation and through this, understanding. Reedy (2005), Whittaker (2004)

and Ziolowski (2004) analyzed changed classroom practice in differing environments and separately concludes that IWB affordances have the potential to prompt changes but only if there is change in pedagogic practice. Starkman (2006) reports positively on the impact of the technology in 40 out of 53 schools within one school district in Canada where backed by effective professional development, and comparable work in schools within the Greater London area (Moss et al., 2007) indicates pedagogic gains although, as yet, limited impact on educational achievement. Smith et al. (2006) after observing 184 primary school lessons conclude that lessons have a faster pace and that discourse is affected by interactive whiteboard use but that the impact on attainment is not yet proven. Shaw (2006) echoes similar views after observation of 122 primary schools, while Greenfield (2006) suggests that investment has been made without proper understanding of changed thinking and learning.

Somekh et al. (2007) analyze two substantial data sets with approximately 2000 primary school pupils. The schools were visited twice in a longitudinal survey which adopted both a descriptive and multi-level modeling approach to ascertain the impact of IWB use as one of several factors affecting attainment. They noted overall gains in pupil motivation and behaviour and in deeper pedagogic thinking by teachers who now use the technology throughout the day rather than in isolated episodes. They suggest that a two-year familiarization period is needed before teacher competence allows creative approaches to interactivity to develop, and that expert teacher support is of value thereafter. At the same time they note the costs of sustaining provision, and the need for continuing professional development opportunities. In attainment terms although unable to be specific, they noted that:

where teachers had been teaching with the IWB for two years, and here was evidence that all children, including those with SEN [Special Educational

Needs], had made exceptional progress in attainment in national tests, a key factor was the use of the IWB for skilled teaching of numeracy and literacy to pairs or threesome of children. (p. 6)

Moss et al. (2007) reporting on IWB use within the London area in 30 secondary schools with 9,000 students cautioned that immediacy in attainment response was not applicable but, for a variety of reasons, were not able to provide evidence of impact on attainment because of the complexity of influences of student attainment, variation in pedagogic approaches and in the professional development offered to teachers.

DIVERSITY IN IWB USE

The use of the IWB varies according to the subject concerned and the potential it offers for the use of visual, auditory and kinaesthetic transmission of concepts and their link to cognitive development. John and Sutherland (2005) consider this in the inter-relationship of the pedagogy of a subject, the culture of the subject identified as its ecology, and the technology available for subject exposition and enhanced understanding. They argue that subject based software is part of a complex affected by the software designers' the teachers' intentions and the teachers' and students' perceptions of how the technology can be used. This is evident in the case studies which offer glimpses of subject use.

Glover et al. (2007) outline research into the teaching of mathematics and modern foreign languages (MFL) and attempt to identify good practice. This accords with the model of enhanced interactivity described earlier. There is some difference between the use of IWBs in different academic subjects. The range is shown with interactivity being driven by the use of vocabulary and through pictures and sound in MFL, and in providing examples and illustration of process and understanding in mathematics. That said there

is evidence of the link between presentational gains and changes in teacher attitudes as they seek to use the affordances of software – more readily in mathematics where more commercial material is available. Gray et al. (2007) identifies the presentational techniques in MFL teaching but found little evidence of transformation in teaching approaches. Cutrim Schmid (2008) outlines the integration of internet resources into English language teaching where voting systems have encouraged student participation and offers some evidence of attainment gain in the pursuit of specified objectives.

Hennessey et al. (2007) focus on the way in which IWB technology has been developed by science teachers. Following observation of "expert" teachers in a variety of learning situations they concluded that there was further need for making connections which built on prior learning e.g. through re-visiting annotated slides; providing opportunities for students to express conceptions in non-verbal and visual ways; developing higher order questioning; increasing opportunities for prediction, interpretation and reflection, and flexibly moving between resources. In all of these areas the socio-cultural interactions within the classroom were seen as essential so that the emphasis shifts to participative learning. This is also reflected by Preston and Mowbray (2008) in considering conceptual and cognitive development in kindergarten science where the IWB has been used as a microscope, internet link and recording medium.

In a summary of subject based case studies Hennessey et al. (2006) show how teachers make differing use of associated technology with CD-ROMs, internet links, PowerPoint presentations, and data projectors all offering the ability to mix oral, visual and auditory resources to support conceptual development. Baker (2007) demonstrates the use of IWBs in music teaching where the potential of internet links and music software for adding pace and understanding is increasingly exploited.

PROFESSIONAL DEVELOPMENT

Professional development is fundamental to competence, confidence and the appropriate use of IWB technology and begins in the initial teacher training stage. Although only limited research has yet been published in this area, Kennewell and Morgan (2003) in a review of potential opportunities of IWB use for all teachers point to the need for teachers to appreciate interactivity, size and visibility, accessibility, and recordability as a basis for effective teaching. After investigation of the gains from IWB use in research schools they concluded that effective use follows initial IWB training before the first school placement so that student teachers are prepared for the use of software and hardware as well as their own ability to develop materials. Allen (2004) sees this initial training as including the use of the virtual pen, highlighting, hide and reveal, and drag and drop with a move to an intermediate level of using the digital notepad and "talking" flipcharts. Hall and Higgins (2005) reporting on interviews with 72 teachers in training found that while there was general enthusiasm for the IWB and the difference it could make to teaching, there was also frustration where students lacked the ICT background or access to equipment once in schools.

In discussion, teachers in the induction phase using new ICT technology look towards a school wide policy that recognizes the need for individual technical and teaching support as exemplified by Lloyd and McRobbie (2005). Time spent in training has to be used effectively and Ganalouli et al. (2004) in recording teachers' perceptions of effective training stress similar needs. However, there are differences between ICT training which tends to be concerned with the computer as the medium, and IWB training. The latter usually offers technical competence in the use of computer software, and subject specific pedagogic training in the use of the IWB. The large-scale introduction of new IWB technology may lend itself to large group lectures and demonstrations by IWB suppliers but there is also a need for deeper subject specific pedagogic training to maximize the teaching and learning potential of the equipment.

There is little reported research into the way in which teachers adapt practice and pedagogy when given the opportunity to make use of IWBs in their classrooms (Glover et al., 2005). Broader research into teacher training for the use of aspects of information and communications technology in schools has led to the conclusion that school-based and essentially individualized support appears to offer the most effective way forward. This is exemplified in the work of Pearson (2003) in Australia, Charalambous and Karagiori (2002) in Cyprus, and Hannele (2003) in Finland. Despite the contextual diversity serving teachers included in these classroom, investigations favor support characterized by "hands-on" constructivist experience (Coupal, 2004; Polyzou, 2005); mentoring, whether by peers or advisory staff (Cuckle & Clarke, 2003); the use of materials underpinning the achievement of competence (Kirschner & Davis, 2003; Kirshner & Selinger, 2003; Bozhuisen & Woperis, 2003) and a shared learning experience (Levy, 2002; Triggs & John, 2004).

There are varying needs in developing programs of continuing professional development for IWB users. Smith et al. (2006) sum up professional development needs in the following way:

Teachers need extended opportunities to think through new ideas and try out new practices, ideally where they get feedback from a more expert practitioner and continue to refine their practice in collaboration with colleagues. Observation, coaching and talk analysis feedback may be useful tools for professional development. (p. 454)

While these approaches can underpin enhanced competence and confidence in technology use Miller et al. (2008) suggests that a schema for development should offer a Skills, Pedagogy, Opportunity, Reflection and Evolution (SPORE) model which moves from technology to an understanding of reasoning and planning so that teachers can use the IWB in a variety of interesting and creative ways. In so doing it creates (new) opportunities for pupils, as well as opportunities for reflection on what is occurring and the consequent evolution of changed approaches.

Miller and Glover (2007) looking at the most successful approaches when interactive whiteboards were being introduced into seven secondary schools, concluded that a model in which all members of a subject department working together was most likely to be successful.

CONCLUSION

The recurring themes of this literature survey highlight the movement from presentation-based didactic approaches to pedagogy to those based on interactivity and an awareness of the classroom as an integrated learning context. As a learning technology the IWB will only be of lasting significance in enhancing student attainment if teachers are prepared to change their teaching approaches to a more interactive mode. Without this change it is possible that the presentational advantages offered by IWBs will soon become commonplace and the potential for understanding and application will be lost, thus inhibiting progress in the long term (Smith et al., 2006; Greenfield, 2006).

In overcoming this Hughes and Longman (2005) argue for the existence of a "connectionist" classroom with the IWB linked to the internet, alongside digital slates or pads and additional networked PCs for individual or pair use. For success a heterarchic rather than hierarchic hardware installation is required so that the interactive whiteboard can function like a hub through which all other items of hardware and software run. This is essential for interactivity. Cutrim Schmid (2008) demonstrates this idea through the use of voting systems but counsels that relatively shallow learning may result where teachers have not structured the alternatives offered for voting decisions. Fry

and Hin (2006) show how wireless communication devices linked to IWBs could be used for peer coaching for groups in different schools marking a move to an intra classroom.

Kennewell (2006) in a review for the Australian Association for Research in Education argues that while teachers who are making good use of the IWB opportunities can make a difference to whole class and individual learning, there is a need to investigate the training and development work which is sufficient to create a critical mass of users within any school so that expert use becomes the norm. Further, he points to the possibility that the IWB is more suited to English-speaking educational cultures where dialogic approaches are encouraged. Barber (2008) also contends that more initial teacher education needs to be directed at both the process and pedagogy of IWB use.

Current research indicates that teachers need to develop competence to use both hardware and software in an integrated way so that the potential of IWB technology can be used to support interactive learning. Failure to do this will result in wasted resources but further research is needed to ascertain the actual rather than perceived impact of changed approaches on student learning. In the UK, Initial evidence suggests that this may be more readily achieved in the primary sector where the IWB is constantly in use rather than in secondary schools where there is great variation in both teacher attitudes and subject compatibility.

REFERENCES

Alexander, R. (2008). *Towards dialogic teaching: Rethinking classroom talk*. Thirsk, UK: Dialogos.

Allen, J. (2004). Getting interactive. *Secondary Education, 29*(6), 243–247.

Armstrong, V., Barnes, S., Sutherland, R., Curran, S., Mills, S., & Thompson, I. (2005). Collaborative research methodology for investigating teaching and learning: The use of interactive whiteboard technology. *Educational Review*, *57*(4), 457–469. doi:10.1080/00131910500279551

Austin, N. (2003, January 7). Mighty white. *The Guardian*. Retrieved November 10, 2008, from http://education.guardian.o.uk/elearning/story/0,869705,00.html

Baker, J. (2007). SmartBoard in the music classroom. *Music Educators Journal*, *93*(5), 18–19. doi:10.1177/002743210709300504

Barber, D. (2008). Learning and teaching with interactive whiteboards. *British Journal of Educational Technology*, *39*(3), 570. doi:10.1111/j.1467-8535.2008.00855_12.x

Bayliss, T., & Collins, L. (2007). *Invigorating teaching with interactive whiteboards: Case Studies 7-10*. Teaching Geography, Geographical Association.

Beastall, L. (2006). Enchanting a disenchanted child: Revolutionising the means of education using Information and Communication Technology and e-learning. *British Journal of Sociology of Education*, *27*(1), 97–110. doi:10.1080/01425690500376758

Beauchamp, G., & Parkinson, J. (2005). Beyond the wow factor: Developing interactivity with the interactive whiteboard. *The School Science Review*, *86*(316), 97–103.

Becta (2003). *What the research says about interactive whiteboards*. Retrieved February 22, 2009, from http://partners.becta.org.uk/page_documents/research/wtrs_whiteboards.pdf

Becta (2004). Getting the most from your interactive whiteboard: A guide for secondary schools. Coventry: Becta. Retrieved February 22, 2009, from http://foi.becta.org.uk/content_files/corporate/resources/foi/archived_publications/getting_most_whiteboard_secondary.pdf

Beeland, W. D., Jr. (2002). *Student engagement, visual learning and technology: Can interactive whiteboards help?* Paper Presented at the Annual Conference of the Association of Information Technology for Teaching Education, Trinity College, Dublin, Ireland.

Bell, M. A. (2001). Update to survey of use of interactive electronic whiteboard in instruction. Retrieved February 22, 2009, from http://www.shsu.edu/~lis_mah/documents/updateboardindex.htm

Birmingham, P., Davies, C., & Greiffenhagen, C. (2002). Turn to face the bard: Making sense of the three way interactions between teacher, pupils and technology in the classroom. *Education Communication and Information*, *2*(2-3), 139–161. doi:10.1080/1463631021000025330

Blane, D. (2003). The whiteboard's a whizz! *Times Educational Supplement*. Retrieved June 15, 2009, from http://www.tes.co.uk/article.aspx?storycode=383940

Blanton, B., & Helms-Breazeale, R. (2000). Gains in self-efficacy: Using SMART board interactive whiteboard technology in special education classrooms. Retrieved February 22, 2009, from http://smarterkids.org/research/paper2.asp

Blanton, P. (2008). Using interactive whiteboard to enhance student learning. *The Physics Teacher*, *46*(3), 188–189. doi:10.1119/1.2840991

Bloom, B. S. (1956). *Taxonomy of educational objectives*. Boston, MA: Pearson Education.

Bourne, J., & Jewitt, C. (2003). Orchestrating debate: A multimodal analysis of classroom interaction. *Reading, 37*(2), 64-72.

Bozhuizen, H. P. A., & Wopereis, I. G. J. H. (2003). Pedagogic benchmarks for information and communications technology in teacher education. *Technology, Pedagogy and Education, 12*(1), 149–159. doi:10.1080/14759390300200150

Branzburg, J. (2008). The whiteboard revolution. *Technology & Learning, 28*(9), 44. Retrieved February 22, 2009, from http://www.wright. edu/~marguerite.veres/SmartWorkshop/white-boardinfo.pdf

Buckinghamshire, L. E. A. (2002). *Developing the use of interactive whiteboards*. Retrieved 22, February 2009, from http://www.bucksict.org.uk/Effective/Whiteboards.htm

Burden, K. *(2002)*. Learning from the bottom up – the contribution of school based practice and research in the effective use of interactive whiteboards for the FE/HE sector. Learning and Skills Research – Making an Impact Regionally Conference. *The Earth Centre: Doncaster.*

Canterbury Christ Church University College (Faculty Learning Technology Team). (2003). *Briefing paper on the application of interactive whiteboards to learning and teaching*. Canterbury Christ Church University College, Learning and Teaching Enhancement Unit. Retrieved February 22, 2009, from http://www.canterbury.ac.uk/support/learning-teaching-enhancement-unit/publications/FLT-briefing-notes/interactive-whiteboards-briefing-note-non-cccuc.pdf

Carr, L. (1999). Bringing lessons to life. *Managing Schools Today*, *9*(1), 14.

Charalambous, K., & Karagiorgi, Y. (2002). Information and communications technology in-service training for teachers: Cyprus in perspective. *Technology, Pedagogy and Education, 11*(2), 197–215. doi:10.1080/14759390200200132

Clemens, A., Moore, T., & Nelson, B. (2001) Math Intervention. *SMART Project Research Report.* Retrieved November 17, 2008, from http://www.smarterkids.org

Cobb, P., & Yackel, E. (1996). Constructivist, emergent and socio-cultural perspectives in the context of developmental research. *Educational Psychologist, 31*(3/4), 175–190. doi:10.1207/s15326985ep3103&4_3

Cogill, J. (2003). The use of interactive whiteboards in the primary school: Effects on pedagogy. *Research Bursary Reports Coventry, Becta*. Retrieved February 22, 2009, from http://publications.teachernet.gov.uk/eOrderingDownload/DfES-0791-2003.pdf#page=54

Coupal, L. V. (2004). Constructivist learning theory and human capital theory: Shifting political and educational frameworks for teachers ICT professional development. *British Journal of Educational Technology, 35*(5), 587–596. doi:10.1111/j.0007-1013.2004.00415.x

Cuckle, P., & Clarke, S. (2003). Secondary school teacher mentors and student teachers views on the value of information and communications technology in teaching. *Technology, Pedagogy and Education, 12*(3), 377–391. doi:10.1080/14759390300200168

Cuthell, J., & Preston, C. (2007). An interactivist e-community of practice using Web 2:00 tools. In C. Crawford et al. (Eds.), *Proceedings of Society for Information Technology and Teacher Education International Conference* 2007 (pp. 2316-2325). Chesapeake, VA: AACE.

Cuthell, J. P. (2003). Interactive whiteboards: New tools, new pedagogies, new learning? Retrieved February 22, 2009, from http://www.virtuallearning.org.uk/2003research/whiteboards_survey.doc

Cuthell, J. P. (2004). Can technology transform teaching and learning? The impact of interactive whiteboards. In J. Price, D. Willis, N. Davis & J. Willis (Eds.), *Proceedings of SITE 2004*. Norfolk, VA: Association for the Advancement of Computing in Education.

Cuthell, J. P. (2005a). The Impact of interactive whiteboards on teaching, learning and attainment. In J. Price, D. Willis, N. Davis & J. Willis (Eds.), *Proceedings of SITE 2005* (pp. 1353-1355). Norfolk, VA: Association for the Advancement of Computing in Education.

Cuthell, J. P. (2005b). Seeing the meaning. The impact of interactive whiteboards on teaching and learning. In *Proceedings of WCCE 05*, Stellenbosch, South Africa.

Cuthell, J. P. (2006). Steering the supertanker: Transforming teaching and learning through the use of ICT computers in schools. *Technology Applications in Education, 23*(1-2), 99–110.

Cuthell, J. P. (2007). Ambassadors for ACTIV-learning. In R. Carlsen, K. McFerrin, J. Price, R. Weber & D. A. Willis (Eds.), *Proceedings of SITE 2007* (pp. 1443–1499) Norfolk, VA: Association for the Advancement of Computing in Education.

Cutrim Schmid, E. (2008). Using a voting system in conjunction with interactive whiteboard technology to enhance learning in the English language classroom. *Computers & Education, 50*(1), 338–356. doi:10.1016/j.compedu.2006.07.001

Damcott, D., Landato, J., & Marsh, C. (2000). *Report on the use of the SMART board interactive whiteboard in physical science*. Retrieved February 22, 2009, from http://smarterkids.org/research/paper3.asp

Davison, I., & Pratt, D. (2003). *An investigation into the visual and kinaesthetic affordances of interactive whiteboards. Report made to Becta.* Retrieved February 22, 2009, from http://publications.teachernet.gov.uk/eOrderingDownload/DfES-0791-2003.pdf#page=31

Dillenbourg, P., & Traum, D. (2006). Sharing solutions: Persistence and grounding in multimodal collaborative problem solving. *Journal of the Learning Sciences, 15*(1), 121–151. doi:10.1207/s15327809jls1501_9

Ekhami, L. (2002). The power of interactive whiteboards. *School Library Media Activities Monthly, 18*(8), 35–38.

Ernest, P. (1994). The impact of beliefs on the teaching of mathematics. In A. Bloomfield, & T. Harries (Eds.) (1994), Teaching and Learning Mathematics (pp. 62-72). Derby, UK: Association of Teachers of Mathematics.

Fry, J. M., & Hin, M. K. T. (2006). Peer coaching with interactive wireless technology between student teachers: Satisfaction with role and communication. *Interactive Learning Environments, 14*(3), 193–204. doi:10.1080/10494820600852969

Ganalouli, D., Murphy, C., & Gardner, J. (2004). Teachers perceptions of the effectiveness of ICT-competence training. *Computers & Education, 43*(1-2), 63–79. doi:10.1016/j.compedu.2003.12.005

Gerard, F., Greene, M., & Widener, J. (1999). *Using SMART board in foreign language classes*. Paper presented at Society for Information Technology & Teacher Education International Conference, San Antonio, TX.

Gibson, I. (2001). At the intersection of technology and pedagogy: considering styles of teaching and learning. *Journal of Information Technology for Teacher Education, 10*(1-2), 37–60.

Glover, D., & Coleman, M. (2005). School climate, culture and ethos: interchangeable or distinctive concepts? *Journal of In-service Education, 31*(2), 251–272. doi:10.1080/13674580500200359

Glover, D., & Miller, D. (2005). Leadership implications of using interactive whiteboards: linking technology and pedagogy in the management of change. *Management in Education, 18*(5), 27–30. doi:10.1177/089202060501800506

Glover, D., Miller, D., & Averis, D. (2004). Panacea or prop: The role of the interactive whiteboard in improving teaching effectiveness. In *Tenth International Congress of Mathematics Education*, Copenhagen. Retrieved February 22, 2009, from http://www.icme-organisers.dk/tsg15/Glover_et_al.pdf

Glover, D., Miller, D., Averis, D., & Door, V. (2005). The interactive whiteboard: A literature survey. *Technology, Pedagogy and Education, 14*(2), 155. doi:10.1080/14759390500200199

Glover, D., Miller, D., Averis, D., & Door, V. (2007). The evolution of an effective pedagogy for teachers using the interactive whiteboard in mathematics and modern languages: an empirical analysis from the secondary sector. *Learning, Media and Technology, 32*(1), 5–20. doi:10.1080/17439880601141146

Glover, D., & Miller, D. J. (2002). Running with technology: The pedagogic impact of the large-scale introduction of interactive whiteboards in one secondary school. *Journal of Information Technology for Teacher Education, 10*(3), 257–278.

Glover, D., & Miller, D. J. (2003). Players in the Management of Change: introducing interactive whiteboards into schools. *Management in Education, 17*(1), 20–23. doi:10.1177/08920206030170010701

Goodison, T. A. (2002). *Looking in classrooms* (8th ed.). New York: Addison Wesley.

Graham, K. (2002). *Switching on switched off children*. Bolton, UK: Promethean.

Gray, C., Pilkington, R., Hagger-Vaughan, L., & Tomkins, S. A. (2007). Integrating ICT into classroom practice in modern foreign language teaching in England: Making room for teachers voices. *European Journal of Teacher Education, 30*(4), 407–429. doi:10.1080/02619760701664193

Greenfield, S. (2006). How will we nurture minds of the future? *Times Educational Supplement*, (4684): 21.

Greiffenhagen, C. (2000). *Interactive whiteboards in mathematics education: Possibilities and dangers*. Paper presented at the working group on The Use of Technology in Mathematics Education held at the 9th International Congress on Mathematical Education, Tokyo, Japan.

Greiffenhagen, C. (2002). *Out of the office into the school: Electronic whiteboards for education*. Retrieved February 22, 2009, from ftp://ftp.comlab.ox.ac.uk/pub/Documents/techreports/TR-16-00.pdf

Haldane, M. (2003). Real-time lesson observation: Using technology in teacher training to learn about technology in the classroom. *Learning and Teaching in Action, 2*(3), 15–18.

Haldane, M., & Somekh, B. (2005). *A typology of interactive whiteboard pedagogies*. Paper presented at BERA 2005, University of Glamorgan, UK.

Hall, I., & Higgins, S. (2005). Primary school students perceptions of interactive whiteboards. *Journal of Computer Assisted Learning, 21*(2), 102–117. doi:10.1111/j.1365-2729.2005.00118.x

Hannele, N. (2003). Towards a learning society in Finland: Information and communications technology in teacher education. *Technology, Pedagogy and Education, 12*(1), 85–103. doi:10.1080/14759390300200147

Hennessy, S., Deaney, R., & Ruthven, K. (2006). Situated expertise in integrating use of multimedia simulation into secondary science teaching. *International Journal of Science Education, 28*(7), 701–732. doi:10.1080/09500690500404656

Hennessy, S., Deaney, R., Ruthven, K., & Winterbottom, M. (2007). Pedagogical strategies for using the interactive whiteboard to foster learner participation in school science. *Learning, Media and Technology, 32*(3), 283–301. doi:10.1080/17439880701511131

Higgins, S., Beauchamp, G., & Miller, D. (2007). Reviewing the literature on interactive whiteboards. *Learning, Media and Technology, 32*(3), 213–225. doi:10.1080/17439880701511040

Higgins, S., Clark, J., Falzon, C., Hall, I., Hardman, F., & Miller, J. (2005). *Embedding ICT in the literacy and numeracy strategies: Final Report*. Newcastle Upon Tyne, UK: Newcastle University.

Hughes, M., & Longman, D. (2005). *Interactive digital display boards and class teaching: Interactive or just another epidiascope*. Paper presented at BERA 2005, University of Glamorgan, UK.

Jamerson, J. (2002). *Helping all children learn: Action research project*. Retrieved February 22, 2009, from http://smarterkids.org/research/paper15.asp

John, P., & Sutherland, R. (2005). Affordance, opportunity and the pedagogical implications of ICT. *Educational Review, 57*(4), 405–413. doi:10.1080/00131910500278256

Jones, S., & Tanner, H. (2002). Teachers interpretations of effective whole-class interactive teaching in secondary mathematics classrooms. *Educational Studies, 28*(3), 265–274. doi:10.1080/0305569022000003717

Kendon, A. (2000). Language and gesture: Unity or duality . In McNeill, D. (Ed.), *Language and gesture* (pp. 47–63). Cambridge, UK: Cambridge University Press.

Kennewell, S. (2001). Interactive Whiteboards – yet another solution looking for a problem to solve? *Information Technology in Teacher Education, 39*, 3–6.

Kennewell, S. (2006). *Reflections on the interactive whiteboard phenomenon: A synthesis of research from the UK Swansea School of Education*. Australia: The Australian Association for Research in Education.

Kennewell, S., & Beauchamp, G. (2007). The features of interactive whiteboards and their influence on learning. *Learning, Media and Technology, 32*(3), 227–241. doi:10.1080/17439880701511073

Kennewell, S., & Morgan, A. (2003). *Student teachers experiences and attitudes towards using interactive whiteboards in the teaching and learning of young children*. Paper presented to Young Children and Learning Technologies Conference. Australia: Australian Computer Society Parramatta.

Kent, M. (2006). Our journey into whiteboard hell. *Times Educational Supplement*, (4703): 40.

Kirschner, P., & Davis, N. (2003). Pedagogic benchmarks for information and communications technology in teacher education. *Technology, Pedagogy and Education, 12*(1), 125–147. doi:10.1080/14759390300200149

Kirschner, P., & Selinger, M. (2003). The state of affairs of teacher education with respect to information and communications technology. *Technology, Pedagogy and Education, 12*(1), 5–17. doi:10.1080/14759390300200143

Levy, P. (2002). *Interactive Whiteboards in learning and teaching in two Sheffield schools: A developmental study*. Department of Information Studies, University of Sheffield.

Lloyd, M., & McRobbie, C. (2005). The whole approach: An investigation of a school-based practicum model of teacher professional development in ICT. *Journal of Educational Computing Research, 32*(4), 341–351. doi:10.2190/623G-MT8A-VC17-R1TA

McCormick, R., & Scrimshaw, P. (2001). Information and communications technology, knowledge and pedagogy. *Education Communication and Information, 1*, 37–57. doi:10.1080/14636310120048047

Miller, D., Averis, D., Door, V., & Glover, D. (2005a). *How can the use of an interactive whiteboard enhance the nature of teaching and learning in secondary mathematics and modern foreign languages?* Report made to Becta. Retrieved February 22, 2009, from http://partners.becta.org.uk/upload-dir/downloads/page_documents/research/bursaries05/interactive_whiteboard.pdf

Miller, D., Averis, D., Door, V., & Glover, D. (2005b). *From technology to professional development: How can the use of an interactive whiteboard in initial teacher education change the nature of teaching and learning in secondary mathematics and modern languages?* Training and Development agency, London. Report made to the Teacher Training Agency. Retrieved February 22, 2009, from http://www.ttrb.ac.uk/attachments/0d65acf3-488a-4fca-8536-918d6dafd694.pdf

Miller, D., & Glover, D. (2004). Enhancing mathematics teaching through new technology: The use of the interactive whiteboard, Summary of a report made to the Nuffield Foundation on completion of a funded two year project (April 2002–March 2004).

Miller, D., & Glover, D. (2006a). *Interactive whiteboard evaluation for the secondary national strategy: Developing the use of interactive whiteboards in mathematics, Final Report for the Secondary National Strategy*. Retrieved February 22, 2009, from http://nationalstrategies.standards.dcsf.gov.uk/node/97754

Miller, D., & Glover, D. (2006b). *Enhanced secondary mathematics teaching: Gesture and the interactive whiteboard*. Keele University BERA: Warwick. Retrieved February 22, 2009, from http://www.keele.ac.uk/depts/ed/iaw/docs/Bera06Enhanced%20secondary%20maths%20and%20gesture.pdf

Miller, D., & Glover, D. (2007). Into the unknown: The professional development induction experience of secondary mathematics teachers using interactive whiteboard technology. *Learning, Media and Technology, 32*(3), 319–331. doi:10.1080/17439880701511156

Miller, D., Glover, D., & Averis, D. (2005). Presentation and pedagogy: The effective use of interactive whiteboards in mathematics lessons. In D. Hewitt & A. Noyes (Eds), *Proceedings of the sixth British Congress of Mathematics Education held at the University of Warwick*, pp. 105-112. Retrieved February 22, 2009, from http://www.bsrlm.org.uk/IPs/ip25-1/BSRLM-IP-25-1-14.pdf

Miller, D. J., Glover, D., & Averis, D. (2008). *Enabling enhanced mathematics teaching: Final Report for the National Centre for Excellence in the Teaching of Mathematics*. Retrieved February 22, 2009, from http://www.keele.ac.uk/depts/ed/iaw/docs/ncetmreport/ncetmreport.pdf

Moss, G., Jewitt, C., Levacic, R., Armstrong, V., Cardini, A., & Castle, F. (2007). *The interactive whiteboards, pedagogy and pupil performance evaluation an evaluation of the schools whiteboard expansion (SWE) project: London Challenge*. London, DfES Research paper 816. Retrieved February 22, 2009, from http://www.dcsf.gov.uk/research/data/uploadfiles/RR816.pdf

Murphy, J. F., Jain, N. L., Spooner, S. A., Hassan, S. W., Schnase, J. L., & Metcalfe, E. S. (1995). Use of an interactive electronic whiteboard to teach clinical cardiology decision analysis to medical students. *Journal of the American College of Cardiology, 25*(2), 238A. doi:10.1016/0735-1097(95)92448-E

Nonis, A., & O'Bannon, B. (2001). *Technology and teacher preparation: Creating learning environments for increasing student involvement and creativity.* Retrieved February 22, 2009, from http://smarterkids.org/research/paper11.asp

Olive, J. (2002). Computer tools for interactive mathematical activity in elementary schools. *International Journal of Computers for Mathematical Learning, 5*, 241–262. doi:10.1023/A:1009813723928

Passey, D. (2002). *ICT and school management: A review of selected literature. Lancaster University.* Retrieved February 22, 2009, from http://partners.becta.org.uk/page_documents/research/ict_sm.pdf

Passey, D. (2006). Technology enhancing learning: Analysing uses of information and communication technologies by primary and secondary school pupils with learning frameworks. *Curriculum Journal, 17*(2), 139–166. doi:10.1080/09585170600792761

Pearson, J. (2003). Information and communications technologies and teacher education in Australia. *Technology, Pedagogy and Education, 12*(1), 39–58. doi:10.1080/14759390300200145

Polyzou, A. (2005). Growth in teachers knowledge while learning to teach with multimedia: What has been learned from concrete educational experiences? *Technology, Pedagogy and Education, 14*(2), 205–223. doi:10.1080/14759390500200202

Preston, C., & Mowbray, L. (2008). Use of SMART Boards for teaching, learning and assessment in kindergarten science. *Teaching Science - the Journal of the Australian Science Teachers Association, 54*(2), 50-53.

Reedy, G. B. (2008). PowerPoint, interactive whiteboards, and the visual culture of technology in schools. *Technology, Pedagogy and Education, 17*(2), 143–152. doi:10.1080/14759390802098623

Reedy, L. (2005). A whiteboard success story. *Media & Methods, 41*(6), 17.

Robison, S. (2000). Maths classes for the twenty first century. *Media and Methods, 36*(4), 10–11.

Roythorne, P. (2006). ABC or ICT. *Times Educational Supplement,* (4691): 5.

Selwood, I., & Pilkington, R. (2005). Teacher workload: Using ICT to release time to teach. *Educational Review, 57*(2), 163–174. doi:10.1080/0013191042000308341

Shaw, M. (2006). Board fun fails to raise game. *Times Educational Supplement,* (4673): 5.

Simpson, M., Payne, F., Munro, R., & Lynch, E. (1998). Using information and communication technology as a pedagogical tool: A survey of initial teacher education in Scotland. *Journal of Information Technology for Teacher Education, 7*(3), 431–446.

Slay, H., Sieborger, I., & Hodgkinson-Williams, C. (2008). Interactive whiteboards: Real beauty or just lipstick? *Computers & Education, 51*(3), 1321–1341. doi:10.1016/j.compedu.2007.12.006

Smith, A. (1999). *Interactive whiteboard evaluation.* Mirandanet. Retrieved February 22, 2009, from www.mirandanet.ac.uk

Smith, F., Hardman, F., & Higgins, S. (2006). The impact of interactive whiteboards on teacher–pupil interaction in the National Literacy and Numeracy Strategies. *British Educational Research Journal, 32*(3), 443–457. doi:10.1080/01411920600635452

Smith, H. (2001). *Smartboard evaluation: Final report*. Retrieved February 22, 2009, from www. kented.org.uk/ngfl/ict/IWB/whiteboards/report. html

Smith, H., Higgins, J., Wall, S., & Miller, K. (2005). Interactive whiteboards: Boon or bandwagon? A critical review of the literature. *Journal of Computer Assisted Learning, 21*(2), 91–101. doi:10.1111/j.1365-2729.2005.00117.x

Somekh, B., Haldane, M., Jones, K., Lewin, C., Steadman, S., & Scrimshaw, P. (2007). *Evaluation of the primary schools whiteboard expansion project*. Centre for ICT, Pedagogy and Learning Education & Social Research Institute, Manchester Metropolitan University.

Starkman, N. (2006). The wonders of interactive whiteboards. *T.H.E. Journal, 33*(10), 36–38.

Stein, G. (2005). *Pedagogy, practice & ICT*. Canterbury Christ Church University.

Tameside, M. B. C. (2003). *Interim report on practice using interactive whiteboards in Tameside primary schools*. Retrieved June 15, 2009, from http://www.tameside.gov.uk/schools_grid/ict/whiteboards.pdf. Accessed 12th. November 2007

Tinzmann, M. B., Jones, B. F., Fennimore, T. F., Bakker, J., Fine, C., & Pierce, J. (1990). *What is the collaborative classroom?* Oak Brook, IL: NCREL.

Triggs, P., & John, P. (2004). From transaction to transformation: Information and communication technology, professional development and the formation of communities of practice. *Journal of Computer Assisted Learning, 20*(6), 426–439. doi:10.1111/j.1365-2729.2004.00101.x

Walker, D. (2002, September). White enlightening. *Times Educational Supplement, 13*(19).

Wall, K., Higgins, S., & Smith, H. (2005). The visual helps me understand the complicated things: pupil views of teaching and learning with interactive whiteboards. *British Journal of Educational Technology, 36*(5), 851–867. doi:10.1111/j.1467-8535.2005.00508.x

Watson, A., & Mason, J. (2002). Student-generated examples in the learning of mathematics. *Canadian Journal of Science . Mathematics and Technology Education, 2*(2), 237–249. doi:10.1080/14926150209556516

Whittaker, M. (2004, October). Students are running the show. *Times Educational Supplement,* (4603): 29.

Williamson, B. (2005). What are multimodality, multisemiotics and multiliteracies? A brief guide to some jargon. *Viewpoint article, 49*(1). Retrieved February 22, 2009, from http://www.futurelab. org.uk/resources/publications-reports-articles/web-articles/Web-Article532

Wood, R., & Ashfield, J. (2008). The use of the interactive whiteboard for creative teaching and learning in literacy and mathematics: a case study. *British Journal of Educational Technology, 39*(1), 84–96.

Ziolkowski, R. (2004). Interactive whiteboards: Impacting teaching and learning. *Media & Methods, 40*(4), 44.

Chapter 2
Policy, Pedagogy and Interactive Whiteboards:
What Lessons Can be Learnt from Early Adoption in England?

Gemma Moss
University of London, UK

Carey Jewitt
University of London, UK

ABSTRACT

This paper will examine the factors that led to the rapid uptake of interactive whiteboards in English schools, the promise they represented to policy-makers and practitioners in those early stages, and how assumptions about their potential to transform pedagogy shaped early use. What can other countries learn from the English experience? Which approaches to IWB use have endured beyond the early stages of uptake? Which have remained unfulfilled, or in the light of experience now deserve to be revised? Where should research and development now focus if "transformative practice" with IWBs remains the policy goal? By reflecting on the history of IWBs in England, their emergence as a focus for policymakers' interests and their use in classrooms, this paper will consider how far such technologies can foster pedagogic change.

INTRODUCTION

The uptake of IWBs has been particularly fast in the English school system, with the primary school sector leading the way. Other countries have turned to England to learn from our experience. Yet as early adopters, many English schools began using IWBs without being able to rely on established and detailed professional knowledge about what the technology's role in enhancing pedagogy might really be and with little available research evidence to define what might constitute best practice. As Hennessy (2008, p. 1) comments, "until recently, assumptions about how [IWBs] have transformed teaching were not based on hard evidence". Since the roll-out of the technology to English schools, the attention of the research community has rested on addressing this deficit. Some of this research has evaluated existing use and its potential impact

DOI: 10.4018/978-1-61520-715-2.ch002

on performance. This work has largely been commissioned by government (see for example Higgins et al., 2005; Somekh et al., 2007; and the study which underpins this chapter, Moss et al., 2007). Other researchers have designed interventions that might enhance technology use in specific pedagogic contexts e.g. the primary classroom, or secondary Maths, Science or History (Kemeny, 2005; Hennessy & Deaney, 2007; Miller & Glover, 2004). They include the active involvement of the research team in developing classroom practice with IWBs.

By contrast, this chapter focuses on the classroom practice of early adopters and analyses this as evidence of what both teachers and policy-makers imagine the technology to be. The working assumption in what follows is that how the technology is imagined will influence how it is deployed. Moreover, in the current policy climate, imagination rather than evidence will often lead uptake, such is the policy premium on speed of change and innovation within education. There are pluses and minuses to this state of affairs. In one sense the need to imagine purpose and function is an intrinsic part of the development and uptake of any new technology (Noss & Pachler, 1999). Given the interest of policy makers in England in ensuring rapid roll-out, a period of extended exploration in which users developed their understanding of what the technology was good for as they tried it out was inevitable. But now that such a period has passed in England what conclusions can be drawn? Which questions have been settled and which remain? Can any of the uncertainties associated with early adoption now be resolved? In all these respects, what are the important lessons second-wave adopters could learn from this experience? This chapter will consider these questions in the light of a study of the introduction of IWBs to London secondary schools[1].

Technology use is here theorized as a social practice, intimately shaped by the social contexts in which such use occurs. In evaluating the introduction of IWBs to London schools the research

design looked for variation in use according to teacher, curriculum subject area and school. We consider that the potential of the technology rests not with the affordance and resistance of the technology considered in the abstract, but with how that potential is both imagined and realized in particular settings (Jewitt, 2002; Moss, 2003). The research design allowed us to investigate these issues.

The analysis of early adoption which follows will explore how competing discourses about the benefits of the technology, the nature of pedagogic practice and the perceived affordance of the technology itself, all jostled to influence practice. There are four distinct communities involved: government and the agencies it has sponsored to foster uptake of new technologies in schools; the private sector which provides the relevant hard and software; the research community which has taken an interest in the potential role of ICT in school settings; and practitioners who use the technology in their classrooms. The chapter maps out similarities and differences in understandings of the technology associated with each of these groups and their respective influence upon classroom practice. In this way, the claims made for the technology and its value are tested against what happened as the technology rolled out in different settings. The discussion of IWBs will be treated as an example of the challenges policy-makers and educators face in modernizing education through the uptake of ICT.

METHODS

The paper draws on data collected as part of an evaluation of the introduction of IWBs to London secondary schools undertaken by a research team based at the Institute of Education, University of London, and commissioned by the Department for Education and Science (for the full report see Moss et al., 2007). The study took place between 2004 and 2006. It followed a decision by the then

Secretary of State for Education to provide a dedicated funding stream for London secondary schools that would fully equip at least one core subject department in each such school with IWBs, ensuring they were present in every teaching room. From this point of view, the policy more than met its objective significantly increasing the number of IWBs in Maths, Science and English. Most boards were installed in Maths and Science, with English generally seen as less of a priority.

The study began with a review of the available policy and research literature which had set the scene for early adoption and which identified various likely benefits. Case studies of the technology in classroom use were conducted in nine London secondary schools, and were based in three Maths, Science, and English departments. The case studies were set alongside statistical analysis of pupil performance data designed to capture any evidence that IWBs had impacted on pupil performance, using a difference in difference design, comparing performance data for groups taught prior to and after the introduction of IWBs. In addition survey data were collected from all London schools on the current distribution of IWBs and how departments perceived their benefits. Finally, informed by the initial analysis from observation of use in the case study sites, a teacher survey on IWB usage was conducted in 27 school core subject departments.

Each case study included classroom observation of one week's sequence of lessons in the core subject (Maths, English or Science). In each site, these were collected from three parallel teaching groups in Year 9 (aged 14 to 15 years), and thus covered teaching across the ability range. In addition, researchers followed one pupil in each subject for all their lessons over two days, thus tracking teaching practice for this Year group with and without IWBs and in a range of other curriculum subjects. All the texts observed in use on the IWBs were collected, and one lesson in the core subject sequence was recorded on video. In addition interviews were conducted with the classroom teacher and the Head of Department. Pupils were surveyed on their view of the technology and a focus group interview was conducted with members of each class. This gave us rich data on how IWB use varied according to the immediate pedagogic context, defined in relation to the curriculum topic as well as curriculum subject and the way in which that topic was tailored to the particular ability group. We were also able to situate our analysis of classroom practice in the context of the longer policy cycle that had made the introduction of ICT to schools a political priority.

Background: Factors Underpinning the Rapid Up-Take of IWBs in England

In many respects, rapid uptake of IWBs in England can be explained by a fortuitous confluence between the development of the technology and the particular point reached in the education policy cycle in England in the 2000s. Policy required what the technology seemed to offer. When New Labour came into office in 1997, they promised to modernize the public sector through investment. Within education more specifically they argued that investment in ICT for schools would re-vitalize the school infrastructure, modernize working practices and equip children for what lay ahead in an increasingly technologically driven society. These motivations have remained relatively constant over the various twists and turns policy has taken.

At the outset New Labour specified a minimum level of ICT infrastructure for every state school, spelt out in terms of internet connection, a dedicated computer suite, and sufficient resources to provide at least one computer in each classroom. A variety of policy levers were introduced to increase the use of ICT across the curriculum in different subject areas, and to increase the time spent by pupils studying ICT as a separate subject. The government also funded initiatives to capacity-build teachers' competence in ICT. These included providing: information and research designed to promote technology use on government-sponsored webpages; e-resources for teachers which could be incorporated into classroom practice; outreach practitioner forums (National Whiteboard Network); programs of in-service training for teachers; and funding for small-scale research into best practice using ICT (Best Practice Research Scholarships; The Review Project, Hull).

ICT IN SCHOOLS: MEASURING THE RETURN ON THE INVESTMENT

As they made the investment, policymakers also tracked the return. This was framed in terms of whether or not ICT impacted on standards of pupil attainment. If it could be shown to have done so then the question, "Is the investment worth the money?", would be clearly answered. Yet getting a certain answer to this question has proved more difficult than policy-makers might have hoped. Government funded research has made it possible to assert that:

School standards are positively associated with the quality of school ICT resources and the quality of their use in teaching and learning, regardless of socioeconomic characteristics. (Pittard et al., 2003)

Nonetheless, there are two important caveats in the research findings. The available data demonstrate statistical association but cannot prove causality. They also indicate that the effect of ICT depends crucially on how it is used not on the mere absence or presence of technology in the classroom. Thus one of the earliest large-scale research projects on the impact of ICT in education reported: "There is no consistent relationship between the average amount of ICT use reported for any subject at a given Key Stage and

its apparent effectiveness in raising standards. It therefore seems likely that the type of use is all important" (Harrison et al., 2002). By 2003, a major review of government policy for ICT in education concluded:

The massive improvements we have seen in the basic ICT-enabled infrastructure for learning now need to be paralleled by a transformation in the use of ICT as a powerful tool for learning, teaching and institutional management - enabling the learning process to be enhanced, extended and enriched. This will require every school to become 'e-confident.' (DfES 2003b, p. 16)

In effect, the disappointment in the low value of the pedagogic return achieved through the high spend on the technology led to a new policy goal: enhanced pedagogic practice with ICT.

The Difference in Use: The Search for the Ingredients Which Deliver Good Practice with ICT

As it became clearer that the technology alone would not transform practice, government-funded research began to look more closely at when and under what conditions ICT might improve learning. Some of this research explored factors extrinsic to the technology. For instance, whether there was a correlation between gains in attainment associated with ICT and the kinds of factors identified as important in the school improvement literature, such as school organization and leadership (Becta, 2003a, 2003b). Could pupil or teacher perceptions and experience of different aspects of the technology explain its high or low use and the quality of its application? (DfES, 2001). How important were the amount of access teachers or pupils had to the relevant resource; their familiarity with the available hard and software; their confidence in and competence with the technology; and their perceptions of the value and relevance of the technology as well as its impact? Four substantial literature reviews brought this evidence together and attempted to lay the foundations for the most profitable directions for future policy (Cox et al., 2003a, 2003b; Jones, 2004; Scrimshaw, 2004).

A general consensus emerged from these studies that training in the technical skills required to work the technology is not sufficient. This has to be combined with a clear understanding on the teachers' part of the pedagogical applications and advantages that ICT can bring. Yet in many respects, precise understanding of the pedagogical applications and advantages of different forms of ICT remains elusive. In part this is because the technology itself continues to develop in new directions, and successively suggests new possibilities for use. IWBs are a good case in point.

IWBS: Technologies in Search of an Application

Interactive whiteboards have their roots in the development of two separate technologies: touch sensitive computer screens and digital projectors. The advent of handwriting recognition systems seems to have been the key element that made harnessing these facilities for education an attractive proposition. The touch sensitive screen allows the presenter to operate from the screen itself without having to go to a computer. By using a hand or pen on the screen like a mouse, the user can then move about within that environment with exactly the same kind of functionality associated with mouse use at a computer terminal: clicking, dropping and dragging, or scrolling. This makes it possible to exploit different kinds of computer software and the choices they offer while any presentation is in process. The handwriting recognition system also makes it possible to annotate what appears on the screen or create new texts at the board which can then be saved

This is the technology's potential. Yet it is also clear from the available information on the commercial development of IWBs that the aptness of the technology for use in education was not immediately obvious. The company which launched IWBs, SMART, comment in their company history: "In those early years no one knew about an interactive whiteboard, much less why they might want or need one, so sales for SMART started slowly. … it took a substantial effort to let people know about the product and the benefits that they could enjoy from using them" (SMART, 2004, n.p.). What the technology can do in the abstract does not clarify its application in particular settings. Indeed, the first attempts to sell touch-sensitive computer screens into the education system via Higher Education met with only limited success. SMART's own account of the history of the product suggests that the potential of the technology really developed in relation to a different context: meetings or presentations organized as part of corporate management where the technology began to act as a computerized flip chart - a system of both creating and storing texts on the computer in real-time - in a context where the texts themselves could later be usefully shared. This apparent crossover in functionality between education, training and business environments was important in sustaining belief in the product's viability. It was simply a matter of finding a market where this potential could be exploited. Such a market began to emerge as the capacity for IWBs to be internet enabled and act as a portal to the internet suggested a new functionality in education.

The Uptake of IWBS in English Schools: Why the Technology Seemed to Fit Here

From a policy-making perspective in England, by the early 2000s some of the drawbacks as well as the advantages of the earlier phases of investment in technology in education had begun to emerge. The decision to invest in ICT suites in both primary and secondary schools was designed to enable all children to acquire a minimum of ICT skills and at least some experience of what the technology could offer. But ICT suites created less than ideal conditions for teaching. Poor sight lines made it hard for teachers to monitor pupil activity or command attention. Access to the facility was itself rationed with teachers competing for time, while the need to relocate to the ICT suite for a set period reinforced the notion that ICT use stood apart from rather than integrated into the normal work of the class or a particular subject area. In 2004 the school inspection service, Ofsted, identified all these issues as distinct problems (Ofsted, 2004). The stress they put on integrating ICT into the broader curriculum re-set the policy objective for ICT use, just at the point when IWBs were beginning to emerge.

As the disadvantages of one technological solution become apparent, the potential of other technologies becomes easier to see. By contrast to PCs, IWBs seemed relatively easy to install in individual classrooms with minimum disruption to the use of the existing space. They seemed to provide an alternative way of facilitating ICT use in group settings while allowing for greater teacher control over the shape and direction of that interaction. They thus opened up the possibility of integrating technology more fully into teaching and learning in every curriculum subject. In addition, within England the reform of teacher pedagogy brought about by the introduction of the National Strategies for Literacy and Numeracy to primary schools had placed great emphasis on interactive, whole class teaching. IWBs seemed to have the capacity to support this objective. The technology matched what the context seemed to require. Indeed, on this basis it was schools rather than government that led the initial uptake of IWBs in England.

Yet once IWBs enter classrooms they compete against older forms of technology - the blackboard, whiteboard, flipchart or overhead projector - as well as newer forms of technology such as networked PCs, laptops, or tablets combined with digital projectors. The precise niche they might best fill only becomes apparent as the technology begins to adapt and respond to the requirements of that setting.

For some producers, adapting the technology more specifically for classroom use has involved developing new and more dedicated platforms that promise easier ways of storing and calling-up a range of e-resources. Companies distinguish their product according to the user interface. Yet clarity of thinking over what kinds of educational content would benefit from being used in this environment has lagged behind. The introduction of the hardware has taken precedence over imagining the most appropriate software. Some IWB manufacturers have solved this dilemma simply by encouraging practitioners to "publish" and share materials they have developed themselves (e.g. SMART). Others are only now beginning to form partnerships with companies with longer histories of producing school-focused content (e.g. Promethean/ Scholastic). In general there continues to be real uncertainty over where responsibility for content production really lies, and whether this is crucial to good use of the technology or not. In England with its particular history of teacher–produced curriculum content, and little use of textbooks, especially in the primary school and humanities subjects, there is not a large and obvious market for commercially-produced materials. Elsewhere companies remain uncertain about the business model that might generate a return from distributing e-resources for any forms of technology associated with educational settings. There are comparatively few incentives for those who already own educational content to transfer it into an IWB compatible resource. Even as the uptake of the technology gathers pace, uncertainties about best use remain.

THE RESEARCH LITERATURE ON IWBS: FEEDING THE POLICY CYCLE, INSIDE AND OUT

At the point of uptake in England, the research literature on IWBs was still relatively underdeveloped, much of it small-scale, and a good deal the result of action research conducted by advocates of the technology either in their own classrooms, or working alongside colleagues during the early stages of implementation (Coghill, 2002). Relatively little had been published in peer-reviewed journals. Details of the research methodologies, the quantity of data collected or how they were analyzed were scant. A few papers cited by government agencies consisted largely of personal testimony from individual users (Smith, 1999; Bell, 2002). The more scholarly work came from those involved in helping practitioners realize the potential of the technology (e.g. Glover & Miller, 2001) in specific pedagogic settings. Nevertheless, such research as there was carried a remarkably similar story about the benefits of the technology for teaching and learning

The Potential of the Technology to Enhance Teaching

A variety of studies reported that the facility of the interactive whiteboard is well adapted to whole class teaching (Glover & Miller, 2001) and encourages an interactive approach in that setting (Ball, 2003). IWBs make it easier to incorporate and use a range of multimedia resources in lessons including: written text; pictures; video; sound; diagrams; online websites (Levy, 2002). They can quicken the pace of lessons through the use of pre-stored materials, which reduce the need to write on the board (Ball, 2003; Miller, 2003). When connected to an intranet they encourage resource sharing among staff, which can reduce teacher workload (Kennewell, 2004). IWBs are easy to use and are more likely to find favor with teachers who

otherwise struggle to incorporate technology into their classrooms (Kemeny, 2004, Smith, 2001). The high production values of the resources are attractive to both teachers and children (Smith, 1999; Ball, 2003; Kennewell, 2004).

The Potential of the Technology to Enhance Learning

In reflecting on learning, a variety of studies reported that IWBs are able to support a range of different learning styles, including visual, auditory and kinesthetic (by physical movement) (Graham, 2003; Ball, 2003). The interactive software available for use on IWBs enables teachers to model abstract ideas and concepts in new ways so that the pupils can respond to the activities and deepen their understanding (Kemeny, 2004; Miller 2003; Richardson, 2002). The facility to save and then re-use materials, which have been created or annotated in lesson time can reinforce and extend learning over a sequence of lessons (Glover & Miller, 2002).

Drawbacks of the Technology

Any drawbacks identified tended to be of a practical or logistical nature: IWBs can be more expensive to purchase than other technologies which might share many of the same affordances (Twining et al., 2005); they may prove difficult to maintain and are difficult to substitute for when out of use; there are difficulties in placing them at the right height for use by both children and adults (Smith et al., 2005); and the mobile versions are time-consuming to install (Brown, 2004; Becta, 2004b).

The terms in which both the potential of the technology and its drawbacks were described and repeated in the government literature devoted to the technology and made available on official websites (DfES, 2004; Becta, 2004a). Promotional material about IWBs provided by suppliers referred to the benefits of the technology in much the same terms (SMART technologies inc, 2004), as did the descriptions of in-service courses designed to encourage the professional uptake of IWBs and their application. In effect, there was a commonsense convergence across these fields on very similar notions of what the technology could do. Substantial reviews of the literature undertaken following the widespread introduction of IWBs in England bore this out (Smith et al., 2005; Glover et al., 2005; Somekh et al., 2007; Higgins et al., 2005). Only Australia provided a significantly different language in which to describe the technology's potential, using the phrase "digital hub" to capture their expectations for teaching and learning with IWBs:

IWBs can be used as simple whiteboards, as interactive whiteboards, as large screen digital convergence facilities and when in the hands of an expert teacher, with an appreciation of the many roles the technology can perform, as a digital teaching and learning hub. .... In the next few years as the IWB and related digital technology develops at pace, the teachers' mastery and expectations of the technology grows and the concept of the digital hub becomes clearer so too will there be the opportunity to enhance the quality of teaching and the level and appropriateness of student learning. (Moss et al., 2007, p. 92)

The very clarity and consistency of expectations led to the assumption that once the technology was made available in classrooms it would reshape teachers' pedagogy through its use. With the right training, the expected effects on the quality of teaching and learning, the motivation and engagement of pupils, increased efficiencies in teachers' work and attendant impacts on pupil performance would all follow.

THE TECHNOLOGY IN CONTEXT: EXPLAINING VARIATION IN USE

As the technology rolled out in England, research began to assess its impact. In many cases this meant extending data collection beyond the self-selecting sample of teachers who had specifically chosen to work with the technology to focus on a broader range of staff now using the technology under different circumstances. Early small scale studies in this area have now been followed by more large scale evaluative research, mainly commissioned by government (e.g. Higgins et al., 2005; Somekh et al., 2007; Moss et al., 2007). These large-scale studies have generally employed robust methodologies for testing impacts on pupil performance. The latter remains a key concern for government.

In general this research has been more cautious about the educational benefits that have flowed from the technology. In particular, uptake has not necessarily changed teaching in the ways that were anticipated. This is in line with earlier work. For instance, Coghill's small scale study (Coghill, 2002) found considerable variation in practice amongst the five teachers in two primary schools who were observed. Coghill comments:

The teachers in this study were all using the interactive whiteboard in different ways and had different views and interests in its potential. ... The participants' pedagogical approach to using the interactive whiteboard varied considerably. (Coghill, 2002, 7.1)

Indeed, part of the point that she makes is that for these teachers it was relatively easy to accommodate the technology to existing ways of working, rather than transform ways of working to accommodate the technology.

One of the main reasons for championing the technology was its potential to directly support interactive whole class teaching (DfES, 2004; Becta, 2004a). However, findings from early studies were mixed in this respect too. Latham (2002) conducted a small-scale study of the introduction of IWBs to a Maths teaching program in North Islington Education Action Zone. She reported that in 4 out of 5 lessons observed, "whiteboards were used to produce appropriate, highly visual, interactive lessons that addressed all the pupils present" (Ibid, p. 5). But in the one exception, the IWB was being used like a traditional chalkboard to present a series of examples. Both Coghill (2002) and Knight, Pennant and Piggot (2004) observed that IWBs were not necessarily used interactively, and indeed, without positive intervention, Knight, Pennant and Piggot (2004) argued that IWBs could reinforce a teacher-centered style of delivery. Interestingly, from this point of view, Beeland's (2002) study of interactive whiteboard use, which correlated attitudinal measures with observed practice, found that pupils were most positive about lessons in which teachers made least use of the interactive potential of the IWBs and most use of their facility to relay multimedia resources.

Overall, the research based on uptake among a broader group than the technology pioneers consistently suggests that the anticipated benefits do not automatically follow. The most common explanation for the lack of transformative impact is the time it takes for teachers to develop the necessary confidence and competence to use it well. For instance, Glover and Miller set out to first identify, next handover and then evaluate a range of approaches which would allow teachers to exploit the potential of IWBs within the Maths curriculum. They report that while in some lessons with IWBs the techniques they advocated were clearly used in a positive way to support learning, this was not inevitably the case. They comment:

In short it would appear that the effective use of the IAW [IWB] in enhancing attainment hinges upon the progress made by teachers in harnessing the additional power of the technology to prompt

analysis of the learning process in the teacher, and appreciation of the concepts and applications by the pupil. (Miller et al., 2004)

The quest for good teaching remains a quest for good teaching with or without the technology. The technology may enhance pedagogy but only if teachers and pupils engage with it and understand its potential in such a way that the technology itself is no longer viewed as the ends but as another pedagogic means. This project concluded that reaching this point in use takes time. The conclusions they draw about the likely sequence involved in the effective appropriation of a new technology mirrors similar conclusions reached elsewhere on the difficulty of developing innovative practice with ICT and the need for a sustained effort on teachers' part if their practice is to be transformed (see Scrimshaw, 2004; Ertmer et al., 1999; Hooper & Rieber, 1995; Twining et al., 2005; Haldane, 2005). This literature describes a successive move away from the status quo to more novel and even transformative practice, with the final stage the desired outcome. The objective is to take more practice through the full sequence to the transformative outcome.

EXPLOITING THE POTENTIAL OF ICT: ARE IWBS SIMPLY ANOTHER CASE IN POINT?

There is a paradox in the research undertaken so far. While there is a clear consensus on what the advantages of IWBs might be in the abstract, observation of the technology in use shows far greater variation in the approach teachers take to the technology than proponents would expect. The anticipated enhancement of practice looks more uncertain. In these respects, the process of transforming teaching practice with IWBs seems to replicate the pattern observed with other technologies (Jones, 2004; Scrimshaw, 2004). Indeed, the clear advantage IWBs seem to have in terms of uptake - that their use fits quite easily with existing patterns of whole class pedagogy – may also be their weakness. Their introduction into classrooms does not guarantee that their potential becomes either immediately apparent to their recipients, nor that it is easily exploited. In the light of this, those most committed to realizing the potential of IWBs as a pedagogic tool have re-doubled their efforts to define good pedagogy and delineate for teachers how it can be achieved. The key objective is to re-direct teachers' attention away from the technology itself to, for instance, what good whole class interactive pedagogy might mean and then how IWBs can be used to achieve this (Hennessy et al., 2007).

We read this contradiction in the research evidence another way. We argue that taking new technologies to the classroom is a process of mutual adaptation, in which the technology inevitably accommodates to the setting and its existing grammar as well as changing it. By looking at the dialectic tussle over the technology as it unrolls into classrooms it is possible to reassess whether the IWB's properties as currently imagined are a useful representation of what the technology could or should do, and whether and how that imagined potential might need to adapt in the light of teachers' existing pedagogic practice. Early use should help define what a process of mutual adaptation might best lead to. This includes reassessing whether the dominant rhetoric about the benefits IWBs bring is either useful or accurate.

Reviewing the dominant rhetoric on the benefits of IWBs in the light of classroom practice

Survey data collected for our study showed that the dominant rhetoric on the benefits of IWBs and their potential to transform pedagogy was very familiar to teachers. The rhetoric converged on these three terms:

- Multimodality: the IWBs' capacity to harness a wider range of multimodal resources in order to facilitate pupil learning

(Kennewell, 2004; Ball, 2003; Levy, 2002; Smith, 1999)

- Pace: its capacity to increase the pace and efficiency of classroom delivery and therefore best use of teacher time (Smith et al, 2005; Becta, 2004a; Ball, 2003; Miller, 2003)
- Interaction: its capacity to enhance interactive whole class teaching (DfES 2004; Ball, 2003; Becta, 2004; Glover & Miller, 2001)

In the classrooms we observed these three concepts often underpinned teachers' selection, use and design of texts for the IWB (Moss et al., 2007). Teachers would invite children to come out to the front and use the board to drag and drop or uncover items that the teacher had embedded in the presentation. Successive screens were often pre-loaded with a variety of multimodal resources, incorporating a range of visual images. In some lessons this seemed to lead to a good deal of emphasis being placed on a brisk pace to classroom interactions. Yet it was no less clear whether these distinctive features of IWB use really led to a transformative pedagogy.

On the contrary, observation of classroom practice suggested that the convergence of much policy, commercial and research literature on the same three aspects of IWBs led to expectations for use that could distort teachers' pedagogic practice. The expectation that appropriate lessons in any subject using IWBs will be visibly and measurably interactive, multimodal, using as many modes as possible, and fast paced does not allow for the varying pedagogic purposes that teachers hold for their subject area or particular curriculum topic. It is a "one-size fits all" prescription which ignores the need to adapt any pedagogic tool to the immediate pedagogic purpose. Pace, multimodality and interaction might be inflected in teacher-designed texts for IWBs and their use of the IWB. Yet good pedagogy did not necessarily follow.

The emphasis on creating an interactive pedagogic teaching style by using features of the board that require hands-on manipulation is a case in point. Drag and Drop and hide and reveal are two distinctive features of the board whose use is strongly associated with constructing an interactive pedagogy. These features were often embedded in the texts we collected, and were widely mentioned by teachers when they described their use of IWBs in our teacher survey. But some of the activities designed in this way seemed to encourage superficial rather than deep interactivity. In Maths and Science lessons we saw hide and reveal used so that the student called to the front could "reveal" whether they or classmates had got the right answer. This kind of use seemed to be governed less by a deep commitment to a conservative model of pedagogy than by the need to be seen to be using the technology in the required way. Provided the boards' distinctive features had been incorporated into the design of resources, then the job had been done. Under these circumstances, the discourse of technological interactivity and its presumed benefits may detract from rather than enhance thinking about what counts as good pedagogy here.

This is not a contrast between novice and experienced users. We saw contrasting styles of use adopted by those who were regarded as the technology champions in their own schools. For instance, we observed a Maths lesson using comparatively few pre-loaded materials, in which the teacher encouraged students to manipulate objects on the board using a remote slate from the body of the class. As they manipulated the display students were expected to comment on what they had changed and talk about its significance. A slow pace enabled the class to work together to build an understanding of the topic at hand led by students' real-time narrative account of their interaction with the board. The teacher had previously used the same activity in class using overhead transparencies. The new technology gave further clarity to the exercise and made it easier for the exercise to be shared in this way. Here the board's potential seemed to come second and the pedagogic intent came first. In the second example, we saw an extremely fast paced class in which the teacher used the facility of the board to pre-load many examples of the same underlying mathematical principles, and then drove the pace at which these were covered in class. Pupil and or teacher use of drag and drop reinforced the teaching points he was already committed to making. The potential of the board was clearly being extensively exploited but for a highly didactic purpose.

What counts as good pedagogy changes from one teacher to another and from one subject domain to another, as well as according to the topic. The presumed value of pace may hold in Maths under certain conditions. Being able to pre-load the board with different examples of the same mathematical procedure and move rapidly through them can allow the teacher to introduce the underlying principle. Through repeated demonstrations of what is involved as different students are asked to complete the calculation, the general principle can be abstracted from the individual case and what has been learnt can be reinforced in this way. Such a pedagogic approach is much less common in English. In general, English as a subject domain puts much less value on speed: speeding through successive Shakespeare sonnets is unlikely to be considered a pedagogic virtue. The presumed benefits of the technology may not apply equally within different domains.

We would argue that there cannot be a simple prescription about what the technology offers to pedagogy. Rather how the technology is understood needs to adapt to the values and pedagogic objectives of the specific subject domain as well as open up new opportunities. Indeed, it may be more pedagogically useful to think of pace, interactivity and multimodality as resources on a continuum which need to be considered as a holistic trio rather than be seen as absolute virtues (Jewitt, Moss & Cardini, 2007). For example, if interactivity is high, then pace may need to be slow. While IWB technology clearly has the capacity to facilitate increased pace of delivery, teachers need to consider when it is in the interest of learners to take advantage of this facility and when it is not. There can be significant pedagogic value in slow real-time board work, when it is used to realize a specific pedagogic aim.

Taking the Old to the New: What Pedagogy without Technology has to Say Back to the IWB

Whatever the pedagogic efficacy of the practice we observed, our research did show high usage of the boards. They were rarely totally ignored. But not all the usage seemed to align with the dominant discourse about their benefits. Take this example. A modern foreign languages teacher entered the classroom to start a lesson and over its course filled the IWB with writing, cleaned the IWB, filled the IWB with writing once again, cleaned the writing off and left the room, the lesson having now finished. Nothing placed on the board was saved or called up from a previously stored file, no other facility of the board except the handwriting recognition system was used. To all intents and purposes, the IWB was functioning as a blackboard. From a policy point of view it looks as if the resource of the IWB is being wasted. For research focused on the transformative benefits of the IWB for pedagogy this looks like an example of a teacher who has not yet taken the first step towards changing what they do. It can be read as proof of the innate conservatism of pedagogic practice, or of the need for those with a clear vision of the technology's benefits to more urgently show the way. Most likely, in the process of research, such evidence would simply be discarded as demonstrating little of interest.

Although this was an extreme example, by keeping this kind of data in the database as part of the analysis we were able to show that such usage has a function of its own which can be pedagogically justified. Writing during the course of a lesson in a publicly shared space, be it blackboard, whiteboard or on an IWB, has a pedagogic function. It captures and solidifies ideas or key points that emerge in the classroom talk. It translates that talk into something visible, crystallizing what otherwise would remain transient. In essence it teaches the students how to pay attention to the talk that they hear. This kind of use of writing to accompany pedagogic talk during real time is quite different from using writing to assemble and sequence the key points ahead of the pedagogic interaction, for instance via a sequence of PowerPoint slides. The second approach presumes that everything of pedagogic interest can be determined ahead of the event. It may also commit the teacher to then delivering everything that has been already set down. Thus minimizing the possibility of teaching itself creating something new through the interaction between pupils and teachers as it unfolds in real time. The pre-prepared delivery model is in fact a very old form of pedagogy, closely identified with working through the textbook, which itself hardly justifies the expense of the IWB.

This is not to argue against the IWB per se. Rather it is to suggest that defining what makes good pedagogy in terms of what the technology can do can limit rather than open up discussion. There may indeed be a value in doing what one did before the new technology arrived, as well as doing new things that the technology allows. From this point of view it makes more sense to consider how IWBs could support, extend or transform existing pedagogy (Twining et al., 2005), under what circumstances, for whom. It is important to recognize that supporting, extending and transforming existing practice can each be justified and have a potential value. They do not form a teleological sequence in which only transformative practice counts.

ADAPTATION AND EVOLUTION: FINDING A NICHE FOR THE IWB

Other countries are now in a position to learn from England's experience with IWBs. In many ways their interest is driven by a shared assumption that education is out of step with new times if it does not incorporate new media and expose children to what those new media can do. From this point of view, IWBs do indeed have a distinct advantage over PCs precisely because of the ease with which they can sit at the front of the class and be absorbed into existing classroom geography. Whether the touch sensitive aspect of the technology really is more useful than the combination of a PC plus data projector and slate remains an open question. Certainly the ability to direct the board via touch seems less essential to pedagogy in the secondary classroom than it might be in the primary setting. This remains an under-researched area which would benefit from greater attention.

What the use of IWBs in English classrooms does demonstrate is that the precise benefits from the technology depend upon the pedagogic intentions of the teachers who use them and the extent to which what the technology offers facilitates rather than obscures or distorts pedagogic thinking. We found that the ways in which teachers use technology is strongly shaped by their existing pedagogic practice, the context of the school, and the demands of particular school subject areas and topics. Given the varied nature of the contexts IWBs enter into, perhaps any potential benefits are best encapsulated by describing the IWB as a "digital hub", rather than too tightly focusing on a particular set of techniques that can be executed at the board (drag and drop; hide and reveal) and which may or may not change pedagogy. As a "digital hub" the IWB brings into the classroom a wider range of resources, from the net, the intra-net, as well as resources that teachers and pupils have fashioned themselves. It allows these resources to be shared in new ways, and become the focus for new kinds of manipulation. It also

allows them to be used in old ways too. Deciding when and under what conditions old ways should be replaced by new ways is a matter of professional judgment. In this respect one interesting development lies with textbook manufacturers in Europe who on the back of the English experience are beginning to try out new ways of combining e-resources as they start to adapt their textbook content to whole class digital use. Companies are re-making the textbook so that teachers can exercise choice over what combination of pages, sound or moving image files they call up, and in what sequence. They are also exploiting a range of tools associated with the computer to navigate around conventional textbook pages in new ways (The Swedish company Natur & Kultur, and the Czech company, Fraus, are two examples). Some of these resources now explicitly anticipate and design for teacher and even pupil annotation of e-materials in real time, thus combining the functionality of the IWB with the functionality of the blackboard. This is a direct outcome of reflecting on actual classroom use, rather than simply anticipating what such use might be from regarding the technology alone.

CONCLUSION

By reflecting on the policy and pedagogic history of IWBs in England this chapter has contributed to the ongoing debate on the extent to which technologies can foster pedagogic change. This chapter has highlighted the factors that led to the rapid uptake of IWBs in English schools. It has sketched the promise they represented to policy-makers and practitioners in those early stages, and how assumptions about their potential to transform pedagogy shaped early use. Policy-driven innovation demands quick returns. It also presupposes that those returns can be measured and identified in advance. Governments like to know precisely what they will get back from the investment made. This produces a curious double-bind for government.

They are more at risk of being unable to demonstrate added-value precisely because of the high premium they put on defining in advance precisely what that added-value will be. Transformative practice as the required outcome is indeed a tall order, whether from IWBs or anything else. Given the continuing uncertainties about the technology's potential, identifying more modest objectives that are within grasp seems more productive. Thinking about technology uptake as a mutually adaptive process provides a way of doing just this.

How a technology is imagined will influence how it is deployed and may well lead to uptake within education. But technologies also need to adapt to the contexts they find themselves in. They need to be tested out in specific contexts where demands are made of the technology too, in line with current practice and clear pedagogic intent. We have shown that the potential of the technology rests not with the affordance and resistance of the technology considered in the abstract, but with how that potential is both imagined and realized in particular curricular contexts shaped by competing discourses and interests. If teachers make something of IWBs then it is because they can adapt them to their own pedagogic purposes as well as finding new pedagogic applications for what the technology can do. This is a form of exploration and adaptation that may or may not transform pedagogy. It will encourage further use of digital texts in the classroom and provide opportunities to develop their pedagogic role.

REFERENCES

Ball, B. (2003). Teaching and learning mathematics with an interactive whiteboard. *Micromath*, *19*(1), 4–7.

Becta (2003a). *Primary Schools – ICT and Standards: An analysis of national data from Ofsted and QCA*. Coventry, UK: Becta.

Becta (2003b). *Secondary Schools – ICT and Standards: An analysis of national data from Ofsted and QCA*. Coventry, UK: Becta.

Becta (2004a). *Getting the most from your interactive whiteboard: A guide for secondary schools*. Coventry, UK: Becta.

Becta (2004b). *Planning to purchase an interactive whiteboard*. Retrieved June 15, 2009, from http://www.becta.org.uk/leas/leas.cfm?section=6_2&id=3160

Beeland, W. D. (2002). Student engagement, visual learning and technology: Can interactive whiteboards help? *Action Research Exchange*, *1*(1). Retrieved June 15, 2009, from http://chiron.valdosta.edu/are/Artmanscrpt/vol1no1/beeland_am.pdf

Bell, M. A. (2002). Why use an interactive whiteboard? A baker's dozen reasons! *Teachers Net Gazette 3*(1). Retrieved June 15, 2009, from http://teachers.net/gazette/JAN02/mabel.html

Brown, S. (2004). *Interactive whiteboards in education. TechLearn Briefing*. UK: JISC Technologies Centre, Joint Information Systems Committee.

Coghill, J. (2002). *How is the interactive whiteboard being used in the primary school and how does this affect teachers and teaching?* Retrieved June 15, 2009, from http://www.virtuallearning.org.uk/whiteboards/IFS_Interactive_whiteboards_in_the_prima ry_school.pdf

Cox, M., Abbott, C., Webb, M., Blakeley, B., Beauchamp, T., & Rhodes, V. (2003a). *ICT and attainment: A review of the research literature. A report to the DfES*. Coventry, UK: Becta.

Cox, M., Webb, M., Abbott, C., Blakeley, B., Beauchamp, T., & Rhodes, V. (2003b). *ICT and pedagogy: A review of the research literature. A report to the DfES*. Coventry, UK: Becta.

DfES (2001). *NGfL Pathfinders: Preliminary report on the roll out of the NGfL programme in ten Pathfinder LEAs.* NGfL Research and Evaluation Series Number 2.

DfES (2003). *Fulfilling the potential.* Policy statement on ICT signed by Charles Clarke.

DfES. (2004). *Interactive whiteboards - frequently asked questions.* Retrieved June 15, 2009, from http://www.dfes.gov.uk/ictinschools/ict_active/factfile.cfm?articleid=511

Ertmer, P., Addison, P., Lane, M., Ross, E., & Woods, D. (1999). Examining teachers' beliefs about the role of technology in the elementary classroom. *Journal of Research on Computing in Education, 32*(1), 54–72.

Glover, D., & Miller, D. (2001). Running with technology: The pedagogic impact of the large-scale introduction of interactive whiteboards in one secondary school. *Journal of Information Technology for Teacher Education, 10*(3), 257–277.

Glover, D., Miller, D., Averis, D., & Door, V. (2005). The interactive whiteboard: a literature survey. *Technology, Pedagogy and Education, 14*(2), 155–170. doi:10.1080/14759390500200199

Glover, D., & Miller, D. J. (2002). The introduction of unteractive whiteboards into schools in the United Kingdom: Leaders, led, and the management of pedagogic and technological change. *International Electronic Journal for Leadership in Learning, 6*(24), University of Calgary Press. Retrieved June 15, 2009, from http://www.ucalgary.ca/~iejll/volume6/glover.html

Graham, K. (2003). *Switching on switched-off children: Does the Promethean ACTIVboard promote lesson participation among switched-off children?* Retrieved June 15, 2009, from http://www.virtuallearning.org.uk/2003research/Switching_Switched_Off.doc

Haldane, M. (2005). *A typology of interactive whiteboard pedagogies.* Paper presented at the British Educational Research Association Conference, Glamorgan, UK.

Harrison, C., Comber, C., Fisher, T., Haw, K., Lewin, C., & Lunzer, E. (2002). *ImpaCT2: The impact of information and communication technologies on pupil learning and attainment. A report to the DfES. ICT in Schools Research and Evaluation Series No 7.* Coventry, UK: Becta.

Hennessy, S. (2008). *Interactivity means more activity for students.* ESRC. Retrieved June 15, 2009, from http://www.esrcsocietytoday.ac.uk/ESRCInfoCentre/PO/releases/2008/september/whitebo ard.aspx

Hennessy, S., & Deaney, R. (2007). *Teacher mediation of subject learning with ICT: A multimedia approach (T-MEDIA).* Retrieved June 15, 2009, from http://www.educ.cam.ac.uk/research/projects/istl/T-MEDIA_Fin_Rep_Main.pdf

Hennessy, S., Deaney, R., Ruthven, K., & Winterbottom, M. (2007). Pedagogical strategies for using the interactive whiteboard to foster learner participation in school science. *Learning, Media and Technology, 32*(3), 283–301. doi:10.1080/17439880701511131

Higgins, S. Clark. J., Falzon. C., Hall, I., Hardman, F., Miller, J., Moseley, D., Smith, F., & Wall, K. (2005). *Embedding ICT in the literacy and numeracy strategies: Final report April 2005.* Newcastle Upon Tyne, UK: Newcastle University. Retrieved June 15, 2009, from http://www.staff.ucsm.ac.uk/rpotter/ict/research/univ_newcastle_evaluation_whitebo ards.pdf

Hooper, S., & Rieber, L. P. (1995). Teaching with technology . In Ornstein, A. C. (Ed.), *Teaching: Theory into practice* (pp. 154–170). Needham Heights, MA: Allyn and Bacon.

Jewitt, C. (2002). The move from page to screen: the multimodal reshaping of school English. *Journal of Visual Communication, 1*(2), 171–196. doi:10.1177/147035720200100203

Jewitt, C., Moss, G., & Cardini, A. (2007). Pace, interactivity and multimodality in teacher design of texts for IWBs. *Learning, Media and Technology, 32*(3), 302–318. doi:10.1080/17439880701511149

Jones, A. (2004). *A review of the research literature on barriers to the uptake of ICT by teachers.* Coventry, UK: Becta.

Kemeny, H. (2004). *Review of some literature and classroom research into IWB use in primary schools.* Unpublished paper produced for the "IWB pedagogy and pupil performance project".

Kemeny, H. (2005). *Transforming learning? Interactive whiteboards in the primary classroom: Case studies from a London school.* Paper included in the proceedings of the CRPP Transforming Pedagogy Conference, NIE June 2005.

Kennewell, S. (2004). *Researching the influence of interactive presentation tools on teacher pedagogy.* Paper presented at BERA 2004.

Knight, P., Pennant, J., & Piggott, J. (2004). What does it mean to 'Use the interactive whiteboard' in the daily mathematics lesson? *MicroMath, 20*(2), 14–16.

Latham, P. (2002). *Teaching and learning primary mathematics: the impact of interactive whiteboards.* BEAM research papers. Retrieved June 15, 2009, from http://www.beam.co.uk/pdfs/RES03.pdf

Levy, P. (2002). *Interactive whiteboards in learning and teaching in two Sheffield schools: A developmental study.* Department of Information Studies, University of Sheffield. Retrieved June 15, 2009, from http://dis.shef.ac.uk/eirg/projects/wboards.htm

Miller, D. (2003). Developing interactive whiteboard activity. *MicroMath, 19*, 33–35.

Miller, D., & Glover, D. (2004). *Enhancing mathematics teaching through new technology: The use of the interactive whiteboard. Summary of a report made to the Nuffield Foundation on completion of a funded two-year project* (April 2002-March 2004). Retrieved June 15, 2009, from http://www.keele.ac.uk/depts/ed/iaw/nuffield.htm, downloadable file at: http://www.keele.ac.uk/depts/ed/iaw/docs/NuffieldReport.pdf

Miller, D., Glover, D., & Averis, D. (2004). *Panacea or prop: the role of the interactive whiteboard in improving teaching effectiveness.* Paper presented at the Tenth International Congress of Mathematics Education, Copenhagen. Retrieved June 15, 2009, from http://www.icme-organisers.dk/tsg15/Glover_et_al.pdf

Moss, G. (2003). Analysing literacy events: Mapping gendered configurations of readers, texts and contexts . In Goodman, S., Lillis, T., Maybin, J., & Mercer, N. (Eds.), *Language, literacy and education: A reader* (pp. 123–137). London: Trentham Books.

Moss, G., Jewitt, C., Levačić, R., Armstrong, V., Cardini, A., Castle, F., et al. (2007). The interactive whiteboards, pedagogy and pupil performance evaluation: An evaluation of the schools whiteboard expansion (SWE) Project: London Challenge. London: DfES.

Noss, R., & Pachler, N. (1999). The challenge of new technologies: Doing old things in a new way or doing new things? In Mortimore, P. (Ed.), *Understanding Pedagogy and its impact on learning.* London: Paul Chapman.

Ofsted (2004). *ICT in schools: The impact of government initiatives five years on.* London: Ofsted.

Pittard, V., Bannister, P., & Dunn, J. (2003). The big pICTure: The impact of ICT on attainment, motivation and learning. London: DfES

Richardson, A. (2002). Effective questioning in teaching mathematics using an interactive whiteboard. *Micromath, 18*(2), 8–12.

Scrimshaw, P. (2004). *Enabling teachers to make successful use of ICT*. Coventry, UK: Becta.

SMART. (2004). *The History of SMART Technologies Inc*. Retrieved June 15, 2009, from http://www.smarttech.com/company/aboutus/history.asp

SMART Technologies Inc. (April 2004). *Interactive whiteboards and learning: A review of classroom case studies and research literature*. White Paper. Retrieved June 15, 2009, from http://dewey.uab.es/pmarques/pdigital/es/docs/Research%20White%20Paper.pdf

Smith, A. (1999). *Interactive whiteboard evaluation*. Retrieved June 15, 2009, from http://www.mirandanet.ac.uk/pubs/SMARTBoard.htm

Smith, H. (2001). *Smartboard evaluation final report, Kent NgfL*. Retrieved June 15, 2009, from http://www.kented.org.uk/ngfl/whiteboards/report.html

Smith, H. J., Higgins, S., Wall, K., & Miller, J. (2005). Interactive whiteboards: Boon or bandwagon? A critical review of the literature. *Journal of Computer Assisted Learning, 21*(2), 91–101. doi:10.1111/j.1365-2729.2005.00117.x

Somekh, B., Haldane, M., Jones, K., Lewin, C., Steadman, S., Scrimshaw, P., et al. (2007). *Evaluation of the primary schools whiteboard expansion project - Report to the Department for Children, Schools and Families*. Retrieved June 15, 2009, from http://partners.becta.org.uk/upload-dir/downloads/page_documents/research/whiteboards_expansion.pdf

Somekh, B., Lewin, C., Mavers, D., Fisher, T., Harrison, C., Haw, K., & Lunzer, E. (2002). *ImpaCT2: Pupils and teachers' perceptions of ICT in the home, school and community. A report to the DfES. ICT in schools research and evaluation series No 11*. Coventry, UK: Becta.

Twining, P., Evans, D., Cook, D., Ralston, J., Selwood, I., Jones, A., et al. with Heppell, S., Kukulska-Hulme, A., McAndrew, P., & Sheehy, K. (2005). *Tablet PCs in schools: Case study report*. Coventry, UK: Becta. Retrieved June 15, 2009, from http://www.becta.org.uk/corporate/publications/documents/tabletpc_report.pdf

ENDNOTE

[1] The Interactive Whiteboards, Pedagogy and Pupil Performance Evaluation was based at the Institute of Education, University of London, between 2004-6. The project directors were: Dr. Gemma Moss, Dr. Carey Jewitt and Professor Ros Levačić. Dr. Vicky Armstrong, Alejandra Cardini and Frances Castle were research officers on the case studies, and statistical analysis was undertaken by Rebecca Allen, Andrew Jenkins, and Maggie Hancock with Sue High. This paper draws on the nine case studies undertaken as part of this report. The full study was published by the DfES and can be downloaded at: http://www.dcsf.gov.uk/research/data/uploadfiles/RR816.pdff

Chapter 3
Interactive Whiteboards and the Discourses of Transformation, Affordance, Orchestration and Participation

Alison Twiner
The Open University, UK

ABSTRACT

This chapter offers a discussion of literature regarding the use of interactive whiteboards in English and Welsh classrooms, focusing predominantly on the primary sector. Broadly speaking a series of shifting terms can be plotted through the research, in how the IWB is characterized within the classroom. This is particularly notable in english and some welsh primary school contexts, in line with changes in curriculum policy and government-introduced national strategy, where the IWB as a particular technological and (arguably) pedagogic tool has been championed by government funding tied to policy change. The discussion reviews shifting characterizations of iwb use in schools, focusing on four key forms of discourse in the literature: transformation, affordance, orchestration and participation. Although discourses are not replaced, the chapter highlights shifts in emphasis from the power of the technology, to the power of the tool when in the hands of teachers and learners.

INTRODUCTION

This discussion of research literature focuses on how characterizations of interactive whiteboard use in education can be seen to vary by project focus and funding source. The descriptors, evident in the research, represent differing views of the relationship between technology and pedagogy, and differing views on pedagogy as for instance au-

thoritative, interactive or dialogic (Scott, Mortimer & Aguiar, 2006). Thus a series of shifting terms can be plotted through the research, in how the IWB is characterized within the classroom and how the tool influences or is influenced by dominant pedagogy. This will be addressed in the context of English primary classrooms (pupils aged 5-11 years), with some research also presented from Welsh primary classrooms. In this context, the IWB as a particular technological and (arguably) pedagogic tool has been championed by government funding tied

DOI: 10.4018/978-1-61520-715-2.ch003

to policy and curriculum change and initiative. While some research has been included in this review from other sectors where salient, take-up and funding for IWBs in secondary schools has been much slower. IWBs were often installed within subject or department areas, according to individual teacher expertise or enthusiasm (Moss et al., 2007).

Curriculum and policy initiatives, including £10m in 2003-4 to install IWBs in primary classrooms discussed below, provide broad scope for research. Inevitably, however, the evaluation of the tool, new to the classroom as it was in the late 1990s and early 2000s, occurred as users were exploring its use and utility within their teaching practices. For some teachers this became an opportunity to broaden their practices; for others it reinforced traditional practices that new educational strategies were attempting to lessen, such as substantial teacher-led instruction, and learning by drill and rote practice. A research-based focus on the IWB offers a useful lens to view how conceptualizations of use and pedagogic value have changed over a relatively short period of time.

The significance and meaning of the term "interactive" in respect of an "interactive whiteboard" is much debated, and perhaps a reason for many construing interactivity as a feature of the IWB rather than a feature of user activity with and around it. In this view, some researchers and practitioners prefer to call it a digital or electronic whiteboard (e.g. Haldane, 2007). Interactivity with regard to "interactive teaching" has been defined by the UK Department for Education and Employment (DfEE, 1998a) as where "pupils' contributions are encouraged, expected and extended" (p. 8). Research has noted however that much "interactive" use of the IWB is still at a surface level: Hargreaves et al. (2003) defined interactivity as either "surface" (quick fire question and answer) or "deep" (extended discussion). With this in mind, many teachers view interactive teaching as the use of question and answer sessions (Cutrim Schmid, 2008a). This

is not a judgment on the inherent interactivity or advantages of question and answer strategies, but falls short of a dream of interactive teaching and learning where users are physically, verbally and conceptually engaged, or interacting with manipulable learning resources and content, in co-constructing their understanding. This "dream" combines Smith, Higgins, Wall and Miller's (2005) technical and pedagogic interactivity, and Jewitt, Moss and Cardini's (2007) technical, physical and conceptual interactivity.

This chapter shows that the roles and responsibilities ascribed to teachers and pupils can vary, depending on the role in which the IWB is cast. Features related to classroom IWB use, commonly multimodality, (fast) pace and interactivity for instance, have been identified by researchers, from different theoretical backgrounds, for a number of years. However, what these features are claimed to add to lessons and learning, or how they are utilized can differ relative to the particular political, financial and theoretical viewpoints within which they are framed. This discussion presents a review of shifts in describing IWBs in schools, focusing on four key forms of discourse in the literature, which at times co-occur: transformation, affordance, orchestration and participation.

Discourses Surrounding IWB Use

Transformation

As IWBs started entering UK schools in the late 1990s, particularly coinciding with the substantial government funding in 2003-4 to install IWBs into primary schools (Primary Schools Whiteboard Expansion project, PSWE), there arose a powerful discourse around the IWB as a "transformative" device. An article entitled, "What the research says about interactive whiteboards" collated in 2003 by the British Educational Communications and Technology Agency (Becta), stated three times in a four-page summary that the IWB could be used to "transform learning". The focus was on how this new educational technology tool could, or in some cases would, "revolutionize" teaching and learning, as also claimed by the then Education Secretary, Charles Clarke, in 2004.

The IWB was considered as a tool for the classroom and a potential vehicle suited to the push toward interactive whole-class teaching with the introduction of the National Literacy and Numeracy Strategies in 1998 and 1999 (Hargreaves et al., 2003). This curricular drive was a response to a perceived need for a standardized and traceable means of improving achievement, particularly in these two subject areas. The push was also supported by international research that interactive whole-class teaching correlated with higher levels of achievement in many Pacific Rim countries (Reynolds & Farrell, 1996).

Before the widespread adoption of IWBs in schools, but aiming to offer advice on the use of ICT in general that would be relatively "future-proof" in respect of technological developments, the DfEE (1998b) encouraged teachers to "use ICT with the whole class or a group for introducing or reviewing a topic and ensuring that all pupils cover the key conceptual features of the topic, e.g. through the use of a single screen or display" (p. 6). Specifically related to the IWB, Smith (2001) presented findings that the most successful pupil interaction was achieved through whole-class teacher-directed use of the IWB from the front of the class, rather than during independent or group activity.

The £10 million of government funding for IWBs in primary schools came at a time when the National Literacy and Numeracy Strategies were being revised into the Primary National Strategy (PNS). With this there was a stronger push toward interactive whole-class teaching which had already been implicated in the original documents. In the new strategy document, Charles Clarke stated, "High standards – especially in literacy and numeracy – are the backbone of success in learning and in life" (Department for Education and Skills, 2003). The tool, the IWB, and the method of

interactive whole-class teaching, were marketed as the perfect combination to meet curricular requirements, assess pupil learning, and above all, increase educational attainment on a national, quantifiable scale. A report by Becta (2004), for example, claimed that:

The key feature of this technology is that it emphasises whole class teaching strategies. These include teacher modelling and demonstration, prompting, probing and promoting questioning, managed whole-class discussions, review of work in progress to reinforce key points emerging from individual and group work, and whole-class evaluation in plenary sessions. (p. 4)

The aim was that the proposed nation-wide introduction of IWBs into primary classrooms would support the achievement of such "high standards", as a tool to support interactive whole-class teaching. A DfES-commissioned pilot study was described within the 2003 report as underway in six Local Education Authorities to identify and disseminate ways in which the tool could be utilized in pursuing this aim. Thus research aligned to the discourse of transformation and revolutionizing learning with the IWB has tended to focus on evidence, impact, and change, addressing quantifiable outcomes and products of teaching and learning.

The benefits of using the IWB, and the potential transformation of teaching and learning through its use were most strongly advocated with respect to what it could add to lessons and learning that was not previously possible. For example, prepared material could be worked through, edited, highlighted, and saved for future revision. These aspects were highlighted by Miller and Glover (2002), who addressed the use of the IWB in five primary schools in an Education Action Zone (EAZ) and Walker (2002) who examined IWBs in the primary school Maths classroom. EAZs funded by the DfEE were permitted to focus on literacy and numeracy, rather than full curriculum coverage, due to being considered challenging areas. They were abolished by the Government in 2001 and replaced with the Excellence for Schools initiative. A further benefit of the IWB was highlighted in the use of multimedia resources to illustrate oral description (Glover & Miller, 2001a).

There was also much discussion of the increased pace resulting from the use of the IWB: Ball (2003) and Miller (2003) commented on this when observing use of prepared IWB resources in Maths lessons; Latham (2002) identified IWB use easing transition between learning points in a case study of primary Maths within a specific EAZ. Such use was considered potentially transformative, bringing new activities into the classroom, or making previous activities easier, quicker, or "better". The importance of pace in teaching and learning cannot be underestimated, particularly in making timely links to previous material to show the alignment of concepts (Alexander, 2000).

Hargreaves et al. (2003) addressed the notion of interactivity within literacy, due to it being identified in the National Literacy Strategy as one of five criteria in "successful teaching". They distinguished between surface and deep interactivity (as described earlier). Deep interactivity was however rarely observed, and considered to occur at the expense of faster pace. This indicated a drive for transformation by quick teacher-led coverage of content, rather than pupil interaction with content. Hardman, Smith and Wall (2003) also reported that "interactive whole-class teaching" had been poorly defined, making it difficult for teachers to interpret and implement, and examples were rarely seen in practice. Assumptions of "transformation" and "interactivity" within this discourse were largely explicated with respect to the potential of the technology, and not concerned with teacher skills or adaptability to new tools, nor teachers' preferred pedagogic approach or desire to alter their practice.

In line with a trend for quantifying and assessing impact, a number of researchers attempted to classify teachers in terms of their proficiency with the technology in class – how they had transformed themselves via the potential of the IWB as a transformative technology. Based on questionnaire responses, they were labeled by Glover and Miller (2001b) as either "missioners", those "transforming" their practice; "tentatives", willing to use technology but unsure how to adapt practice; or "luddites", resistant to technological change. Further to this, a transitional framework was identified by Beauchamp (2004) through class observation and semi-structured interviews with teachers in a technology-rich primary school, to categories teachers' use of the IWB, from blackboard/whiteboard substitute, apprentice user, initiate user, advanced user, to synergistic user. Once again transformation was depicted as a bottom to top process, with synergistic users presented as examples of "transformed" practitioners. Still addressing IWB use, but with a view to whole-class interaction rather than a focus solely on the teacher, a Five-level framework was devised by Tanner, Jones, Kennewell and Beauchamp (2005). This aimed to describe whole-class teaching by the apparent locus of control, from lecture through to collective reflection, based on reflections on practice and policy guidelines introduced in the PNS.

Frameworks and categorizations of teachers' practice with the IWB began to extend beyond a transformative discourse, though perhaps still rooted within a technological view of the tool. Research building on these categories or hierarchies allowed consideration of how such categories fit within the wider school environment. Glover and Miller, in 2007, shifting focus more toward the learning environment in which lessons occur, collected video recordings of 46 Maths lessons in seven secondary schools, six months after IWB installation. From this data they aimed to categories "the culture of the learning experience", which for each observed lesson was then coded as traditional, transitory or interactive using a list of key features identified by the researchers from viewing the videos. They found that most teachers across different lessons could be coded under different categories, shifting according to need/purpose, and highlighting that practice was not necessarily a static quality of an individual teacher. While still discretely coding teachers' practice as belonging to one category or another, Glover and Miller's coding was located within the wider "culture" of the school, recognizing that teachers demonstrated different practices on different occasions.

Tanner and Jones (2007) used Tanner et al.'s (2005) framework described above for classifying teachers' practice, to provide an updated review of the literature concerning IWB use. They argued that there were tensions between implicit assumptions of what the IWB can do and guidance within National Strategy documents, concerning: the need for a fast pace against allowance for thinking time/reflection; the need to meet lesson objectives against exploration of pupils' methods; and the use of factual recall against constructive use of pupil error. Such findings suggest a link between the discourses of transformation and affordance, in the challenges that can be posed and potential solutions provided by use of the tool when viewed in the curricular context.

Affordance

Developing from this largely technology-driven view of the introduction and initial reaction to IWBs in the classroom, many researchers began viewing the tool in terms of affordances, potential and constraints. Kennewell (2001) defined affordance as "the attributes of the setting which provide potential for action" (p. 106). This view allowed some researchers to focus on technical affordances: what the tool could do, such as the partnership research agenda between the IWB manufacturer Promethean and the MirandaNet fellowship – a group represented by numerous professions aiming to promote ICT use in education. Other researchers adopted a user-focused stance, observing what teachers and learners could,

wanted to, and actually did do with the IWB (e.g. Smith et al., 2005).

Smith et al. (2005) in a literature review of IWB use since its widespread introduction offered a distinction concerning some of the cited "affordances" of the IWB, in terms of technical and pedagogic interactivity:

We would argue that the uniqueness and the "boon" of IWB technology lies in the possibility for an intersection between **technical** *and* **pedagogic** *interactivity; in other words, in the opportunities this technology holds for collective meaning making through both dialogic interaction with one another, and physical interaction with the board. (p. 99, authors' emphasis)*

The IWB was portrayed as a tool that could enhance teaching through technical interactivity with the board – by both teacher and pupil – but also pedagogic interactivity between teacher and pupils, as well as pupils among themselves. In this process, the pupils attempts to construct meaning together and further their joint and individual understanding by explaining their own ideas and concepts to one another. Smith et al. noted that pedagogic interactivity and social (re)construction of meaning was relatively rare in lessons observed, supporting Hargreaves et al.'s (2003) finding of a predominance of surface interactivity. This potentially suggested that classroom focus was still largely on notions of transformation and technical interactivity – such as "drag and drop" activity – rather than using the IWB to facilitate the joint construction of meaning.

Regarding Smith et al.'s (2005) distinction, Kennewell, Tanner, Jones and Beauchamp (2008) argued that there can be confusion when using IWBs between technical and pedagogic interactivity, regarding the structure and potential of tools to support task completion and/or learning gains, i.e. how to address product and process. Within this study, the researchers analyzed data against a framework model for teaching and learning (Kennewell, 2001). Other researchers have highlighted teachers' concerns over the prevalence of testing and external assessment, wherein a certain focus on learning products and outcomes and getting the "right" answer is inevitable (Wood & Ashfield, 2008). Teachers may not necessarily feel this is the "best" way to teach their pupils, but utilize the IWB as affording easy display of information to meet curriculum requirements.

The concept of affordance seemed to be a midway point for some researchers, reflecting on the discourse of transformation, often more tentatively than earlier claims, and looking toward teacher orchestration and pupil participation. Somekh (2007) proposed that "[t]he development of new social practices will therefore be transformative to varying degrees, depending on the affordances of the tool, the skill with which human agents learn to use them and their ability to imagine new possibilities" (p. 13). This is supported by Laurillard (2002) within Higher Education. This brings into question where affordances of technology use, such as multimodality, pace and interactivity, are attributed: as within the technological tool, or under the teacher's control in managing lesson activity. Agency therefore, being in control or just watching, is critical: Jewitt et al. (2007) for instance stated that "a multimodal, interactive and a fast-paced pedagogy are not necessarily good in and of themselves" (p. 316). Reviewing this dilemma in terms of affordance and agency, Kennewell, Beauchamp et al. (2008) concluded that teachers "need to become attuned to the affordances and constraints of ICT's features so that they can orchestrate these effectively in support of task goals and learning goals" (p. 22). Thus the relationship of the tool's affordances to how to orchestrate them in class was a pedagogic challenge teachers were addressing.

This suggests a contrast between the discourses of transformation and affordance, and two complementary forms of discourse concerning the orchestration of resources and pupil participation. These two discourses in particular tend to co-occur, seeing both teacher and pupils as active agents in perceiving and utilizing affordances and functionalities of the IWB which support the current learning situation and need – any transformation is that which is orchestrated by users of the tool.

Orchestration and Participation

In general research has been moving toward discourses of orchestration of resources and learner participation. Research questions within these two discourses frequently explore the nature of interaction and dialogue around such tools and use of additional resources, describing processes and pedagogies rather than quantifying outcomes. Focus has been shifting from the power of the technology to the role of the teacher and involvement of the class. Researchers using these discourses have argued against a notion that the IWB will replace other resources and have adopted a sociocultural framework to suggest the IWB will be a tool within the teacher's toolkit, thus enabling teachers to orchestrate a rich interplay of various modes and media while using the most appropriate method for each task (e.g. Littleton, Twiner & Gillen, in press). Gillen, Littleton, Twiner, Kleine Staarman, and Mercer (2008) also drew on Wertsch's (1991) notion of the "mediational toolkit", to view the IWB both as a toolkit encapsulating a number of functionalities or affordances of which the teachers and learners can use the most relevant, and as one tool among numerous others available to the class as a whole. This was applied in the context of a primary Science classroom. In Wertsch's terms, the tool or toolkit only has purpose and potential when brought into interaction.

Littleton et al. (in press) defined orchestration as:

a metaphor that captures the teachers' pursuit of overall goals, weaving together of themes and sub-themes, while allowing some flexibility of responsiveness in the dialogue with students. Or-

chestrating is not just about putting the resources in play, it is also about acknowledging and making useful pupils' contributions, as significant evidencing of a process. (n.p.)

As alluded to above, the IWB is one resource among many, available to the teacher and pupils, to be foregrounded and backgrounded as appropriate: orchestration can occur at the level of the activity, as well as across various resources.

Kennewell, Beauchamp et al. (2008) linked notions of affordance to orchestration and participation in stating "ICT supports dialogic teaching by providing affordances for learning interaction: about … with … through ICT" (p. 15). This particular reference however is ambiguous as to what or who is the active agent in providing this "support". Adopting a sociocultural and sociolinguistic framework, Alexander (2008) argues that dialogic teaching focuses on "the quality, dynamics and content of talk, regardless of the way classrooms and lessons are organised. And it challenges us to re-assess attendant notions of time and pace" (p. 23). Glover, Miller, Averis and Door (2007) contended that "research during the first phase of IWB installation in schools concentrated on the benefits accruing from the technology rather than on analysis of the ways in which pedagogy may need to be changed" (p. 6). A similar thought to that expressed by Kennewell, Beauchamp et al. (2008) above, worded slightly differently by Lewin, Somekh and Steadman (2008), placed the onus clearly with the teacher: "it is the teacher who, when teaching, mediates all the many kinds of interactivity that an IWB, as a mediating artefact, can facilitate to stimulate and support learning" (p. 301).

Orchestration

The notion of IWB use and utility via the lens of teacher orchestration emphasizes that it is in the teacher's hands to employ the technology to complement learning goals. It also highlights the

inherent dangers of an assumption that technology will drive the lesson rather than the learning: "Since the technology allows a seamless access to multimedia resources, there is a potential danger of using the technology mainly to give lessons a crisp pace, instead of focusing on making the best pedagogical use of these resources" (Cutrim Schmid, 2008b, p. 1566). This identifies the concern raised by Hargreaves et al. (2003), that fast pace at the expense of deep interactivity, is still an issue. Cutrim Schmid's paper addressed how international students at a British university on a pre-sessional English course used IWBs. Cutrim Schmid defined multimedia as the "use of computers to present text, graphics, video, animation, and sound in an integrated way" (p. 1553). This suggests the advantage of such multimedia resources lies in how they are orchestrated together and with other resources, to present a fuller picture of content being covered. She pinpointed research stating that IWB and multimedia were well-suited "because it [the IWB] enables a seamless and easy access to multimedia resources … in conjunction with the facility to highlight, annotate, drag, drop and conceal linguistic units" (p. 1554). These arguments draw on a number of other researchers (Gray, Hagger-Vaughan, Pilkington & Tomkins, 2005; Hall & Higgins, 2005; Moss et al., 2007; Walker, 2003). While many would claim these are not "revolutionary" uses of the IWB, the critical factor for Cutrim Schmid lay in how these functions were employed within the learning experience. Thus the teacher could use this technological tool to address the educational challenge of achieving coherence between learning points, which calls for the virtues of the IWB to be considered in its context of use.

Cleaves and Toplis (2008) presented a cautionary note as trainee secondary Science teachers in their study reported on use of dataloggers with the IWB. A datalogger is a tool for automating data collection and calculation, and producing graphs that can easily be manipulated. In interview the trainee teachers claimed that although a datalogger combined with the IWB could save time, there was some reluctance as it masked much of the process, removing the need for pupils to estimate, plot graphs or work with data. The trainee teachers also recounted that multimedia and animations were used to demonstrate concepts, but could be misleading as they rarely presented "noisy" data. Reporting on use of simulations presented on the IWB, Hennessy, Wishart et al. (2007) commented that the teacher's role changed from helping with problems doing the task such as in practical experiments, to helping discussion of learning points evidenced in the simulation. Teachers also reportedly facilitated discussion of discrepancy in simulated models, encouraging critical thinking of the learning material and content contained in the display, and showing a means of addressing Cleaves and Toplis' concern through dialogue around the resource. Thus orchestration occurred in the form of "connection building" (Gee & Green, 1998): a crucial part of the teacher's role, and of critical educational significance for developing pupils' cumulative understanding (Littleton et al., in press).

Many teachers and researchers would be keen to highlight however that the IWB is an addition, not a replacement to other tools in the teacher's toolkit, and that simulations or animations would be used alongside practical experimentation, such as in Science. Hennessy and Deaney (2006) identified such a concept in terms of "matched resources", where content presented or referred to in different modes can offer different avenues to the same objective. The alignment and discussion of these complementary resources requires the teacher's timely orchestration to have the most benefit for pupils' learning and understanding.

Regarding classroom talk and teacher orchestration, teachers' use of the IWB in capturing the ephemeral aspects of classroom dialogue was noted by Haldane (2007): "because of the transient nature of the spoken word, during the process of dialogue, key points are often captured and converted to some more stable format by the teacher" (p. 260). She considered the IWB as a "stable" medium, unlike talk which is an "unstable" medium and disappears once spoken. Thus the stability of the IWB can be a backdrop on which to record significant ideas.

The notion of pace remained but was reframed within the discourse of orchestration by Kennewell, Beauchamp et al. (2008), reporting that speed was useful in providing instant feedback, but potentially distracted attention from learning goals encouraging task completion rather than understanding of processes behind the learning activity. Within their study some pupils were found to subvert tasks, particularly if a trial and error strategy allowed them to arrive at the "answer". Where the teacher was available they could re-direct attention to the learning intentions and underlying understanding. Thus teacher orchestration was critical to pupils gaining more than just a performance score from such tasks.

Within these examples, orchestration can be seen through observed responses to educational challenges, such as aligning key concepts, and assisting cumulative understanding. The overarching discourse of orchestration was played out through teachers' use of tools and strategies such as integration, connection building, and matched resources, to encourage pupil participation in dialogue and tasks leading to the co-construction of knowledge.

Participation

Despite Cleaves and Toplis' (2008) reported concern over use of dataloggers and their automated output data, it has been noted that in terms of a discourse of participation, using pupils' own data in spreadsheets displayed on the IWB for instance offered pupils a stronger sense of ownership of lesson content (Cutrim Schmid, 2008a). How learners' data are used however is critical, employing both the teacher's orchestration of the data, and the space given for pupil participation and involvement with their data. Cutrim Schmid

(2008b) employed cognitive learning theory in addressing learners' articulations of two dangers in teachers' IWB use and multimedia presentation of information. Firstly, there is a danger of cognitive overload. Equally there is danger of teachers doing too much and so "spoon feeding" explanations without much need for the learner to engage with or actively process the content, resulting in lack of cognitive engagement. Both dangers imply minimal pupil participation.

Warwick (2008, personal communication) reporting on an ongoing study observing Science in six primary schools, identified that at present the capacity for IWBs to support pupil collaborative work was not being utilized. The study found that most pupils had not previously collaborated at the IWB, and while some could use it well from observing teachers' use, others had difficulty. Seeing the IWB as a vehicle to enhance pupil participation promotes the notion of dialogic teaching, and begins to address the relationship between pedagogic interactivity, as acknowledging alternative ideas by teachers and pupils in collective meaning making; dialogic teaching, facilitating genuine openness and discussion; and interactive teaching, via deep interactivity such as extended discussion. Petrou, Kerawalla and Scanlon (2009) devised software for the IWB ("Talk Factory") to scaffold development of pupils' argumentation strategies in group work to design, conduct and evaluate primary Science investigations. This combination of task and technology aimed to address the educational challenge that pupils often do not possess or use discursive strategies for argumentation (Mercer & Littleton, 2007), as well as the goal of encouraging pupil participation.

On a more conceptual level, Scott et al. (2006) provided a framework for considering teachers' encouragement and allowance for pupil contribution, offering two continua of authoritative/dialogic, and non-interactive/interactive communicative approach. Thus a teacher could use an authoritative, largely instructive approach, or a dialogic approach, drawing on pupil contributions, which may be invited at the time or invoking earlier contributions. At the same time this can be interactive, with pupil involvement at the time, or non-interactive, where pupils listen. In presenting the framework Scott and colleagues acknowledged that all approaches will be more suited to certain activities, and so there is no hierarchy of a better or worse approach, merely a need to consider which is the most appropriate to the task and context. Concerning the IWB therefore, using a prepared presentation file may be suited to an authoritative, non-interactive approach in introducing new material, in a period of minimal pupil participation. The same file could be re-used to encourage participation within a more dialogic, interactive manner to be reviewed and revisited, queried and altered as pupils become more familiar with the material (Gillen, Kleine Staarman, Littleton, Mercer & Twiner, 2007).

The nature of participation that can be beneficial to learning has been discussed in terms of pupils' physical interaction with the IWB; as guided participation (Rogoff, 1995) with teachers encouraging pupils to move from the periphery to take on greater responsibility for their learning; and vicarious participation in pupils watching peers complete tasks or provide explanations to the whole class (Hennessy, Deaney, Ruthven & Winterbottom, 2007). Hodge and Anderson (2007) emphasized the importance of a dialogic, interactive approach and pupil participation, in that if not careful it can be easy for teachers to use the IWB as a means of classroom management.

Cutrim Schmid (2008a) for instance highlighted the importance of providing opportunities for "socio-cognitive interactivity associated with learning processes involving co-construction of knowledge between teacher and learners" (p. 342), drawing on cognitive load theory and sociocultural theory. Hennessy, Deaney et al. (2007) also claimed that "the strength of the IWB lies in its support for shared cognition, especially articulation, collective evaluation and reworking of pupils' own ideas, and co-construction of new knowledge" (p. 298), which they linked back to Hargreaves et al.'s (2003) concept of "deep interactivity". Such findings indicate how the IWB can be used by teachers to generate and resource discussion, prompting pupils' meaningful participation in the topic.

Pupil participation and response to IWB material was highlighted by Gillen et al. (2007) as a means of contesting or re-ordering planned content. Within observed lessons, Gillen et al. identified two occasions in a literacy lesson where pupils queried the teacher's prepared content on the IWB display. On the first occasion, in discussing a recipe as an instructional text, a pupil suggested that an instruction within the specific recipe was missing. The teacher acknowledged the pupil's contribution as valid, but the IWB slide remained unchanged: a relatively authoritative, interactive approach to use Scott et al.'s (2006) term. On the second occasion, when a pupil asked a question about the task referenced on the IWB, the teacher took this as an opportunity to add to his IWB slide, adopting a more dialogic, interactive approach. Therefore whilst the IWB can be considered stable, as above, it can support the provisionality and mutability of presented material. Pupils' ideas can be explored, and teachers' plans updated in class, evidencing orchestration of resource and dialogue which both influence and are influenced by pupil participation, without fear that writing something means it is the final or "right" answer. This calls for teachers to be flexible between planned structure and spontaneity, and offers learners opportunities to respectfully challenge authority and discuss material.

Regarding such flexibility, Sawyer (2004) queried the metaphor of teaching as performance, suggesting instead that teaching be considered as *improvisational* performance which frames learning as a social activity, in line with social constructionist accounts of teaching and learning and allowing for spontaneous and creative teaching practice still within the confines of the curriculum,

thus termed "disciplined improvisation". This specific research was not related to the IWB, but addressed creative teaching by comparing the dialogue of improvising actors to classroom dialogue, where responses cannot be predicted and are contingent on earlier discursive moves.

A discourse of participation therefore emphasizes the roles of the pupils and teacher, through dialogue, technical and pedagogic interactivity, in encouraging learners to be active in developing individual and shared knowledge. It demonstrates how the IWB can be used to support, display and record developing understanding, but that the power of any tool is in the hands of the teachers and learners using it.

A Note on Methodology and Methods

A lot of the research deploying the discourse of transformation has been based on large-scale studies, presented with statistics or frequency analysis of survey data (e.g. Glover & Miller, 2001a), with government department or agency-funded focus on attainment scores (e.g. Crowne, 2008). Research questions have often addressed measures of impact or improvement: other key terms in evidencing change through the use of the technology, as reported by Lewin et al. (2008) in presenting a portion of data from a government-funded study.

Research deploying a discourse of affordance around the IWB has largely been based on relatively small-scale case study evidence and some use of mixed methods, with some drawing on frameworks or categorizations of IWB users, or types of use (Kennewell, 2001). Such studies utilized pre- and post-assessment tests, teacher interviews and pupil focus groups, and lesson observations often with two cameras to address activity both at and away from the IWB (Kennewell, Beauchamp et al., 2008). This demonstrates a sense of quantifying or categorizing use, but also a move away from the sole focus on the IWB as the source of activity, and a recognition of pupil voice in analysis.

Research reflecting discourses of orchestration and pupil participation has adopted predominantly qualitative methods, using small-scale case studies (e.g. Gillen et al., 2007, 2008), and some Video Stimulated Reflective Dialogue with teachers and occasionally pupils, recognizing the importance of user perception in the use of this particular technological tool (Hargreaves et al., 2003; Kennewell, Beauchamp et al., 2008; Kennewell, Tanner et al., 2008). Moreover, funding has typically been provided by research councils rather than government departments or agencies (e.g. Hennessy, Wishart et al., 2007). Research questions have focused on the interplay between teachers, pupils, resources used in the classroom including but not limited to the IWB or ICT, and the wider environment (e.g. Littleton et al., in press). Research behind these two discourses has predominantly drawn on sociocultural theory, emphasizing the teacher's role in scaffolding (Wood, Bruner & Ross, 1976) learning for the pupils, through orchestration of activity and resource, encouraging pupil participation to allow the scaffold to be faded, and for the group and individual to construct their own knowledge of the specific subject.

MOVING FORWARD

What Areas are Missing, Outlined in the Research?

Much of the research into IWB use in classrooms has been from a teacher or learner perspective, but rarely both. Studies have mostly been situated in primary or secondary schools, and within this predominantly primary. Although not the focus of this chapter, there has been minimal exploration of IWB use in further or higher education, with the exception of Cutrim Schmid for example, or informal learning environments. Studies suggest a difference in IWB use between primary and secondary schools: specifically in Science,

Beauchamp and Parkinson (2008) found that there can be a move from the generic tool of the IWB in primary which offers simulated access to concepts, to a mix of subject-specific, practical tools in secondary which may offset the need for or dominance of a single device such as the IWB. It is also often the case that primary schools are more likely than secondary schools to have an IWB in every class, whereby secondary teachers may not be able to rely on having access to an IWB. The experience of IWB use in primary and secondary school can therefore vary substantially.

Within the research there has tended to be a focus on English, Maths and Science lessons. This is perhaps as these are the easiest to gain "baseline" measurements from, in the form of national tests, and lessons are also more likely to cover similar material across a range of schools and Local Authorities due to the need to cover curriculum content and prepare pupils for assessment. Owing to their status in the curriculum, as identified by the Education Secretary at the time (DfES, 2003), it is also likely that there are more commercially-developed resources available for these subjects, for use with an IWB. Researchers have addressed the use of commercial IWB resources in class, compared with teachers' and pupils' attitudes and practices in using resources developed themselves, but a discussion of these issues is beyond the scope of this chapter (for a discussion see Jewitt et al., 2007).

In terms of temporality, the projects often conducted observations over a series of lessons, but few have used this to view the progression and accumulation of ideas. Though there are some exceptions to this, including our own paper (Littleton et al., in press) and Hennessy and Deaney's (2005-2007) T-MEDIA project in secondary schools, Glover et al. (2007) stated that "there has, however, been little attempt to explore sequentiality in concept development and the ways in which the IWB can foster responses to a range of learning processes" (p. 6). Some projects focusing on a series of lessons honed in on consistency of practice, or development of teachers' skills, but lessons were not necessarily consecutive or on a continuous topic. Further observation of consecutive topic lessons would allow insight into development as well as revising of ideas and resources across time.

CONCLUSION

Transformation Revisited

A discourse of transformation is not unique to the IWB. Other technologies including Personal Computers (Shields, 1995) have been heralded for their potential to radically reform the nature of education. And this pattern does not stop, as Crook (2008) identified in a report on use of Web 2.0 technologies in schools: "It is encouraging that individual innovators and some whole institutions are making progress with an obviously promising technology. But one thing that must be better understood is how the transformation possibility of Web 2.0 practices are realised" (p. 55).

It can be noted that within certain areas of IWB research, notably those more concerned with the development of technology, the discourse of transformation is still very evident, if perhaps a little more muted than previously. In a one-page document authored by the Becta chief executive, the "transformation" discourse was still evident. The closing argument stated: "technology can and should transform schools and colleges … [in terms of management and record keeping]. But, most important, it transforms the learning experience of our children, young people and adult learners" (Crowne, 2008, p. 10). Thus the need to drive change was still central, but the discourse of transformation was not seen as solely based on assessment scores and quantifiable measures, and had shifted to consider the learning process as an important area of observation.

As mentioned, the curriculum and policy initiatives of the 1980s and 90s provided fertile ground for research into the use of the IWB in the classroom context, but inevitably the evaluation of the tool, new to the classroom as it was in the late 1990s, occurred as teachers and learners were exploring a new resource in the context of an evolving curriculum. Unsurprisingly, some teachers embraced this time as an opportunity to broaden their practices; for other teachers the introduction of the IWB and coinciding policies inadvertently and perhaps comfortingly reinforced traditional practices that new educational strategies were attempting to lessen, such as substantial instruction, learning by drill and rote practice. Again, as Glover et al. (2007) claimed, in looking back over research conducted in the early days of IWBs in schools, "research during the first phase of IWB installation in schools concentrated on the benefits accruing from the technology rather than on analysis of the ways in which pedagogy may need to be changed" (p. 6).

This chapter has offered a way of reading the literature on IWBs in teaching and learning, through a shifting view of how it has been represented, the agency it has been accorded, and the research and funding agenda in which it has been situated. Viewing the literature in this way allows the shift in emphasis to be seen, from the IWB as a transformative device, irrespective of use or user, through a consideration of it as a tool with functionalities and affordances that may or may not be apparent to users, and on to a more user-oriented view of the IWB as one resource amongst many to be foregrounded and backgrounded as appropriate, as the backdrop for learning material and concepts, and as one site for encouraging and hosting pupil participation in class discussion. Notions of participatory culture are increasingly occurring in literature regarding the IWB and other classroom technologies (Crook, 2008), whereby practice with and research around the IWB are mirroring trends of other technological developments, and reflecting more general changes in pupils' in and out-of-school experiences.

REFERENCES

Alexander, R. (2000). *Culture and pedagogy: International comparisons in primary education.* Malden, MA: Blackwell Publishers.

Alexander, R. (2008). *Towards dialogic teaching: Rethinking classroom talk* (4th ed.). York, UK: Dialogos.

Ball, B. (2003). Teaching and learning mathematics with an interactive whiteboard. *Micromath, 19*(1), 4–7.

Beauchamp, G. (2004). Teacher use of the interactive whiteboard in primary schools: Towards an effective transition framework. *Technology, Pedagogy and Education, 13*(3), 327–348. doi:10.1080/14759390400200186

Beauchamp, G., & Parkinson, J. (2008). Pupils' attitudes towards school science as they transfer from an ICT-rich primary school to a secondary school with fewer ICT resources: Does ICT matter? *Education and Information Technologies, 13*(2), 103–118. doi:10.1007/s10639-007-9053-5

Becta (2003). *What the research says about interactive whiteboards.* Coventry, UK: Becta. Retrieved October 21, 2008, from http://partners. becta.org.uk/upload-dir/downloads/page_documents/research/wtrs_whiteboards.pdf

Becta (2004). *Getting the most from your interactive whiteboard: A guide for secondary schools.* Coventry, UK: Becta. Retrieved December 8, 2008, from http://foi.becta.org.uk/content_files/ corporate/resources/foi/archived_publications/ getting_most_whiteboard_secondary.pdf

Cleaves, A., & Toplis, R. (2008). Pre-service science teachers and ICT: Communities of practice? *Research in Science & Technological Education, 26*(2), 203–213. doi:10.1080/02635140802037344

Crook, C. (2008). *Web 2.0 technologies for learning: The current landscape – opportunities, challenges and tensions.* Coventry, UK: Becta.

Crowne, S. (2008). 'Next generation learning' – promoting the benefits of technology in schools and FE. *Education Journal, 109,* 10.

Cutrim Schmid, E. (2008a). Using a voting system in conjunction with interactive whiteboard technology to enhance learning in the English language classroom. *Computers & Education, 50*(1), 338–356. doi:10.1016/j.compedu.2006.07.001

Cutrim Schmid, E. (2008b). Potential pedagogical benefits and drawbacks of multimedia use in the English language classroom equipped with interactive whiteboard technology. *Computers & Education, 51*(4), 1553–1568. doi:10.1016/j. compedu.2008.02.005

Department for Education and Employment. (1998a). *The national literacy strategy: A framework for teaching.* London: HMSO.

Department for Education and Employment. (1998b). *Initial teacher training national curriculum for the use of information and communication technology in subject teaching. Circular 4/98, Annex B.* Department for Education and Employment.

Department for Education and Skills. (2003). *Excellence and enjoyment: A strategy for primary schools.* London: Department for Education and Skills. Retrieved October 28, 2008, from http:// www.standards.dfes.gov.uk/primary/publications/literacy/63553/pns_excell_enjoy037703v2. pdf

Gee, J., & Green, J. (1998). Discourse analysis, learning, and social practice: A methodological study. *Review of Research in Education, 23*(1), 119–169. doi:10.3102/0091732X023001119

Gillen, J., Kleine Staarman, J., Littleton, K., Mercer, N., & Twiner, A. (2007). A 'learning revolution'? Investigating pedagogic practice around interactive whiteboards in British primary classrooms. *Learning, Media and Technology, 32*(3), 243–256. doi:10.1080/17439880701511099

Gillen, J., Littleton, K., Twiner, A., Kleine Staarman, J., & Mercer, N. (2008). Using the interactive whiteboard to resource continuity and support multimodal teaching in a primary science classroom. *Journal of Computer Assisted Learning, 24*(4), 348–358. doi:10.1111/j.1365-2729.2007.00269.x

Glover, D., & Miller, D. (2001a). Running with technology: The pedagogic impact of the large-scale introduction of interactive whiteboards in one secondary school. *Journal of Information Technology for Teacher Education, 10*(3), 257–276.

Glover, D., & Miller, D. (2001b, October). *Missioners, tentatives and luddites: Leadership challenges for school and classroom posed by the introduction of interactive whiteboards into schools in the UK.* Paper presented at the British Educational Management and Administration Society conference, Newport Pagnell, UK.

Glover, D., & Miller, D. (2007). Leading changed classroom culture: The impact of interactive whiteboards. *Management in Education, 21*(3), 21–24. doi:10.1177/0892020607079988

Glover, D., Miller, D., Averis, D., & Door, V. (2007). The evolution of an effective pedagogy for teachers using the interactive whiteboard in mathematics and modern languages: An empirical analysis from the secondary sector. *Learning, Media and Technology, 32*(1), 5–20. doi:10.1080/17439880601141146

Gray, G., Hagger-Vaughan, L., Pilkington, R., & Tomkins, S. (2005). The pros and cons of interactive whiteboards in relation to the key stage 3 strategies and framework. *Language Learning Journal, 32*(1), 38–44. doi:10.1080/09571730585200171

Haldane, M. (2007). Interactivity and the digital whiteboard: Weaving the fabric of learning. *Learning, Media and Technology, 32*(3), 257–270. doi:10.1080/17439880701511107

Hall, I., & Higgins, S. (2005). Primary school students' perceptions of interactive whiteboards. *Journal of Computer Assisted Learning, 21*(2), 102–117. doi:10.1111/j.1365-2729.2005.00118.x

Hardman, F., Smith, F., & Wall, K. (2003). 'Interactive whole class teaching' in the National Literacy Strategy. *Cambridge Journal of Education, 33*(2), 197–215. doi:10.1080/03057640302043

Hargreaves, L., Moyles, J., Merry, R., Paterson, F., Pell, A., & Esarte-Sarries, V. (2003). How do primary school teachers define and implement 'interactive teaching' in the national literacy strategy in England. *Research Papers in Education, 18*(3), 217–236. doi:10.1080/0267152032000107301

Hennessy, S., & Deaney, R. (2006, September). *Integrating multiple teacher and researcher perspectives through video analysis of pedagogic approaches to using projection technologies.* Paper presented at British Educational Research Association conference, Warwick, UK.

Hennessy, S., & Deaney, R. (2005-2007). *T-MEDIA: Exploring teacher mediation of subject learning with ICT: A multimedia approach.* ESRC-funded project: RES-000-23-0825.

Hennessy, S., Deaney, R., Ruthven, K., & Winterbottom, M. (2007). Pedagogical strategies for using the interactive whiteboard to foster learner participation in school science. *Learning, Media and Technology, 32*(3), 283–301. doi:10.1080/17439880701511131

Hennessy, S., Wishart, J., Whitelock, D., Deaney, R., Brawn, R., & la Velle, L. (2007). Pedagogical approaches for technology-integrated science teaching. *Computers & Education, 48*(1), 137–152. doi:10.1016/j.compedu.2006.02.004

Hodge, S., & Anderson, B. (2007). Teaching and learning with an interactive whiteboard: A teacher's journey. *Learning, Media and Technology, 32*(3), 271–282. doi:10.1080/17439880701511123

Jewitt, C., Moss, G., & Cardini, A. (2007). Pace, interactivity and multimodality in teachers' design of texts for interactive whiteboards in the secondary school classroom. *Learning, Media and Technology, 32*(3), 303–318. doi:10.1080/17439880701511149

Kennewell, S. (2001). Using affordances and constraints to evaluate the use of ICT in teaching and learning. *Journal of IT and Teacher Education, 10*(1/2), 101–116.

Kennewell, S., Beauchamp, G., Jones, S., & Norman, N. Parkinson, J., Tanner, H., et al. (2008). *The use of ICT to improve learning and attainment through interactive teaching: Full research report.* Economic and Social Research Council end of award report. RES-139-25-0167-A. Retrieved October 20, 2008, from http://www.esrcsociety-today.ac.uk/ESRCInfoCentre/ViewOutputPage.a spx?data=v9XrjLJ6xhGKkb12HPJ7W5ye0b9qtr 8%2fqVQxkan2L1TIciduxIHf6agYU3K1R1Cc1 XeShX2F5UjcyVTLWid0cK3oi%2bu3Y8Y1%2 fejJYVW6gMQ%3d&xu=0&isAwardHolder=&i sProfiled=&AwardHolderID=&Sector=

Kennewell, S., Tanner, H., Jones, S., & Beauchamp, G. (2008). Analysing the use of interactive technology to implement interactive teaching. *Journal of Computer Assisted Learning, 24*(1), 61–73.

Latham, P. (2002). *Teaching and learning primary mathematics: The impact of interactive whiteboards*. North Islington Education Action Zone: BEAM research papers. Retrieved October 13, 2008, from http://www.beam.co.uk/pdfs/RES03.pdf

Laurillard, D. (2002). *Rethinking university teaching: A conversational framework for the effective use of learning technologies* (2nd ed.). London: RoutledgeFalmer.

Lewin, C., Somekh, B., & Steadman, S. (2008). Embedding interactive whiteboards in teaching and learning: The process of change in pedagogic practice. *Education and Information Technologies, 13*(4), 291–303. doi:10.1007/s10639-008-9070-z

Littleton, K., Twiner, A., & Gillen, J. (in press). Instruction as orchestration: Multimodal connection building with the interactive whiteboard. *Pedagogies: An International Journal, 5*(4).

Mercer, N., & Littleton, K. (2007). *Dialogue and the development of children's thinking: A sociocultural approach*. London, New York: Routledge.

Miller, D. (2003). Developing interactive whiteboard activity. *Micromath, 19*(3), 33–35.

Miller, D., & Glover, D. (2002). The interactive whiteboard as a force for pedagogic change: The experience of five elementary schools in an English education authority. *Information Technology in Childhood Education, 1*, 5–19.

Moss, G., Jewitt, C., Levacic, R., Armstrong, V., Cardini, S., & Castle, F. (2007). *The interactive whiteboards, pedagogy and pupil performance evaluation: An evaluation of the Schools Whiteboard Expansion (SWE) Project: London Challenge. Research report 816*. London: Department for Education and Skills.

Petrou, M., Kerawalla, L., & Scanlon, E. (2009). *The talk Factory software: Scaffolding students' argumentation around an interactive whiteboard in primary school science. Paper submitted to the Computer Supported Collaborative Learning conference*. Greece: Rhodes.

Reynolds, D., & Farrell, S. (1996). *Worlds apart? A review of international surveys of educational achievement involving England*. London: HMSO.

Rogoff, B. (1995). Observing sociocultural activity on three planes: Participatory appropriation, guided participation, and apprenticeship . In Wertsch, J. V., Del Rio, P., & Alvarez, A. (Eds.), *Sociocultural studies of mind* (pp. 139–164). Cambridge, MA: Cambridge University Press.

Sawyer, R. (2004). Creative teaching: Collaborative discussion as disciplined improvisation. *Educational Researcher, 33*(2), 12–20. doi:10.3102/0013189X033002012

Scott, P., Mortimer, E., & Aguiar, O. (2006). The tension between authoritative and dialogic discourse: A fundamental characteristic of meaning making interactions in high school science lessons. *Science Education, 90*(4), 605–631. doi:10.1002/sce.20131

Shields, J. (1995). Now appearing on the big screen… . *Technology and Learning, 15*(6), 38–43.

Smith, H. (2001). *Smartboard Evaluation: Final Report*. Retrieved January 10, 2006, from http://www.kented.org.uk/ngfl/ict/IWB/whiteboards/report.html#6

Smith, H., Higgins, S., Wall, K., & Miller, J. (2005). Interactive whiteboards: Boon or bandwagon? A critical review of the literature. *Journal of Computer Assisted Learning, 21*(2), 91–101. doi:10.1111/j.1365-2729.2005.00117.x

Somekh, B. (2007). *Pedagogy and learning with ICT: Researching the art of innovation*. London, New York: Routledge.

Tanner, H., & Jones, S. (2007). How interactive is your whiteboard? *Mathematics Teaching Incorporating Micromath, 200*, 37–41.

Tanner, H., Jones, S., Kennewell, S., & Beauchamp, G. (2005, July). *Interactive whiteboards and pedagogies of whole class teaching*. Paper presented at Mathematics Education Research Group of Australasia conference, Melbourne, Australia. Retrieved April 19, 2007, from http://www.merga.net.au/documents/RP832005.pdf

Walker, D. (2002, November 1). Meet whiteboard Wendy. *Times Educational Supplement*. Retrieved October 13, 2008, from http://www.tes.co.uk/article.aspx?storycode=371268

Walker, R. (2003). Interactive whiteboards in the MFL classroom. *TELL and CALL, 3*, 14–16.

Wertsch, J. (1991). *Voices of the mind: A sociocultural approach to mediated action*. Hemel Hempstead, UK: Harvester Wheatsheaf.

Wood, D., Bruner, J., & Ross, G. (1976). The role of tutoring in problem-solving. *Journal of Child Psychology and Psychiatry, and Allied Disciplines, 17*(2), 89–100. doi:10.1111/j.1469-7610.1976.tb00381.x

Wood, R., & Ashfield, J. (2008). The use of the interactive whiteboard for creative teaching and learning in literacy and mathematics: A case study. *British Journal of Educational Technology, 39*(1), 84–96.

Chapter 4

Designing Resources for IWBs:
The Emerging Roles of Educational Publishers and Materials Writers

Byron Russell
Woodstock Publishing Partnership, UK

ABSTRACT

The following chapter will be of interest to all those involved in creating resources for the Interactive Whiteboard with a view to commercial publication, either via an established publishing house or via the web as an open resource. It will also inform those who are already involved in digital publishing or who are considering implementing a digital publishing strategy. It is not aimed at providing solutions, but at stimulating publishers and authors to ask the right questions and to consider the management of change that may be required within their company. The chapter will look at the challenge from organizational, creative, production and commercial standpoints. It will conclude with an examination of the emerging role of the teacher as an IWB materials writer, and how new paradigms are emerging which may increasingly mesh the parts played by the practicing user and the commercial publisher of IWB resources.

INTRODUCTION

The growing demand for digital resources in the field of education poses a range of new challenges for mainstream educational publishers. This is especially true for those creating materials intended for the Interactive Whiteboard. This is partly because among all the innovative tools being deployed in the classroom, the IWB has the most rapidly grow-

ing presence. There are a number of reasons for its popularity. A full discussion of these issues is outside the scope of this article, but they range from the simple "wow!" factor to the political agenda, with the bulk acquisition and installation of IWBs being presented as visible evidence of government spending on education. At the 2006 IATEFL (International Association for Teachers of English as a Foreign Language) conference, it was mooted that IWBs would "fail" in the marketplace for three basic reasons – high cost, inadequate teacher training and

DOI: 10.4018/978-1-61520-715-2.ch004

poor commercial content (for a discussion of this, see Bax, 2006). The prediction of lack of take up has proved to be anything but true, as increasingly individual schools and entire education ministries rush to provide IWBs for staff and students; but while the costs are falling dramatically (it is now possible to buy an excellent portable IWB for under $600, or even to make one yourself – see Lee, 2007) there remain the twin issues of effective training and medium-appropriate content from commercial publishers.

Demand for appropriate software resources is increasing, yet in business terms publishing for IWBs is unlikely to be a highly profitable revenue stream in its own right. Another factor is the growing expertise of teachers themselves – the more technically aware are quite capable of producing their own quality web-based resources and in effect becoming their own publishers, potentially to a very wide audience. For publishers creating materials for the digital environment new paradigms are needed for both business and editorial operations. My own background is in educational publishing, particularly in the field of English as a Foreign or Second Language, and it is fascinating to observe the new dynamism – and the new challenges – faced by the educational publishing industry as digital content and its delivery becomes increasingly part of the mainstream.

From the business standpoint, commercial publishing for the education and training market has remained largely unchanged over the years. Educational publishing is, overall, a conservative industry. Consequently, many of the publishers currently recognized in the field of IWB software, such as 2Simple (www.2simpleshop.com) and Espresso (www.espresso.co.uk), are what might be termed publishing's "digital natives" – those who have grown up with digital technology and to whom this world is utterly familiar (for more on the term "digital natives", see Prensky, 2001). These publishers pursue little or no commercial activity outside software publishing and had no existence before the widespread introduction of the IWB and class PCs. They are not involved in major textbook publication, as textbooks and supplementary materials continue to be mainly paper-based (though it will be interesting to see what changes the steadily-growing adoption of e-book players such as the Kindle have on the paper-based textbook market). The business models of such digital publishers depend not on the sale of class adoptions of course books, but on the sale (and renewal) of site licenses – a system whereby a piece of software, such as an IWB resource, is licensed to multiple users within a school for a limited or unlimited period, in return for a relatively substantial (three to four figure) license fee. Critical revenue mass is achieved from sales to multiple institutions, and profitability through sales volume coupled with low costs, other than initial development (the cost of hosting or even CD-ROM storage is negligible compared to the cost of maintaining book stocks in a warehouse depository). There are, of course, many educational publishers with their feet in both the paper and digital camps – notable examples are Macmillan Education, Pearson, Oxford University Press and Cambridge University Press. Alongside the aforementioned digital publishers, which tend to be smaller commercial operations, these well-known publishing houses already have a range of digital material available on CD-ROM or for installation on a local school intranet, featuring interactive games and activities. This chapter is primarily aimed at those working with or for established publishers in the textbook/supplementary materials market, who are relatively new to IWB publishing.

BACKGROUND

Resources for the IWB may be stand-alone products or supplement main course material, which is generally delivered in traditional paper format. In order to contrast the established paper-based publishing model with emerging new paradigms in a digital age, it will be worth summarizing the current processes which see supplementary paper-based course material, such as activity books, pass from the concept to the publication stage.

Initially, as a result of market feedback, learning materials are commissioned. Generally supplementary material will be published to accompany a specific textbook rather than as a stand-alone resource. It may be very much an afterthought – if the course book is highly successful, a wide range of supplementary materials may be subsequently commissioned to strengthen the course book's "brand" and secure greater customer (i.e. teacher) loyalty.

Once it has been commissioned, the material will pass through various authorial and editorial stages and processes before final publication. Now at final manuscript and design stage, the material will pass to production, and will be printed, perhaps at a low-cost printing house in Asia. In advance of actual publication, the sales and marketing teams will be informed about publication and stock dates, and they will in turn inform customers, distributors and retailers. Customer mailings will be prepared, and advanced information sheets sent to retailers and distributors. Finished stock will then be shipped back to the publisher's main warehouses, and from them on to national and overseas distributors, in the case of materials destined for the international market. Finally, the resulting publication will be sold at a discount to book shops or direct to the schools concerned. Schools will have adopted the related textbooks as a result of visits and presentations by field sales representatives, who have an in-depth knowledge of their local market and the teachers who make up their customers.

This overview outlines in a few words what is, of course, a lengthy and complex process. From the mind of the commissioning editor to the hand of the practicing teacher can easily take two years. It is also very costly, but the ROI (Return on Investment) can be very high in the long term. A successful textbook series may have an extremely long life, once adopted. For example, the current highly successful adult ESL/EFL title Headway (Oxford University Press), now in a new and revised edition, was first launched in 1986. It has spawned a broad range of accompanying materials, from activity books to posters and wall charts. However, such supplementary material is commercially of far less value to the publisher than the main textbook, and may be given away free as an adoption incentive to teachers. In particular, posters and wall charts – which in some ways may be considered analogous to IWB software - are often not perceived as real publications in their own right. Though for cataloguing and administrative purposes they may be allocated an ISBN (International Standard Book Number - a unique, numeric commercial book identifier), they may well have no independent existence outside the course book they are intended to accompany. The publication of such supplementary material (and this is how major text book publishers may tend to perceive IWB material) is therefore seen as subordinate to the publication of the textbook, whereas for the digital native publisher it will be a core business.

Another factor affecting publishers is that increasingly the textbook is no longer king. Teachers are dealing with highly specific core curricula, for specific training purposes. Published paper-based resources such as textbooks and their accompanying materials may be either less than adequate for purpose or become rapidly outdated. Relatively few teachers may use commercially available IWB material (perhaps under 45% - see Moss et al., 2007), and will supplement this with material sourced from the web. An ideal presentation format for topical web-sourced material is of course the IWB.

Finally, publishers need to consider that they are coming up against unexpected competition – from the teachers themselves. It is perfectly within the technical competence of an increasing number of teachers to create their own materials for the IWB that both meet their precise requirements and that look reasonably attractive and "professional". Enthusiastic teachers may then go on to make such material available to all, free, via the web. However, presentation of unmoderated material on the IWB presents its own problems, and there is some concern that material that has not been professionally created (in the sense of having been professionally published) may under-use the potential of the medium (see Moss et al., 2007). The professional design of didactic content is of great importance if the material is to be used at its most effective, and "do-it-yourself" resources may not be adequate in core areas – for example, teachers may lack the technical skills needed to create fully interactive resources. Teachers making texts for use in the classroom is not new, of course, and is a long-established practice with paper-based and photocopied resources. However, the introduction of IWBs into schools impacts on this practice in a number of ways. Teachers now have an increasing role to play in digital text design and the potential of text design as a pedagogic tool for change, but of course teachers are not primarily resource designers. Moss et al. (2007) in their review of the use of IWBs in London secondary schools, point out that changes to design and display format (i.e. from the printed page or worksheet and the blackboard to the IWB screen, with its easy access to multimedia resources) may bring new potential for teacher text design for IWBs, but will also lead to challenges for the teachers concerned. The resources they produce may have little legacy outside their own classroom: when creating their own texts, many teachers struggle to incorporate principles of design which can establish clear reading paths for pupils. Lack of familiarity with such principles of design may make it much harder for teachers to create and share resources that can be used independently of their author (Moss et al., 2007). Even the creation of an animated PowerPoint slide, with embedded video/audio content, may be outside the technical capabilities of many teachers working in today's classrooms. Nevertheless, there are

strong indications that teachers continue to use and prefer "home made" resources over commercially available materials. The Moss evaluation carried out a survey of IWB use in all London secondary schools in the autumn term 2004/5 (the response rate was 41%). The results make interesting reading for those creating commercial IWB software. Moss' analysis of the teacher survey found that the majority of teachers (78%) reported that they created their own resources to use on the IWB, and about two-thirds of teachers (64%) reported that they used content copied from the internet as a resource. But less than half of all teachers (45%) surveyed were using commercial software. For those who can create attractive, interactive material and who then make them available web-wide, there is the unresolved issue of digital rights. The majority of free material incorporates no anti-piracy tools, and can therefore be freely copied, used and – by the unscrupulous - passed off as "their own work".

Teacher-created IWB content therefore involves technical expertise and is time consuming. There is also an element of copyright risk involved. However technically competent, teachers will therefore continue to look for commercially-produced IWB content, but ideally this should be material that:

- can be edited to suit class needs
- saves preparation time
- improves the effectiveness of delivery
- is high quality, and professionally designed
- integrates into a core curriculum

How will mainstream educational publishers and their authors, driven by an increasingly informed and demanding teacher workforce, usefully meet these needs? How will they ensure that the IWB content they publish fully exploits the new medium, and is not simply a reworking or digitization of page-based content? Publishers, being market-driven, will need to re-assess working practices if they are to create IWB materials that really meet classroom requirements. We shall look at the challenge from four standpoints:

- Organizational
- Creative
- Publishing/production
- Commercial

THE ORGANISATIONAL STANDPOINT

As has been shown, commercial publishers are organised as manufacturers of high quality, traditionally produced books. A move to the publishing of digital materials brings its own set of issues which will need to be effectively addressed. These fall into three key areas:

1. Appropriate inter-departmental communication
2. Digital awareness
3. Training

Inter-Departmental Integration/ Communication

Paper-based educational publishing, unlike software publishing, is generally not the preserve of small independent organizations. Commercial publishing for the educational market is a profitable business, and dominated by large companies such as Oxford University Press, Pearson and Macmillan Education – all corporations with a global presence. Organizationally, their sheer size leads to compartmentalism as a variety of editorial groups – each of which may be unaware of what the others are engaged on – work away at market-specific or segment-specific projects. Publishing is therefore a compartmentalized series of processes – a linear progression from concept to publication. Though there may be a unifier among some groups, from over twenty years of

personal experience I know how difficult it can be for the various sub-groups within a large publishing house to engage with each other, resulting in much reinvention of the wheel. One way to circumvent this would be the appointment of a digital tsar with sufficient authority and cross-departmental knowledge to pull the various groups together. Alternatively publishers may create the role of cross-curricular IWB-specific editors (the revenue from IWB material alone may well not justify the employment cost of a subject-specific IWB editor). It takes a team to work on an IWB task, with appropriate input from the content, functionality and technical standpoints.

Digital Awareness

Publishers are experts in publishing, and know what is market-appropriate – it is after all their job. But they may have very limited experience of producing digital content. Before they can think about what they can publish, editors and authors need to know about what is feasible and what "works". It is still easy to find resources supposedly for the IWB that are little more than projected worksheets, with inappropriate font sizes and limited links or interactivity. In order to commission appropriate resources, editors need to know what can be achieved, what is practical – and what is not.

Though very creative within narrow spheres, in my experience editorial departments in large publishing houses tend to be fundamentally conservative. This is perhaps in the nature of the business – teachers themselves tend towards the conservative, maneuvered into being so by the strictures of educational curricula and budgetary constraints. Many editors are themselves former teachers, but – having been out of the classroom for years (or decades, in some cases!) are unaware of the real practical impact the introduction of the IWB is having on everyday teaching. Or rather, though they may be aware of the growth of the IWB phenomenon, they have very little if any practical experience of actually using an IWB in the classroom. Publishers will need to invest in appropriate training for those involved in the business of commissioning and editing. Additional fieldwork needs to be done by all those involved in the editorial process – from editorial assistant up to publishing director - to fully understand the ways in which the IWB is changing classroom pedagogy, and thereby to begin to put together publishing strategies that truly meet market needs.

Training

Training is at the heart of this required change. Promethean runs multilevel training courses in the use of basic IWB tools expressly for publishers, to assist editors working on IWB material in gaining an understanding of what is (and is not) possible (see www.prometheanlearning.com/uk/index.php). At least one primary publisher has chosen to put all its editors through level one of the Promethean online learning program. Such training – or at the very least consultancy from an appropriate IWB expert - is essential for a publisher to successfully marry the task in hand with the actual capabilities of the IWB. The need for basic training can be difficult to accept for an editor with years of experience and market knowledge – and the training itself may present a sharp and difficult learning curve for the technophobic.

Knowledge is not the only area in which there may be a shift of control. In the case of a course or activity book, the author and editor largely manage both input and output. IWBs are by their nature more class/user centric – as we shall see later, it is the teacher (or the student) who may take control of how material is used (or adapted) in the classroom. Beauchamp (2004) argues that the transition from traditional modes of teaching to the totally integrated use of IWBs in classrooms demands a shift in the pedagogical style of the teacher, and that there needs to be considerable investment for teachers to learn to develop their technical competence alongside their pedagogical skills. Such investment – a new skill set, blending both pedagogical and technical awareness - is also required on the part of editors who are aiming to develop effective material for teachers and their students to use.

THE CREATIVE STANDPOINT

In addition to the organizational issues summarized above, there are creative factors which need to be addressed before the commissioning of truly appropriate material, which fulfils the needs of teachers in terms of content relevance and exploits the new pedagogical aspects of learning which are inherent in the IWB. This aspect of training so seldom features in the programmes run by the IWB manufacturers themselves – actual training in how to use IWBs effectively is often ignored (see Dudeney & Hockly, 2007). Unfortunately, it is still common for publishers to bring out what is essentially the textbook, on screen. In some cases the textbook pages may have been "tweaked" with some basic interactive devices, such as the ability to zoom in and out of sections of the text or click on embedded audio/video, which may be useful for presentational purposes, but nevertheless in effect it reduces the role of the IWB to that of a costly overhead projector.

A fundamental issue is that editors and authors need to be fully aware of the potential, and limitations of the IWB, in order to commission and produce materials which – though they may well be intended to complement to the textbook – nevertheless deliver on the promise of the new medium. As Tanner and Jones point out, learning to use the IWB effectively requires more than simply technical training (see Tanner & Jones, 2007) and technical skills need to go hand-in-hand with awareness of how the material may actually be used in class. One basic issue is that publishers do not "create" on the IWB itself. And frequently the material being developed might be nearing publication stage before it is actually seen on the board.

It is therefore very important for editors/authors to think in terms of digital delivery, even at the commissioning stage. Instead of a cohesive, linear learning program – which is the way traditionally-minded course book publishers work – editors will increasingly have to think in terms of Learning Objects (LOs). The definition of the term "Learning Object" is complex. Chiappe has defined LOs as digital, self-contained and reusable entities, with a clear educational purpose and having at least three editable components - content, learning activities and contextual elements. To aid digital storage and retrieval, each must incorporate metadata tagging: every LO has embedded electronic tags which allow it to be found easily (see Chiappe, Segovia & Rincon, 2007). The concept of LOs as small pieces of instructional media which can be re-used (Wiley, 2003) is a relatively novel way of considering learning content; it has been suggested that LOs have the following key characteristics (see Beck, 2007):

- Learning Objects are small (typically 2 to 15 minutes) units of learning, not a single, long linear program
- They are self-contained and each can be used independently
- An individual learning object may be used in a variety of contexts for a variety of educational objectives (the concept of re-usability)
- Though not linear, they can be grouped into larger collections, including traditional course structures
- They are tagged with descriptive metadata

Resources for the IWB should therefore be considered as individual LOs rather than a "course", and may be understood as reusable assets within different learning contexts and course structures.

Editors will have to think more visually and even spatially – the IWB is, after all, a whole class tool. Carey, Moss and Cardini (2007) point out that the transitions in design and display, from traditional formats (marker whiteboard, worksheet) to the IWB, with its easy access to a variety of resources and formats including audio and video, allow new potential for text design. Currently, if IWB resources are considered at all during the editorial process, it is as an adjunct to an established course book or – in a very few rare cases – as a standalone product. As has been described in the introduction, the majority of textbooks in use today were commissioned several years ago, when IWBs were still the preserve of the few. Those commissioning the course books of tomorrow should consider today what IWB support these new products will have, and plan for the simultaneous availability of book and IWB resource. Other assets may need to be embedded in the final IWB product, such as video, audio and animated graphics; however, over-complexity may be detrimental to effectiveness of the medium.

One of the simplest and most flexible set of tools available is provided on the Teachit website (www.teachit.co.uk), a peer-to-peer site for teachers of English working within the UK education system and teaching English to native speakers. An international version, Teachitworld, is aimed at ESL/EFL teachers (www.teachitworld.com). Subscribers to either site can use the tools, which include an automatic IWB stop-watch and "fridge magnets" – flexible language building blocks which can be deployed and animated by the teacher to support the teaching of sentence construction to foreign language vocabulary. These simple applications are very good examples of IWB toolsets provided by a commercial publisher which can be edited by the teachers themselves to fit the needs of their students.

Where the material itself is professionally authored, the editor managing the project will need to be even more conscious of the importance of design for projected content. Fortunately, educational publishers have been design-conscious for decades. For reasons of motivating students and maximizing the amount of learning material within a given space, much more effort is given to creating attractive, easy to follow page layouts, with stimulating and appropriate graphics. However, material for use on an IWB will need to be given extra attention in a variety of areas; most importantly, it will need to be tested pre-publication on an IWB, and in an actual classroom environment. Considerations will include font size and the use of colour and white space, but may also include attention to animation and interaction types, such as the use of voting pods and touch-screen membranes. Voting tools are particularly interesting examples, as it this relatively new interactive element is quite outside the experience of many of the editors with whom I have spoken. The voting tool or learner response system, employed by Promethean among others, enables active participation in the learning process by individual learners and the whole class. Individuals can "take control" of board functions, and whole groups can analyze, predict and vote on the outcomes of activities: "the electronic voting system was seen to increase considerably the scope of interactivity during the lessons by helping students to enhance their development into active participants" (see Schmid, 2008, p. 338). Touch-screen membranes, such as those employed in SMART boards, encourage participation front-of-class by individual students and can be particularly useful for younger learners.

THE PUBLISHING AND PRODUCTION STANDPOINT

The third issue commercial publishers will need to address is that of actual publication. At a fundamental level, there will be the need for the integration of IWB packages into publishing schedules for new textbooks, but of course the most pressing commercial need may be for the publication of add-ons for existing course materi-

als, and supplementary, standalone products for specific subject areas.

One additional challenge publishers face in this area is the fast changing pace of the technology. Though by and large what works on one IWB will work equally well on another, differing features may require a different publishing approach. As an example, products tuned for SMART boards, which employ touch-sensitive membranes instead of interactive pen tools, may require a different product design and different interactivity types from Hitachi pen-driven boards. Indeed, the SMART UK software catalogue for materials from accredited publishers is dominated by products for the primary market, as SMART boards tend to predominate in the primary (5–11) age segment (the rationale is that touch-sensitive screens are easier for children to use than pen boards – for example, my local primary school has SMART boards throughout, positioned at child-height). Similarly Promethean employs voting software and voting pods (though of course not all users will have these) which have considerable pedagogical opportunities for teaching at secondary/adult level. This complexity compounds the problem for the publisher – when creating material for the junior secondary/K12 market, do they create products which can best make use of student interaction via touch-sensitive screens, or voting pods, or both? It is of course in the interest of IWB manufacturers to work with publishers to ensure that appropriate materials are created for their products. Both the UK market leaders – Promethean and SMART – employ business support models which make life easier for the publisher, and it is worth looking at these in more detail, as this will help to highlight the difficulties – and choices – publishers have to make when creating content for specific boards.

SMART

SMART aim for content to be embedded in their platform, so would naturally prefer publishers to work creatively with SMART software tools such as Notebook (Smart Notebook software is – at the most basic level – like a simple version of Power-Point, and enables the user to create graphic items, use templates and otherwise manipulate the board, saving all the results for future use or adaptation – a key feature for effective use). As early as 2006 teachers could download the software onto a PC to create and prepare IWB lessons outside school, and students can review their IWB class work and do extra work at home (see Starkman, 2006 for a further interesting discussion of this aspect of IWB work outside the classroom). In addition to offering an extensive set of software tools, the SMART Development Network (SDN) offers a range of resources which have been designed to help publishers create content and software applications that are compatible with SMART IWB products.

SMART offers two membership levels for the SMART Development Network. Commercial membership involves what is described as a "modest annual fee" – currently $3,000. Membership includes access to development tools and technical support from SMART, and an evaluation system to ensure that the multimedia content or software that the publisher creates effectively complements SMART IWBs (the SMART Software Accreditation Program). Though acceptance via the SMART Software Accreditation Program (http://education.smarttech.com/ste/en-US/Ed+Resource/SAP/default.htm) does not mean in any way that SMART will actually sell the software itself (though their resellers may), SMART accreditation is clearly something a potential purchaser will look for when evaluating materials. There are currently three levels of accreditation; to date SMART has accredited approximately 150 titles from over 50 companies:

1. "Ready" is the basic accreditation level for content, indicating that SMART has approved the title for use with its products. This is very straightforward – essentially,

it appears that almost any IWB-targeted software will meet the standards of this base level.

2. "Enabled" products meet the requirements of the Ready level and are also integrated with SMART tools, enabling the products to use a digital ink feature called SMART Ink Aware. Ink Aware integrates SMART Board software with many types of applications, including Microsoft Word, Excel or PowerPoint – whatever you write or draw on the board becomes embedded in and part of the actual file, rather than an external note created over the file

3. "Select" accredited products meet all requirements of the Enabled level and are specifically designed for use with SMART Notebook software – and consequently may not be fully compatible for use on other boards.

Here, of course, lies one of the challenges facing publishers. Should a primary publisher (for example) focus on producing only material that meets SMART Select accreditation levels, because – as is the case in the UK – SMART are the market leaders in the primary sector? If this is the case, then the relationship between publisher and manufacturer has become truly symbiotic and mutually supportive. Such symbiosis is not, of course, a wholly new concept for educational publishers, who may well publish a specific textbook which fits the curriculum of a single important market, and is therefore not sellable elsewhere, or who for market or cost reasons may produce software that is compatible with PCs, but not with MACs.

Promethean

Promethean's approach is subtly different, focusing on educating and training the author and publisher rather than assessing what they may have already published to ascertain its compatibility with Promethean boards. In effect, they provide a personal consultancy service for publishers creating materials for the IWB. A full-time Publisher Support Specialist works closely with leading publishing houses, advising editors on what will and what will not work on the whiteboard and offering hands-on training in IWB use. Promethean also offers a very helpful showcase for publishers – Promethean Planet (www.prometheanplanet. com). This is a free, simple-to-navigate Web 2.0 online community for teachers. It was originally launched in September 2006 and was redesigned – effectively a relaunch – in June 2008. The aim of Promethean Planet is to support teachers in using technology effectively, but of course it is an extremely useful platform for educational publishers and authors. Users are encouraged to interact with each other using online tools such as forums, blogs and conferencing, and professional development is provided via a broad range of online courses. The "shop" allows users to browse published material, download samples and link to publisher sites. Though publishers who make use of Promethean's Activ software are specifically encouraged, it is possible for any resources to be showcased on the site – and for teachers to critically review the resources they have purchased, and post their comments.

THE COMMERCIAL STANDPOINT

In the world of traditional educational publishing, sales channels are well established. Promotion of the product range is carried out via catalogues and book displays at conferences, plus consultative sales visits from educational publisher's representatives who are knowledgeable about their product ranges. The actual purchasing of published materials is typically via a local bookshop, which may or may not be a specialist educational supplier, or direct from a local distributor or online retailer. In the case of IWB material, purchase may be via subscription, download, CD-ROM,

or resource websites belonging to the IWB manufacturer. SMART, for example, publishes catalogues of SMART-approved material from third party publishers, and Promethean offers an excellent shop window via Promethean Planet. On the commercial side, two issues are emerging; the first is that of the actual purchasing process and the second is that of marketing. The second is far more important, for once teachers find that they want a specific product, they can usually source it, and there will inevitably be resellers who want to profit from the situation. There is certainly scope for IWB resellers to act as software distributors too, and a number of traditional publishing distributors are starting to act as agents for IWBs. However, in order to decide whether they want a particular product, teachers will need to see and understand it in action, and generally it is up to the sales representatives to demonstrate and explain the product. In the case of IWB software, sales representatives – like editors – may have little understanding of the possibilities of the IWB, much less be able to demonstrate it adequately. Even were this not the case, it is in the sales representatives' best interests (and frequently s/he will have little time available) to focus on products which are high volume and high margin, which means course books. Supplementary materials such as activity books will come second, and anything else a very poor third in the representative's order of priorities. Publishers will therefore need to address the challenge of how to best make teachers aware of the IWB products they have available; again, as with editors, this may mean a separate sales force, focused on (and expert in) digital products. However, the financial returns on published IWB resources are, as we have seen, very low. It may be that publishers, under the weight of free material available on the web and the low volume/ low margin business that IWB resources currently represent, will simply provide resources for free, as stand-alone or additional marketing support for books. This is already beginning to happen under a SMART-led initiative – a very ambitious program called the Global Grid for Learning, which is open to both commercial publishers and teachers.

In collaboration with Cambridge University Press, SMART aims to "connect a billion digital resources to education in the next ten years". It is claimed that this will provide a huge, almost limitless range of open educational content and associated professional development. In addition to actually providing ready-made learning objects on a searchable database, the project aims to establish collaborative ventures between educators and schools worldwide in order to develop open interactive resources. A building program will provide free online training opportunities for teachers, publishers and authors in order to develop content creation and usage skills. Registered users will be able to upload and download education resources for free, typically under an open content license which allows for unrestricted use within an educational and non-commercial context. The service is actually not entirely open; a subscription fee is required, but once that is paid subscribers are free to download the resources as needed. In other words, rather than aiding professional publishers to create and actually sell commercial content SMART are hoping that teachers will themselves become developers, and furthermore will upload content for sharing in this way. The two open questions are whether a critical mass of teachers will be prepared to share their content royalty-free in this way and who – if anyone - will moderate the content.

PUBLISHING IWB RESOURCES AND WEB COMMUNITIES

Following the SMART/Global Grid concept through to a logical conclusion, it may be that in fact the future for IWB content publication lies not so much with commercial publishers at all, but with teachers themselves. We can all be publishers now. Through YouTube, anyone can be a broadcaster; through blogs, wikis and MySpace,

anyone can publish. In a December 2007 interview with the present author, Catherine Howard (Business Manager at Steljes Ltd., the UK distributor for SMART interactive whiteboards) questioned whether, as teachers become more adept in using specific platforms, there will be a real need for published materials for the IWB. This will increasingly be the case as "digital natives" rise through school and university to the teaching profession. So is there a need for publishers to create and sell IWB materials, and are schools going to be willing to spend their budgets on site licenses?

Whiteboard manufacturers themselves are, in their own interest, making it ever easier for users to create IWB resources. In the 2007 evaluation of IWB use in London secondary schools (see Moss et al., 2007) the observers saw the following variations in the kind of texts used in the case study classrooms:

- Pre-prepared sequential texts using applications such as PowerPoint and Promethean's ACTIVstudio software tools
- Texts produced through technologies of display in real-time. e.g. the use of a microscope or a scanner to throw an image onto the screen
- Adapted texts produced by teachers or pupils in real-time through adding and changing elements of a text. e.g. through the use of highlighting
- Emergent texts produced by teachers or pupils in real-time. e.g. texts created on the board during a lesson
- Commercially made software with the form and function of traditional print texts such as textbooks or worksheets
- Subject specific software designed to fully exploit the interactive functionality of the IWB
- Generic software using Microsoft Office applications such as spreadsheets
- Sites that are accessible via the Internet and can be surfed in real time

- Texts that exploit the manipulation of digital materials.

In the above summary, only one use refers to commercially available teaching resources; the others are all teacher-created, or adaptations of pre-existing resources that may or may not have been designed for classroom exploitation.

I believe that publishers may have to look very carefully at established author models as the teaching body becomes increasingly sophisticated. One possible future, I believe, lies in web-based teacher communities and moderated peer-created content. This is the underlying concept behind SMART's ambitious project, but were I a practicing teacher/contributor I might question why others would benefit financially from original work that I had created. There are practical reasons for teachers becoming author/publishers; "teachers are the critical agents in mediating the software, the integration of the software into the subject aims of the lesson and appropriate use of the IWB to promote quality interactions and interactivity" (see Armstrong et al., 2005, p. 455). At the current generational level, practicing teachers have far more experience of the IWB in action – what it can and cannot do – than the majority of publishing editors. They also have a clear understanding of what their students need, and how the IWB can help. In an increasing number of cases, commercially available content can already be edited or adapted, but downloaded content frequently can only be modified within the constraints of the publisher's EULA (End User License Agreement).

EULAs typically refer to "authorized users" or those working within an authorized educational institution. The authorized user can exploit the resources for education or research during the subscription period, but other than presentation and illustration, use is generally limited to browsing, copying and reproduction for course work. Actual editing of content, however desirable that might be from the teacher's point of view, may be limited (if allowed at all) to adding usage notes.

From the teacher's point of view, publishers may have to accept that teacher editing of content may be both acceptable and desirable, but may have to be moderated in some way – design, for example, may have to conform to an automated style guide. There is reciprocity between the technology and the user (be it teacher or learner) where "the user adapts the tools they use according to their everyday practice and preferences in order to carry out their activities; and how, in turn, the tools themselves also modify the activities that the user is engaged in" (Scanlon et al., 2005). Further, the shift of focus from the teacher to students who may be able to take greater control of the technology, may be more enabling for learners, but this aspect of pedagogy needs to be understood and taken on board by those who are creating the source material (see Zevenbergen, 2008). Developing and publishing material for the IWB which can be controlled and adapted by the user therefore demands a sea-change in the way publishers traditionally create their materials.

An interesting community-based business model is currently provided by Teachit (www.teachit.co.uk), a small independent UK publisher which we have met earlier. Teachit has evolved entirely around peer-created and peer-adapted content. There are two key differences between the SMART/Global Grid for Learning proposition and the Teachit model. The first is that Teachit's in-house editors and designers professionally moderate and may design the teacher-submitted content; the second is that Teachit operates a royalty-share co-operative business model. The process is as follows. A teacher will send in a resource, typically as a Word document. If approved, the resource may then be edited to provide several different resources on the same theme. A dialogue, or example, can be re-edited to become an interactive gap-fill activity on the IWB. Access to the various resources is via a simple range of differentiated subscription levels. At the premium level, teachers have access to all the resources on the site; these may (depending on the appropriateness of the resource) be available as pdfs, editable Microsoft Office documents and interactive IWB resources. The revenues are then pooled and shared proportionately between the contributors and the Publisher. The result is a cooperative publishing operation by teachers and for teachers in which everyone wins. A key "selling point" of this model is that all the resources have been created by practicing professionals, and teacher trust of peer-created resources may be evidenced from the site's subscription rates (an October 2008 Press Release for the company claims Teachit.co.uk is "the most widely used resource for English teaching in the UK").

Teachit provides a model which other publishers could emulate – teachers might submit resources based on existing textbooks to the relevant publisher's resource website, which is accessible to all via a small annual subscription. The resource is then edited by the publisher's in-house design team, to ensure relevance and design harmony. Peer created materials are also an important resource for the publishing editor/author. It is a given that editors will carefully evaluate what rival publishers are producing in their segment. They now also need to have a careful look at what teachers themselves are creating.

CONCLUSION

No publisher can afford to ignore the IWB phenomenon, and the new electronic literacies that define our times (see Warschuaer, 2005). Despite the fact that such products are never likely to make a profit, publishers will need to produce IWB resources, if only as an essential adjunct to successful mainstream textbooks. The issue is how to create effective resources that can contribute - albeit marginally - to the publisher's bottom line. The peer-to-peer, moderated content model on which Teachit has built a business is interesting and innovative. There may well be space for publishers to think creatively about new business models which build on teacher expertise, tying teacher-contributed content firmly in with their core textbook products. There will also be greater opportunities for teachers to turn authors, possibly challenging established royalty models, and for professional trainers to offer appropriate courses for in-house editors.

I asked Julia Glass, Publisher Support Specialist at Promethean, what her advice would be to neophyte publishers working on IWB learning materials. Her view was that publishers should be prepared to take informed advice from appropriate specialists, and be ready to change established work patterns in order to build a knowledgeable team. In order to become effective producers of digital media for the IWB, commercial publishers will need to re-examine their current working practices and business models, and be prepared to ride the learning curve.

REFERENCES

Armstrong, V., Barnes, S., Sutherland, R., Curran, C., Mills, S., & Thompson, I. (2005). Collaborative research methodology for investigating teaching and learning: The use of interactive whiteboard technology. *Educational Review*, *57*(4), 457–469. doi:10.1080/00131910500279551

Bax, S. (2006). Interactive whiteboards: Watch this space. *California Law Review*, (Summer): 5–7.

Beauchamp, G. (2004). Teacher use of the interactive whiteboard in primary schools: Towards an effective transition framework. *Technology, Pedagogy and Education*, *13*(3), 327–348. doi:10.1080/14759390400200186

Beck, R. (2003). *What are learning objects?* Center for International Education, University of Wisconsin-Milwaukee. Retrieved November 10, 2007, from http://www.uwm.edu/Dept/CIE/AOP/LObib.html

Chiappe, A., Yasbley, S., & Yadira, R. (2007). Toward an instructional design model based on learning objects. [Boston: Springer.]. *Educational Technology Research and Development, 55,* 671–668. doi:10.1007/s11423-007-9059-0

Dudeney, G., & Hockley, N. (2007). *How to teach English with technology.* Harlow, UK: Pearson Longman.

Jewitt, C., Moss, G., & Cardini, A. (2007). Pace, interactivity and multimodality in teachers design of texts for interactive whiteboards in the secondary school classroom. *Learning, Media and Technology, 32*(3), 303–317. doi:10.1080/17439880701511149

Lee, J. C. (2007). *Using infrared (IR) light pens and the Wii Remote, it is possible to create very low-cost multi-point interactive whiteboards and multi-point tablet displays.* Retrieved April 10, 2009, from http://www.youtube.com/watch?v=5s5EvhHy7eQ

Moss, G., Carey, J., Levaãiç, R., Armstrong, V., Cardini, A., & Castle, F. (2007). The interactive whiteboards, pedagogy and pupil performance evaluation: An evaluation of the schools whiteboard expansion (SWE) project: London challenge. School of Education and Policy Studies, Institute of Education, University of London, Research Report 816.

Prensky, M. (2001). Digital natives, digital immigrants. *On the Horizon, 9*(5). Retrieved July 10, 2009, from http://www.marcprensky.com/writing/Prensky%20-%20Digital%20Natives,%20Digital%20Immigrants%20-%20Part1.pdf

Scanlon, E., Jones, A., & Waycott, J. (2005). Using a PDA as a learning or workplace tool. *Learning, Media and Technology, 30*(2), 107–130.

Schmid, E. C. (2008). Using a voting system in conjunction with interactive whiteboard technology to enhance learning in the English language classroom. *Computers & Education, 50*(1), 338–356. doi:10.1016/j.compedu.2006.07.001

Sharma, P., & Barrett, B. (2007). *Blended learning.* Oxford, UK: Macmillan Education.

Starkman, N. (2006). The wonders of interactive whiteboards. *T.H.E. Journal, 33*(10), 36-38. Retrieved March 14, 2009, from http://www.thejournal.com/articles/18500

Tanner, H., & Jones, S. (2007). How interactive is your whiteboard? *Mathematics Teaching Incorporating Micromath, 200,* 37–41.

Warshauer, M. (2002). A developmental perspective on technology in language education. *TESOL Quarterly, 36*(3), 314–328.

Wiley, D. (2000). *Connecting learning objects to instructional design theory: A definition, a metaphor, and a taxonomy.* Retrieved March 1, 2009, from http://www.reusability.org/read/chapters/wiley.doc

Zevenbergen, R., & Lerman, S. (2008). Learning environments using interactive whiteboards: New learning spaces or reproduction of old technologies? *Mathematics Education Research Journal, 20*(1), 108–126.

WEBSITE REFERENCES

Espresso: http://www.espresso.co.uk

Headway ESL/SFL course series: http://www.oup.com/elt/global/products/headway

Hitachi: http://uk.hitachisoft-interactive.com/Templates/Type2_English.asp?modeID=Content&uID=43&DoLoginLe Petit

Promethean: http://www.prometheanplanet.com and http://www.prometheanlearning.com/uk/index.php

2Simple Software. http://www.2simpleshop.com

SMART. http://smarttech.com/

SMART. accreditation program: http://education.smarttech.com/ste/en-US/Ed+Resource/SAP/default.htm

Teachit: http://www.teachit.co.uk

Teachitworld: http://www.teachitworld.com

Part 2
Classroom Research

Chapter 5

Meeting Teachers' Real Needs:
New Tools in the Secondary Modern Foreign Languages Classroom

Carol Gray
University of Birmingham, UK

ABSTRACT

This chapter uses a narrow geographical and subject-specific focus to discuss factors affecting teachers' preferred use of Interactive Whiteboards in situ. It highlights tensions between political rhetoric concerning the power of ICT to transform teaching and learning, subject-specific pedagogy, and the industrial realities of teaching in the compulsory secondary sector in the UK. Case studies are used to investigate ways in which individual teachers maneuver their way through these tensions, identifying and developing uses of the new technology to meet their own immediate concerns in the situated reality of their classrooms. The chapter concludes that the popularity of the IWB may stem from the fact that whereas previous ICT applications encouraged greater freedom on the part of the learner, the Whiteboard by contrast can be used to increase teacher control of both content and behaviour, thus better meeting teachers' immediate needs within their context. Although very specific in its focus, the chapter highlights the need for sensitivity to the sociocultural environment when introducing new technology into teaching and learning environments.

INTRODUCTION

Discussion of UK government policy for education is complicated by degrees of devolution to Northern Ireland, Wales and Scotland, whereas England has no independent governing body. Educational policy in England, therefore, is decided by the UK govern-

ment, whereas other areas of the UK have degrees of independence. The following refers only to policy as implemented in England. Readers from beyond the UK might also need to know that the government department responsible for English education policy has been renamed several times in recent decades; relevant for this chapter are the changes from Department for Education and Employment (DfEE) to Department for Education and Skills

DOI: 10.4018/978-1-61520-715-2.ch005

(DfES) through to the most recent Department for Children, Schools and Families (DCSF).

In recent decades the UK government has stated in numerous papers its faith in the power of ICT to contribute to its agenda of raising standards in schools, using the rhetoric of "transformation". It has invested more than any other European government in equipping schools with hardware, software and Broadband access, and in training teachers to use new technologies in their classrooms. Only since the appearance of the Interactive Whiteboard, however, does there appear to have been widespread enthusiasm among the teaching profession in England for the integration of computers and digital technology into their pedagogy. In Modern Foreign Language teaching in particular, only the most ardent technophiles accepted the challenge of working in computer suites or with clusters of computers; IWBs, however, are becoming a departmental priority. This chapter discusses possible reasons for such popularity and uses a small number of case studies to demonstrate how individual teachers interact with technology to address their own priorities in the classroom.

BACKGROUND

The Raising Standards Agenda

Like governments around the world, the UK authorities have over recent decades taken increasing control of education and its agenda as major tools for developing and sustaining a robust economy – plus, perhaps, as "easy" areas to demonstrate determined and effective political intervention and win public sympathy and votes. Since the early 1980s regulation has increasingly reduced the autonomy of higher education institutions in teacher education, and this has been accompanied by tightening control over content of the school syllabus. In the late 1990s a number of both compulsory and recommended "strategies" were introduced to exercise detailed control over the very act of

teaching, their implementation supported by an inspection regime which might be said to make nonsense of any non-compulsory status.

A key refrain in government educational policy and directives since 1998 has been that of harnessing the power of ICT to provide wider opportunities for pupils as well as to create virtual national and regional networks of and for teachers. Standards for new teachers entering the profession from 1998 included a stringent set of requirements for ICT skills (DfEE, 1998a, 1998b), which were to be expected of all practicing teachers by 2002. Resources were created for experienced teachers to identify and address their training needs (Teacher Training Agency, 1999) and a range of training initiatives developed. The era of compulsory technology in the school classroom had begun.

The Potential of Information and Communications Technology

The government's faith in ICT to raise standards in education is reflected both in financial investment in the compulsory education sector and in the rhetoric of official publications. Since 1997 hundreds of millions of pounds per year have been spent equipping both primary and secondary schools with hardware, software and reliable Internet access and creating online resources and networking sites for teachers. According to Jones and Coffey (2006):

The UK is at the forefront of integrating ICT skills in schools. We are, for example, the only European country to have installed IWBs on a massive scale and to have made ICT a National Curriculum requirement at both primary and secondary levels. The government has invested millions of pounds in developing ICT for education (£700m for 2005-06 in England alone!). (p. 121)

This investment is accompanied by a determination that all teachers should "learn to use ICT as a significant and integral part of their teaching" (TTA, 1999, p.1). The rhetoric of recent government publications reveals the motivation behind such investment: Transforming the Way We Learn: a Vision for the Future of ICT in Schools (DfES, 2002, 2005). ICT is seen as potentially transformative, a central tool in the national agenda of school reform (Deaney, Ruthven & Hennessy, 2006; McCarney, 2004). The supporting evidence base is limited, however, and in contrast to the speed of policy implementation, slow to emerge (Smith, Higgins, Wall & Miller, 2005). Even the government's main ally in the achievement of its transformational goals, the British Educational and Communications Technology Agency, seems recently to reflect discomfort with this thrust and to reassess the centrality of technology in the process of transformation: "the focus needs to be on the development of and transformation of learning and teaching for the 21st century. Technology must become secondary to a larger teaching and learning agenda" (BECTA, 2007, p. 15). This position still, however, maintains the rhetoric of transformation; learning and teaching must change radically and fundamentally to meet the needs of a new century.

The terminology of transformation suggests fundamental changes in the nature of teaching and learning. A key component of this desired transformation seems to be the individualization, or in the most recent government sound bite "personalization" of learning (DfES, 2007). Jones and Coffey (2006) summarize this as "the capacity to facilitate more individualized styles and rates of learning" (p. 123). Pupils, assisted by technology, can become more autonomous and self-directed, making use of automatic feedback and the interactivity of resources to plan and manage their own learning path (BECTA, 2003a; Kennewell, Parkinson & Tanner, 2003). There is a sense in the literature of the power of technology to promote learner freedom from the tyranny of the teacher. As Smith et al. (2005) found in their critical review of literature, "the success of new technology is

perceived as inevitable" (p. 93). Disagreement or resistance are seen as outmoded conservatism; here as elsewhere, government discourse creates "the impression that anyone disagreeing with government strategies could not be considered 'effective' " (Boag-Munro, 2005, p. 135).

There is also, however, a general feeling of disappointment at the pace of transformation and acknowledgement that it is a "long term project" (Moss et al., 2007, p. 4). Contextual constraints working against such transformation are being recognized. An International Certificate Conference (ICC) report commissioned by the European Directorate General of Education and Culture in 2003 highlighted the need for a "major change in the culture of learning" (p. 9) because of a mismatch between the promised potential of ICT and the traditional structure and accountability systems of compulsory education. BECTA (2003a) has also acknowledged the contextual constraints of the school as an institution and the difficulty of developing appropriate independent learning skills in pupils engaged in compulsory education, as have Kennewell et al. (2003). Hall and Higgins (2005) point out that if independent access and self access learning are to play "key roles in improving the quality of students' experiences and learning", then "realizing the benefits of ICT requires more flexible curricula and changes in teacher and student roles" (p. 111). There are voices questioning the notion that bringing the modern world of technology into the classroom will automatically encourage pupils to become more autonomous and motivated learners, and we must also bear in mind that "learning is not the highest priority for many children" (Driessen, Smit & Sleegers, 2005, p. 536).

Despite acknowledgement of these contextual constraints, there persists a tendency to reduce significant obstacles to a simple need for retraining of a conservative profession. Things will improve as "the conservative world of education begins to catch up with the world inhabited by its students" (Gill, 2000, p. 7). Hall and Higgins

(2005) emphasize the responsibility of teachers to adapt to the demands of new technology so as not to waste its potential benefits. The technological determinism implied here leads to the logical conclusion that teachers are duty bound to ensure that the affordances of new technologies are put into operation, regardless of their own priorities or preferences or the existing dynamics of the sociocultural situation. Causality appears to be located in the technology (Fisher, 2006). Even pupils seem to subscribe to this "fantasy of a teacher-proof curriculum" represented by the computer (Pinar, 2005, p. 34) in that they themselves talk of "computers and IWB in an anthropomorphic fashion" (Tanner & Jones, 2005, p. 330).

This approach, in fact, continues the second long-standing strand of government rhetoric which labels teachers and their teaching as deficient (Hall, Collins, Benjamin, Nind & Sheehy, 2004; Heilbronn, 2004) and in need of prescription and retraining. Considerable frustration has been expressed at the resistance of a conservative profession to change at the pace required by short-term political imperatives. Perhaps the technological determinism identified by Fisher (2006) in government discourse, linking ICT directly with transformation and thus ascribing agency and causality to the tool rather than to the expert teacher, allows a frustrated political master neatly to bypass a well established profession with strong power to resist within individual classrooms (Ollin, 2005). It also, of course, allows government to blame teachers for a failure of its policies and lack of return for its substantial investment. It is not the policy at fault, but the teachers who have failed to learn to use the new technology to best advantage. Early initiatives designed to train the teachers have had varied and partial success (see Conlon, 2004; Galàn & Blanco, 2004; OFSTED, 2004) and the promised transformation is, perhaps not surprisingly in the light of the complexity of issues involved, still awaited (Beastall, 2006; OFSTED, 2005).

THE GOVERNMENT UNDERMINES ITS OWN RHETORIC

There appears, in fact, to be a potential conflict between two major thrusts of government intervention into classroom life. Simultaneously with the requirements for computers to become a significant tool for learning in the classroom, the authorities introduced a raft of 'strategies' to dictate the shape of lessons in both primary and secondary schools. The compulsory National Literacy Strategy (DfES, 1998c) and National Numeracy Strategy (DfES, 1998d) plus the "recommended" Key Stage Three National Strategy (DfES, 2001) set the tone with a strong emphasis on interactive whole class teaching (see Smith, Hardman & Higgins, 2006, 2007; Tanner & Jones, 2007). Such an approach of necessity involves an emphasis on direct teaching and instruction, as opposed to task-based and discovery learning approaches which might be more readily associated with the use of ICTs. A further thrust of the strategies is the expectation that teachers take full control of their pupils' learning and behaviour in order to achieve pre-determined outcomes. A key principle of the Key Stage Three National Strategy, recommending "best practice" to teachers of pupils aged 11-14, is the setting, sharing and monitoring of clear, precise objectives for each individual lesson (DfES, 2001). This emphasizes a "highly instructional objectives-based pedagogy", placed firmly within a "heavily accountable teaching culture" (Burns & Myhill, 2004, p. 47). The classroom teacher is left in the unenviable position of reconciling opposing strands of rhetoric in the daily challenge to teach as effectively as possible within given constraints.

A BRIDGE BETWEEN TWO RHETORICS: THE INTERACTIVE WHITEBOARD

The IWB is a tool which allows teachers to meet the potentially conflicting demands of harnessing technology and increasing their control over learning and behaviour. It promises both support for and enhancement of whole class teaching. Moss et al. (2007), evaluating the use of IWBs in core subjects (Maths, English and Science) in secondary schools in the London area, pointed out that: "banks of computers … create less than ideal conditions for teaching"; the IWB, however, offers an "alternative way of facilitating ICT use in group settings whilst allowing for clearer teacher control over the shape and direction of that interaction" (p. 90). They describe the IWB as "easy to use and more likely to find favour with teachers who otherwise struggle to incorporate technology" (p. 91). In contrast to the focus in a computer suite on "learning", the IWB is a "teaching" tool. It is precisely its easy integration into existing practice which initially led some ICT language pioneers to reject it, preferring to focus on the development of practices offering different opportunities for pupils to learn such as computer suites fitted with language practice software (Myers, 2003).

The IWB has been seized upon by the UK government as an ally in its mission to transform teaching and learning. It has been made widely available as "a pedagogic tool for promoting interactive whole class teaching" (Smith, et al., 2007, p. 455), particularly linked with the National Literacy and Numeracy Strategies in the primary sector and core subject teaching at secondary level (Moss et al., 2007). The latter draw attention to its capacity to "bring the functionality of the computer into whole class settings" whilst simultaneously solving "some of the perceived difficulties associated with the previous deployment of PCs in schools" (p. 12).

There is a plethora of publications advocating the merits of IWBs and exemplifying "good use". BECTA have produced online advice in a variety of documents (BECTA, 2003b, 2004) and a major funded project resulted in a cross-curricular CD-ROM supplied free to secondary schools (Walker, 2004). Moss et al. (2007) group the affordances offered by the IWB into three key themes: "increased pace of delivery; increased use of multimodal resources, incorporating image, sound and movement in new ways; and a more interactive style of whole class teaching" (p. 6). For the MFL teacher, the following might be seen as key affordances:

- The ease of integrating images, sound and the written word in a multi-sensory presentation to support the development of grapheme/phoneme relationships
- The potential for the use of colour, font size and animation to draw attention to particular features of language; "noticing" being a key aspect of language acquisition (Lightbown, 2003; Skehan, 1998)
- The ease of electronic storage allowing rapid access to a range of multimodal resources for adaptation in lesson planning and for impromptu revision of earlier work
- The potential for display of pupils' work, both written and oral, to support peer assessment with a focus on language quality
- The potential for a "classroom without walls" (Hall & Higgins, 2005, p.107) through easy access to authentic multimodal materials integrating cultural aspects and allowing "virtual travel" (Lawes, 2000, p. 50)
- The possibility for allowing "fairly mundane drills to pass as fun" (Jones & Coffey, 2006, p. 125) through the use of interactive language games employing technical interactivity (Smith et al., 2005)
- The potential for video-conferencing allowing real-time interaction with native speakers

In summary, Hall and Higgins (2005) describe the IWB as a "conglomeration of all previous educational technologies" (p. 106), which is viewed very favorably for its versatility by both teachers and students. This list could be divided into affordances which increase teacher control over the learning process and affordances which open up the classroom to the outside world and to more flexible approaches.

Other more sophisticated claims for the IWB are linked with its professed ability to enhance the nature of classroom interaction by helping teachers to make students' thinking visible (Goodison, 2003), by focusing on reasoning rather than on answers (BECTA, 2003a,) and by leading to increased interactions between teachers and pupils prompted by the dynamic interaction between pupils and computers (BECTA, 2003a). Smith et al. (2006) point out, however, that there is a "lack of empirical evidence to support many of the assertions made about the benefits of IWBs in promoting teacher pupil interaction" (p. 445), and there are debates about the nature and quality of such interaction (Smith et al., 2005; Tanner & Jones, 2007).

With such potential on offer, the teacher is often positioned as deficient for failing to capitalize on the wealth of educational opportunities offered by this amazing tool; technological determinism is well entrenched. Moss et al. (2007) warned that the low take up of externally offered training courses and the tendency for teachers to create their own materials for their classes "may reinforce a relatively conservative use of the technology as teachers adapt it to their existing teaching style" (p. 9). This "transformative" device must not be stymied by conservative, old-fashioned pedagogy. The assumption is that technology can transform any teaching, anytime, anywhere, and that transformation is always good.

THE REALITY OF THE MODERN LANGUAGES CLASSROOM

A sociocultural approach cautions that context is paramount; it can therefore be useful to look in detail at the reality of a contextually situated case to identify the interacting factors affecting teachers' work. These include the political and social expectations placed on them as educators, the requirements of the national and local systems, school ethos, pupil/teacher/community relationships and subject-specific differences in pedagogy.

Generalizations about the need to transform pedagogy make no reference to existing subject-specific differences. Hall and Higgins (2005) are right to point out that there is "really no comparison between the plain whiteboard and the IWB" (p. 106). MFL teachers, however, already have an extended repertoire of resources beyond the board and the textbook and have long been effective users of "low tech" techniques such as audio recordings and the overhead projector to promote speaking skills (OFSTED, 2002, p. 8). This same Office for Standards in Education report highlighted the superior effectiveness of such techniques over newer technologies, though it also raised the as yet unexplored potential of the IWB. The language teacher's traditional repertoire contains:

- Flashcards, i.e. pictures representing meaning plus word cards that can be manipulated by both teacher and pupil for kinesthetic involvement and physical language games such as "human sentences", where several individuals rearrange themselves into correct word order
- Pair work activities using cut-up sentences, maps and dice games to promote interactive language practice
- Aural and video recordings, television and satellite programmes, newspapers, magazines, menus and shopping brochures plus photographs and postcards
- Real objects in the classroom such as pupils' own belongings, food from the target country which can be tasted and described
- Physical activity such as miming, Physical Education and cookery lessons to learn and practice verb forms
- Genuine interpersonal communication in the target language to exchange information

and jokes, either as incidental use of language or in the conduct of class surveys

Some of this can be replicated and even enhanced by use of the IWB; however there are clearly instances where "traditional" non-technological activities have the advantage. Whereas Smith et al. (2005) write that the IWB has been used on occasions to eliminate "the disruption associated with movement around the classroom" (p. 94), many MFL teachers use pair work and survey work precisely to move pupils out of their seats and encourage them to interact with a wider range of peers in the target language. What the IWB does offer for the language teacher is the ease of access to a wide range of resources and the potential to integrate a number of these effective "low-tech" devices smoothly into a highly responsive digital environment. The technology can be useful and motivating as part of a "blended" approach, but even without it, MFL teachers in England have been described as experts in interactive whole-class teaching (Mitchell, 2000, p. 10). Moss et al. (2007) in their investigation of the use of IWBs in core subjects warned against prioritizing technical interactivity over clear pedagogical intent (p. 41); certain aspects of pedagogical intent in MFL teaching and learning are best served without electronic support.

This leads to the question of what actually constitutes an effective MFL teaching methodology in the compulsory secondary classroom. This question has long been the subject of much debate (Van Essen, 2002; Lodge, 2000; Mitchell, 2000). Language teachers are renowned for a very teacher-centered pedagogy, an approach which has been severely criticized in certain quarters and identified as one of the sources of disaffection in boys in particular (Harris, 1998; Jones & Jones, 2001; OFSTED, 2003). Skehan (1998) has been particularly scathing about the persistence of the "presentation, practice, production" approach to teaching languages employed by a "conservative

profession" which is "out of touch with language acquisition studies" (p. 94).

Once again there emerges a deficit model of the teaching profession. Such criticisms seem to ignore the specific conditions of the compulsory secondary classroom within a highly controlled, highly accountable teaching profession. Bruton (2005) has questioned how realistic it is to advocate the implementation of suggestions for alternative methodology which stem mainly from classrooms focused on English as a Second or Foreign Language, and which are not necessarily transferable to school classrooms in England. A closer look at conditions within those classrooms might help to explain the tenacity of the "presentation, practice, production" sequence and the consequent popularity of the IWB by contrast with other electronic resources.

Firstly, an underlying theme within second language acquisition theory is that of the central importance of motivation. Motivation is not an automatic ingredient in a compulsory classroom, particularly in a country where the home language of many learners is the major international vehicle for business and leisure. One of the major advantages of the IWB for beleaguered teachers is its support in enhancing learner motivation. In the absence of motivation, coercion must be used; coercion is "a pervasive characteristic of formal schooling in almost every culture" (Wells, 1999, p. 362). Managing behaviour becomes a key aspect of the teacher's role. Language lessons have been shown to demonstrate the lowest levels of on-task behaviour (Banner & Rayner, 2002. p. 39). If language learning is "90% practice after 10% presentation" (Davies & Rendall, 2004, p. 9), the challenge is to motivate or coerce pupils in compulsory language classrooms to engage in such intense practice. When left to their own devices many pupils opt out of practice situations, and practice does not necessarily mean learning; Laurillard (1997) found that when working alone at a computer without teacher input a considerable number of pupils resort to guessing. Deaney et al. (2006) referred to tensions between "encouraging more autonomous, self-paced, exploratory activity, and ensuring that pupils' attention was drawn to salient elements of the topic" (p. 475). Attention to detail is even more important with beginner language learners, where there is inevitably a "preponderance of accuracy work early on" to establish good foundations for developing independent language use (Hedge, 2000, p. 61). In a sixty minute lesson, minus time to enter the classroom, do the compulsory register, organize children, pack away and dismiss the class, without any whole-class teacher input each child in an average-sized class would receive a maximum of one and a half minutes of individual teacher time for monitoring, feedback and queries. This hardly seems sufficient to support optimum effective learning. The easiest way to monitor and enforce accurate repeated practice with unmotivated learners, or with a mixture where the experience of the motivated is at risk from poor behaviour by others, may at times be to engage in interactive whole-class teaching using question and answer techniques and games to insist on language production by pupils.

Secondly, the secondary school teacher has a syllabus to teach, a scheme of work to cover in a very limited time, and works within a competitive marketplace where the effectiveness of schools and individual teachers is measured by a quantitative comparison of outcomes in terms of public examination results and national test results. Teachers thus operate within a heavily accountable teaching culture based on a rather too simple equation of teaching intervention with outcomes which ignores the complexity of the teaching and learning process and militates against any form of risk-taking (Munn & Lloyd, 2005; Burns & Myhill, 2004). Teachers are expected to be firmly in control of outcomes. They cannot take the chance that pupils will "notice" grammatical forms and useful vocabulary within a communicative exchange or during task achievement.

The school timetable allows for as little as one or two hours of language lessons per week, in an atmosphere where only a minority of pupils will have an interest in accessing the language outside of those times. Directive teaching may seem to be the only way to meet the expectations placed on teachers, and recent government initiatives place strong emphasis on such directive teaching with clear, shared objectives and the use of well-paced, lively and interactive whole-class work, not only in the Numeracy and Literacy Strategies but also in the Key Stage 3 Strategy Framework for MFL (DfES, 2003).

Thirdly, teachers' intense workloads and their need to rely on established routines and practices to survive their days with dignity also militate against innovation. Even committed enthusiasts find it hard to make the time to innovate, and the pace of externally imposed change in recent decades exacerbates this situation. Asking for a radical change of pedagogy and methodology when teachers are so busy and their prime concern in selecting pedagogy is often control (Ireson, Mortimore and Hallam, 2002), seems unreasonable. After all, in many situations and done well, the teacher-fronted approach seems to work (Bruton, 2005).

In summary, the persistence of teacher-fronted presentation, practice and production as a teaching methodology underlines its perceived usefulness by teachers and teacher educators within the conditions peculiar to compulsory secondary sector language teaching. It is not surprising, then, that the one technological tool developed to enhance whole-class teaching has become the most coveted in language classrooms. In order to understand how it is used and to what extent the transformational rhetoric can be believed, we need to look at the precise situational circumstances within which teachers make their decisions about pedagogy and resources.

AN INVESTIGATION INTO WHAT GUIDES TEACHER DECISION-MAKING WHEN EMPLOYING NEW TECHNOLOGICAL TOOLS

An opportunity to investigate such decision-making arose when I was invited in 2002 by a local language college to support a developmental plan for the 17 members of its languages department involving the wholesale installation of IWBs to replace traditional whiteboards and overhead projectors. Curriculum managers were keen to ensure that the integration of new technology and the changes in methodology which it might provoke should have a firm focus on pedagogy and should undergo a clearly structured evaluation process. The return for my involvement would be access to a range of teachers as they integrated new tools and the agreement that, subject to the permission of individual participants and with due regard to ethical considerations, my research team would be allowed to use any data collected. With the curriculum managers we devised a range of procedures and data collection tools to support the teachers in exploring their thinking and decision-making, such as: baseline questionnaires to assess their levels of skill and confidence with a variety of ICT applications; teaching logs to record the use of ICT; video snippets of lessons selected by participants to represent their priorities; group meetings to discuss pedagogy and progress; and individual interviews to explore thinking. A first round of log keeping and interviewing was compulsory for the teachers as part of their departmental development plan, though all willingly granted permission for collected data to be used by the researchers. A second round was voluntary. For details of the research tools and of the resolution of potential ethical conflicts plus fuller information concerning the overall research outcomes see Gray, Hagger-Vaughan, Pilkington and Tomkins (2005), Gray, Pilkington, Hagger-Vaughan and Tomkins (2007) and Pilkington and Gray (2004).

The overall outcomes of the project generally reflected those discussed in Chapter 1 of this volume (Miller & Glover). After initial frustration with technical aspects of the technology, enthusiasm for use of the boards was unanimous. This enthusiasm was primarily rooted in the perception of easier classroom management – pupils paid greater attention, were focused more uniformly and with greater concentration on the front of the class, and were generally more amenable about engaging with the teacher and the lesson. Teachers felt that they were spending less time coercing the pupils into paying attention and had more time to interact positively with them, with clear benefits for the pace of the lesson. In some cases this allowed the teacher to capitalize on the new balance in the relationship to push pupils into increased use of the target language, in others it allowed them to explore reasoning in order to justify correct answers and identify why others were wrong. Increased focus and motivation were seen to result in faster learning, speedier syllabus coverage and more effective lessons.

In teaching logs the participants classified their role when using new technology with pupils. The most frequent classification was that of "facilitator", supporting pupils in more individual or autonomous work, even during whole class cycles of presentation, practice and production. The teacher seemed to be taking second place on the stage to the computer. This was seen in a variety of ways, not always positively. One teacher seemed to see herself as pushed into the role of "deliverer of material" with some loss of her persona as an imaginative actress. She did, however, feel better organized when using the IWB and wasted less time in transitions. Most teachers were overwhelmingly positive about being able to share the stage and the responsibility for motivating and enthusing pupils, with one at least seeing it as a license to step back and leave the pupils to their own devices. In all cases this was less to do with a more self-directed style of learning, and more to do with a reduction of the need for coercion to engage in learning activities. The "autonomy" described was not about pupils making choices and planning their learning, it was simply about deciding to engage with what the teacher offered rather than having to be coerced into compliance. In the lessons demonstrating the clearest learning outcomes, this apparent absence of leadership was in fact an illusion: pupils thought they were interacting with the computer rather than the teacher, whereas they were in fact interacting with the teacher through the medium of resources carefully compiled to guide their learning inexorably towards the teacher's goals. The control effected by the teacher in the most effective lessons was actually far stronger than in lessons using paper resources, though carefully disguised. One teacher pointed out that practically the whole of her lessons from start to finish was planned step by step within a PowerPoint presentation. The resources, videos, lesson plans and logs provided by several other teachers along with their comments about the intensity and time-consuming nature of preparation confirmed the impression that the IWB was used to increase rather than to decrease control over the learning process and behaviour. Teachers were not changing their style of teaching; those who most readily engaged with pedagogical discussion in interviews were paralleling their established methodology of presentation, practice and production. One commented that "much of this could be done with an overhead projector and other resources, but it would have been less fun, less smooth and have had less impact", mirrored by a second who stated that "in the past it would have taken much longer to achieve it and it wouldn't have captured the imagination of the children as much – I don't think they would have picked things up so quickly". A third described her ongoing challenge in language teaching as "finding a new way all the time to attract their attention", and a fourth commented on the faster pace of syllabus coverage and consequent reduction of boredom. A fifth teacher, who had previously worked in adult education, lamented

this need to "become an entertainer", to be "extremely quick" so as to avoid discipline problems. The contribution of PowerPoint shown through the IWB to maintaining a smooth, fast pace in the lesson was a vital advantage for her and had revived her enjoyment of teaching. All five of these teachers were exploiting the features of dynamic display offered by the IWB, mainly in the form of PowerPoint presentations and interactive games, to draw pupils' attention to specific aspects of the language content and push them into practicing sentence building in the whole-class setting. A group of teachers of community languages were exploiting the features of the IWB to increase pupil motivation for reading and writing, as these were their pupils' least advanced skills. Only one of the teachers interviewed seemed to favour a more "open" approach to learning, making use of web-based materials in order to reduce his preparation time, and even here the emphasis was on "better control of behaviour" due to the "improved quality of activities". All teachers prioritized in their interviews the advantages offered by the IWB, mainly through use of PowerPoint, for managing pupil behaviour. It was described as "highly effective in establishing a concentrated learning atmosphere". Several explicitly stated control of behaviour as their priority in deciding how to use the IWB: "I've concentrated more on developing my ICT skills with the less able to manage the behaviour"; and "it really has improved my lessons, definitely – I feel I'm assisting their learning rather than forcing it down".

The particular approaches used by participants in their early integration of IWB for the most part fell into the category of an increase in control rather than an opening of the classroom to the outside world. All but one expressed caution about the use of authentic materials from the Internet, and indeed about any resources which they had not themselves created. Tensions between the expectations on teachers to produce results demonstrating progress and the "opening" affordances offered by the technology were clear in the words of one of our teachers: "by creating your resources you really target the levels and needs of your kids". Where Internet material was used, it was primarily in the guise of tried and tested practice games recommended by trusted colleagues, with several teachers still expressing a note of caution about the limitations of such mainly word level work, or in the use of specific websites again tested by trusted colleagues and linked very precisely to explicit tasks and outcomes. Most teachers favored the creation of their own carefully targeted materials, including where appropriate their own photography and video recordings of the target country, and in effect were creating their own flexible and adaptable electronic textbook. They were using the IWB to implement their existing methodology and meet their own pedagogical aims in a more interesting and motivating way both for themselves and their pupils in order to increase their ability to move the pupils inexorably and with less conflict towards the required outcomes. As they did so they discovered new ways of meeting their existing goals.

The timescale for this project covered the early years of teachers' implementation of the electronic whiteboards, and it is possible that their practice may have developed in later years to integrate more of the "opening" features of the technology. However, even during the period of the research, the attention of the participating teachers and their curriculum managers had begun to move from the potential of the IWB to newer possibilities opened up by the use of digital recording devices such as mobile telephones, iPods and cameras, as well as the creation of an electronic learning platform for use beyond the classroom. The pace of electronic change and the expectations of school managers and the wider community appeared to demand a relentless rush onwards without the time or space to consolidate and develop current patterns of practice. Without a longitudinal study it is impossible to draw reliable conclusions about whether the practice of these individuals continued to develop towards the promised transformation, or

whether it began to fossilize once the teachers had learnt how to employ their existing methodology to maximum effect. Logic tells us that the survival needs of these teachers in a challenging inner city school might well place a limit on the development of their pedagogical direction. In fact, several of the participants commented on the unsustainable drain on their personal resources required to create the materials which they were using, and many implied that they were only prepared to commit so much time because this would become a flexible, reusable resource for future years: "once you've done it, it's done, it doesn't get tatty and you can't lose it"; "next year's going to be a piece of cake because I've got it all there"; "preparation takes a lot of time but once it's there it will be a bank of resources for use in following years". Longitudinal research into the use of IWB in the primary classroom has yielded conflicting results concerning the long term effects on classroom interaction. The strong pedagogical beliefs of our participating teachers, and the apparent insularity of certain belief groups from one other even within the same department, seem to argue against the type of transformation of pedagogy prophesied by advocates of technological determinism. These deeply rooted pedagogical beliefs did not seem open to influence from any quarter, though it did appear from the discussions that the technology was sometimes limiting or steering practice in certain ways which were not always completely positively valued. Several of our teachers felt that although they were gaining in terms of managing behaviour more easily, they were perhaps in danger of losing some of the enjoyable practices of their pre-IWB days and had to remind themselves to re-integrate such work and create opportunities to do so: "with Year 7 I can be a bit silly". In a later project with a smaller number of these teachers investigating the combined use of a variety of ICT resources including digital voice and video recorders, the role of the IWB was to draw pupils together after more independent and creative work to focus them on linguistic accuracy and language quality and to "close down" the work which had been "opened up" by the use of other electronic resources.

Facilitating Independent Learning? Or Increasing Teacher Control?

In our small-scale investigation, the IWB was mainly used as a tool for increasing control over pupil behaviour and learning rather than for opening up the classroom to the outside world or for increasing pupil autonomy. The "autonomy" targeted by these teachers was not autonomy in choice of resources or of what or how to learn, rather linguistic autonomy reached through carefully controlled practice. Where greater autonomy in the more traditional sense was pursued, there was less evidence of satisfactory measurable outcomes and in some cases a sense of dissatisfaction expressed by both teachers and pupils with the quality of both product and learning. Successful language lessons seemed to require a clearly defined learning path with visible measurable outcomes. The technology was being used to meet the immediate needs of both teachers and pupils within the sociocultural conditions of their world. Is this a case of skilful teachers subverting the paradigm of technological determinism (Fisher, 2006) to meet their own professional aims? As indicated earlier, however, the affordances of the technology also appeared to interact with those aims to limit some possibilities and steer the outcomes towards particular directions.

Subverting the Power of Information and Communications Technology?

It is of course impossible to draw generalizations from such small-scale, localized investigations. Nevertheless, one cannot help but see irony in the fact that the much vaunted power of technology to transform teaching and learning has in reality been diverted by most of the teachers in this project to increase rather than reduce their control over

pupils and their learning, to meet the expectations and exhortations voiced by government agencies in the various "strategies" and their own survival needs in the busy classroom. It is no coincidence that the most popular technological application so far in schools has been one which meets many teachers' desire for control over content, learning and behaviour rather than those which promote independent learning. Learning may be improved, but perhaps not in the ways first envisaged by the technophiles. Even within our own projects, the types of application which appealed to the ICT experts within our research group were questioned by the MFL methodologists in terms of perceived learning potential and outcomes. As with any new initiative, policy makers need to understand the realities of practitioners and the ways in which individuals and communities of practice within specific institutions and systems interact with tools to address priorities. It may be that interaction with those tools eventually leads to some changes in practice, and perhaps even to a widening of practice. It is highly unlikely, however, that the imposition of tools will lead users to abandon their hard won and deeply engrained beliefs about the values and procedures of their practice or take risks with their precious and fragile classroom authority in order to adapt wholesale to the tool or to the expectations of a technological determinism tradition. Users select tools to meet their own perceived needs, or make selective use of tools imposed upon them. Developments in practice may come from the interaction between current practice and new tools, but whether this might be called "transformation" is a different matter. Once users have exhausted the tool's potential to enhance their practice, having taken as many risks as they are prepared to, use may fossilize. The teachers in our projects, having once mastered the basics of using the IWB in their classrooms, were prompted by the local City Learning Centre and their school curriculum managers to move on to other challenges involving digital recording, the use of iPods and mobile telephones, the development of podcasts and interactive websites. The limited time available for developmental thinking in a busy profession was thus directed away from conscious ongoing experimentation with their IWBs.

FUTURE RESEARCH DIRECTIONS

It would be useful to pursue a longitudinal study of individual MFL teachers' developing use of IWBs over several years to verify or refute the suggestions above that use might fossilize rather than develop. Large scale longitudinal studies of IWB use in core subjects have provided conflicting evidence; the development of high level IWB teaching skills seems to be closely linked with ongoing professional development opportunity (Smith, et al., 2006, 2007; Somekh et al., 2007). Time, energy and funding for continuing professional development is limited, and with the entire English educational system in constant flux as new initiatives continue to be introduced at breathless pace, the priority for many may be directed towards different challenges. Research from other educational systems would be useful to help tease out the interplay between factors in the complexity of a given sociocultural situation.

CONCLUSION

As summarized above, the use of ICT has been vaunted in England as a way of empowering learners, of developing learner independence and offering wider opportunities for learners both within and beyond the classroom. Many of our project participants claimed to see themselves more as "facilitators" than "directors" when using a range of technological applications in their classrooms. When investigated in detail, however, the practice of the majority did not demonstrate the facilitation of autonomous learning in its traditional interpretation, rather its opposite: increased control over

lesson content, pupil activity, pupil behaviour and learning and performance outcomes. In a sense, these teachers were subverting the emancipatory power of technology to increase their control over pupil learning rather than reduce it, in order to meet their own needs as defined by the system within which they worked and the expectations of their communities. Statements about the power of technology to widen horizons and increase pupil responsibility may in fact be justifiably rejected by teachers who see their main challenge as to mould the pupils in their classroom into the compliant, responsive beings which the system requires of them in order to meet externally imposed achievement targets for pupils, teachers and schools.

REFERENCES

Banner, G., & Rayner, S. (2002). Learning language and learning style: Principles, process and practice. *Language Learning Journal*, *21*, 37–44. doi:10.1080/09571730085200091

Beastall, L. (2006). Enchanting a disenchanted child: Revolutionizing the means of education using information technology and e-learning. *British Journal of Sociology of Education*, *27*(1), 97–110. doi:10.1080/01425690500376758

BECTA. (2003a). *ICT and pedagogy: A review of the research literature. National Grid for Learning Research & Evaluation Series, Report No. 19*. London: DfES/BECTA. Retrieved January 29, from http://www.becta.org.uk/resarch/reports

BECTA. (2003b). *What the research says about interactive whiteboards*. BECTA. Retrieved January 29, 2004, from http://www.becta.org.uk/research/reports

BECTA. (2004). *Getting the most from your interactive whiteboard: A guide for secondary schools*. Coventry, UK: BECTA.

BECTA. (2007). *Harnessing technology review 2007: Progress and impact of technology in education. Summary report.* Coventry, UK: BECTA. Retrieved February 11, 2008, from http://www.becta.org.uk/research/

Boag-Munro, G. (2005). 'The naming of cats is a difficult matter' – how far are government and teachers using the same words to talk about educational concepts? In J. Satterthwaite & E. Atkinson (Eds.), Discourses of education in the age of new imperialism (pp. 131-150). Stoke on Trent, UK: Trentham Books.

Bruton, S. (2005). Task-based language learning: For the state secondary FL classroom? *Language Learning Journal, 31,* 55–68. doi:10.1080/09571730585200091

Burns, C., & Myhill, D. (2004). Interactive or inactive? A consideration of the nature of interaction in whole class teaching. *Cambridge Journal of Education, 34*(1), 35–49. doi:10.1080/0305764042000183115

Conlon, T. (2004). A failure of delivery: The United Kingdom's new opportunities fund programme of teacher training in information and communications technology. *Journal of In-service Education, 30*(1), 115–139. doi:10.1080/13674580400200286

Davies, G., & Rendall, H. (2004). *ICT4LT module 1:4. Introduction to computer assisted language learning (CALL).* Retrieved January 29, 2004 from http://www.ict4lt.org/en/en_mod1-4.htm

Deaney, R., Ruthven, K., & Hennessy, S. (2006). Teachers' developing 'practical theories' of the contribution of information and communication technologies to subject teaching and learning: an analysis of cases from English secondary schools. *British Educational Research Journal, 32*(3), 459–480. doi:10.1080/01411920600635460

DfEE. (1998a). Circular 4/98 teaching: high status, high standards. London: DfEE

DfEE. (1998b). Initial teacher training National Curriculum for the use of information and communications technology in subject teaching. DfEE Circular 4/98, Annexe B. London: DfEE.

DfEE. (1998c). The national literacy strategy: A framework for teaching. London: DfEE

DfEE. (1998d). The national numeracy strategy: A framework for teaching. London: DfEE

DfES. (2001). The key stage 3 national strategy. London: DfES.

DfES. (2002). Transforming the way we learn: A vision for the future of ICT in schools. DfES Report No: 0008/2002. London: DfES.

DfES (2003). *The key stage 3 national strategy. Framework for teaching modern languages: Years 7, 8 and 9.* London: DfES.

DfES. (2005). Harnessing technology: Transforming learning and children's services. London: DfES.

DfES. (2007). Teaching and learning in 2020 Review. DfES Report No: 6856/2007. London: DfES.

Driessen, G., Smit, F., & Sleegers, P. (2005). Parental involvement and educational achievement. *British Educational Research Journal, 31*(4), 509–532. doi:10.1080/01411920500148713

Field, K. (Ed.). (2000). *Issues in modern foreign languages teaching.* Cambridge, MA: Cambridge University Press.

Fisher, T. (2006). Educational transformation: Is it, like 'beauty', in the eye of the beholder, or will we know it when we see it? *Education and Information Technologies, 11*(3-4), 293–303. doi:10.1007/s10639-006-9009-1

Galàn, J. G., & Blanco, S. M. (2004). Design of educational web pages. *European Journal of Teacher Education, 27*(1), 99–103. doi:10.1080/0261976042000211793

Gill, C. (2000). *Improving MFL learning through ICT. Dunstable & Dublin*. Ireland: Folens Limited.

Goodison, T. (2003). Integrating ICT in the classroom: A case study of two contrasting lessons. *British Journal of Educational Technology, 34*(5), 549–566. doi:10.1046/j.0007-1013.2003.00350.x

Gray, C., Hagger-Vaughan, L., Pilkington, R., & Tomkins, S. (2005). The pros and cons of interactive whiteboards in relation to the key stage 3 strategy and framework. *Language Learning Journal, 32*, 38–44. doi:10.1080/09571730585200171

Gray, C., Pilkington, R., Hagger-Vaughan, L., & Tomkins, S. (2007). Integrating ICT into classroom practice in modern foreign language teaching in England: Making room for teachers' voices. *European Journal of Teacher Education, 30*(4), 407–429. doi:10.1080/02619760701664193

Hall, I., & Higgins, S. (2005). Primary school students' perceptions of interactive whiteboards. *Journal of Computer Assisted Learning, 21*, 102–117. doi:10.1111/j.1365-2729.2005.00118.x

Hall, K., Collins, J., Benjamin, S., Nind, M., & Sheehy, K. (2004). SATurated models of pupildom: assessment and inclusion/exclusion. *British Educational Research Journal, 30*(6), 801–817. doi:10.1080/0141192042000279512

Harris, V. (1998). Making boys make progress. *Language Learning Journal, 18*, 56–62. doi:10.1080/09571739885200271

Harrison, C., Comber, C., Fisher, T., Haw, K., Lewin, C., Lunzer, E., et al. (2002). ImpaCT2. The impact of information and communication technologies on pupil learning and attainment. (ICT in Schools Research and Evaluation Series No. 7). London: DfES/BECTA.

Hedge, T. (2000). *Teaching and learning in the language classroom*. Oxford, UK: Oxford University Press.

Heilbronn, R. (2004). The national strategy for key stage 3 and its application to modern foreign language teaching. *Language Learning Journal, 30*, 42–49. doi:10.1080/09571730485200221

International Certificate Conference (2003). *The impact of information and communications technologies on the teaching of foreign languages and on the role of teachers of foreign languages. A report commissioned by the Directorate General of Education & Culture*. Retrieved February 26, 2004, from http://icc-europe.com/ICT_in_FLT_Final_Report_Jan2003/ICT_in_FLT_in_Europe.pdf

Ireson, J., Mortimore, P., & Hallam, S. (2002). What do we know about effective pedagogy? In Moon, B., Shelton Mayes, A., & Hutchinson, S. (Eds.), *Teaching, learning and the curriculum in secondary school: A reader* (pp. 64–69). London, New York: Open University/Routledge Falmer.

Jones, B., & Jones, G. (2001). *Boys' performance in modern foreign languages. Listening to learners*. London: CILT.

Jones, J., & Coffey, S. (2006). Modern foreign languages 5-11: A guide for teachers. London: David Fulton.

Kennewell, S., Parkinson, J., & Tanner, H. (Eds.). (2003). *Learning to teach ICT in the secondary school*. London: RoutledgeFalmer.

Laurillard, D. (1997). *The TELL consortium – formative evaluation report*. Hull, UK: University of Hull. Retrieved January 29, 2004, from http://www.hull.ac.uk/cti/tell/eval.htm

Lawes, S. (2000). Why learn a foreign language? In Field, K. (Ed.), *Issues in modern foreign languages teaching* (pp. 41–51). Cambridge, MA: Cambridge University Press.

Lightbown, P. M. (2003). Second language acquisition research in the classroom/second language acquisition research from the classroom. *Language Learning Journal, 28*, 4–13. doi:10.1080/09571730385200151

Lodge, A. (2000). Higher Education . In Green, S. (Ed.), *New perspectives on teaching and learning modern languages* (pp. 105–123). Clevedon, UK: Multilingual Matters Ltd.

McCarney, J. (2004). Effective models of staff development in ICT. *European Journal of Teacher Education, 27*(1), 61–72. doi:10.1080/0261976042000211801

Mitchell, R. (2000). Research, inspection and teacher education: The quest for a consensus on effective MFLs pedagogy. *Links (New York, N.Y.), 21*, 5–12.

Moss, G., Jewitt, C., Levaãic, R., Armstrong, V., Cardini, A., & Castle, F. (2007). The interactive whiteboards, pedagogy and pupil performance evaluation: An evaluation of the schools whiteboard expansion (SWE) project: London challenge. DfES Research Report RR 816. London: DfES.

Munn, P., & Lloyd, G. (2005). Exclusion and excluded pupils. *British Educational Research Journal, 31*(2), 205–221. doi:10.1080/0141192052000340215

Myers, H. (2003). *Case study 5: The Ashcombe School, Language College. Information and Communications Technology for Language Teaching (ICT4LT) Module 3:1. Managing a multimedia language centre*. Retrieved 26 February, 2004, from http://www.ict4lt.org/en/en_mod3.1.htm

Office for Standards in Education. (2002). *ICT in schools: the effect of government initiatives. Secondary modern foreign languages (HMI 706)*. London: Her Majesty's Inspectorate.

Office for Standards in Education. (2003). *Modern foreign languages (MFL). Progress and improving boys' achievement in modern foreign languages*. Ofsted subject reports conference series 2002/2003 (HMI 1641). London: Her Majesty's Inspectorate.

Office for Standards in Education. (2004). *ICT in schools – the impact of government initiatives. Secondary modern foreign languages. HMI 2191*. London: Her Majesty's Inspectorate.

Office for Standards in Education. (2005). *Embedding ICT in schools – a dual evaluation exercise*. London: Office for Standards in Education.

Ollin, R. (2005). Professionals, poachers or street-level bureaucrats: government policy, teaching identities and constructive subversions. In J. Satterthwaite & E. Atkinson (Eds.), Discourses of education in the age of new imperialism (pp. 151-162). Stoke on Trent, UK: Trentham Books.

Parry, J. (2004). Pupil authors and teacher innovators. *European Journal of Teacher Education, 27*(1), 83–98. doi:10.1080/0261976042000211810

Pilkington, R., & Gray, C. (2004). Embedding ICT in the modern foreign language curriculum: pedagogy into practice . In Cook, J. (Ed.), *Research proceedings of ALT-C 2004. Blue skies and pragmatism* (pp. 270–283). Exeter, UK: ALT-C.

Pinar, W. (2005). Curriculum studies and the politics of educational reform. In J. Satterthwaite & E. Atkinson (Eds.), Discourses of education in the age of new imperialism (pp. 25-46). Stoke on Trent, UK: Trentham Books.

Skehan, P. (1998). *A cognitive approach to language learning*. Oxford, UK: Oxford University Press.

Smith, F., Hardman, F., & Higgins, S. (2006). The impact of interactive whiteboards on teacher-pupil interaction in the National Literacy and Numeracy Strategies. *British Educational Research Journal, 32*(3), 443–457. doi:10.1080/01411920600635452

Smith, F., Hardman, F., & Higgins, S. (2007). Gender inequality in the primary classroom: Will interactive whiteboards help? *Gender and Education, 19*(4), 455–469. doi:10.1080/09540250701442658

Smith, H. J., Higgins, S., Wall, K., & Miller, J. (2005). Interactive whiteboards: Boon or bandwagon? A critical review of the literature. *Journal of Computer Assisted Learning, 21*, 91–101. doi:10.1111/j.1365-2729.2005.00117.x

Somekh, B., Haldane, M., Jones, K., Lewin, C., Steadman, S., & Scrimshaw, P. (2007). *Evaluation of the primary schools whiteboard expansion project. Report to the DfES*. Manchester, UK: Manchester Metropolitan University.

Tanner, H., & Jones, S. (2007). Using video-stimulated reflective dialogue to learn from children about their learning with and without ICT. *Technology, Pedagogy and Education, 16*(3), 321–335. doi:10.1080/14759390701614454

Teacher Training Agency. (1999). *The use of information and communications technology in subject teaching. Identification of needs: Secondary modern foreign languages. TTA 13/3/1999*. London: Teacher Training Agency.

Van Essen, A. (2002). A historical perspective. In M. Grenfell (Ed.) (2002). Modern languages across the curriculum (pp. 10-25). London & New York: RoutledgeFalmer.

Walker, R. J. (2004). *The review project*. Hull, UK: The University of Hull. Retrieved February 26, 2004, from http://www.thereviewproject.org/

Wells, G. (1999). *Dialogical inquiry: Towards a sociocultural practice and theory of education*. Cambridge, MA: Cambridge University Press.

Chapter 6

The Impact of Interactive Whiteboards on Classroom Interaction and Learning in Primary Schools in the UK

Steven Higgins
University of Durham, UK

ABSTRACT

The UK Government's Primary National Strategy undertook a pilot programme "Embedding ICT in the Literacy and Numeracy Strategies" where interactive whiteboards were installed in the classrooms of teachers of 9-11 year old students in more than 80 schools in six regions of England. Research to evaluate this project collected multiple sources of data, including students' attainment, structured lesson observations and the perceptions of teachers and students. Results suggest that the use of the interactive whiteboards did lead to significant changes in teachers' practices in the use of technology and in aspects of classroom interaction, and that the perceptions of those involved were overwhelmingly positive, but that the impact in terms of students' attainment on national tests was very small and short-lived. This raises questions about the integration of new technologies into classroom teaching and how such technologies might improve teaching and learning.

INTRODUCTION

The aim of this chapter is to present a critical analysis of the findings from a large-scale research project in the UK where electronic or interactive whiteboards were introduced into over 200 classrooms of the teachers of 9-11 year olds in England (Higgins et al., 2005). The initiative was explicitly designated as a national pilot project with the key goal of raising levels of attainment in the pilot schools in literacy and mathematics, which are the central curriculum focus of the UK Government-funded Primary National Strategy (i.e. strategy for raising standards in primary or elementary schools across England). Some aspects of the project have been published elsewhere, such as the initial literature scoping to identify likely issues with the evaluation

DOI: 10.4018/978-1-61520-715-2.ch006

(Smith, Higgins, Wall & Miller, 2005), changes in patterns of interaction identified through systematic observation over the course of the research (Smith, Hardman & Higgins, 2006), two analyses of students' perceptions using different methodologies (Hall & Higgins, 2005; Wall, Higgins & Smith 2005), an analysis by gender of the impact on classroom interaction (Smith, Higgins & Hardman 2007) and a discussion of the limitations of analysis of question types without investigating the subsequent discourse moves (Smith & Higgins, 2006). This chapter therefore aims to synthesize key aspects of the findings in relation to the overall objectives of the research in terms of its national policy objectives and to identify key issues for wider research into the use of interactive whiteboards in education. The process of the research also raises wider questions about the way that educational research is valued and used at policy level in the UK and more general challenges in evaluating the impact of technologies on education.

BACKGROUND

The UK has invested heavily in promoting the use of educational technologies in primary or elementary schools. Initiatives such as training for teachers in the use of information and communications technology in the late 1990s aimed to offer a course of training to all serving school teachers in the UK at a cost of about $800 million. Additionally investment in hardware, software and networking (such as the development of a "National Grid for Learning") have similarly seen considerable sums (over $3 billion up to 2008).

At the policy level, the introduction of interactive whiteboards was seen as a way to integrate technology into teaching in primary or elementary schools and at the same time support the development of "whole class interactive teaching" (Reynolds & Muijs, 1999) in order to improve standards of attainment. Other goals were infor-

mally identified, such as greater engagement of boys in lessons to address their perceived under-achievement. These aims were discussed with the funders of the research and this helped to shape the development of the research methodology.

The implementation of training and the support for the teachers involved was also studied as part of the research. A model was developed in the project where one full-time specialist teacher supported groups of about 20 teachers in each region. Training materials were developed centrally, then revised as they were used locally. A temporary website was created to exchange ideas and teaching resources (used mainly by the specialist teachers, but also by a number of classroom teachers in the project). In addition, most regions established support groups which met more informally on a regular basis. The approach to supporting teachers in using the technology effectively was a key part of the pilot programme.

RESEARCH APPROACH

The research team adopted a pragmatic approach to the evaluation of this major national initiative working within the limitations imposed by the sponsors and the funding available. The main driver of the research was to evaluate the impact of the initiative on national test results with an implicit rationalist paradigm (Young, 1999) but influenced by post-positivist approaches such as scientific realism (Pawson & Tilley, 1997) and responsive evaluation (Stake, 2004). Working with the sponsors of the pilot project, the team planned a multi-method approach to the evaluation using complementary qualitative and quantitative methods. The model of impact the research team used involved short-term indicators (participants' perceptions and changes in patterns of classroom interaction) as well as outcomes (students' attitudes and attainment). A review of the available evidence at the outset of the project indicated that the perceptions of those involved in the introduction of such technologies is generally positive, but that information about the impact in terms of changes of patterns of classroom interaction or measures of attainment were scarce (Smith et al., 2005). This remains the trend in research in this area (Higgins, Beauchamp & Miller, 2007).

The research approach was influenced by this existing evidence about the use of interactive whiteboards in education. The team attempted to design the research to address some of these shortcomings similar to the approach advocated by Blatchford (2005) in terms of the balance of evidence types. The evaluation also took into account aspects of the process of the initiative (such as technical and logistical issues) which were fed back to the sponsors and participants as the research developed. The main focus of this chapter, however, is the perceptions of the teachers and students involved of the impact of the technology, the actual changes found in classroom interaction through systematic observation and then the analysis of attainment data for literacy and mathematics, first after one, and then after two years of use.

The research team therefore used a multi-method approach to the evaluation of the impact of the technology on teaching and learning. Quantitative data was collected about aspects of classroom discourse and interaction and about students' attainment using national test data. In addition the perceptions of teachers, students and others involved in the initiative were included as an important aspect of the project methodology (van den Berg & Ros, 1999). In the sections which follow, summaries are presented of some of the data published elsewhere (Hall & Higgins, 2005; Higgins et al., 2005; Smith et al., 2005; Smith et al., 2006; Smith & Higgins, 2006; Wall et al., 2005) to provide a background for the discussion of issues concerning the synthesis of evidence in relation to the impact on students' attainment which has not been previously integrated into the overall analysis.

Daily Use of Interactive Whiteboards for Literacy and Mathematics

Descriptive data about the day-to-day use of the whiteboards was collected for two six-week periods one year apart using online diary forms. The weekly records contain data for about 100 teachers' self-reported use of the interactive whiteboards (about half of the participating teachers) representing about 8,800 lessons in literacy and mathematics. These teachers were volunteers and this may therefore over-estimate the actual usage (assuming the volunteers were more willing participants in completing the online forms and in participating in the project overall). The records indicate that the teachers reported using their interactive whiteboards in just over two thirds of their lessons (66%) in the first year of the project and nearly three-quarters of their lessons (74%) one year later. Interactive whiteboards were used slightly (and significantly) more often during mathematics lessons compared with literacy in the first year of the project. This had evened out a year later (with a 6.3% increase in reported use in mathematics and a 9.7% increase in literacy), resulting in no significant difference in reported use by subject after two years. This suggests that either the teachers were initially more confident to use the IWBs for mathematics teaching or that there were more activities or software available in this area of the curriculum at the start of the project.

Consistent patterns of use were reported over the course of the week, with a steady decline in reported use from Monday to Thursday (from about 80% of lessons at the beginning of the week to about 73% of lessons on a Thursday) and significantly fewer teachers reporting using IWBs on Fridays (about 67% of lessons).

Use increased in all parts of lessons (whole class introduction, group and plenary phases) and patterns of software use indicated that teachers were involved in developing or adapting resources more in the second year of the research, suggesting greater levels of confidence and skill in using the technology (for further details see Higgins et al., 2005). These data indicate that the pilot project was successful in developing use of the technology to a point where it was being used in nearly three-quarters of lessons of the teachers who completed the weekly records.

Changes in Patterns of Classroom Interaction

Structured observations of classroom interaction were undertaken in early 2003 and again a year later in early 2004. A total of 184 lessons of a random sample of 30 teachers were observed; the research focused on differences between lessons where teachers taught literacy and mathematics with and without an interactive whiteboard and on any changes in patterns of interaction a year later. This enabled us to investigate potential differences in classroom interaction between those teachers when using whiteboards and when they were not. Our sample size was also large enough to compare literacy and mathematics lessons and to examine any interaction effect between lessons with and without an interactive whiteboard and subject area (literacy or mathematics). The structured observation system was developed from that of Mroz, Smith and Hardman (2000) and Smith, Hardman, Mroz and Wall (2004), based on earlier classroom observational research (Croll, 1986; Flanders, 1963; Galton, Hargreaves, Comber, Wall & Pell, 1999; Good & Brophy, 1991). Full details of the findings from this aspect of the research are published elsewhere in terms of general patterns of interaction (Smith et al., 2006) as well as an analysis in terms of gender (Smith et al., 2007), and a summary of these findings is presented below.

Overall the interactions in lessons were fairly typical of the kinds of patterns in primary schools identified in this earlier research. For example, the most frequent discourse moves were *explaining* by the teacher (135 'moves' per hour, each lasting

on average 12 seconds and accounting for 28% of lesson time), *closed questions* by the teacher (62 per hour, each lasting on average only 3.5 seconds), *evaluation* by the teacher (62 per hour, on average 4.7 seconds long and accounting for 7.5% of lesson time), and *direction* (51 per hour, lasting 8.1 seconds on average and comprising 9.4% of lesson time). A typical *pupil answer* lasted for 4.4 seconds and such answers accounted for about 17% of the duration of a lesson overall.

The use of interactive whiteboards did seem to make a difference to aspects of classroom interaction. Some of these were relatively short-lived, others appeared over time as the use of the technology became embedded. From both years of observations, there were fewer pauses and uptake questions in interactive whiteboard lessons; but an embedding effect was observed in the second year of the project whereby there were also more open questions, repeat questions, probes, longer answers from students, and general talk in these lessons. There was almost twice the amount of evaluative responses from teachers in interactive whiteboard lessons. Teachers using interactive whiteboards after a year of use tended to focus their uptake or follow-up questions on the whole class rather than on an individual student.

There was a faster pace in the interactive whiteboard lessons (as measured by total number of discourse moves) in 2004 compared with the non-whiteboard lessons in 2003. Nearly 100 more discourse moves were found per lesson (such as explanations, questions, evaluations and answers). However, answers from students were also longer in whiteboard lessons compared to non-whiteboard lessons. The initial decrease in the amount of explanation by the teacher was short-lived (it increased again in 2004).

There were a number of statistically significant differences between mathematics and literacy lessons. For example, closed questions made up 9.5% of an average mathematics lesson but only 3.4% of a literacy lesson. Open questions constituted 3.1% of a literacy lesson but only 0.9% of a mathematics lesson. Presenting from pupils and uptake questions by the teacher both had larger percentage contributions in literacy lessons; and teacher direction (such as giving instructions) had a larger percentage contribution in mathematics lessons. These differences were consistent, however, between whiteboard and non-whiteboard lessons suggesting a strong subject pedagogy with clear patterns of interaction associated with the different lessons in literacy and in mathematics.

In the first set of observations, interactive whiteboard lessons contained about five minutes more whole class teaching and five minutes less group work than lessons without an interactive whiteboard. This difference was found in both literacy and mathematics. After a year the amount of group work had decreased further (this time a difference of nearly seven and a half minutes). This difference was found in the classes of 9-10 year olds (Year 5) and of 10-11 year olds (Year 6) classes.

The patterns of interaction in lessons by boys and girls remained consistent across both interactive whiteboard lessons and lessons where such technology was not used. There was no difference in who initiated or who received questions and answers between interactive whiteboard and non-interactive whiteboard lessons. Although there are clear differences in patterns of interaction and response between boys and girls (Smith et al., 2007), particularly in terms of the greater amount of attention boys receive, the introduction of the interactive whiteboard did not make a significant difference to these patterns.

Interpretation of these findings is challenging. Some of the changes suggest an increase in the kinds of interaction associated with more effective teaching (e.g. Muijs & Reynolds, 2001; Nystrand & Gamoran, 1991), although the relationship between observed teacher and learner behaviors and teaching effectiveness is an elusive one (Rex, Steadman & Graciano, 2006). In particular the increase in open questions, length of answers and use of "probes" or follow-up questions indicate

a more interactive style of classroom discourse (Galton et al., 1999). Others may or may not be so beneficial. Pace of lessons is an example of this (Muijs & Reynolds, 2001, p. 9) as pace of interaction must be balanced with students' level of understanding. Inspection reports in the UK often comment favorably on one of the benefits of information and communications technology as enabling a faster pace of lessons (e.g. Ofsted, 2005, p. 16). The research reported here confirms that the use of interactive whiteboard technology is indeed associated with faster pace (at least in terms of the number of interactions in lessons). However, overall it is difficult to determine from the observational evidence alone whether the introduction of IWBs had a positive impact on interaction in these classes.

Teachers' Perceptions

Structured interviews were undertaken with a random sample of 68 teachers to determine their perceptions of the impact of the technology on their teaching and their views of the training and support they had received. Checks were made to ensure that the sample was broadly representative of the group of teachers as a whole (Higgins et al., 2005). These interviews were conducted by telephone and covered areas such as teaching and ICT experience, training and more detailed exploration of their use of the technology and their perceptions of its impact.

Overall, the teachers interviewed were extremely positive about the impact of interactive whiteboards on their teaching. They were also positive about the training and support that they had received as part of the pilot project with the majority of teachers reporting that using the interactive whiteboard had improved their confidence. All of them felt that the interactive whiteboard helped them to achieve their teaching aims and cited a number of factors such as the wealth of resources available, the stimulating nature of the presentation and the flexibility that the technology offers. The overwhelming majority (99%) believed that using the interactive whiteboard in lessons improved students' motivation to learn. Eighty-five percent thought that interactive whiteboards would lead to improvements in student attainment, though some felt that this would be dependent on how the interactive whiteboard was used and that such impact might not be evident immediately.

In terms of patterns of working, the teachers were asked how the interactive whiteboard had affected their teaching and just over 70% reported that they were doing more teaching of the whole class together (as opposed to setting group or individual work) and a greater majority (81%) thought that their workload had increased since the introduction of the interactive whiteboard, one of the few negative comments in relation to the new technology, though about one third of these believed (or hoped) that the increase would be only temporary in nature as they developed, stored and shared their digital resources.

Fifty-six percent of respondents said they had not noticed any differences between boys and girls in relation to interactive whiteboard use while 44% said they had noticed differences, usually commenting on a positive impact on boys such as that they were more motivated and interested or more focused and involved.

Overall the responses were overwhelmingly positive about the introduction of this technology in the classroom, with by far the majority of teachers commenting that they believed that the interactive whiteboards helped them to achieve their teaching aims and to improve students' motivation.

Student's Views

Twelve sets of student interviews were conducted between March and April 2004 with groups of students who had been in classes where interactive whiteboards had been used for two years. The schools were chosen at random, but each school selected the group to be interviewed. In total, 72

students were involved in the group interviews. The interviews were taped and transcribed, then analyzed for the responses to each of the questions as well as for any further themes which emerged (Hall & Higgins, 2005).

The students were very positive about the use of interactive whiteboards, they particularly liked the multimedia potential of the technology and believed that they learned better when an interactive whiteboard was used in the classroom. In particular, most of the student groups interviewed believed that the interactive whiteboard helped them to pay better attention during lessons. Their reasons for this appear to revolve around the opportunities for a wider range of resources and multi-media being used, though they generally also liked having their work shown on the interactive whiteboard. It was widely seen as an opportunity to learn and to improve their work. Students also said that they would like to use the interactive whiteboard themselves more than they currently had opportunities to and that they would like it if their teachers used the interactive whiteboard more in lessons. The consensus seemed to be that mathematics was the most popular lesson among those students interviewed although students also readily identified other lessons that they enjoyed when an interactive whiteboard was used.

Students identified a number of common problems which were encountered by their teachers. Apart from the interactive whiteboard breaking down entirely or having to be recalibrated (which they universally found frustrating), students mentioned difficulties seeing the interactive whiteboard when sunlight shone through the windows. They also noted that sometimes moving objects on the board could be difficult to manipulate or to see clearly and that some colors of text were hard to read.

Asking pupils whether there were any differences between boys and girls in connection with interactive whiteboards sparked off a level of rivalry between them (all of the groups were mixed), which made it difficult to tease out whether

Figure 1. The IWB pupil views template

there are any real differences in their perceptions. Student responses fell into four distinct themes: specific pupils are chosen more than other pupils to answer questions; boys use the interactive whiteboard more than girls; girls use the interactive whiteboard more than boys; everyone gets an equal chance to use the interactive whiteboard. There was no clear consensus over this theme.

An innovative methodology was also used to record pupils' views using templates of a classroom scene with an IWB and showing children with speech and thought bubbles (see Figure 1) to try to elicit their thoughts about learning with IWBs (Wall et al., 2005; Wall et al., 2007) as opposed to simply what they thought of them. Eighty pupils (46 boys and 34 girls) in three LEAs completed the pupil views templates.

The responses were broken down into 1,568 individual statements for analysis, ranging from single words to whole sentences. The split between responses in the thought and speech bubbles was approximately equal (51% and 49% respectively). The statements were then categorized according to whether they were positive, negative, or neutral, with the majority positive (56%) and neutral (32%).

The use of the cartoon structure seemed to facilitate discussion and recording of thinking processes such as remembering, understanding and concentrating in relation to the use of the IWB. Other areas recorded corresponded more closely to the findings from the focus group discussions such as enjoying the variety and the multimedia features of the boards as well as some of the challenges and difficulties in their use (such as technical difficulties, frequent recalibration, visibility of text and the like).

The overall impression from both sets of interviews was of a positive reaction to the technology, particularly in terms of their motivation and learning, but of informed and critical comments about the use of the technology more generally. These findings are broadly consistent with the wider research on students' and teachers' perceptions of interactive whiteboard use in education (Higgins et al., 2007).

Impact on Student Attainment

Data at student level from the national tests in English, mathematics and science for 11 year olds were provided by the UK's Department for Education and Skills (DfES) for 2003 and for 2004. Data were provided for both the project schools and a further matched control group of schools in the same Local Education Authority (LEA) as a comparison. These data were then analyzed to identify any impact of the use of interactive whiteboards in the project schools and to see if there was any difference in impact according to gender or for high or low attaining students.

The group of the pilot project schools and matched control group consisted of 67 of the schools in the six LEAs who participated in the project, while the control group consisted of 55 schools from the same LEAs. As the use of interactive whiteboards started in most schools early in 2003, the schools were matched on the basis of their 2002 national test performance, using both mean points score and mean percentage of students achieving level 4 and above (this is the target level for 11 year olds). As the interactive whiteboard schools had test scores about five points above the national average, it was not possible to constitute a control group of the same size as the interactive whiteboard group, nor to include all project schools in the experimental group. Schools were also included only if test data were available for all three years from 2002-2004. The matching was carried out so as to ensure similar proportions of schools in each of eight percentile bands and where there were more potential control group schools than required in a band, the selection was carried out using random numbers. Checks were made so that the two groups were well matched on the following additional criteria: mean number of students on roll 2002, mean proportion of students with Special Educational Needs, patterns of attendance in 2002 and national test performance in 2001. In all cases the two groups were seen to

be equivalent, with no differences approaching statistical significance.

The 2003 national tests were taken in May, after approximately five to seven months of use of interactive whiteboards in the project schools. This is a relatively short time for any effect to become apparent, but as shown in Table 1, the mean raw test scores in the interactive whiteboard schools are slightly higher than in the control schools, with statistically significant margins for mathematics and science. However, the effect size in each case is very small.

A year later, in 2004, raw test scores were again made available by the DfES and the overall comparison of interactive whiteboard and control samples is presented in Table 2. Here it can be seen that there are no significant differences between the two groups and the effect sizes are negligible. The small benefit for the interactive whiteboard schools seen in mathematics and science test results in 2003 was not sustained. Analysis of teacher assessments in 2004 yield a very similar set of results, with non-significant between-group differences and very small effect sizes of 0.06 for English, 0.04 for mathematics and 0.01 for science.

When the 2004 Reading and Writing test components for English are compared separately, the effect sizes for between-group differences are -0.01 for Reading and 0.05 for Writing.

Although some of the initial differences were statistically significant the extent of the difference (the effect size) was small. The early improvement seen after the first few months may have been a novelty or Hawthorne effect of some kind (Gilliespie, 1991). It did not lead to further improvement in the following year, which might have been expected on the hypotheses that students were taught more actively, and therefore perhaps more effectively, in interactive whiteboard classes. The initial small improvement in mathematics and science did not seem to provide a platform for continued improvement for students the follow-

Table 1. Comparison of 2003 student attainment data

Subject	Group	No of students	Mean test score	s.d.	t	p	Effect size (Cohen's d)
ENGLISH	IWB	2879	58.69	16.39	1.28	n.s.	0.04
	Controls	2085	58.09	16.32			
MATHS	IWB	2892	63.93	21.00	3.62	<0.001	0.10
	Controls	2094	61.75	21.06			
SCIENCE	IWB	2921	59.42	11.94	3.79	<0.001	0.11
	Controls	2108	58.10	12.30			

(Raw national test scores: interactive whiteboard and controls - student level)

ing year. It therefore appears that, after two years, the impact of the use of interactive whiteboards is not identifiable in the levels of attainment of students, at least as measured in national tests. While the nature of the evaluation design (without random allocation) means it would not have been possible to claim a clear causal inference had a significant and substantial difference been found (there may have been systematic bias in the allocation of schools to the IWB intervention for example), the absence of a clear difference is indicative (or at least strongly suggestive) of a *lack* of direct effect.

Issues and Challenges

The analysis indicates that it is important to consider the multiple sources of data in evaluating the impact of the introduction of educational technology on this scale. The teachers involved all rated the introduction of the interactive whiteboards, the training in its use and the support from

the specialist teachers very highly. There can be no doubt that the technology had a real impact on the primary or elementary school classrooms where they were introduced. The response of the teachers and students involved in the project was overwhelmingly positive. Both of these groups reported that they were convinced that these changes were improving the teaching and learning in lessons where they were used.

The observations confirmed that there were significant differences in patterns of classroom interaction, both as the teachers learned to use the technology and a year later as the use of interactive whiteboards became more "embedded" in literacy and mathematics lessons. Overall interactive whiteboards did seem to make a difference to aspects of classroom interaction. Some of these were relatively short-lived, others appeared over time as the use of the technology became embedded. For example, there were fewer pauses and uptake questions in lessons where an interactive whiteboard was used and an embedding effect

Table 2. Comparison of 2004 student attainment data

Subject	Group	n students	Mean test score	s.d.	t	p	Effect size
ENGLISH	IWB	2763	55.36	15.08	0.63	n.s.	0.02
	Controls	1965	55.08	14.89			
MATHS	IWB	2824	66.53	21.41	0.09	n.s.	0.00
	Controls	1980	66.47	21.20			
SCIENCE	IWB	2850	57.29	12.45	1.16	n.s.	-0.03
	Controls	1944	57.71	11.99			

(Raw test scores: IWB and controls - student level)

was observed in the second year whereby there were also more open questions, repeat questions, probes, longer answers from students, and general talk in these lessons. This suggests a stronger lesson "flow" (Jewitt, Moss & Cardini, 2007; Kounin, 1970). There was almost twice the amount of evaluative responses from teachers in whiteboard lessons. The indications from these observations also suggested that the changes in questioning by the teachers and the responses from their students were consistent with the kinds of interaction associated with effective teaching and in particular teacher questioning (e.g. Muijs & Reynolds, 2001; Nystrand & Gamoran, 1991). The enthusiasm of the teachers and the early data from the evaluation convinced policy-makers that the approach was successful and plans to widen the pilot began before the final analysis of national test data were available.

This analysis of students' performance in literacy, mathematics and science tests at first suggested that the impact of the introduction of interactive whiteboards was associated with some small improvements in children's learning. The aggregated national test results show that after one year the pilot project schools made slightly more progress overall than a matched group of schools not involved in the project, with a rather small effect size of 0.09. However, these differences were not found after the second year of the project, suggesting that the early improvement was due to the initial intervention or that sustained improvement is harder to achieve, especially in relatively high performing schools and as measured by national tests.

Implications and Issues for Future Research

This chapter has presented findings from a major national policy initiative in the UK where educational technology was introduced to improve standards of attainment. The research findings indicate that caution is needed in introducing such new technologies, if the aim is to improve student's levels of tested attainment. Initial indicators from the innovation were positive, yet the final outcomes of the research suggest that the overall impact on standards was negligible. The technological validity (Strassmann, 1974) of the study is demonstrated through similar findings being repeated both in other similar evaluations of IWB technology and in more general implementation studies of educational technology more broadly.

As in the US, current political pressures on the educational research community are such that research should meet the demands of evidence-based and scientifically-based inquiry, however the policy drive by the Primary National Strategy in England has been to continue to promote the 'embedding' of such technologies in schools, despite the lack of convincing evidence of impact on student attainment or more developmental research into how teachers' can best be supported in getting the best from the technology. This raises questions about how educational research is valued and used at policy level and more broadly about educational research and its utility.

THE FUTURE OF IWB RESEARCH

One direction for further research is in the nature of the technology itself. Interactive (single-touch) surfaces to control a computer and to display information are clearly welcomed by both teachers and students. Multitouch interfaces are the focus of much current development (such as Microsoft's Surface™ or even Apple's iPhone). The development of multi-touch interfaces for computer displays for use by both teachers and learners is likely therefore to be motivating and productive. If the lessons from the introduction of IWBs are learned, then educational impact will be achieved by identifying a match between the affordances of the technology with the pedagogical affordances of its introduction into educational settings. The stage after this is perhaps the development of multi-user, multi-touch environments, such as the prototype SynergyNET environment (see http://tel.dur.ac.uk/) where networked multi-touch tables are the basis of a classroom environment supported with interactive technologies. Here again the emphasis must be on the pedagogical possibilities, rather than the technological capabilities.

A clear indication from the findings from this project is that research in embedding new or developing technologies in education needs a pedagogical design phase as well as a technological one. The levels of enthusiasm for the technology suggest that this could have been achieved with the support of the teachers (and students) involved. The pedagogical intervention in this project could be described as negligible in that the technology was used to support existing approaches to teaching literacy and mathematics. There was no exploration or evaluation of how the technology might have supported changes or improvement to teaching and learning approaches, such as through improved modeling or the use of dynamic images for example. This is an area which still needs further research (Higgins et al., 2007).

It may be, of course, that the introduction of the technology was beneficial for learning, but that the indicators used to assess outcomes did not capture the changes that resulted. Certainly national test performance represents only a limited assessment of learning in mathematics or literacy (see, for example, James & Brown, 2005). It focuses impact narrowly on a range of quantifiable outcomes, usually with a particular curriculum content focus (often heavily weighted towards the knowledge domain). The use of digital technologies may be beneficial because it develops deeper knowledge, more positive attitudes or learning dispositions, more creative and flexible learners, or better social learning situations; indeed there is evidence that such approaches are associated with higher attainment in specific subjects of the curriculum (Voogt & Knezek, 2008).

There is a general assumption that new technologies can (or even will) improve learning; however on occasion the different enthusiasts seem to talk over each other without exploring how their different conceptions of learning are affecting their interpretation of the existing evidence and current use of technology in schools. From the learner's point of view, there are those who see the availability of technology as a means to altering the curriculum and certainly the means of accessing the curriculum (Loveless, DeVoogd & Bohlin, 2001; Nachimias, Mioduser & Forkosh-Baruch, 2008). This stance can perhaps be identified as aligned with the "pupil-empowerment' dimension and connected with primary or elementary school teachers' thinking about educational technology and learning (Higgins & Moseley, 2001). From this viewpoint ICT offers a way to enable children to learn by giving them access to information (Law, 2004), tools (Jonassen, 2000) or to take control of aspects of their learning (Smeets & Mooij, 2001) in a way that is educationally more desirable. The introduction of IWBs in the UK was clearly not aimed at achieving this goal.

ASSESSING THE IMPACT OF TECHNOLOGY USE ON LEARNING

It is therefore possible to conceptualize new approaches in terms of their view of pedagogy (or pedagogies) for educational technologies. Most advocates of digital technologies see them as a way of altering aspects of teaching and learning, particularly in terms of empowering pupils through the use of technology as Scrimshaw's (2004) analysis identifies. This could perhaps be characterized broadly as having a view of a prospective pedagogy (Higgins & Moseley, 2001) in which technology is used to develop or re-shape aspects of teaching and learning. This position is hard to counter as it takes the view that technology can support the development of a more effective curriculum (e.g. Loveless et al., 2001). Since it implicitly advocates changes in the curriculum or pedagogy, the use of outcome indicators from the current position form only part of the case (or perhaps the "cause" more accurately): it may be that the effectiveness of the introduction of technology, for example in developing more independent learners, can only be judged after a longer period of time. It is therefore possible to take up a position that the use of technology in this way cannot be effectively evaluated until its impact upon the curriculum or upon the learners is complete. Others may see this as a dangerous position (e.g. Cuban, 2001) as criteria to judge the effectiveness of ICT are always in the future and the promise is always of "jam tomorrow" (Blamires, 2004).

It is therefore necessary for those of us who advocate the use of technology in schools to be clear about what it might achieve and to identify some indicators to assess its impact. These might be characterized as follows:

1. **The technology will help do what you have to do now, but better (either more efficiently or more effectively).** This could be evaluated by pupils' achieving either greater success on conventional outcome measures or achieving equal success, but with less teaching, or with greater understanding, or with more positive attitudes or dispositions towards learning. This rationale should identify the means by which the technology will improve upon existing pedagogy, such as through more effective feedback as simply replacing current practices with technology is unlikely to provide benefits.

2. **The technology will help you achieve other things that you value educationally and be as effective or more effective on conventional measures;** or, if less effective on conventional outcomes, it should be possible to justify why the benefits outweigh the disadvantages. This might

be through developing more effective patterns of talk or collaborative skills or better understanding.

3. **Technology will help you develop the curriculum and its assessment to something that you value more.** The development of new approaches such as digital portfolios for incremental or ipsative self-assessment by learners may be considered to be of sufficient benefit that the impact of their introduction is worth pursuing to achieve long-term aims of improving important aspects of teaching and learning. In this position it is incumbent on the proponents of such a change to argue clearly what the likely impact is to be and to be clear about the costs and benefits (human as well as financial) of such change at each stage of the process.

4. **Technology will help you explore how teaching and learning may be changed.** The process of change offers the opportunity to explore how ICT can affect pedagogy (e.g. Loveless et al., 2001). The main issues here are moral ones about how those involved in such an exploration understand and have given consent to be involved. Again the onus is on the advocates to be clear about their theoretical and practical rationale as to why such changes are likely to be beneficial (and then in what way they are actually beneficial) as well as what the disadvantages might be.

CONCLUSION

The challenge of this evaluation of the introduction of interactive whiteboards into primary schools in the UK was in integrating the data and findings from the various sources over the course of the evaluation. The short and medium term indicators were positive. Teachers' and learners' perceptions were overwhelmingly positive with very few negative points raised in the interviews and were supported with what appeared to be positive and quantifiable changes in patterns of classroom interaction which might be associated with more effective teaching. Use of the technology increased, again suggesting a positive trend. The initial impact on tested attainment was small, but positive. However, there was no sustained improvement in test scores once the technology was embedded in the classrooms of the schools where it had been introduced.

Of course the study also had significant limitations. There was no random assignment of schools or teachers to the intervention with interactive whiteboards. The schools chosen were already above the norm in terms of their test results. The pedagogic model of use was determined by the Primary National Strategy and involved direct translation of the existing approach to teaching advocated by the former Literacy and Numeracy Strategies without interactive whiteboards and without any exploration of how learning interactions might be enhanced by the new technology such as by applying aspects of multimedia learning theory (Mayer, 2001). Exploration of such variation in use is essential to explore in any variation of impact of new technologies. We need to know not just whether they are more effective (in some way) than what went before, but also the ways in which the range of ways they can be used is related to aspects of learning. The policy adoption of the technology and its subsequent uptake in the UK made it impossible in a relatively short time to evaluate the contribution that interactive whiteboards make to learning. There are now an average of 18 interactive whiteboards in every primary school in England, at least according to recent figures (Smith, Rudd & Coghlan, 2008, p. 19).

Technology on its own does not change pedagogy. It is clear from the observations that the characteristic patterns of interaction in primary school classrooms remain constant in whole class teaching with or without interactive whiteboard technology. These patterns of interaction are led by teachers with largely responsive behaviors by both boys and girls (though with boys getting more of the teachers' attention). There are also characteristic patterns of interaction in mathematics and literacy lessons (such as the pattern of open and closed questions) which are also affected very little by interactive whiteboards. Both the classroom and subject pedagogies are more robust that the opportunities offered by technology. Though there were some changes in teachers' practice in terms of the balance of lessons between whole class and individual or group work and in an overall increase of 'pace' (the number and type of questions and responses) these were not sufficient to bring about identifiable changes in students' learning as measured by national standards.

Future studies of technology implementation need to have a clear hypothesis about *how* technology is likely to improve learning. This could include increased time spent on learning, or the development of better understanding through more effective modeling. Moreover, it would require researchers to undertake a design which investigates this hypothesis within the evaluation or research, such as by investigating correlations between increased time spent learning with greater knowledge acquisition or an association between the assessment of richer understanding with increased use of modeling or visualization activities. Evaluation of pedagogical change is at least as important as evaluation of technological change.

REFERENCES

Blamires, M. (2004). Virtual learning or real learning? In Hayes, D. (Ed.), *The Routledge-Falmer guide to key debates in education*. London: Routledge.

Blatchford, P. (2005). A Multi-method approach to the study of school class size differences. *International Journal of Social Research Methodology, 8*(3), 195–205. doi:10.1080/13645570500154675

Clark, R. E., & Sugrue, B. M. (1991). Research on instructional media, 1978-1988. In Anglin, G. J. (Ed.), *Instructional technology: Past, present, and future* (pp. 327–343). Englewood, Colorado, USA: Libraries Unlimited.

Cuban, L. (2001). *Oversold and underused: Computers in the classroom*. Cambridge, MA: Harvard University Press.

Galton, M., Hargreaves, L., Comber, C., Wall, D., & Pell, A. (1999). *Inside the primary classroom: 20 Years On*. London: Routledge.

Gillespie, R. (1991). *Manufacturing knowledge: A history of the Hawthorne experiments*. Cambridge, UK: Cambridge University Press.

Hall, I., & Higgins, S. (2005). Primary school students' perceptions of interactive whiteboards. *Journal of Computer Assisted Learning, 21,* 102–117. doi:10.1111/j.1365-2729.2005.00118.x

Higgins, S., Beauchamp, G., & Miller, D. (2007). Reviewing the literature on interactive whiteboards. *Learning, Media and Technology, 32*(3), 213–225. doi:10.1080/17439880701511040

Higgins, S., Falzon, C., Hall, I., Moseley, D., Smith, F., Smith, H., & Wall, K. (2005). *Embedding ICT in the literacy and numeracy strategies: Final report*. Newcastle upon Tyne, UK: Newcastle University. Retrieved January 27, 2009, from: http://www.becta.org.uk/research/research.cfm?section=1&id=4971

Higgins, S., & Moseley, D. (2001). Teachers' thinking about ICT and learning: Beliefs and outcomes. *Teacher Development, 5*(2), 191–210. doi:10.1080/13664530100200138

James, M., & Brown, S. (2005). Grasping the TLRP nettle: Preliminary analysis and some enduring issues surrounding the improvement of learning outcomes. *Curriculum Journal, 16*(1), 7–30. doi:10.1080/0958517042000336782

Jewitt, C., Moss, J., & Cardini, A. (2007). Pace, interactivity and multimodality in teachers' design of texts for interactive whiteboards in the secondary school classroom. *Learning, Media and Technology, 32*(3), 303–317. doi:10.1080/17439880701511149

Jonassen, D. (2000). *Computers as mindtools for schools: Engaging critical thinking* (2nd ed.). New Jersey, USA: Prentice Hall.

Kounin, J. S. (1970). *Discipline and group management in classrooms*. New York: Holt, Rinehart & Winston.

Law, N. (2004). Teachers and teaching innovations in a connected world . In Brown, A., & Davis, N. (Eds.), *World yearbook of education 2004: Digital technology, communities and education* (pp. 145–163). London: RoutledgeFalmer.

Loveless, A., DeVoogd, G. L., & Bohlin, R. M. (2001). Something old, something new… Is Pedagogy affected by ICT? In Loveless, A., & Ellis, V. (Eds.), *ICT Pedagogy and the curriculum: Subject to change* (pp. 63–83). London: RoutledgeFalmer.

Mayer, R. E. (2001). *Multimedia learning*. New York: Cambridge University Press.

Mroz, M. A., Smith, F., & Hardman, F. (2000). The discourse of the literacy hour. *Cambridge Journal of Education, 30*(3), 379–390. doi:10.1080/03057640020004513

Muijs, D., & Reynolds, D. (2001). *Effective teaching: Evidence and practice*. London: Paul Chapman Publishing.

Nachimias, R., Mioduser, D., & Forkosh-Baruch, A. (2008). Innovative pedagogical practices using technology: The curriculum perspective . In Voogt, J., & Knezek, G. (Eds.), *International handbook of information technology in primary and secondary schools* (pp. 163–179). Guildford, UK: Springer Science. doi:10.1007/978-0-387-73315-9_10

Nystrand, M., & Gamoran, A. (1991). Student engagement: When recitation becomes conversation . In Waxman, H. C., & Walberg, H. J. (Eds.), *Effective teaching: Current research.* Berkley, CA: McCutchan.

Ofsted, (2005). *The annual report of her majesty's chief inspector of schools.* London: Ofsted.

Pawson, R., & Tilley, N. (1997). *Realistic evaluation.* Thousand Oaks, CA: Sage.

Rex, L., Steadman, S., & Graciano, M. (2006). Researching the complexity of classroom interaction . In Green, J., Camilli, G., & Elmore, P. (Eds.), *Handbook of complementary methods for research in education.* Washington, DC, USA: American Educational Research Association.

Reynolds, D., & Muijs, D. (1999). The effective teaching of mathematics: A review of research. *School Leadership & Management, 19*(3), 273–288. doi:10.1080/13632439969032

Scrimshaw, P. (2004), *Enabling teachers to make effective use of ICT.* Becta, Coventry, UK. Retrieved January 27, 2009, from: http://www.becta.org.uk/page_documents/research/enablers.pdf

Smeets, E., & Mooij, T. (2001). Pupil-centred learning, ICT, and teacher behaviour: Observations in educational practice. *British Journal of Educational Technology, 32*(4), 403–417. doi:10.1111/1467-8535.00210

Smith, F., Hardman, F., & Higgins, S. (2006). The impact of interactive whiteboards on teacher-pupil interaction in the National Literacy and Numeracy Strategies. *British Educational Research Journal, 32*(3), 443–457. doi:10.1080/01411920600635452

Smith, F., Hardman, F., Mroz, M., & Wall, K. (2004). Interactive whole class teaching in the National Literacy and Numeracy Strategies. *British Educational Research Journal, 30*(3), 395–411. doi:10.1080/01411920410001689706

Smith, F., Higgins, S., & Hardman, F. (2007). Gender inequality in the primary classroom: Will interactive whiteboards help? *Gender and Education, 19*(4), 455–469. doi:10.1080/09540250701442658

Smith, H., & Higgins, S. (2006). Opening classroom interaction: The importance of feedback. *Cambridge Journal of Education, 36*(4), 485–502. doi:10.1080/03057640601048357

Smith, H. J., Higgins, S., Wall, K., & Miller, J. (2005). Interactive whiteboards: Boon or bandwagon? A critical review of the literature. *Journal of Computer Assisted Learning, 21,* 91–101. doi:10.1111/j.1365-2729.2005.00117.x

Smith, P., Rudd, P., & Coghlan, M. (2008). *Harnessing technology: Schools survey 2008 report 1: Analysis national foundation for educational research September 2008.* Retrieved April 7, 2009, from http://partners.becta.org.uk/upload-dir/downloads/page_documents/research/ht_schools_survey08_analysis.pdf

Stake, R. (2004). *Standards-based and responsive evaluation.* California, USA: Sage.

Strassmann, W. P. (1974). Technology: A culture trait, a logical category, or virtue itself? *Journal of Economic Issues, 8*(4), 671–687.

van den Berg, R., & Ros, A. (1999). The permanent importance of the subjective reality of teachers during educational innovation: A concerns based approach. *American Educational Research Journal, 36*(4), 879–906.

Voogt, J., & Knezek, G. (Eds.). (2008). *International handbook of information technology in primary and secondary education.* New York: Springer. doi:10.1007/978-0-387-73315-9

Wall, K., Higgins, S., & Packard, E. (2007). *Talking about learning: Using templates to find out pupils' views.* Devon, UK: Southgate Publishers.

Wall, K., Higgins, S., & Smith, H. (2005). 'The visual helps me understand the complicated things': Pupil views of teaching and learning with interactive whiteboards. *British Journal of Educational Technology, 36*(5), 851–867. doi:10.1111/j.1467-8535.2005.00508.x

Young, M. D. (1999). Multifocal educational policy research: Towards a method for enhancing traditional educational policy studies. *American Educational Research Journal, 36*(4), 677–714.

Chapter 7
Using the Interactive Whiteboard to Stimulate Active Learning in School Science

Sara Hennessy
University of Cambridge, UK

Rosemary Deaney
University of Cambridge, UK

Chris Tooley
Bottisham Village College, UK

ABSTRACT

This case study is set in the context of an extraordinarily rapid influx of interactive whiteboards in schools in the UK. The focus is on pedagogical strategies used to harness the functionality of this powerful technology to support teaching and learning in science. The study offers a vivid example of how one expert secondary teacher used the IWB technology and other digital resources to support "active learning" about the process of photosynthesis by a class of students aged 14-15. Collaborative thematic analysis of digital video recordings, teacher diary, field notes and post-lesson interview data from a sequence of six lessons yielded detailed, theorized descriptions of the teacher's own rationale. The chapter concludes by highlighting a multimedia resource produced as an outcome of this case study in order to support professional development of practitioners working in other contexts.

CONTEXT OF THE T-MEDIA PROJECT

This research took place in the UK educational context where there has been substantial government investment and policymakers' interest in interactive whiteboards and a sixfold increase in their numbers in UK schools (sixfold between 2002-05: Kitchen,

Mackenzie, Butt, & Finch, 2006). The UK is in fact the most prominent investor globally in IWBs in education; virtually all schools now possess a number of boards (primary schools have a mean of 9 each and secondaries have 24) and many have one in every classroom. In notable contrast with many other educational technologies, IWBs are not only present but actually used regularly. For example the Evaluation of Curriculum On-

DOI: 10.4018/978-1-61520-715-2.ch007

line survey of schools found that 69% primary and 42% secondary teachers use them in at least half of all lessons, although only about a third of teachers use subject-specific software (Kitchen et al., 2006). A similar proportion of secondary teachers still feel that they need more whiteboards in order to "deliver the curriculum adequately" (Becta, 2008, p.20).

Despite their meteoric rise in popularity, penetration of IWBs took place before the implications for teaching and learning were properly understood or even investigated (e.g. Smith, Higgins, Wall, & Miller, 2005). Assumptions about "transforming pedagogy" were not empirically based although Government-commissioned evaluations (Moss et al., 2007; Somekh et al., 2007) and other recent research (see reviews by Glover, Miller, Averis, & Door, 2005; Smith et al., 2005, and Sept. 2007 issue of Learning, Media and Technology) are now providing insights. The research to date shows that teachers and students are enthusiastically adopting this powerful tool, which appears ideally suited to supporting interactive whole class teaching, where learners express, collectively evaluate and reformulate their ideas to build new knowledge. However it seems in practice to be associated with superficial collaboration, motivation and participation at the expense of uptake questioning (Higgins et al., 2005), student talk and reflection (Gillen, Kleine Staarman, Littleton, Mercer, & Twiner, 2007; Kennewell, Tanner, Jones, & Beauchamp, 2008; Smith, Hardman, & Higgins, 2006). This may be at least partly related to the implementation of a national curriculum in England and Wales in 1989 and increasingly centralized control of its delivery and assessment of achievement in recent years, at least in England. Research by Moss et al. (2007) shows that pressure to maintain lesson pace and "get through" curriculum content means that IWB use may decrease thinking time and opportunity for learner input, resulting in teacher-only operation, particularly in secondary schools where our study was likewise situated. In our own earlier studies of IWB use in secondary

science, students' physical manipulation of objects was desired by teachers but constrained by systemic school and subject cultures, and curricular and assessment frameworks (Hennessy, Deaney, Ruthven, & Winterbottom, 2007).

RATIONALE OF THE T-MEDIA PROJECT

The T-MEDIA[1] project used digital video to analyse and document how secondary teachers exploit the use of IWBs, data projectors and other digital resources to support subject learning. The work investigated the evolving pedagogy underlying classroom practice. It focused on understanding how and why successful approaches work (not on developing them), and explored how other resources and activities are complementary. The research took a collaborative approach to the systematic analysis of video recordings of classroom activity in a small number of cases. The methodology built upon that of related studies employing video as a key tool in capturing the complexity of teaching and learning processes and revisualizing the practices captured (Armstrong & Curran, 2006; Powell, Francisco, & Maher, 2003; Sorensen, Newton, & Harrison, 2006). Video-stimulated recall is believed to provoke reflective, dispassionate and considered responses and to help overcome working memory limitations on introspective reasoning (Lyle, 2003). It is inevitably selective and thus ideal when provoking evaluation and rethinking of what teachers normally take for granted is desirable (as in our case) rather than pure recall. Our goals were to assist teachers in making explicit their pedagogical rationale and, uniquely, to engage them in collaborative theory building about strategic technology use. The purpose was to understand, question, describe and disseminate classroom practice – with researchers and teachers acting as "co-enquirers". Teachers who took part were all experienced, reflective practitioners who used technology in their everyday practice.

This chapter presents one of the four case studies within the project, characterizing the pedagogical approach taken by an expert science teacher to enhance teaching and learning through strategic integration of IWB technology.

The core collaborating team in each case included the classroom teacher, a departmental colleague (nominated by the teacher) and two researchers (the first two authors). A sociocultural framework provided the initial theoretical language, central constructs and lens through which to begin our joint analysis. The ideas were then recontextualized within different settings involving use of similar technologies, as we explored the data together. Through the processes described later on, our various interpretations were made visible, contrasted and debated, systematically tested, iteratively refined and extended. The aim was to integrate the scholarly knowledge of university researchers and academic subject specialists with teachers' perspectives on how technology supports learning, and the professional "craft knowledge" underlying their everyday practice. In this way, "intermediate theory" was co-constructed by the teachers and university researchers – bridging between teachers' perspectives on supporting learning in specific settings and key sociocultural constructs. (The theory building process is described in detail by Hennessy & Deaney, 2009a.).

THE SCIENCE CASE STUDY: TEACHING AND LEARNING OBJECTIVES

The lesson sequence captured for this study focused on the development of understanding the photosynthesis process, the plant cell and leaf structure (Table 1). In this chapter we illustrate how the teacher, Chris Tooley, used technology to further his objectives "to explore the topic of photosynthesis in an active and stimulating manner" and to encourage students to "express their thinking through engagement with both whole class and small group activities." He aimed to use the IWB extensively with "every opportunity taken to make the sequence as interactive as possible" and vary the use of its features so as to maintain student interest. Chris considered the IWB as a tool for "vivid expression of the teacher's passion" and a means to "overcome the inertia of resistance to learning and so inspire the learner and, in so doing, the teacher".

Participants included a designated "low ability" class of 22 students aged 14-15 years. Most were white, native English speakers. One boy had specific educational difficulties and received support from a special needs assistant in the classroom during each lesson. This was described as a challenging group with some recent temporary exclusions from school.

Chris had worked as an Advanced Skills Teacher[2] and was designated by the county as a leading science teacher in relation to his extensive expertise with the IWB. He also had a particular interest in the development of pedagogy through practitioner research. At the time of filming he had taught for 15 years at the same school, and was central in introducing ICT across the curriculum. The school was a mixed sex 11-16 college specializing in both Technology and Modern Foreign Languages and serving a very wide rural area. Achievement standards were above the national average. Chris provided all staff with training in the use of IWBs and had been instrumental in securing a large number of IWBs and data projectors in classrooms.

TECHNOLOGY RESOURCES

Chris's classroom was equipped with a network computer linked to the internet, a mobile interactive whiteboard and data projector. Other peripherals included a digital microscope and a visualizer with flexible camera mounting used to display children's work (Episode 1.2), live images

Table 1. T-MEDIA Science lesson sequence: Aims and outlines

Aims	Content
Lesson 1 To understand structure and function of plant cell and differences to animal cells.	Review of the structure of animal cells through guided visualization. Teacher draws diagram of plant cell on IWB. Students develop personal visualizations of key elements: cell wall; sap vacuole and chloroplast. Students draw examples on IWB and explain to class. Flexible camera used to project examples from exercise books. Equation of photosynthesis introduced on IWB; students sort elements using paper mini-diagrams. Student moves elements to correct positions in equation on IWB.
Lesson 2 To understand structure of leaf; importance of chlorophyll; how a variegated leaf responds to being tested for presence of starch; process of starch testing.	Review of equation of photosynthesis and role of starch. Practical method introduced using large digital images on IWB. Students use iodine to test leaves for presence of starch, teacher discusses results and highlights features on projected example. Students record methods on "fill the gap" handouts. IWB equation revisited during plenary.
Lesson 3 To understand that plants need sunlight to photosynthesize and the link between breaking down glucose, respiration and release of energy.	Discussion of survival of Arctic plants with limited light exposure; Students suggest their own theories. Practical experiment to test effect of light deprivation using normal leaf as control. Starch test as in Lesson 2. Use of IWB to consider the fate of glucose made in photosynthesis (and chlorophyll). Student drags labels on IWB to match products with functions. Return to Arctic plant issue using IWB images.
Lesson 4 To examine whether carbon dioxide is needed for photosynthesis and whether plants give out oxygen.	Square of Truth starter activity on IWB to recap previous lessons. Discussion of statement: "Plants are very clever." Spotlight on individual elements of equation on IWB to recap. Students predict effect of (3 days) CO_2 deprivation on a photosynthesizing leaf. Teacher demonstrates outcome of starch test, using visualizer. Further demonstration testing for O_2 as product of photosynthesis. Simulation on IWB to model the effect of altering light, temperature and CO_2 intensity on the rate of photosynthesis and oxygen production in Elodea (pondweed) sample and in commercially grown tomatoes (with associated profit/loss).
Lesson 5 Plant detectives 1 For students to suggest ideas and theories about leaf structure and color (what veins carry, how light is absorbed etc.) from clues.	Brief recap using photosynthesis equation. Analogy of dismantling a car to find out how it works. Small groups investigate the leaf to see how it is well designed for photosynthesis: examining veins; color of leaf surfaces; how oxygen leaves the leaf. IWB used to summarize each aspect; flexible camera used to illustrate branching veins. Film clip & animation for consolidation and conclusion. Brief intro to next lesson.
Lesson 6 Plant detectives 2 To identify key parts of leaf and consider their functions; to draw all the learning together and apply knowledge in a new context.	Brief recap: matching pairs activity on IWB. Students examine cross-sections under microscopes. Teacher demo/explanation using flexible camera image of magnified leaf on IWB. Teacher discusses 3-D model of plant leaf with groups during practical work. Teacher relates 2-D images of leaf structure diagram on IWB to 3-D model; clicks on labels and reveals functions in turn. Question-and-answer, explanation and visualization using model & IWB images as stimuli. Consolidation using "fill in the blanks" task on IWB, revealing annotated written descriptions/functions for each element. Teacher teaches mime of photosynthesis process in order to "fix it in students' minds."

or specimen slides. Specific uses made of these technologies across the six lessons are evident from Table 1. A systematic categorization (using the video data) of teaching mode across the six 1-hour lessons we filmed showed that the IWB was used for direct whole class teaching for 43% of the total lesson time. 9% was individual/pair work directly referring to the IWB, 42% no IWB use, 6% mixed mode activity.

Chris devised or sourced (from the internet) most resources himself rather than making use of science educational software. Even where he employed a commercial simulation package he edited the scenarios to suit his own purposes. He used generic IWB software (SMART Notebook) purposefully to create engaging, generative learning objects (interactive, self-contained media with built-in learning or revision objectives) that were

Figure 1. Paired statements activity

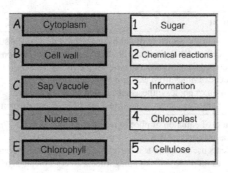

Figure 2. Interactive Square of Truth activity

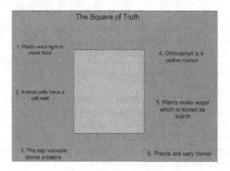

Figure 3. Fate of Glucose matching activity

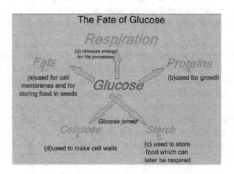

adaptable to different topics and provided task structure. These content-independent resources offered instant feedback to learners and included a paired statements activity (Figure 1), the Square of Truth (Figure 2) and a diagram (Figure 3) with images and statements to be matched.

These were complemented by a deliberately wide range of content-specific learning objects, including high quality visual images and dia-grams (such as the equation of photosynthesis), a video clip he had created (showing gas flow), and an interactive animation of a journey into the microscopic structure of a leaf, allowing students to visualize themselves "seeing the whole leaf and actually diving into it." The resources used collectively exploited the dynamic visual presentation, provisionality, manipulability and immediate feedback affordances of the IWB, as

Table 2. IWB features used in the lesson sequence

IWB feature	Description of use	Example
Textual annotation	To support knowledge building especially through use of labels and links	Episode 1.2
Handwriting conversion	To aid legibility and/or student spelling – and "implicitly reinforce" the aim of quality presentation	Episode 1.1
Freehand drawing	To support teacher and student generation of diagrams / sharing of multiple representations	Episode 1.2
Shrinking images and text	To create board space while keeping objects accessible	Episode 1.2
Enlarging and zooming	To focus attention and examine detail; also used with iCam	Investigation of leaf in Lesson 5
Graphical annotation	To draw attention to key concepts / features / components by colored circling and highlighting	Evaluating experiment results in Lesson 2
Spotlight / shaded box / hide and reveal	To orient (conceptually or within lesson sequence); also to create suspense and as a prompt, e.g. displaying steps of practical method	Episode 1.1 Episode 1.2
Drag and drop	To support interactive displays and demonstrations; also sorting and matching activities	Episode 1.3 Figures 1-3, 6

elaborated in Table 2 (and referenced to episodes discussed under Outcomes).

EVALUATION AND ANALYSIS OF PRACTICE

We observed Chris and video recorded[3] his class over a unit of work lasting six lessons (plus one familiarization lesson) and we interviewed him three times during the study. Learner perspectives were sought through two focus group interviews conducted by trained peers.[4] Chris kept an unstructured diary recording his planning, decision-making, post-lesson reflections and suggested modifications. Screen displays and annotations were saved and copies made of student work, lesson plans, handouts etc.

The research was evaluated against its own objectives of developing a shared analytical framework and language, identifying pedagogical strategies for making use of IWB technology effective in the specific educational context, and characterizing more generalizable strategies. This was achieved through a phased process of video

review using a clearly formulated set of criteria for identifying key episodes and eliciting the rationale underlying the practice depicted, and through soliciting additional feedback from the teacher and students during interviews and meetings.

Video Review and Data Analysis Procedure

Chris, his colleague, Ruth, and the two researchers reviewed the lesson videos. Phase 1 of this iterative process included individual review, generating analytical commentary and describing strategies and interactions on time-coded grids containing video summaries, plus provisionally identifying "critical episodes". These were defined as actions, interventions or student-initiated interactions that were key in using technology effectively and/or promoting learning of the topic. Analytic commentary described what key part the technology and the teacher played, and the effectiveness of the supporting teaching approach. Phase 2 involved independent review of grids combining all four sets of comments and selected excerpts from interviews and diaries, plus comments made independently by a science teacher educator. Four recorded joint meetings (3 hours each) followed (Phase 3), where we progressively negotiated a consensus account and thematic coding scheme (sample codes appear in italics below). In Phase 4, the team identified overarching themes and potential exemplars for dissemination, clarifying selection criteria and negotiating content and structure of multimedia outcomes (see Implications section). Interview transcripts, individual commentary, meeting notes and diaries were ultimately analyzed systematically by the researchers using HyperResearch™ software.

A further in-depth semi-structured interview carried out 1 year after the collaborative analysis evaluated the impacts of the process of critical reflection during T-MEDIA on the teacher's pedagogical thinking and practice, and the supporting or constraining factors. (Note that all of Chris's time on project activities was funded by the grant.)

OUTCOMES OF THE CASE STUDY

The Teacher's Approach to "Active Learning" Using the IWB

Chris construed his own role and that of the IWB as facilitating the students' learning journey, namely a scaffolded pathway towards developing new knowledge and skills during this six-lesson sequence. His first key strategy for facilitating the journey was fostering active involvement in learning through participation in IWB-supported activity, discussion and scientific thinking. His general approach was one of:

using the technology to provoke thinking and not to tell the answer ... to see as many ways as possible in which you can get them to see the mystery of what there is there, and to make them want to find the answer.

Chris planned to use the IWB as interactively as he could – moving away from its use as a "glorified overhead projector". However he mainly operated the IWB himself since physical manipulation by students (illustrated below in Episode 1.2) was deemed to be "of secondary importance" and giving everyone a turn at the board was time consuming: "The most important thing is that they're actively learning in whatever sense ... It can be interactive at a cognitive level rather than a physical level." Students invited to the board were chosen at random (or if they had been less active beforehand) "to keep them on their toes" and build up their confidence. Certainly students appeared highly motivated and engaged in all of the activities, and teacher-student rapport was impressive.

Importantly, Chris tried to ensure that all students remaining seated were involved in the process and had "a personal stake in the outcome", for example by asking students to vote or canvassing opinions after a peer had sorted or responded to statements on the IWB. This created a safer forum for these (often self-conscious) adolescents to express their thinking than speaking out in class or coming up to the board. Instead "everyone is in the spotlight." He also challenged the whole class by asking "Which ones do you think are wrong?" and soliciting explanations. "You are engaging them all in that sort of browsing through the provisional nature of the knowledge before you then start showing them ... a way through [that has] been developed as a class."

We now illustrate these and further elements of Chris's approach using three critical episodes collectively identified in the first lesson.

Episode 1.1: Plant Cell Introduction

Chris described Lesson 1 as aiming to "reactivate students' earlier knowledge of the animal cell and extend it to cover the plant cell." In this initial episode he began by explaining (with the aid of displayed diagrams and the Hide and Reveal tool

Figure 4. Plant cell diagram and Mandy's and Rowena's IWB representations of sugar storage

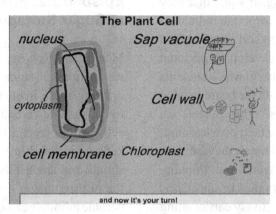

to create suspense) that the aim of the next few lessons would be looking at the plant cell and the process of photosynthesis – how plants make food. After introducing the plant cell by drawing a freehand diagram on the IWB (Figure 4, left side), students helped (verbally) to label the image. Chris used this activity to gauge their levels of recall; their contributions concerning differences between plant and animal cells formed a critical part of the diagram. Then he introduced the functions of a new component: the cell wall. He handed over responsibility and challenged students to "create their own imagery" and record it in their exercise books so that they would remember the protective and supportive function. He gave examples from previous classes, offering guidance and scaffolding for students to use in generating their own aides-memoires. Students produced a variety of colorful and personally meaningful images (e.g. Figure 5); some drew heavily on the given examples while others expressed ideas more creatively.

Asking learners to construct their own representations and notes as aides-memoires was part of a wider view of the IWB as an aid to cognitive engagement through encouraging students to visualize themselves in a particular scenario or to relate a concept to themselves. Chris felt that his approach to whole class teaching was subtly different from the traditional sense in which the teacher would be trying to get all learners to come to the same understanding: it was "pupilcentric". He commented: "You are actually addressing a class of individuals and trying to challenge them

Figure 5. Lucy's representation of sugar storage in her exercise book

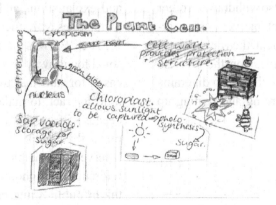

individually in their learning. It's just that they are doing it together. So it's corporate individual learning that you are trying to sort of set up."

His notion of students "developing personal memory" highlighted the ways in which students "translate what's going on with the board to what they produce in their books." The students are taking more responsibility for their own learning: "There are clues there, but ultimately they are actually making it into their own work" and "thinking for themselves." In this and other lessons Chris ensured that learners were "actively participating rather than copying and cutting off from the class" by requesting students' representations or notes to be recorded as "rough work" or plans in the backs of their books. As he went around the room he challenged any evident direct copies from the board, prompting students to consider what was happening and why.

Active learning meant that support from Chris was not only measured but withdrawn or faded once it was no longer needed, as he described in relation to this episode, where the students' representations offered them permanent records:

You can really model what you are doing on the board and then talk through different examples, but very much the emphasis [is] on them to think about what for them will be memorable and for them to take control of their learning ... we've led them up to this point but it's time for me to fade now and then even to withdraw from it.

Teacher assistance was also withdrawn in other lessons through giving direct instructions on carrying out a practical experiment, then deliberately displaying only hints and ideas on the IWB so that students had to generate their own diagrams and comments during recording and writing up ("It's your notes").

Episode 1.2: Sharing Images of Sugar Storage

Mandy and Rowena shared their personal representations of sugar storage with the class by drawing them freehand on the IWB (Figure 4, right side) and verbally explaining them (e.g. the cell wall protects a football player from a ball kicked towards him). Chris discussed, grouped, shrunk and labeled the diagrams. This left room for further images – so that the working space became infinitely expandable while visual prompts remained. The tool for converting handwriting into typed text was used to aid legibility of plant cell labels and student spelling – and "implicitly reinforce" the aim of quality presentation. Three students' illustrations (e.g. Figure 5) were instantly projected for the class to see by placing their books under the flexible camera (iCam) and the students explained them to the class.

This episode illustrates how learners actively participated in collective whole class activity around the IWB. Chris clearly legitimated the diversity and drawing on of peers' ideas. He and Ruth asserted that this public sharing and showcasing of student work was popular and both gave students confidence to articulate their reasoning ("because they produce much higher quality work using pencils and colors in their books than when using the board directly") and prompted other students' thinking. This relates to the notion that IWB use supports scaffolding of learners' thinking by hearing others' suggestions and explanations and comparing them to one's own (Jones & Tanner, 2002).

The IWB was thought to take some of the personal focus away from the teacher and to make it easier for students "to engage much more openly ... to interact, to make comments and take risks because it's a [neutral] physical object there" rather than a teacher awaiting a correct answer. It served as a visible, manipulable object of joint reference throughout, with the teacher exploiting this by publicly interpreting the display to explain

Figure 6. Template for constructing photosynthesis equation

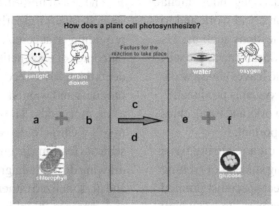

key concepts and helping learners to explain their own, pertinent ideas to the class. In subsequent lessons digital images of practical methods were considered effective in "setting visual bookmarks in students' minds to guide the next stage of the practical. This process frees me up to circulate with students." Dispensing with written instructions (often copied verbatim) also involved "much more processing" by learners. In discussing the next episode we see how a graphical representation of the photosynthesis equation was also employed as an object of joint reference.

Episode 1.3: Constructing the Photosynthesis Equation

Chris introduced the equation of photosynthesis for the first time using color pictorial images of its components and an equation template on the IWB (Figure 6). The class were given paper mini-diagrams that replicated the IWB component images in miniature and asked to cut up and order them into a correct equation, justifying their arrangements and discussing them with peers. Chris circulated, talking to small groups, strategically questioning and challenging their ideas, with the intention of provoking student evaluation of their current frameworks and active, higher level thinking. The task presented opportunities for learners to apply their knowledge and for Chris to formatively assess their individual understandings and offer responsive assistance as he circulated. Diary and observation data showed that these interactions solicited some clear student misconceptions about the roles of gases. However Chris deliberately withdrew his support (fading again), not divulging correct answers too easily, leaving some students with temporary uncertainty. This reportedly motivated students to "want to know the answer" and primed them for the subsequent manipulation on the IWB.

One girl then came up to the board and completed the equation by dragging and dropping the elements. Students verified their own diagrams against her model and revised them before sticking the correct version into their books. This relates to the research literature which suggests that testing viability of conjectures and understandings against corporate meaning is an important component of interactive teaching (Jones & Tanner, 2002). Chris finally summarized the equation and highlighted the need to verify it empirically next time, introducing the uncertainty of scientific theory.

This episode illustrates how the equation displayed on the IWB was used to stimulate thinking and support stepwise knowledge building, a central theme throughout the whole lesson sequence. The equation served as a pivotal support to make a normally invisible process explicit. It was used to connect activities or lessons together, to represent visually the principles underlying phenomena observed during students' practical work and to prompt them to consider questions such as: "Is light really necessary? Why doesn't an arctic willow die without light? Why do leaves have a waxy cuticle? How do we know oxygen is produced?" Knowing how the equation works and using clues to find out were deemed important.

Displaying the equation on a recurring basis played a major role in orienting students or "setting the scene" (Ruth). Our subject specialist pointed out that it was helpful for learners "to see where they are on the journey and where this lesson fits in." Students similarly pinpointed "breaking [the material] down so it's easier to digest" as important in making complex concepts accessible and memorable. Chris tried to show, however, that understanding of photosynthesis is not a linear process of acquiring discrete facts and he aimed to deepen links between facets of a larger, complex body of underlying knowledge. This notion of using the IWB as a powerful tool for orienting and constructing layers of increasingly sophisticated ideas was generalized to other science topics too. It highlighted the major role played by the equation and other visual cues in "reigniting" prior learning, an evocative term coined by Chris and subsequently adopted as part of the wider project terminology.

The equation was used in every lesson although in different ways, and with various IWB tools (e.g. it was enlarged or annotated, components were revealed or spot-lit and discussed in turn) for different purposes: it was in fact continually deconstructed and reconstructed. Revisiting of this screen in subsequent lessons exploited a key feature of the technology and was described by Chris as "like seeing the same person but knowing them better each time – seeing new dimensions of the same thing". Revisiting was considered to combine continuity with familiarity, easing students into the lesson and "reactivating the memory," clearly important for subsequent knowledge building.

The use of mini-diagrams in this episode (and several others) greatly assisted this process by providing a succinct, permanent record of the outcomes of class activity in exercise books. Students themselves recognized the transience of ICT products and wanted records "for reference" and as memory aids. These matched resources were used by Chris to draw students into the activity, scaffold learning, minimize time spent copying or drawing difficult diagrams (they can be annotated and personalized rather than starting from scratch) and increase "thinking time." (In other lessons they helped to structure experimental method write-ups.) They were also physically manipulated by students, with the equation template on the IWB acting as a scaffold. Chris additionally used matched resources because:

- a "multi-sensory exercise book" offers sophisticated color images, modeling high standards of presentation and accuracy which seems to motivate students to take more care too
- images are more powerful and succinct than text; they create "visual anchor points in lessons," particularly useful for revision or stimulating instant recall of previous lessons

Students confirmed these points in interview. They particularly appreciated the public visibility of projected images, texts, videos and demonstrations, and the clarity and quality of "proper diagrams from the Internet" rather than "sketches onto the whiteboard." This reportedly "made us remember it easily and it stays in our mind, so come examination time we know all the answers." Indeed the group's final Biology test scores were significantly higher than those of the parallel "low ability" group in the other half year (students were randomly assigned to the two classes, both ranked 4th out of 5 ability levels): $t(37) = 2.57$, $p < 0.005$. The parallel group was taught by a different teacher, also using an IWB. (Chris's classes had higher test scores than those of other teachers generally, hence his Advanced Skills Teacher status. We acknowledge that his innovative and supportive pedagogical approach may have increased scores regardless of technology use, however this difference was widely attributed within the school to his effective integration of digital technology.[5] Participation in the research is unlikely to explain the difference in any case since the teaching filmed was naturalistic and our analysis and reflections followed it.)

Students also told us "He gives us everything in picture form so it's much more easy to remember." "It's less writing." In Lesson 5 Chris himself referred a student to the image of the equation stuck in his exercise book, using it as an aide-memoire to help him think about the role of veins in the leaf.

Use of matched resources as a pedagogical strategy was highly unusual; we and other researchers have found that saving or printing IWB work for later use is an underdeveloped practice at present. Offering mini-diagrams or images could be construed as providing a bridge between activity within the public classroom arena and private learning spaces (Hennessy et al., 2007).

Finally there was some further (albeit cautious), qualitative evidence for learning in the final teacher interview:

It's hard to say how much they actually learned until later lessons, where you start more formally assessing and seeing if they can apply those ideas. But certainly ... they were starting to take discrete bits of information and apply them. And they were sort of able to put together the information from the equation that they'd actually met beforehand, and starting to reason about what things actually were. So rather than a surface understanding ... we're developing real long-term learning ... It's still got to be reinforced as they go through. But I was pleased with the start that we made and pleased with the evidence of earlier learning.

CONCLUSION

The teacher's pedagogical, subject and technical expertise meant that he was able to devise and source a wide range of sophisticated technological resources and to use these strategically and with great fluency, to support development and deepening of understanding of the photosynthesis process. The case study demonstrates some "advanced pedagogical practices" (Ilomaki et al., 2003; 2006) employing these resources to help in reigniting learners' prior knowledge, visualizing thinking and complex concepts and supporting collaborative activity directed towards student explanation and stepwise knowledge building. The IWB and other digital resources played many roles in facilitating both authoritative exposition of scientific concepts and more active learning in this context: describing a procedure, sharing objectives with students and charting the learning journey, supporting storytelling, priming for activity, setting the context for provoking thinking, offering a forum for making explicit, manipulating, challenging, connecting, evaluating and synthesizing ideas. While most of the activities could potentially have been carried out without an IWB (using the data projector and computer alone, or paper resources), Chris exploited the powerful technology present in his classroom; teacher and student interviews and observations corroborated previous research findings that the IWB offered significant advantages in terms of ease and speed of use, direct manipulability, student motivation, etc. (space precludes elaboration of this evidence here, where our emphasis is on pedagogy, although Table 2 offers some relevant information). However, improving technical facility alone does not transform teaching and learning, and as always, the pedagogical strategies employed by the teacher were pivotal in making use of the technology effective and in ensuring that individual learning outcomes were recorded and consolidated. By distilling out these strategies through thematic analysis of this case study, we hoped to offer some ideas that could be generalized to other subject, topic and learner contexts.

IMPLICATIONS AND RESOURCES FOR PROFESSIONAL DEVELOPMENT

Aside from the substantive findings, the research has illustrated how collaborative microanalysis of lesson videos renders implicit rationale, values and routine practices more explicit and can be used to engage teachers in deep reflection, critique and debate. We know that the rich opportunities afforded for engagement in professional dialogue and scholarly analysis were highly valued by Chris and Ruth and the other T-MEDIA teachers (Hennessy & Deaney, 2009b). This approach offers a significant professional development opportunity – both for the participant who is filmed, and subsequently for other practitioners viewing the material, as we describe in turn in this section. In the former case it is of course costly in terms of filming and time for participation and thus difficult to extend to typical schools, raising an important ethical issue. However it offers some implications for devising professional development activities that integrate theory and practice and support development of an analytical scrutiny of classroom teaching, so it seems worthwhile to share the outcomes briefly.

Impact on the Participating Teacher

The follow-up interview carried out with Chris a year later yielded strong evidence of a perceived impact of involvement in the research in terms of a much more reflective outlook on his practice. Chris described how although "things don't necessarily fit neatly into categories," the collaborative thematic analysis allowed him to "identify what you were trying to achieve with one technique over another" and "to rethink, to re-sort my tool kit, to

realize I had these individual tools [strategies] and I could use them to different respects."

In the interim Chris had become Deputy Principal in a new school; he struggled to balance a very demanding job (and limited teaching time) with putting into practice the "many opportunities and thought processes opened up by the project." The 14-16 science curriculum had radically altered too since filming, reducing the photosynthesis topic profile, however the pedagogical and technological techniques that Chris used were already generalized to other science topics. Moreover, the deeper insights he felt he had gained reached far beyond the strategies for using technology that were our original research focus, and offered implications for other teachers' professional learning and metacognitive development:

It's moving to this level of metacognition ... standing back and thinking "why am I thinking that?" ... so much of it has now become ingrained. ... So the process was very useful, not just in planning for teaching, but in preparation for being a Deputy Head ... [Instead of simply reacting] everything is treated as provisional while you stand back and consider all the aspects first. It has ... helped me to help other teachers I'm working with and line managing about how to think about situations themselves.

Chris also described a strong impact on his new school and its practice as a result of devising a staff training programme that models classroom use of IWBs: "I use that basis to deliver some of what has come from the project ... suggesting how they can start using it [to intervene] in the way in which [students] think." Back in his old school, there was a notable impact upon his colleague Ruth too, who had explicitly drawn on the pedagogical strategies that Chris had modeled, both when revising the department's schemes of work and in her own teaching. She had also become more responsive to students and confident in allowing them to write on the IWB rather than just "moving things from one place to another." Students had become more comfortable with this too. Ruth now used the IWB to build up a picture of "what's going on" during a lesson or over several lessons, through revisiting student contributions for revision purposes – an extension to Chris's original approach.(Further findings from the follow-up study are reported by Hennessy & Deaney, 2009b.)

Development of Multimedia Professional Development Materials

The case study findings were exploited much more widely too, through co-construction and dissemination of a low-cost interactive CD-ROM[6] intended to support professional development of other practitioners. This resource characterizes the key themes and strategies emerging from the case study, with illustrative video sequences and associated analytic commentary, in turn hyperlinked to built-in discussion activities plus relevant sections of the narrative account. It does not offer a model of "best practice" for replication per se, but rather an accessible framework that might guide teachers' questioning and reflective thinking about how IWB technology can support effective pedagogy, the extent of its perceived "added value," and when alternative approaches may be more fruitful. This unique resource is aimed at practitioners, teacher educators and researchers. It may be used by (a) individuals viewing or downloading examples of teaching resources to support new approaches and trying these out in the classroom, (b) individuals independently reflecting on the issues and then debating them with colleagues, or (c) groups of colleagues or teacher educators/advisers working with groups of trainees or experienced practitioners.

It has been trialed with student teachers and embedded in a Masters degree course in Science Education at Cambridge University, with the aim of supporting teachers in developing effective ways to exploit the IWB to enhance learning within their own classrooms. Although our evidence for success here remains limited, responses so far are positive and presenting footage of lessons filmed in a real classroom with students at the lower end of the attainment range, and offering a wide choice of flexible or structured routes through the multimedia resource, have particularly been found to appeal to teachers.

ACKNOWLEDGMENT

The researchers are extremely grateful to the teacher, Chris Tooley, who willingly devoted his time and energy to our research and from whom we learned so much. We acknowledge the participation of the students, and the roles of Theresa Daly and Bryony Horsley-Heather in managing the data and preparing this chapter for publication. We also thank Elaine Wilson, the science specialist colleague who shared her helpful insights into our video data, and an anonymous reviewer who provided valuable feedback on an earlier draft of this chapter. The research and writing were funded by two grants from the UK Economic and Social Research Council (RES000230825 and RES063270081).

REFERENCES

Armstrong, V., & Curran, S. (2006). Developing a collaborative mode of research using digital video. *Computers & Education*, *46*(3), 336–347. doi:10.1016/j.compedu.2005.11.015

Becta. (2008). *Harnessing Technology: Next Generation Learning 2008-14*. Coventry, UK: Becta.

Gillen, J., Kleine Staarman, J., Littleton, K., Mercer, N., & Twiner, A. (2007). A 'learning revolution'? Investigating pedagogic practice around interactive whiteboards in British primary schools. *Learning, Media and Technology, 32*(3), 243–256. doi:10.1080/17439880701511099

Glover, D., Miller, D., Averis, D., & Door, V. (2005). The interactive whiteboard: a literature survey. *Technology, Pedagogy and Education, 14*(2), 155–170. doi:10.1080/14759390500200199

Hennessy, S., & Deaney, R. (2009a). 'Intermediate theory' building: Integrating multiple teacher and researcher perspectives through in-depth video analysis of pedagogic strategies. *Teachers College Record, 111*(7), 1753–1795.

Hennessy, S., & Deaney, R. (2009b). The impact of collaborative video analysis by practitioners and researchers upon pedagogical thinking and practice: A follow-up study. *Teachers and Teaching: Theory and Practice, 15*(5), 617–638.

Hennessy, S., Deaney, R., Ruthven, K., & Winterbottom, M. (2007). Pedagogical strategies for using the interactive whiteboard to foster learner participation in school science. *Learning, Media and Technology, 32*(3), 283–301. doi:10.1080/17439880701511131

Higgins, S., Falzon, C., Hall, I., Moseley, D., Smith, F., Smith, H., et al. (2005). Embedding ICT in the Literacy and Numeracy Strategies. Final Report. Newcastle, UK: Centre for Learning and Teaching, School of Education, Communication and Language Sciences, University of Newcastle upon Tyne.

Ilomaki, L., Jaakkola, T., Lakkala, M., Nirhamo, L., Nurmi, S., Paavola, S., et al. (2003). *Principles, models and examples of designing learning objects (LOs). Pedagogical guidelines in CELEBRATE. Working paper for the European Commission, CELEBRATE Project, IST-2001-35188.* Retrieved 9 February 2009, from http://www.helsinki.fi/science/networkedlearning/texts/principlesforlos.pdf.

Ilomaki, L., Lakkala, M., & Paavola, S. (2006). Case studies of learning objects used in school settings. *Learning, Media and Technology, 31*(3), 249–267. doi:10.1080/17439880600893291

Jones, S., & Tanner, H. (2002). Teachers' interpretations of effective whole-class interactive teaching in secondary mathematics classrooms. *Educational Studies, 28*(3), 265–274. doi:10.1080/0305569022000003717

Kennewell, S., Tanner, H., Jones, S., & Beauchamp, G. (2008). Analysing the use of interactive technology to implement interactive teaching. *Journal of Computer Assisted Learning, 24*(1), 61-73(13).

Kitchen, S., Mackenzie, H., Butt, S., & Finch, S. (2006). *Evaluation of Curriculum Online report of the third survey of schools.* London: National Centre for Social Research.

Lyle, J. (2003). Stimulated recall: a report on its use in naturalistic research. *British Educational Research Journal, 29*(6), 861–878. doi:10.1080/0141192032000137349

Moss, G., Jewitt, C., Levacic, R., Armstrong, V., Cardini, A., Castle, F., et al. (2007). The Interactive Whiteboards, Pedagogy and Pupil Performance Evaluation: An Evaluation of the Schools Whiteboard Expansion (SWE) Project: London Challenge (No. RR816). London: DfES.

Powell, A., Francisco, J., & Maher, C. (2003). An analytical model for studying the development of learners' mathematical ideas and reasoning using videotape data. *The Journal of Mathematical Behavior, 22*, 405–435. doi:10.1016/j.jmathb.2003.09.002

Smith, F., Hardman, F., & Higgins, S. (2006). The impact of interactive whiteboards on teacher-pupil interaction in the National Literacy and Numeracy Strategies. *British Educational Research Journal, 32*(3), 443–457. doi:10.1080/01411920600635452

Smith, H. J., Higgins, S., Wall, K., & Miller, J. (2005). Interactive whiteboards: boon or bandwagon? A critical review of the literature. *Journal of Computer Assisted Learning, 21*(2), 91–101. doi:10.1111/j.1365-2729.2005.00117.x

Somekh, B., Haldane, M., Jones, K., Lewin, C., Steadman, S., & Scrimshaw, P. (2007). *Evaluation of the Primary Schools Whiteboard Expansion Project (SWEEP): Report to the Department for Education and Skills*. London: Becta.

Sorensen, P. D., Newton, L. R., & Harrison, C. (2006, September 2006). *The professional development of teachers through interaction with digital video*. Paper presented at the Annual Conference of the British Educational Research Association (BERA), University of Warwick.

ENDNOTES

[1]   Exploring teacher mediation of subject learning with ICT: A multimedia approach (2005-2007). Funded by the UK Economic and Social Research Council (RES000230825).

[2]   Advanced Skills status is awarded to recognize expert UK teachers and partly release them from teaching in order to share their practice with others.

[3]   The main (mobile) video camera was positioned mainly at the back of the classroom, and followed the teacher. A (fixed) second camera at the front captured students' faces.

[4]   British Educational Research Association ethical guidelines were followed throughout the study, particularly with respect to

Chapter 8
Enhanced Interactivity in Secondary Mathematics

Dave Miller
University of Keele, UK

Derek Glover
University of Keele, UK

ABSTRACT

This chapter outlines the background to the development of changed pedagogy by mathematics teachers within a secondary school in England. It relates this development to the enhanced understanding of the use of interactive whiteboards, initially as a presentational and motivational support but then as the basis of more effective conceptual and cognitive learning by students. The experience of teachers within the school and members of a research group points to the importance of the integration of interactive whiteboards, desk work and thinking in the planning of mathematics lessons. It also discusses emerging evidence that effective whiteboard use requires an understanding of the role of individual learning style, gesture, and artifact use in reflective and stepped teaching and learning situations.

INTRODUCTION

During the past decade the interactive whiteboard has passed from being a novelty to being part of the equipment of many mathematics teaching rooms within the UK, and to a much lesser extent, parts of Western Europe, North America, South East Asia and Australasia. In part this is a response to government educational policy aimed at learning for the globalized digital age but it is also a reflection of self-government within schools and their intention

to support individualized student motivation and learning through more appropriate pedagogy. Early evidence suggests that practitioners pass through stages of developing both technology and pedagogy moving from the use of technology for presentational purposes to its use as a stimulus for interactive learning (Glover et al., 2003). The availability of equipment alone is no guarantee of enhanced teaching and learning (Miller et al., 2004). Government reports by the inspectorate and the Qualifications and Curriculum Authority (QCA) in England in 2005 point to the need for teachers to become more aware of the inherent value of interactivity at the heart of

DOI: 10.4018/978-1-61520-715-2.ch008

a changed pedagogy. This view has been reflected in a number of research reports with varying sized cohorts of users (Hall & Higgins, 2005; Hennessey et al., 2007; Smith et al., 2006). In this chapter we are concerned with establishing the basis of interactive learning and then using the outcomes of recent research undertaken at Keele University on behalf of the National Centre for Excellence in Teaching Mathematics (NCETM) to illustrate how a pedagogic emphasis on interactivity has enhanced teaching in mathematics (Miller et al., 2005; Miller et al., 2008).

Our case study traces the introduction of IWB use in a secondary comprehensive school in Cambridgeshire, England (subsequently referred to as the "school" in this chapter). The co-author of this chapter (hereafter called the lead teacher because of her role in developing new ways of working) is an Advanced Skills Teacher (AST) in the school and became involved with the research group at the University of Keele that was concerned with establishing the practical issues and teaching and learning responses in promoting interactivity in mathematics teaching. The school experience was one of several case studies underpinning the recommendations to the NCETM. Case studies are by their nature descriptive but the experience of the mathematics teachers in the school offers some valuable pointers to the management of professional development for pedagogic change.

THE BACKGROUND TO INTERACTIVE LEARNING IN MATHEMATICS

There are two levels to our understanding of the incorporation of interactive learning in mathematics teaching. These are the learning context within which IWB use is to occur and then the practical level concerned with the way in which IWB use can support interactive learning. The context is concerned with the socio-psychological basis of mathematical learning. The starting point is Vygotsky's (1978) theory of social constructivism which argues that effective learning occurs in those situations where there is interaction between teacher and taught, or between students, so that the problem is commonly understood and the solution collaboratively determined. Tinzmann et al. (1990) extend this notion to the organization of collaborative classrooms and point to the need for teacher and students to share the knowledge, and more importantly, the authority underpinning learning. This requires teacher understanding of the process of facilitation and support, and leads, perhaps more contentiously to the view that diverse groupings of students are more effective in promoting individual development through the use of modeling responses. Ernest (1994) urges that there is a need for the human face of mathematical learning and stresses the requirement for dialogic intercourse as the basis of enjoyment and hence, learning. Taylor (1996) extends this to argue that the context within which mathematical learning occurs must promote such interactions so that learning is targeted at conceptual change. Schussler et al. (2007) relate this concept of interactivity into classroom management contexts. They offer a model called:

hypertextual function ... to consider teachers' thinking, practice, and development in the use of technology. Hypertextual function is a multidimensional model linking a teacher's knowledge about students (familiarity) and technology (facility), with a teacher's teaching practice of integrating technology with content (transparency) and across disciplines and experiences (connectivity), and a teacher's sense of support (collegiality). Additionally, a teacher's context affects each of these. Such a model is important as technology becomes more pervasive and integrating technology into classrooms adds another layer of complexity to teaching. (p. 572)

This is the point at which understanding IWB integration becomes important – our second level of incorporation. The IWB has to be considered within the context of mathematics teaching. The Office for Standards in Education (OfSTED) report for mathematics teaching for ages 14-19 in May 2006 found that there were several factors which contributed to high achievement in mathematics teaching. These factors included the secure subject knowledge (of the teacher) underpinning an approach to mathematics in which all topics are seen as part of a coherent set of related ideas and a style of teaching that focuses on developing mathematical concepts and enhances critical thinking and reasoning with a spirit of collaborative enquiry. This can occur where there are well-paced lessons, where there is effective use of ICT and other high quality resources and where there is a range of learning programs suited to all ability levels. Where the interactive whiteboard is available such teaching can be enhanced both through enhanced kinaesthetic presentation and the use of alternative strategies to present concepts and processes, and through staged conceptualization.

In a report on improving learning in mathematics for the Department for Education and Science, Swan (2005) offers strategies by which these changes can be facilitated. He argues that teaching can be more effective when it:

- builds on the knowledge that students already have
- exposes and discusses common misconceptions, uses higher order questions
- uses co-operative small group work
- encourages reasoning rather than answering
- uses rich collaborative tasks
- creates connections between topics
- uses technology

Swan suggests that appropriate teaching activity should include classification, interpretation of multiple representations, evaluation of statements, the creation of problems and analyzing,

and reasoning and solving. One of the tasks of the Keele research group was to ascertain exactly how the teaching potential of the IWB was being realized in all of these spheres through alternative presentations and the use of kinaesthetic as well as verbal and visual learning.

Davison and Pratt (2003) argue that teachers who are both competent and confident in the use of IWB technology look initially at the presentation of material but then change as they move from offering purely static visual support to the use of kinaesthetic affordances with enhanced student participation. Beauchamp and Parkinson (2005) see this as moving beyond the "wow" factor as teachers explore the potential of interactivity for enhanced learning. Cuthell (2006) demonstrates that the IWB can be interactively used to enhance conceptual and cognitive development in a range of subject areas. Latane (2002) and Hennessey et al. (2006) after observation of lessons taught in traditional and interactive ways, show that interactivity springs from heightened student-student and student-teacher relationships. Jones and Tanner (2002) show that this interactivity is most effectively sustained through effective questioning as well as a wider range of activity in lessons and Simpson et al. (1998), Cogill (2003), Robison (2000) and Damcott et al. (2000) all argue that the movement from didactic to experiential and interactive approaches offers enhanced mathematical understanding.

There are however a number of issues in providing effective professional development to assist this process. The literature suggests that the starting point for changed pedagogy occurs when the IWB has been identified as the visual focus in the classroom. Materials can then be presented in visual form and software programs used to mediate learning between teacher and students through a variety of techniques. Glover and Miller (2002), basing their work on Gardner's concept of multiple intelligences (1991), have indicated the need for the IWB to be used to give an immediacy of response and the opportunity to explore ideas as an adjunct to the varied and enhanced presentation of material. Iding (2000) has shown the need for the co-ordination of pictorial, textual and audio materials in fulfilling teaching aims. There has however been little attempt to explore sequentiality in concept development and an understanding of the ways in which the IWB can foster responses to a range of learning processes. For many teachers interactivity has been seen as an aid to traditional teaching rather than as the driving force for conceptual development. If interactivity is only understood in terms of a question and response process, the potential for effective learning is consequently reduced.

Underpinning this though, is an understanding of interactivity in mathematics. Where teachers are gaining confidence in the technology they also appeared to show increasing awareness of a variety of learning styles and used this to underpin their lesson planning. In part this stems from whole school professional development work in ICT as described by Terrell and Capper (2003), and in part form a desire to exploit the kinaesthetic capacity of the IWB software. Research into the introduction of IWBs into schools in England in 2005-6 (Miller et al., 2006) identified the following elements in progressing from presentational use to enhanced pedagogy:

- *Planning for cognitive development.* A striking feature of enhanced interactivity was the way in which the IWB was being used to underpin lesson structure and to enhance students' thinking skills and the development of their mental powers. This reflected much tighter planning as materials were organized to support learning.
- *Clear visual representation of concepts.* Teachers commented on the particular advantages for some students who needed reinforcement through the presentation of data or processes with more than one learning style. The ease of visually demonstrating principles on the IWB encourages

those teachers working at the most interactive stage to use it more and incidentally work with a wider armory of illustrative Web 2.0 techniques including animation, internet linkage, video clips and overwriting of board based text.

- *Activities that encourage an active, thinking approach.* In all the observed lessons it was clear that teachers were using the learning of concepts as a basis for cognitive understanding. As a result there were discernible cognitive aims and a series of activities to explore, develop, explain and reinforce subsequent understanding.
- *Progression.* This stems from teacher awareness of the conceptual paths being followed, allows for revisiting of ideas that may not have been fully appreciated, and offers opportunities for assessment.
- *Illustrating concepts in different ways.* In addition to the preparation or use of commercially prepared software materials showing the same ideas in verbal, pictorial, numeric, algebraic or kinaesthetic ways, simpler approaches such as over-writing offer scope for assisting cognitive and conceptual development according to varying student needs.
- *The importance of sequencing.* The way teachers structure the material or ideas that they are presenting is crucial to motivation, offers a scaffold for progression and enables individuals or groups within a class to move at a faster or slower rate.
- *Immediate feedback.* The possibility of immediacy of feedback, either through programmed software or through the use of presentational tools, may aid conceptual development. This also prompts requests for explanation and opens the way for more general discussion. Because of the facility of virtual manipulation, where students can move items on the IWB with immediate responses on the board, this was regarded as

being easier to do, and far more effective than with other presentational means.

- *Recall to strengthen learning.* The existence of a library of program resources offers teachers an opportunity to structure lessons in such a way that recall can be used as the lesson progresses – again enhancing assessment where voting systems or simple whiteboards are being used.

The research group sought to identify the "Eureka" moment when teachers recognize the place of the IWB in securing cognitive development and integrate these approaches into their approaches. Our case study illustrates progressions from didactic to interactive use alongside gains in teachers' understanding of pedagogic approaches.

Introducing Technology

When interactive technology was first offered to schools, the school was quick to look at the range of technology available and choose the one which the staff thought would have the most impact on their teaching. Teachers from the school were all invited to try out the boards when the salespeople demonstrated them and a consensus was taken about which boards would be used the most. It was decided to use one particular type of technology so that teachers would be comfortable with them wherever they were teaching. The school decided to install the Promethean Activboard as almost all agreed that the software seemed to have greater potential. Each faculty designated one teacher to have the board in their room for the first, trial year. A confident and innovative user of ICT, was chosen to trial the board for the Mathematics Faculty. Her confidence in working with ICT and her experimental approach to learning meant that she quickly grasped the basic skills needed to work with the board. Writing using the pen, typing text and simple drawing skills were quickly mastered. Regular meetings, both formally and informally between the teachers within each faculty to share

knowledge and newly acquired skills helped to maintain the initial fervor of learning experienced by the teachers. Effective peer professional development occurred with teachers sharing new skills or tools used in their lesson preparation. Within this first wave of development, this informal development opportunity fuelled the greatest progression. As a teacher in one faculty discovered a particular use of the interactive whiteboard they were quickly identifying ways in which other subjects could make use of it too. Over the next three years, all faculties were equipped with interactive whiteboards and all reached a good standard of use. One benefit of this approach to introducing the interactive whiteboards was that it brought faculties together. It became clear, to those using the boards during the first year, that the techniques most were using were specific to their subject but were generic techniques that could be used by lots of different subjects. This resulted in an early shift from technical knowledge of board use to concerns with the way in which the IWB could promote more effective learning.

Developing Individual Practice

The principles of progression noted in the literature were put into action through support for individual users within the mathematics department at the school. The lead teacher quickly became confident in creating simple, text-based lessons and then began to experiment with drawing lines and using grids. Her lessons always used the IWB, although she often only displayed work or wrote on the IWB in the way that a normal board would be used while she gained confidence. She records that she found it useful that she saved what had been written after each use. Within a short time, she developed a format of working in which she created topic resources rather than lesson resources and significantly reduced her use of textbooks and worksheets. However, she recalls that the way in which she was using the board was not particularly interactive and, although it saved money and reduced wasted paper, it did not seem to add much to the learning of the students although it did seem to affect their engagement. This realization was possibly highly significant in prompting more interactive approaches.

Once interactive whiteboards were introduced into the faculty, they began to explore the different ways in which teachers were developing resources for lessons. In meetings, teachers shared their experiences, asked for help in creating a particular resource that they wanted and began to create a faculty style of lessons. However, the use remained mostly static and failed to make full use of the software's potential. It was felt that there was a need to identify what it was about the IWB technology that was capable of affecting the learning in a lesson. This became the focus of some action research projects. Lessons were observed and recorded, students interviewed and the findings analyzed. Initially, the lead teacher had focused on the actual board use, looking for some breakthrough in how she had prepared activities that made a difference. From her time sharing her experiences with other "missioner" users it became clear that it was not about this at all, although some things such as color use had helped but largely in a presentational manner.

It was the type of activity that she had been using that was making the difference to student understanding. Almost all of the activities used in the training started with the interactive whiteboard being used to set a task. Then teachers worked on the problem themselves. After this phase, the board then became the focus for discussion and reflection. This led to shared understanding, generalization and understanding for those engaged in the problem. By interacting with the activities on the board, it often created a resolution of some conflict or confusion about a mathematical concept. Actually seeing something move or match up on the board helped make sense of the mathematics. In addition, it was clear that this discussion phase was critical in achieving understanding by those engaging with the problem.

Thus the use of an interactive whiteboard could promote greater mathematical discussion, not just between teachers and students, but between students themselves. This would allow student ownership of their understanding and create an environment of thoughtful questioning and collaboration in class. The conclusions from this element of the research were that:

- the type of activity that the teacher uses is the most important consideration
- by interacting with mathematical ideas, through movement, use of color, highlighting key points and the ability to correct mistakes students gain a greater understanding of how the mathematics works, what it is for and how the concepts can be applied to situations
- reflection and discussion enables learning to become a socially constructed experience
- students' engagement increases through being involved in the lesson, particularly when working at the board and this enhances their ownership of the ideas from the lesson.

Developing Techniques in Others

At school the process by which others became involved showed recognition of the need for training in both hardware and software use. As interactive whiteboards have spread throughout schools in the UK, there has been an overwhelming need for training, though this has not always been reflected in practice. The companies supplying schools with interactive whiteboards often provide training on how to use the tools on their software without considering how the technology is most effective in increasing learning. Teachers who came early to the technology led the way in offering this aspect of training. The lead teacher was amongst those teachers offering support to others and leading training through effective peer support. She records that a number of teachers were reluctant users and did not appreciate the importance of interactivity in learning. To establish competence and confidence in the first phase of training events, she concentrated more on the tools of the board, rather than challenging teachers' teaching styles. Through demonstrating skills, however, she was able to offer a range of activities, many of which were unfamiliar to those receiving the training. In some cases, teachers were delighted with their new skills and inspired by the activities they had witnessed but, more often, the teachers could not see why these activities would be useful or successful. In fact, she records that it was quite normal to hear teachers remarking that it was all very good to "play" with the mathematical ideas but they still had to teach students the methods so they could answer examination questions. Somehow teachers had to be helped to the realization that the "play" would enable students to grasp the concepts in a deeper way. This would then facilitate their learning of the alternative methods and perhaps remove the need for repetitive algorithmic teaching.

The lead teacher and a colleague organized an IWB Network to try to address both the issue of competence in skills and developing pedagogy to bring interactive learning to the forefront. This network seemed a sensible course of action given the amount of outreach work that both the advanced skills teacher and her colleague were undertaking where the focus was on using the interactive technology effectively. This work spread from the school when teachers from all schools in the county were invited to attend a twilight session where they could share their experiences of using different resources for the interactive whiteboard. At first, only a few experienced teachers attended, but word spread and others started to join out of interest rather than coercion and the focus quickly shifted to sharing ideas and approaches.

Developing New Pedagogies

As a self-selected group, the teachers who attended often had different needs and used different platforms from session to session. Thus, rather than focus on specific skills, the group began to focus on activities for each curriculum area. This provided a range of ideas that teachers could use, which itself focused discussion on pedagogy. It became clear that within these examples there was a particular style of activity which was seen again and again. A number of these styles were very similar to the Swan (2005) materials as they included card sorts and categorization activities. Discussion highlighted these similarities, but there was insufficient momentum of understanding about why these make a difference to learning. In many ways, the teachers continued to see these as "just fun" activities which their students enjoyed but by working jointly under expert guidance they moved from the technology and development of materials to the incorporation of heightened objectives of conceptual awareness and cognitive development as objectives in all mathematics planning. At school the furthering of this process of integration was outlined as follows:

The network needs to discuss how teachers have or could use existing resources in class. The leaders of the network aim to develop this discussion to identify the power of the actual interactions. The group already recognized that movement on the board assists students to understand geometrical ideas and the aim is to show how these movements can be used outside of the most obvious curriculum areas. Ideally, once the resources are analyzed, the group will be able to suggest teaching episodes that maximize the impact of the resource which may involve identifying key questions, desk activities and discussion points that will achieve this. The network will then build in some aspect of this into their lessons. The impact of these can be discussed in subsequent meetings. It is here that there is a real opportunity to develop interactive learning as a realistic teaching style. (Evidence given to NCETM Keele Research Group, 2008)

This stage is also marked by considerable teacher-teacher interchange (Levy, 2002; Glover et al., 2004, 2005). This is happening in many schools as individual members of staff recognize that the potential for enhancing their own skills in the preparation of materials and their subsequent use in a variety of teaching situations. These action research attempts are recorded online (ftp://ftp.promethean.co.uk/research_pdfs/) but are echoed in a growing research literature including Hinostroza and Mellar (2001) in their work on computer studies teaching, and the work of Ligorio (2001) who has looked at the way in which learning styles variety can be built into materials. A counter argument is given in the unpublished work by Cardini who argues that the current pressure for examination results in the United Kingdom may lead teachers to make too much use of pre-prepared resources and their implied pace and structure. Current research by the Keele team suggests that this may be a feature of the development stage but that once teachers feel competent with technology and materials they revert to a more relaxed mode (Miller & Glover, 2006). The consensus view of the Keele team when discussing the case study evidence is that effective IWB use requires a change of emphasis for a number of teaching skills.

Emerging Approaches

The case study outlined above identifies the need for both the will to change approaches and awareness of techniques for interactivity. Kennewell (2001, 2004) with continuing work suggests that the IWB offers a number of affordances which teachers may or may not use. By this we mean in mathematical education something (object, tool, artifact, instrument) affording the ability of the user to understand concepts. In brief these include the mechanical gains of speed, calculations and

materials storage; the teaching gains of easy recall of materials, interactivity, clarity, and focusability, and the pedagogic gains of authenticity, multi-modality, collatability from differing sources and shareability. Although largely working within the primary field his work shows that teachers grow to appreciate and then use or reject these affordances over time. The extent to which they can recognize affordances and maximize their potential may well be the most significant element in enhanced student achievement. To these we would add the following arising from work with the group of staff involved in Developmental Work Research at Keele (Glover & Miller, in press):

a. The importance of understanding and using questioning based upon Bloom's (1956) taxonomy. Questioning played a significant role in effective lessons and we found that teachers making use of the interactive board for more than presentational purposes used very few closed questions and moved quickly in any exposition from the closed to open questions and then as the lesson progressed fostered higher order questioning and the development of discussion. Such progression appeared to be supported where teachers were aware of the structure of learning and they had followed the Cognitive Acceleration in Mathematics Education course (CAME) which stresses the relationship between classroom practice, conceptual and cognitive development. While the IWB does not appear of itself to change the responsiveness of students it appears to be of greatest benefit when questioning is adapted to move from closed questions to those that require reasoning in the development of a process or the building up of an argument because the visual stimulus is still available. It was noted that where there has been some change of questioning techniques by linking conceptual development, student assessment and the provision of alternative explanations when needed the classroom focus has shifted to learning accessed through the IWB - an improvement on traditional practice where questions are only used for recall.

b. The inculcation of an approach to lesson planning. Our observations suggest that teachers are intuitively responding to opportunities for interactivity. Where it is clear students have understood material, they are being invited and encouraged to present their work and conjectures to the whole class. The use of questions by the teacher such as "Can you explain?" and "Why did you?" lets students clarify and confirm points in their own mind thereby increasing their own understanding before moving to the next stage of development. Additionally, when students need help, it is possible to revisit material to reconsider learning points from a different standpoint. Such experiences suggest that there is increased effort to match teaching method by the teacher to learning styles of students. Teachers are recognizing that the IWB is a medium to be used to stimulate learning and reinforce understanding according to the range of learning styles. It is not only the students but also the teachers who are going through a learning process linking technology and pedagogy. Our observations suggest that the focus and duration of lesson phases becomes more obvious as the use of the IWB increases. There is some evidence that each of these has appropriately structured "episodes" of interaction within them. As we continue to collect evidence we anticipate that teachers will become more fluent in managing these "episodes" and that this will allow us to develop a more coherent framework linking interaction, pedagogy and learning.

c. Appreciation of the way in which IWB use can be enhanced by the use of gesture. In an analysis of over 100 video-recorded lessons (Miller et al., 2006) it became clear that teachers develop a set of gestures when using the IWB. This was an aspect of the role of "teacher as performer" in both exposition and reinforcement of learning. Abrahamson (2003) argues that gesturing "plays a crucial role in establishing shared meanings for new artifacts" (p. 792). It may be that too much information is being given and that students may be encountering too much data too quickly before they have learnt to handle it – gesture then allows them to supplement what is being said and to overcome frustration. Radford (2003) has shown how gesture is used in the understanding of algebraic notation. He suggests that students need the guidance of semiotic (sign based) representation of ideas and that these can be developed within the mathematics discourse as understood by all engaged in the process of learning. This requires understanding of ideas, their reinforcement through artifacts and the transition into objectification as students make new understandings apparent – it is only then that generalizations can develop. Throughout this process gestures are used and students develop their own gesture vocabulary relating to pointing, movement and transitional processes. The hand movements that mediated technology and learning through movements were:

○ invitational, with the use of movement linking students to the IWB, offering the pen for use, showing a step and offering an opportunity for participation – often encouraged with IWB software e.g. mathematics games, plenary summary

○ displaying, with hand gestures pointing to material on the IWB and then using movement, highlighting or overwriting to indicate content or process

○ blocking, with hand gestures putting a barrier between the students and the IWB as a result of mistakes or the need to re-think a process and then followed by an invitational reinforcement of process and use of drag and drop and over-writing to support this

- ○ sequencing, with the gestures to indicate progression e.g. with tapping the IWB for successive digits or parts of an equation; measurement e.g. with work on angles of a polygon, and "what if" discussion related to the development and solution of equations using gestures to pose the question and then to work through sequence.

d. Integration into learning. The gains listed above can only be achieved if teachers are aware of deeper pedagogic issues. Enhanced learning is not simply a matter of using new technology effectively, but of considering the way in which interactivity can be achieved. We believe that there is a "triangulation" here:

- ○ At the board – teachers are recognizing that the learning process is changing and there is evidence that they are constantly developing a new vocabulary of explanations linking concept and explanation for a variety of learning styles. Their thinking is however not directed towards alternative verbal or verbal-visual explanations but to the incorporation of kinaesthetic momentum

- ○ On the student's desk – teachers note a changed practice away from the use of the IWB as a source of explanation but with continuing use of conventional textbooks and worksheets on the desk, towards tasks that emulate similarly lively techniques so that learning can also involve manipulations and virtual manipulatives

- ○ In the head – our subsidiary investigation of student attitudes to learning

mathematics has shown that motivation and attainment are fostered where the teacher provides frequent opportunities for assessment of what has been understood. This is often intuitive as shown in the way in which observed teachers worked differently with individuals in the group, but is increasingly focused on understanding rather than calculation capability

This three-way relationship offers a framework for re-thinking approaches to pedagogy in mathematics teaching and has led us to suggest that effective continuing professional development requires attention to the following aspects of teaching. An important feature of all teaching is the liveliness of interaction between teachers and students and this requires some understanding of the culture of a classroom where the interactive whiteboard is the focus of so much activity. This was noticed in a positive way in one classroom in our research where the board was situated so that all students could have ready access, where trays of materials were readily available and regularly used, and where the displays were based on "screens" that had been developed and used on the interactive whiteboard. In short, the interactive whiteboard was used to orchestrate students' learning and offered a bridge between ICT and interactive learning.

Pedagogy for Interactivity

The work outlined above at the school, together with the outcomes of research by others point to the need for a fuller understanding of a range of concepts to underpin lesson planning and the preparation of materials. These include activity theory (Kaptelinin, 1997; Chinnappan & Thomas, 2003). This is based upon an understanding of schema as meaningful wholes of concepts and relies on the spread of networks, and the strength of links. Digital technologies can enhance these if the software promotes challenge through scaffolded learning. Complexity theory also offers a starting point for devising learning materials and approaches. This refers to internal diversity, internal redundancy, distributed control, organized randomness (or enabling constraints) and neighbor interactions – otherwise seen as a learning system. The theory argues that any innovation, or new learning concept must be seen in relationship to the whole learning situation and so is affected by contextual conditions (Davis & Simmt, 2003).

CONCLUSION

Our experience is that teachers' use of IWBs is still in its infancy and that their understanding of pedagogy is hampered by technological fluency. There is a need to move emphasis from basic skills associated with using the IWB's functionality to a framework of knowledge, skills and understanding related to interactivity (teacher-student and student-student), that can help promote future work. The school experience has shown that it is important that teachers working with IWBs remain flexible and open to ideas. We question whether it is appropriate to continue to apply traditional templates to lessons when initial evidence suggests that there is the potential for further gains if one adopts new approaches. One example is the opportunity to use the dynamic and "replay" facility offered by the IWB to explore students' conjectures and misconceptions. The ease of use of these facilities means that teachers now have an opportunity to explore new ways to develop topics based on students' thoughts and ideas. This might have considerable implications for student empowerment.

REFERENCES

Abrahamson, D. (2003). Embodied spatial articulation: A gesture perspective on student negotiation between kinaesthetic schemas and epistemic forms in learning mathematics. In D. E. McDougall & J. A. Ross (Eds.), *Proceedings of the 26th Annual Meeting of the International Group for the Psychology of Mathematics Education, 2,* (pp. 791-797).

Beauchamp, G., & Parkinson, J. (2005). Beyond the 'wow' factor: Developing interactivity with the interactive whiteboard. *The School Science Review, 86,* 316.

Bloom, B. S. (1956). *Taxonomy of educational objectives.* Boston: Pearson Education. reprinted 1984

Chinnappan, M., & Thomas, M. (2003). Teachers' function schemas and their role in modelling. *Mathematics Education Research Journal, 15*(2), 151–170.

Cogill, J. (2003). *The use of interactive whiteboards in the primary school: Effects on pedagogy. Research Bursary Reports.* Coventry, UK: Becta.

Cuthell, J. (2006). Tools for transformation: The impact of interactive whiteboards in a range of contexts . In Crawford, C. (Eds.), *Proceedings of society for information technology and teacher education international conference 2006* (pp. 1491–1497). Chesapeake, VA: AACE.

Damcott, D., Landato, J., & Marsh, C. (2000). *Report on the use of the SMART board interactive whiteboard in physical science.* Retrieved February 15, 2008, from www.smarterkids.org.

Davis, B., & Simmt, E. (2003). Understanding learning systems: Mathematics education and complexity science. *Journal for Research in Mathematics Education, 34*(2), 137–167.

Davison, I., & Pratt, D. (2003). *An investigation into the visual and kinaesthetic affordances of interactive whiteboards. Research Bursary Reports.* Coventry, UK: Becta.

Ernest, P. (1994). The impact of beliefs on the teaching of mathematics . In Bloomfield, A., & Harries, T. (Eds.), *Teaching and learning mathematics.* Derby, UK: Association of Teachers of Mathematics.

Gardner, H. (1991). *The unschooled mind: How children think and how schools should teach.* New York: Basic Books Inc.

Glover, D., & Miller, D. (2002). Running with technology: The impact of the large-scale introduction of interactive whiteboards in one secondary school. *Journal of Information Technology for Teacher Education, 10*(3), 257–276.

Glover, D., & Miller, D. (in press). Optimising the use of interactive whiteboards: An application of developmental work research (DWR). *Journal of In-service Education.*

Glover, D., Miller, D., & Averis, D. (2003). The impact of interactive whiteboards on classroom practice: Examples drawn from the teaching of mathematics in secondary schools in England. *The Mathematics Education into the 21st Century Project: Proceedings of the International Conference The Decidable and the Undecidable in Mathematics Education* (pp.181-5). Brno, Czech Republic.

Glover, D., Miller, D., & Averis, D. (2004). Panacea or prop: The role of the interactive whiteboard in improving teaching effectiveness. Paper presented at the Tenth International Congress of Mathematics Education, July 4-11, Copenhagen, Denmark.

Hall, I., & Higgins, S. (2005). Primary school students' perceptions of interactive whiteboards. *Journal of Computer Assisted Learning, 21*(2), 102–117. doi:10.1111/j.1365-2729.2005.00118.x

Hennessey, S., Deaney, R., & Ruthven, K. (2006). Situated expertise in integrating use of multimedia simulation into secondary science teaching. *International Journal of Science Education, 28*(7), 701–732. doi:10.1080/09500690500404656

Hennessey, S., Wishart, J., & Whitelock, D. (2007). Pedagogical approaches for technology-integrated science teaching. *Computers & Education, 48*(1), 137–152. doi:10.1016/j.compedu.2006.02.004

Hinostroza, J. E., & Mellar, H. (2001). Pedagogy embedded in educational software design: Report of a case study. *Computers & Education, 37*(1), 27–40. doi:10.1016/S0360-1315(01)00032-X

Iding, M. (2000). Is seeing believing? Features of effective multimedia for learning science. International . *Journal of Instructive Media, 27*(4), 403–416.

Jones, S., & Tanner, H. (2002). Teacher's interpretations of effective whole class interactive teaching in secondary mathematics classrooms. *Educational Studies, 28*(3), 265–274. doi:10.1080/0305569022000003717

Kaptelinin, V. (1997). Activity theory: Implications for Human-Computer Interaction . In Nardi, B. A. (Ed.), *Context and consciousness: Activity theory and Human-Computer Interaction.* Boston: MIT Press.

Kennewell, S. (2001). Interactive whiteboards – yet another solution looking for a problem to solve? *Information Technology in Teacher Education, 39,* 3–6.

Kennewell, S. (2004). Researching the influence of interactive presentation tools on teacher pedagogy. Paper presented at BERA.

Latane, B. (2002). Focused interactive learning: a tool for active class discussion. *Teaching of Psychology, 29*(1), 10–16. doi:10.1207/S15328023TOP2901_03

Levy, P. (2002). *Interactive whiteboards in learning and teaching in two Sheffield schools: A developmental study*. Department of Information Studies: University of Sheffield.

Ligorio, M. B. (2001). Integrating communication formats; synchronous versus asynchronous and text based versus visual. *Computers & Education, 37*(2), 103–125. doi:10.1016/S0360-1315(01)00039-2

Miller, D. J., Averis, D., Door, D., & Glover, D. C. (2005). *How can the use of an interactive whiteboard enhance the nature of teaching and learning in secondary mathematics and modern foreign languages?* Retrieved February 15, 2008, from http://www.becta.org.uk/page_documents/research/bursaries05/interactive_whiteboard.pdf

Miller, D. J., Averis, D., & Glover, D. (2008). *Professional development for teachers of mathematics using interactive whiteboards: Report to National Centre for Excellence in Teaching Mathematics. Keele*. Staffordshire, UK: Keele University.

Miller, D. J., Glover, D., & Averis, D. (2006). *Interactive whiteboard evaluation for the secondary national strategy: Developing the use of interactive whiteboards in mathematics. Final Report for the Secondary National Strategy*. Retrieved February 15, 2008, from http://www.standards.dfes.gov.uk/keystage3/downloads/ma_IWB_eval_rpt.pdf

Miller, D. J., Glover, D. C., & Averis, D. (2004). *Enhancing mathematics teaching through new technology: The use of the interactive whiteboard*. Retrieved February 15, 2008, from http://www.keele.ac.uk/depts/ed/IWB/nuffield.htm

Radford, L. (2003). Gestures, speech and the sprouting of signs: a semiotic-cultural approach to students' types of generalisation. *Mathematical Thinking and Learning, 5*(1), 37–70. doi:10.1207/S15327833MTL0501_02

Robison, S. (2000). Math classes for the 21st century. *Media and Methods, 36*(4), 10–11.

Schussler, D., Poole, I., Whitlock, T., & Evertson, C. (2007). Layers and links: Learning to juggle 'one more thing' in the classroom. *Teaching and Teacher Education, 23*(5), 572–585. doi:10.1016/j.tate.2007.01.016

Simpson, M., Payne, F., Munro, R., & Lynch, E. (1998). Using information and communication technology as a pedagogical tool: A survey of initial teacher education in Scotland. *Journal of Information Technology for Teacher Education, 7*(3), 431–446.

Smith, F., Hardman, F., & Higgins, S. (2006). The impact of interactive whiteboards on teacher–student interaction in the national literacy and numeracy strategies. *British Educational Research Journal, 32*(3), 443–457. doi:10.1080/01411920600635452

Swan, M. (2005). *Improving learning in mathematics: Challenges and strategies*. Nottingham, UK: University of Nottingham, Standards Unit.

Taylor, P. C. (1996). Mythmaking and myth-breaking in the mathematics classroom. *Educational Studies in Mathematics, 31*(1-2), 151–173. doi:10.1007/BF00143930

Terrell, I., & Capper, S. (2003). *The Hedley Walter High School: Cultural change in learning through the use of new technologies. Research Bursary Reports*. Coventry, UK: BECTA.

Tinzmann, M. B., Jones, B. F., Fennimore, T. F., Bakker, J., Fine, C., & Pierce, J. (1990). *What is the collaborative classroom?* Oak Brook, IL: NCREL.

Vygotsky, L. S. (1978). *Mind in society*. Cambridge, MA: Harvard University Press.

Chapter 9
Interactive Whiteboards and Student Achievement

Karen Swan
University of Illinois at Springfield, USA

Annette Kratcoski
Kent State University, USA

Jason Schenker
Kent State University, USA

Mark van-'t Hooft
Kent State University, USA

ABSTRACT

This study explored the effects of teachers' use of interactive whiteboards on students' reading/language arts and mathematics performance. Reading/language arts and mathematics achievement test scores of all students in the third through eighth grades in a small urban school district in northern Ohio, United States, were compared between students whose teachers used interactive whiteboards for instruction and those whose teachers did not. A statistically significant but not meaningful positive main effect of whiteboard use on mathematics achievement was found. A statistically significant main effect on reading achievement was not found, although the reading/language arts scores of students whose teachers used whiteboards were slightly higher than those of students whose teachers did not use them. In addition, statistically significant and meaningful interactions between whiteboard use and grade levels were found, leading to a more careful look at differences in the ways teachers employed whiteboards in their instruction. A within-group comparison of such usage between teachers whose students scored above the mean on standardized tests and those whose students scored at or below the mean revealed that teachers of high-scoring students used interactive whiteboards more frequently and in more creative and constructivist ways than did teachers whose students performed at or below the mean. The results suggest that the use of interactive whiteboards can enhance student learning of mathematics and reading/language arts when teachers use them in a manner that takes advantage of their unique capabilities.

DOI: 10.4018/978-1-61520-715-2.ch009

INTRODUCTION

Interactive whiteboards are a relatively new instructional technology that is being used in many schools as a replacement for the traditional chalk and blackboard. Many educators see these electronic boards as a versatile digital tool that can help them in increasing student achievement levels. The research reported in this chapter takes a look at a small city school district in Ohio that has invested heavily in interactive whiteboards in the hope that their integration in its classrooms will improve student scores on the mandatory state achievement tests. More specifically, the objective of this study was to explore the effects of teachers' use of interactive whiteboards on student performance in mathematics and reading/language arts.

BACKGROUND

Current theories of learning emphasize the importance of actively engaging children in the learning process (Bransford, Brown & Cocking, 1999), and a variety of digital technologies has been introduced in schools to support active engagement in learning (see Swan et al., 2007; van 't Hooft & Swan, 2007). One recently introduced technology is the interactive whiteboard. Interactive whiteboards allow teachers and students to interact with content projected from a computer screen onto a whiteboard surface. Virtually anything that can be done on a computer can be done on an interactive whiteboard. The advantage of an interactive whiteboard is that the interaction with the digital content involves manipulation of information with fingers and pens, making learning with an interactive whiteboard more active, kinesthetic, and engaging. In addition, drawing, marking, and highlighting of any computer-based output is supported; a whole class can follow all such interactions; and lessons (including audio) can be saved and replayed at a later time.

Initial research on the use of interactive whiteboards in both K-12 and higher education, albeit still fairly exploratory, has been promising. Studies have documented that both teachers and students like the technology (Beeland, 2002; Hall & Higgins, 2005; Kennewell & Morgan, 2003; Smith, Higgins, Wall & Miller, 2005), and that students are more engaged and motivated to learn when whiteboards are employed (Beeland, 2002; LeDuff, 2004; Miller, Glover & Averis, 2004, 2005; Painter, Whiting & Wolters, 2005; Smith, Hardman & Higgins, 2006). Moreover, several research studies have noted that the use of whiteboards shifts instruction from presentation to interaction, and moves students' focus away from teachers and onto content, making interactive whiteboard lessons more student-centered than traditional ones (Cuthell, 2005; Miller, Glover & Averis, 2003, 2004; Painter, Whiting & Wolters, 2005).

Additionally, there is some data-based evidence that the use of interactive whiteboards can increase student achievement. Zittle (2004), for example, explored the effects of whiteboard lessons on the geometry learning of Native American elementary students by comparing pre- to post-test gains of 53 students whose teachers used interactive whiteboards with 39 students whose teachers did not. He found statistically significant differences in gain scores between the interactive whiteboard group (average gain score of 20.76) and the control group (average gain score of 11.48). Similarly, Dhindsa and Emran (2006) compared pre- to post-test gains between college classes that were taught six organic chemistry lessons, either with or without interactive whiteboards. Here too, the authors found statistically significant differences in gain scores between students taught with interactive whiteboards, averaging a mean effect size of 2.68 and the control group, averaging a mean effect size of 2.16.

Two large-scale investigations of the effects of the use of interactive whiteboards on teaching and learning undertaken in the United Kingdom are particularly relevant to the research reported in this chapter. In the Embedding ICT in the Literacy and Numeracy Strategies pilot project (Higgins et al., 2005), whiteboards were installed in year 5 and 6 classrooms in 12-15 schools in each of six Local Education Authorities (LEAs). Reporting positive teacher and student responses to the use of interactive whiteboards, this two-year study also investigated the effects of whiteboard use on student performance by comparing the mean progress on national tests between students in whiteboard and non-whiteboard schools in the same districts. Findings from the first year of the study show a slight positive advantage for students using interactive whiteboards for learning (ES = .09), but in the second year of the study this trend was reversed (ES = -.10). In the Primary Schools Whiteboard Expansion project, interactive whiteboards were installed in 172 classrooms in 97 primary schools in 20 LEAs. Researchers from the Centre for ICT, Pedagogy and Learning at Manchester Metropolitan University used multilevel modeling to compare the achievements of students learning with whiteboards with students learning without them. Findings showed significant gains in mathematics achievement for high and middle achieving students, but no gains for low achieving students. Findings for science and English language arts were mixed.

The promise of interactive whiteboards as a technology that has the potential to increase student achievement has led many US schools and districts to similarly purchase and install them in K-12 classrooms in the hope that their use will improve student scores on standardized tests. In this study we report on research examining the impact of one such district-wide implementation. Specifically, the research questions asked were:

- Do students whose teachers use interactive whiteboards to support instruction perform better on standardized tests of mathematics and reading/language arts than those who do not?

- Among classes where interactive whiteboards are used, are there differences in the ways in which teachers use whiteboards between classes whose average test scores are above grade level means and those whose aren't?

SUBJECTS AND SETTING

The research study reported in this chapter took place in a small city school district in northern Ohio (~7,500 students, K-12), which is in Academic Watch under the State of Ohio's accountability system[1]. One-third of the school district's student population are minorities, with the largest number (21%) being African-American. Eight percent of the district's students live below the poverty line. The research was undertaken as part of a larger evaluation of interactive whiteboard use in the district. Because Ohio Achievement Tests (OAT) are given in grades three through eight, the results provided here come from a comparison of OAT scores between students in those grades whose teachers used interactive whiteboards in mathematics and reading/language arts instruction, and students in those same grades whose teachers did not use them. In all, the study involved over 3,000 students enrolled in 11 elementary schools, 3 junior high schools, and 1 alternative school. More specific demographics are provided in Figure 1.

Every school in the district was participating in the interactive whiteboard program at the time of the study, although it was implemented first in a few schools and then rolled out across the district. Teachers who received whiteboards were selected by school principals through a variety of methods ranging from voluntary participation and arm twisting to selection by administrators, although implementation across all grade levels was required. All teachers who received whiteboards had to participate in initial teacher professional development and monthly Saturday

*Figure 1. Demographic data for students partici-
pating in the smartboard study*

Mathematics (n=1392)		Reading/Language Arts (n=1352)	
Gender		Gender	
Female	1573	Female	1558
Male	1619	Male	1594
Grade Level		Grade Level	
3	510	3	454
4	519	4	524
5	560	5	565
6	565	6	567
7	521	7	511
8	517	8	531
Smartboard		Smartboard	
Yes	1379	Yes	1466
No	1813	No	1686

meetings throughout the first year they had the boards.

A total of 72 out of 79 teachers in grades 3-8 who had whiteboards in their classroom participated in the research, including 15 male (20.8%) and 57 female (79.2%) teachers. More specific demographics are provided in Table 1. Their teaching approaches ranged from teacher-centered to student-centered.

DATA SOURCES AND ANALYSIS

Data sources for the research included the mathematics and reading/language arts scores of all third through eighth grade students in the district on the Ohio Achievement Test (OAT) for the 2006-2007 school year, as obtained from district administrators. The district also provided demographic information, including students' schools, teachers, grade level, gender, race/ethnicity, and IEP status. In order to determine the relationship between interactive whiteboard use and student achievement in mathematics and reading/language arts, the OAT scores of students whose teachers

used interactive whiteboards in mathematics and reading/language arts instruction were compared with the scores of students whose teachers did not use them, using analysis of variance (ANOVA). Post-hoc T-tests were run separately for each grade level to look for statistically significant differences at individual grade levels.

In addition, data concerning teachers' use of interactive whiteboards was obtained through an online survey completed weekly by teachers using whiteboards in their classes, from February 2007 through April 2007. Data collected via these self-reports included the frequency of interactive whiteboard use in mathematics, in reading/language arts, and for classroom management. Respondents were also asked to note effective or otherwise interesting uses made of interactive whiteboards during the previous week in mathematics instruction, in reading/language arts instruction, or for classroom management. Out of a total of 142 teachers using interactive whiteboards in the entire district a total of 109 teachers responded (77% response rate), with weekly responses varying between 30 and 67. For grades 3 through 8 only, a total of 79 teachers used whiteboards and 72 responded (91% response rate). While not all teachers replied each week, a majority of the teachers responded at least once a month.

Researchers also conducted two focus groups with participating teachers to obtain additional data regarding instructional use of the interactive whiteboards and teachers' perceptions regarding the impact of this technology on teaching and learning. The focus groups were conducted in conjunction with Saturday teacher meetings in the district and provided data that was triangulated with the survey responses.

To explore potentially more effective uses of whiteboards, whiteboard teachers whose students scored above overall district means on standardized tests of mathematics and/or reading/language arts were identified. These included 19 teachers whose students' scores were higher than the general mean in reading/language arts and

Table 1. Demographic data for teachers participating in the smartboard study

Grade Level	Number of Male Teachers	Number of Female Teachers
3	1	9
4	2	10
5	1	8
6	2	7
7	5	10
8	3	11
6-8	1	1
7-8	0	1
Total	15	57

17 teachers whose students' scores were higher than the overall mean in mathematics. Self-report survey data for these teachers were descriptively compared with self-report data from teachers who used interactive whiteboards but whose students scored at or below the district mean in reading/language arts and/or mathematics. First, weekly frequency of whiteboard use was averaged for each teacher across the ten-week reporting period and then average use was compared between teachers with high-achieving students and all other teachers, in three categories – frequency of use for mathematics instruction, frequency of use for reading/language arts instruction, and frequency of use for classroom management. In addition, teachers' comments concerning whiteboard usage in each category were qualitatively analyzed for themes and trends and similarly compared between high achieving and average and/or below average classes.

RESULTS

In the sections that follow, findings from statistical comparisons of standardized test scores between students whose teachers employed interactive whiteboards and those whose teachers did not are summarized – first in terms of mathematics performance and then for reading performance. Finally, comparisons in usage between high achieving whiteboard classes and other classes using the technology are summarized.

Between-Group Comparisons of Achievement Test Scores

Mathematics Achievement

A total of 1379 students in the data set were enrolled in the classes of the 31 teachers who used interactive whiteboards for mathematics instruction in grades three through eight, while 1813 students were enrolled in the classes of the 43 teachers who did not use interactive whiteboards in those grades. When comparing students whose teachers used interactive whiteboards for mathematics instruction to those whose teachers did not, the interactive whiteboard group performed slightly better (M = 415.81) on the Ohio Achievement Mathematics Tests than the group that did not use interactive whiteboards (M = 414.63) across all grades. This difference was statistically significant, $F(1, 3168) = 5.591$, $p = .018$, $d = .08$ Additionally, there was a statistically significant interaction between interactive whiteboard use and grade, $F(5, 3168) = 2.925$, $p = .012$. As shown in Figure 2, students in mathematics classes with interactive whiteboards

Figure 2. Comparison of standardized mathematics scores across grade levels by whiteboard usage

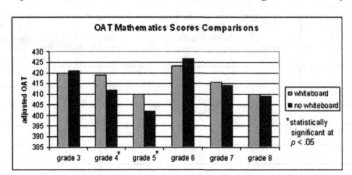

outperformed students in classes without them in all grades except grade 6. T-tests run separately for each grade level showed statistically significant differences for grades 4 and 5 only, t(516) = 2.987, p = .003, d = .26, and t(558) = 2.879, p = .004, d = .25 respectively.

No interactions between gender and interactive whiteboard use were found at particular grade levels.

Reading Achievement

A total of 1466 students in the data set were enrolled in the classes of the 35 teachers who used interactive whiteboards for reading/language arts instruction in grades three through eight, while 1686 students were enrolled in the classes of the 45 teachers who did not use interactive whiteboards in those grades. When comparing students whose teachers used interactive whiteboards for reading instruction to those whose teachers did not, the interactive whiteboard group performed slightly better (M = 416.95) on the Ohio Achievement Reading Tests than the group that did not use interactive whiteboards (M = 415.55) across all grades. This difference was not statistically significant, F (1, 3128) = 1.477, p = .224, d = .004. However, a statistically significant interaction was found between interactive whiteboard use and grade in school, F (1, 3128) = 2.238, p = 0.048. As shown in Figure 3, students in reading/language arts classes with interactive whiteboards

outperformed students in classes without them on Ohio Achievement Tests of reading/language arts in all grades except grades 3 and 7. T-tests run separately for each grade level showed statistically significant differences for grades 5 and 8, t(563) = 2.063, p = .04, d = .20 and t(529) = 2.438, p = 0.015, d = .29 respectively.

No interactions between gender and interactive whiteboard use, or gender, grade level, and interactive whiteboard use were found.

Summary

Slight positive differences in performance were found between students whose teachers used whiteboards and the students of teachers who did not on standardized tests of reading/language arts and mathematics. The results were only statistically significant for mathematics achievement and not meaningful for either discipline. However, statistically significant and meaningful differences were found at specific grade levels in both mathematics and reading/language arts performance. One explanation for this might be that due to the number of tests undertaken, the possibility of finding a statistically significant difference increased, so we approached our findings with caution here (Sakoda, Cohen & Beall, 1954). Even so, while these findings in some respects mirror those of large scale UK studies (Higgins et al., 2005; Somekh et al., 2007) in that they tend to show more positive effects in the lower grades,

Figure 3. Comparison of standardized reading/language arts scores across grade levels by whiteboard usage

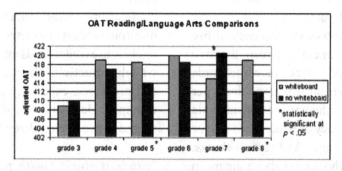

they are not consistently so. These anomalies led us to consider how individual teachers used interactive whiteboards to explore the possibility that particular kinds of use were more effective than others.

Within-Group Comparisons of Whiteboard Use

The differences in outcomes of whiteboard usage detailed above, especially the significant positive effects at certain grade levels, prompted us to look more closely at how whiteboards were used by different teachers to see if there might be more and less effective ways of integrating such use into classroom routines. In particular, we compared the ways in which interactive whiteboards were used by teachers whose students scored above district means on standardized tests with how they were used by teachers whose students scored at or below the means on standardized tests, using the data from teachers' self-reported weekly usage.

Overall, teachers in the district who had interactive whiteboards reported using them quite frequently, averaging roughly three times per week. Across schools, subject areas, and grade levels, they expressed overwhelmingly positive attitudes toward using the boards. Generally speaking, interactive whiteboard use tended to be more frequent in the elementary grade levels than in higher grades for both mathematics and

reading/language arts. However, the frequency of use of interactive whiteboards for classroom management purposes was more consistent across grade levels. Whiteboards were used slightly more often in mathematics teaching than in the teaching of reading/language arts, and they were generally used a little less for classroom management than for either mathematics or reading/language arts teaching. While many teachers simply used their interactive whiteboards as substitutes for chalkboards or overhead projectors, many others reported using them for a variety of purposes, including displaying charts and graphs, connecting to online activities and sources of information, videoconferencing, preparing for the OAT using questions from previous tests, playing educational games, classroom assessment, and student presentations.

Frequency of Use

To explore possible differences in frequency of use of interactive whiteboards between high achieving whiteboard classes and other classes using the same technology, teachers whose average student scores were higher than the mean for all classes on standardized tests of mathematics and reading/language arts were identified. Frequency of whiteboard use among these teachers for mathematics instruction, reading/language arts instruction, and classroom management was compared with frequency of use among teachers whose students scored at or below the mean on the same standardized tests.

There was no difference in frequency of use for classroom management between the two groups. Average use of interactive whiteboards for classroom management was three times per week in both. However there was a considerable difference in the frequency of whiteboard use for instruction between groups. As Figure 4 shows, teachers of students who scored above the mean on standardized tests of mathematics reported using interactive whiteboards an average of 4.7 times per week, while the teachers of students who scored at or below the mean on the mathematics test reported using them only about 3.1 times per week. Similarly, teachers of students who scored above the mean on standardized reading/language arts tests reported using interactive whiteboards an average of 4.6 times per week, while the teachers of students who scored at or below the mean in reading reported using them an average of only 2.9 times per week.

Characteristics of Use

Teachers' descriptions of the uses they made of interactive whiteboards were qualitatively coded and analyzed for emerging themes. Emerging themes were organized in the general categories "whiteboard functions employed" and "instructional uses" and compared between teachers whose students scored above the mean on standardized tests in each subject area and teachers whose students scored at or below the mean, first in mathematics and then in the area of reading/language arts.

In mathematics classes, teachers reported using whiteboards for simple display, for interacting with charts, graphs, and manipulatives, and to connect to the Internet to access information and interactive activities such as math games. These whiteboard functions were employed to motivate, present subject matter, support preparation for standard-

ized tests, play games, and facilitate whole-group practice and/or assessment activities.

Teachers whose students scored above the mean on standardized mathematics tests were more likely to use whiteboards interactively and to focus whiteboard activities on visualization of concepts and processes, especially problem solving. For example, elementary teachers whose students scored above standardized test means noted:

"Students worked with pattern blocks on the board to build fractions using different values, i.e. triangle = 1/4 build a polygon worth 3 3/4; hexagon = 1 what is the value of two rhombuses + 3 trapezoids? etc."

"I've been using it to show students how to get to web-sites for problem solving. We also use the strategies of how to 'think through' a problem by modeling it with the actual problems the kids are doing on paper. We did several strategy puzzles too."

Similarly, a middle school teacher reported:

"I used it to teach solving and graphing an inequality on a coordinate graph. I also have my students go to the SmartBoard and complete the x/y table and graph the results."

The teachers of high achieving mathematics classes also seemed more likely to encourage their students to become active participants in the teaching and learning process. Two teachers in this group, for example, had students create math games they shared with their classmates. One teacher commented:

"This type of medium holds interest more than any other I've used in 28 years of teaching. Children take to it so quickly and come up with ideas and alternatives in lessons that I have prepared that we can change on the spot."

Figure 4. Comparison of frequencies of whiteboard usage in reading and mathematics by average test scores

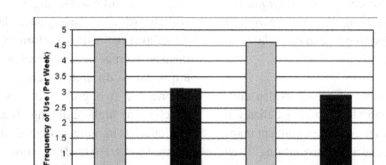

In contrast, although teachers whose students scored at or below the mean on mathematics assessments also were most likely to use the interactive features of whiteboards, they tended to use these for more teacher-centered activities. For example, mathematics teachers in this group reported:

"We are in the fractions unit. I designed a PowerPoint presentation called 'Fraction Action' to encourage students to get more excited about fractions."

"I used the ruler to demonstrate how to line up for measuring and explained 1/2 inch."

Teachers in this group also seemed more likely to use whiteboards to access Internet activities, such as math games than teachers in the high achieving group. Moreover, many of them commented on the motivational aspects of interactive whiteboard use, whereas none of the teachers with high achieving students did. One teacher in this group wrote, for example,

"The Smartboard serves as an incredible incentive for positive behavior. My students are well aware that coming to the Smartboard is a privilege and only students who are quiet and follow instructions are allowed to engage in this activity."

In reading/language arts classes, teachers reported using whiteboards for simple display, displaying graphic organizers, connecting to the Internet to access information and online activities, and videoconferencing. These functions were employed to motivate, present subject matter, support preparation for standardized tests, play games, for student presentations, and to support special needs students.

Perhaps even more so than in mathematics, the contrast between reading/language arts teachers whose students scored above the mean on state assessments and teachers whose students scored at or below the mean seemed to be between student-centered and teacher-centered uses of the whiteboards. For example, teachers whose students scored above the reading/language arts mean were more likely to use whiteboards to support student presentations:

"Students gave PowerPoint presentations they created for a book share, using Inspiration webs and propaganda techniques to persuade others to read the books."

In contrast, teachers whose students scored at or below the mean were more likely to use interactive whiteboards in their own presentations, for example:

"I used it to practice singular and plural possessives. I wrote sentences and children put the apostrophe where it belonged. I could move the apostrophe from before the 's' and after the 's' to demo the difference."

Teachers of high-achieving students also tended to use the whiteboards to support visualization of concepts with activities such as concept mapping, brainstorming, and interactive editing. They used their whiteboards in incredibly creative ways including videoconferencing with other classes to support group work over distance and for developing and presenting poetry as music videos. One of these teachers, for example, wrote:

"During the week we correct grammar sentences, we rearrange words too as part of peer editing; we take notes, watch movies, share student PowerPoints and graphic organizers."

In contrast, teachers whose students scored at or below reading/language arts means on the state test often used the whiteboards for more mundane tasks such as simple display of assignments, vocabulary words, and worksheets. Many of these teachers also used the interactive whiteboards to play a variety of language games and used the built-in timer function for timed seatwork. For example, two teachers in this group reported:

"Timer to keep students on track; daily list of what will be covered in class; sharing vocabulary words on the board."

"We complete workbook pages at the SmartBoard rather than individually at seats."

Summary

When differences in the ways in which the teachers used whiteboards were compared between teachers of high-achieving students and teachers whose students scored at or below district means,

several important differences surfaced. First, the teachers of high-achieving students used their whiteboards almost every day, whereas the teachers of average or low-performing students used them an average of three times per week. Second, a qualitative difference between usage patterns among the two groups of teachers emerged. Teachers of high-achieving students used their whiteboards in more student-centered ways than did the teachers of students who scored at or below the means. In addition, teachers of high-achieving students reported usage that tended toward employing whiteboards to support the visualization of concepts and creativity, whereas teachers of students who scored at or below district means tended to use them mainly for presentation and motivation.

DISCUSSION

The results of this exploratory study show a small statistical difference in achievement between students whose teachers used interactive whiteboards for reading/language arts and mathematics instruction and students whose teachers did not use them. The overall differences were quite small and not really meaningful, and are statistically significant only in mathematics. However, statistically significant and meaningful differences between groups were found at specific grade levels – at the fourth and fifth grade levels in mathematics, and at the fifth and eighth grade levels in reading/language arts. These differences, combined with significant interactions between grade level and whiteboard use, prompted us to explore the possibility that differences in the ways in which teachers used interactive whiteboards made a difference in their effectiveness. The results of these comparisons suggest that they do.

When teachers were grouped by their students' mathematics and reading/language arts performance on the state achievement tests, teachers whose students scored above the district mean on one or both assessments were found to use the whiteboards more frequently (almost every day) than the teachers whose students scored at or below the means on these tests. More importantly, the teachers of high-achieving students used their whiteboards qualitatively differently from teachers in the comparison group. Teachers in the former group used whiteboards in a more student-centered manner and primarily to support the visualization of concepts, while teachers in the latter group used whiteboards in a more teacher-centered manner and primarily for presentation and motivation purposes. Thus it may be that certain kinds of teaching strategies resonate more with the particular affordances of interactive whiteboards to better enhance learning.

FUTURE RESEARCH DIRECTIONS

The findings thus suggest that the ways in which interactive whiteboards are used affects their efficacy. Findings concerning frequency of use may indicate a kind of tipping point in usage that needs to be reached first, or alternatively, that the more integral a part of daily classroom activities whiteboard usage becomes the more effective they are in enhancing learning. Findings concerning the ways in which whiteboards are used suggest that more active and constructivist uses are more effective, as are uses that focus on the visualization of concepts. These results seem to build on findings from the literature which suggest that whiteboard use can lead students to refocus their attention away from the teacher and onto academic content, perhaps suggesting that this only happens when teachers allow it. They may also indicate that the most effective uses of the technology are those that take advantage of its more unique capabilities, such as support for visualization and interactivity.

Of course, the nature of our study makes it impossible to tell whether the teachers whose students excelled on district tests were just bet-

ter teachers than the comparison teachers. As Higgins, Beauchamp and Miller (2007, p. 217) remark, "Good teaching remains good teaching with or without the technology." However, even if we could tell the difference, the results then indicate that better teachers take full advantage of interactive whiteboards by making their use a more integral part of their classroom activities and by capitalizing on their unique affordances.

In any case, the results are provocative and clearly indicate that further investigation of the more effective uses of interactive whiteboards should be undertaken. For example, quantitative research is needed to investigate how frequency of use, types of use, or a combination of both affect student learning, and in particular, what types of learning. Second, investigations that look more specifically at the affordances that interactive whiteboards provide can yield useful information, particularly in the areas of digital visualization and human computer interaction, including direct manipulation of objects on the screen (i.e. without an intermediary input device such as a mouse, keyboard, or stylus). Third, research needs to determine best practices for teaching with interactive whiteboards, in order to inform practitioners as well as professional development efforts.

CONCLUSION

This study explored the effects of teachers' uses of interactive whiteboards on student performance in reading/language arts and mathematics. Reading/language arts and mathematics achievement test scores of all students in the third through eighth grades in a small urban school district in northern Ohio were compared between students whose teachers used interactive whiteboards for instruction and those whose teachers did not. Statistically significant and meaningful interactions between whiteboard use and grade levels were found, leading to a more careful look at differences in the ways in which whiteboard-using teachers employed them in their instruction. A within-group comparison of such usage between teachers whose students scored above the mean on standardized tests and those whose students scored at or below the mean revealed that the teachers of high-scoring students used interactive whiteboards more frequently and in more creative and constructivist ways than did teachers whose students performed at or below the mean.

In sum, the results from our study show that the use of interactive whiteboards can make a difference in academic achievement, but that such a difference seems dependent on how teachers use them. As more and more classrooms, schools, and school districts are acquiring digital technologies like interactive whiteboards, this is perhaps our most important finding. For teachers and schools to make good use of what can be a considerable investment, effective uses of interactive whiteboards should be more thoroughly and robustly explored.

REFERENCES

Beeland, W. D. (2002). *Student engagement, visual learning, and technology: Can interactive whiteboards help?* Retrieved October 8, 2007, from http://chiron.valdosta.edu/are/Artmanscrpt/vol1no1/beeland_am.pdf

Bransford, J. D., Brown, A. L., & Cocking, R. R. (1999). *How people learn: Brain, mind, experience and school.* Washington, DC, USA: National Academy Press.

Cuthell, J. P. (2005). The impact of interactive whiteboards on teaching, learning, and attainment. [Phoenix, AZ: AACE.]. *Proceedings of SITE, 2005,* 1353–1355.

Dhindsa, H. S., & Emran, S. H. (2006, March). Use of the interactive whiteboard in constructivist teaching for higher student achievement. *Proceedings of the Second Annual Conference for the Middle East Teachers of Science, Mathematics, and Computing* (pp. 175-188). Abu Dhabi, UAE: METSMaC

Hall, I., & Higgins, S. (2005). Primary school students' perceptions of interactive whiteboards. *Journal of Computer Assisted Learning, 21,* 102–117. doi:10.1111/j.1365-2729.2005.00118.x

Higgins, S., Beauchamp, G., & Miller, D. (2007). Reviewing the literature on interactive whiteboards. *Learning, Media and Technology, 32*(3), 213–225. doi:10.1080/17439880701511040

Higgins, S., Falzon, C., Hall, I., Moseley, D., Smith, F., Smith, H., & Wall, K. (2005). *Embedding ICT in the literacy and numeracy strategies: Final report. Centre for Learning and Teaching. Newcastle, UK: University of Newcastle upon Tyne.* Retrieved May 7, 2009, from: http://partners.becta.org.uk/page_documents/research/univ_newcastle_evaluation_whiteboards.pdf

Kennewell, S., & Morgan, A. (2003). Student teachers' experiences and attitudes towards using interactive whiteboards in the teaching and learning of young children . In Wright, J., McDougall, A., Murnane, J., & Lowe, J. (Eds.), *Young children and learning technologies* (pp. 71–76). Sydney, Australia: Australian Computer Society.

LeDuff, R. (2004). Enhancing biology instruction via multimedia presentations. In C. Crawford et al. (Eds.), *Proceedings of the Society for Information Technology and Teacher Education International Conference 2004* (pp. 4693-4695). Chesapeake, VA: AACE. Retrieved October 8, 2007 from http://www.edcompass.de/NR/rdonlyres/B65DEF10-F8F0-40A3-B91A-A892BED75292/0/LeDuff_Jan04.pdf

Miller, D., Glover, D., & Averis, D. (2003, March). *Exposure: The introduction of interactive whiteboard technology to secondary school mathematics teachers in training.* Paper presented at CERME3: Third Conference of the European Society for Research in Mathematics Education, Bellaria, Italy.

Miller, D., Glover, D., & Averis, D. (2004). *Motivation: The contribution of interactive whiteboards to teaching and learning in mathematics.* Retrieved October 8, 2007, from http://cerme4.crm.es/Papers%20definitius/9/Miller-Glover-Averis.pdf

Miller, D., Glover, D., & Averis, D. (2005). Presentation and pedagogy: The effective use of interactive whiteboards in mathematics lessons. In D. Hewitt & A. Noyes (Eds.), *Proceedings of the sixth British congress of mathematics education* (pp. 105-112). Coventry, UK: University of Warwick.

Painter, D. D., Whiting, E., & Wolters, B. (2005). The use of an interactive whiteboard in promoting interactive teaching and learning. *VSTE Journal, 19*(2), 31–40.

Sakoda, J. M., Cohen, B. H., & Beall, G. (1954). Tests of significance for a series of statistical tests. *Psychological Bulletin, 51,* 172–175. doi:10.1037/h0059991

Smith, F., Hardman, F., & Higgins, S. (2006). The impact of interactive whiteboards on teacher-pupil interaction in the National Literacy and Numeracy Strategies. *British Educational Research Journal, 32*(3), 443–457. doi:10.1080/01411920600635452

Smith, H. J., Higgins, S., Wall, K., & Miller, J. (2005). Interactive whiteboards: Boon or bandwagon? A critical review of the literature. *Journal of Computer Assisted Learning, 21,* 91–101. doi:10.1111/j.1365-2729.2005.00117.x

Somekh, B., Haldane, M., Jones, K., Lewin, D., Steadman, S., & Scrimshaw, P. (2007). *Evaluation of the primary schools whiteboard expansion project.* Manchester, UK: Centre for ICT, Pedagogy and Learning, Education & Social Research Institute, Manchester Metropolitan University.

Swan, K., Kratcoski, A., van 't Hooft, M., Campbell, D., & Miller, D. (2007). Technology support for whole group engagement: A pilot study. *International Journal on Advanced Technologies for Learning, 4*(2), 68–73.

van 't Hooft, M. A. H., & Swan, K. (2007). *Ubiquitous computing in education: Invisible technology, visible impact.* Mahwah, NJ: Lawrence Erlbaum Associates.

Zittle, F. J. (2004). *Enhancing native American mathematics learning: The use of Smartboard-generated virtual manipulatives for conceptual understanding.* Retrieved October 8, 2007, from http://edcompass.smarttech.com/NR/rdonlyres/3E2A063B-6737-400F-BD07-1D239C428729/0/Zittle.pdf

ENDNOTE

[1] Ohio's accountability system ranks schools and districts according to their performance on a combination of academic indicators, a performance index score, and adequate yearly progress. Possible rankings include Excellent, Effective, Continuous Improvement, Academic Watch, and Academic Emergency. A school or district in Academic Watch has met 31.0-49.9% of academic indicators or has a performance index score of 70-79.9 (on a scale of 0-120), *and* has not met the adequately yearly progress. For more information see: http://www.ode.state.oh.us/GD/Templates/Pages/ODE/ODEDetail.aspx?Page=3&TopicRelationID=1266&ContentID=52790&Content=52818

Chapter 10
Effective Implementation of Learner Response Systems:
Moving Beyond the Right Response

Diana Bannister
University of Wolverhampton, UK

Andrew Hutchinson
University of Wolverhampton, UK

Helen Sargeant
University of Wolverhampton, UK

ABSTRACT

This chapter is based upon research from the REVEAL Project - a REVIEW of Electronic Voting and an Evaluation of Uses within Assessment and Learning. The REVEAL Project was a two-year development and research project across the UK funded by the Bowland Charitable Trust, (UK) that focused upon understanding the effective use of one of Promethean's Learner Response Systems (LRS) called Activote, across seventy primary and secondary schools within eleven local authorities. Led by the Learning Technologies Team, Midlands Leadership Centre, University of Wolverhampton, the project aimed to define and disseminate best practice in the use of Learner Response Systems, highlighting key uses and creative ways of working. This chapter summarizes the key themes and findings that have emerged from the project, providing an overview for teachers and practitioners including a suggested model of implementation for the Learner Response Systems. The work from this project would be beneficial to developments on classroom interaction and collaboration as well as teacher training and related continuing professional development for the effective use of interactive technologies within learning and teaching.

INTRODUCTION

During the last decade, teachers have been faced with an abundance of technology. While some embrace the latest equipment and quickly move on to the next kit, others are keen to embed the use of technology within their practice. The interactive whiteboard first appeared in UK classrooms in the late 1990s, but more than ten years later, it has taken considerable

DOI: 10.4018/978-1-61520-715-2.ch010

investment to demonstrate consistency and the full potential of whole class interactive technologies. Consequently, peripheral devices have received a similar reception, schools have bought or loaned learner response systems, but there is work to be done to ensure that they can be successfully integrated across different institutions. Teachers need both training and continuing professional development to determine whether such technologies are fit for their intended purpose, or indeed if there is another approach available.

Some teachers are confident enough with their own abilities to start with the technology and decipher the technical jargon. With most new technologies in the classroom, a framework for effective use is developed long after the initial experimentation from the teacher. This means that the teacher's use of the technology can plateau quite easily and in some cases, leads to lack of use rather than progress. However, in order to achieve the balance of the pedagogy alongside the new technology, it would seem more appropriate to have a framework to follow. Regardless of the technology; it is always useful to have a guide for implementing ideas in the classroom.

Historically, Learner Response Systems have been designed around the concept of providing an audience with a simple multiple choice keypad that allows questions to be answered during a lesson or lecture. Response data is collected and projected via a graph or histogram and discussed within the group. Some manufacturers, such as Promethean, have created hybrid software that allows for the creation of lessons where interactive whiteboard and a learner response system are used seamlessly, together. Key classroom applications of the Activote system include use in supporting Assessment for Learning, for the engagement and motivation of students, to encourage interaction between teacher and learner, and peer to peer dialogue.

For the purpose of this development and research project, all schools had been identified by the commercial supplier Promethean (UK) and

were using one particular system called Activote. At the time of this study Activote was the market leader in primary and secondary education within the UK, Europe, Africa and the Middle East (Decision Tree Consulting 2007). The multiple choice based learner response system is commonly sold in class sets of thirty-two devices to primary and secondary schools. It comes with a radio receiver and software that works in conjunction with an interactive whiteboard of any brand or ceiling mounted projector. Responses are collected by a USB radio receiver or a similar unit embedded in the IWB. Activote consists of a rubberized handset with six response buttons labeled A-F. Two other flashing panels inform the user whether their vote has been sent and received. Questions can be prepared in advance of a session, using a built in Question Master software application. This allows the teacher to input multiple choice options, set correct answers, give a time limit or countdown and add other resources to the displayed page.

The Activote device also allows for spontaneous questions where the teacher can write a question with a pen onto the interactive whiteboard. The software provides question template pages, that a teacher can click to edit and voting clipart images in the form of labeled Venn diagrams, Likert scales or Carroll diagrams, which can be dragged onto the screen and used on the spur of the moment. Teachers can use 'Voting' button images to drag and drop onto diagrams or pictures before asking questions. Advanced users have also been observed to use the system to gain responses to spontaneous verbal questions that they pose.

Following each question a data panel appears. Response data can be displayed in a variety of formats, these include:

- Answers in a graph (A-F)
- Who answered what?
- Right / Wrong (pie chart)
- Response Summary (all questions asked)
- Overall scores
- Response times

At the end of a session, the teacher can export a complete summary of the response data to a spreadsheet such as Microsoft Excel in order to conduct further analysis.

This chapter goes beyond the use of the interactive whiteboard to explore other technologies that can be embraced to demonstrate how the teacher can make a continual assessment within the classroom environment and how the learner can benefit. It begins with a review of the literature, with a particular focus on learner response technology. The authors then describe the work of the REVEAL Project, looking specifically at the key themes that emerged through the two year study. They also consider the model for implementation: the Response Technology Pyramid; this framework was developed by the REVEAL Project team and has helped to determine how teachers can improve their practice. Finally, the chapter offers some suggestions for the teacher, and the commercial supplier, on how effective use of this technology can be taken forward.

Throughout this chapter, any references made are in relation to evidence gathered from teachers using the Activote system; however, the project team believe that because of the current lack of evidence and guidance for the effective use of Learner Response Systems, this research will inform the users and suppliers of other devices.

Literature Review

The huge field of literature concerned with Information and Communications Technology within the education sector, stems from a wide range of sources and is multifaceted due to the continued drive to embed ICT within educational institutions. The literature available in relation to Learner Response Systems is limited, particularly when compared to other technologies, and research has so far predominantly been small-scale studies that focus on one type of device, subject area and age phase. In part, this is because the technology is considered to be at an embryonic stage in schools

and there is a lack of an agreed definition. To assist the reader, the literature review has been separated into the emerging themes within the research, but it will be absolutely essential to do additional reading in relation to each of the areas below.

Pre-Conditions

Much of the literature reviewed is concerned with technologies once they have been implemented and are being used at a competent level. There are, however, organizational and individual issues and factors that influence the reaching of this competence level, which can be described as pre-conditions.

These include e-maturity (the level of capability available to apply technology) (Becta, 2007), infrastructure (Draper & Brown, 2004), the existence of a strategic level e-strategy in schools (Condie & Munro, 2006) and the level of effective use of an interactive whiteboard. The readiness of teachers to implement ICT and how quickly and successfully they move through levels of implementation is also considered by Osborne and Hennessy (2003) to be a combination of numerous factors including pedagogy, institutional characteristics and attributes, personal attributes, learner profile, curriculum requirements and educational and political agendas.

A large body of research is also concerned with how and why some teachers successfully implement aspects of ICT while others have less success, which is clearly relevant in terms of pre-conditions. A key model here is the Integration of ICT developed by Hooper and Reiber (1995). Their model describes a teacher's journey towards the successful integration of emerging technologies through five levels: Familiarisation, Utilisation, Integration, Reorientation and Evolution.

Response technology, like many other technologies cannot by and large be considered to be a stand-alone solution to issues or contributor to success. Draper and Brown (2004) indicate from their research into the use of LRSs that: "success depended on putting pedagogy first, technology second" (p. 93). Similarly, Wasteney (2004) states that the technology itself is not a panacea, but how it is used is the important factor. The research suggests that the use of LRSs can facilitate effective teaching and learning and have an encouraging impact, but that it is still dependent on effective pedagogy and the use of the technology to facilitate successful outcomes. It has therefore been important to consider the perspectives of the teacher and the learner in relation to some of the other areas of literature which impact upon the use of learner response systems.

Learning and Teaching

The literature also identifies a range of uses for LRSs within learning and teaching. Roschelle, Penuel and Abrahamson (2004) state that: "Researchers report that instructors use the novel technological capabilities to enhance questioning and feedback, to motivate and monitor the participation of all students, to foster discussions of important concepts, and to energise and activate students' thinking" (p. 1).

Similarly, Bruff (2007) suggests that such technology might be used to increase attention, engagement, interaction, discussion and collaboration, anonymity, checking for understanding and adapting teaching accordingly.

Many other commentators also suggest positive impacts are seen in relation to the use of LRSs from both the teacher and learner perspective including increased enjoyment, participation, motivation and engagement, higher levels of attainment, active learning, effective questioning, immediate feedback, increased understanding, self-assessment, the promotion of discussion and the facilitation of monitoring (Draper & Brown, 2002; Penuel, Abrahamson & Roschelle, 2005; Roshcelle, Penuel & Abrahamson, 2004; Sillman & McWilliams, 2004). However, these positive

impacts are lost, or not fully exploited, if the use of the technology is infrequent (Duncan, 2006).

Although the concept of learning and teaching is integral to many of the areas that are explored, it is also referred to more explicitly in relation to ICT by Becta (2007). They suggest that technology is not enough on its own, but that it must fit with the learning and teaching taking place.

The literature reviewed also suggests a range of barriers to use from both an organizational and individual perspective. These include time, the production and sharing of resources, system failures, designing questions, and the implications for classroom management and lesson pace (Bruff, 2007; Draper & Brown, 2002; Sillman & McWilliams, 2004; Wasteney, 2004).

Personalizing Learning Using Technology

One of the key features of the learner response system is that it allows all pupils to participate in learning and perhaps therefore, begins to address some of the main aspects of personalizing learning. As a key commentator in the field of personalizing learning with the use of technologies, Hargreaves (2004), states that "Personalising teaching and learning is realised through nine interconnected gateways" (p. 1). It is noteworthy that these include "student voice", "assessment for learning" and "new technologies". In general terms, Hargreaves argues that, "There is a growing confidence in the profession that they [new technologies] are a powerful aid to better teaching" (p. 4). While "personalizing" learning is an area that still requires definition within some classrooms, there are examples of classroom research where teachers are beginning to explore how technology can help them to improve their understanding of individual learning needs.

The personalization of learning and teaching is described by the DFES (2006) as: "taking a highly structured and responsive approach to each child's and young person's learning, in order that all are able to progress, achieve and participate" (p. 6). This definition was part of the DfES 2020 Review of Teaching and Learning (2006) which focused on personalizing teaching and learning. In the report Gilbert stated that: "Personalising learning is a considered response to the opportunities and challenges of the future, and to ensuring that all children and young people make good progress at school" (p. 3).

Questioning

An integral and fundamental purpose of LRSs is the facilitation of questioning. This area attracts a wide range of literature, although, at present, it is limited in terms of the relevance to LRSs. Thalheimer (2007) suggests that in order to ensure meaningful learning teachers must become effective and competent in the use of questioning and discussion techniques. The importance and usefulness of effective questioning is supported by many other commentators including McCabe, Heal and White (2001), Ward (2005) and Hargreaves (2004).

The specific importance of student generated questions is considered important by Chin, Brown and Bruce (2002) who state that: "Students' questions play a significant role in meaningful learning and motivation and can serve different functions for them" (p. 251).

Cutrim-Schmid (2008) looks at the increase in the level of interactivity when using LRS and concludes within her research that "the voting system used in conjunction with IWB technology forced them to become more actively involved in the learning process, especially those who tended to be more passive in other lessons" (p. 355).

Stuart, Brown and Draper (2004) also comment that the learner response system prevents students from being passive as it: "facilitates an interaction between the students and lecturers, which keeps the students thinking and concentrating on the material throughout the lesson" (p. 99).

The issue of discussion is considered to be important by Beatty (2004) whose research focused specifically on learner response systems. He suggests that when using the technology, questioning is most effective if correct or incorrect answers are not given or displayed until a discussion is had around each one. Later work by Beatty, Gerace and Leonard (2006) also focused on designing effective questions when teaching with LRSs which they acknowledge as having the potential to be difficult and as different to designing other forms of questions.

A number of suggestions for effective questioning have links to the principles of Bloom's Taxonomy (Business Balls, 2006). It was created to categorize and classify levels of intellectual learning in the classroom and consists of three overlapping domains. Within the cognitive or knowledge domain, Bloom identified six levels that are known as Bloom's Taxonomy: knowledge, comprehension, application, analysis, synthesis and evaluation. The model suggests that if these levels are considered when planning lessons and devising questioning, a wider range of lower and higher order thinking skills are addressed. In the 1990s Anderson and Krathwohl (Oz-TeacherNet, 2006) from Australia developed Bloom's Revised Taxonomy, which incorporates both the knowledge domain and the process used to learn i.e. the cognitive process. This is seen by many as being more relevant for modern teaching and easier to practically apply, as the nouns have been changed to verbs to reflect the active nature of thinking.

Assessment

One of the main functions of LRSs is their ability to operate as an assessment tool. Not surprisingly, there is a huge field of literature available regarding assessment and all the factors it involves. Assessment has attracted increasing attention over the last few decades and in recent years the term "Assessment for Learning" has become a key focus for education, particularly within the primary and secondary sectors. Black and Wiliam (1998) suggest that "Assessment for Learning" is a significant factor in improving learning and increasing standards, with formative assessment being at the core of effective teaching.

The very broad field of assessment for learning can be broken down into smaller areas. McTighe and O'Connor (2005) suggest three categories: summative, diagnostic and formative, with each having distinct purposes. Put simply, they suggest that summative assessment is evaluative and often "formal" or external in nature. However, in later work, McTighe and O'Connor (2007) suggest that on its own, summative assessment does not maximize learning and can be too late to address issues. Some work has been carried out specifically in terms of assessment and LRSs. Ward (2005) acknowledges that using learner response technology can help with assessment through the efficient capture of data, because it is a challenge for teachers to collate and analyze.

It is clear from this brief review that there is limited research and direct comment on the use of LRSs and the literature available is often linked closely with ICT research. Where specific literature does exist, it generally indicates positive impacts from all perspectives. However, the research often has a commercial bias or was carried out with e-confident teachers. As with all technology, there are some limitations and barriers to use and issues exist in relation to attributing benefits to the technology itself as opposed to the pedagogical applications it facilitates and supports.

Despite these limitations, the literature review provided a contextual framework and informed the focus areas for the research. It also suggested, given the lack of an existing framework, that the development of a model of implementation would be helpful to users. The REVEAL Project has subsequently made a significant contribution to the field of literature and practical classroom application of the technology; it also presents a number of additional focus areas which would benefit from additional future work.

The Work of the REVEAL Project (UK)

Review of Electronic Voting and an Evaluation of Uses within Assessment and Learning

The REVEAL project was a two-year development and research project across the UK, funded by the Bowland Charitable Trust, that focused upon the effective use of one of Promethean's Learner Response Systems called Activote. The methodology within this work could be applied to other projects, indeed, the REVEAL Project team recognize that there is much to be learned from using the data collection process to ensure that effective use and application of technology is evident. While this research examined the use of only one learner response system, the project team believe because of the current lack of literature and evidence for the effective use of the devices, that this research will do much to inform users of other systems because of their generic functionality.

Research Methodology

The research team adopted a mixed methods approach to maintain a development focus within their work to cultivate the use of the technology by the teachers. The team were able to collect and analyze the data from 100 questionnaires, over 130 lesson observations with 70 teachers and 80 interviews with teachers, learners and local authority advisers. These have been gathered from three phases of visits.

Before embarking on the main programme of research, a pilot study provided opportunities to test the observation form and interview questions while allowing the project team to consider the logistical and technical issues. Subsequently, a number of interview questions were revised and the observation procedures were reviewed to ensure minimum disruption to teachers and learners. The research team were also able to look at issues in relation to training; including being able to determine their own professional development needs, in order to be able to support teachers throughout the project.

The purpose of the questionnaires as a method of data collection was to enable the project team to gather evidence from a wider audience than the eleven local authorities within the scale of the project. Eight hundred questionnaires were distributed to existing users and it was also made available electronically on the project website. The project team received approximately 100 responses prior to the school visits. Using this evidence, an analysis of both quantitative and qualitative data allowed the research team to begin to identify key themes and common strands that could be investigated further within observations and interviews.

The observations were also supported by interviews with teachers and pupils. These served the purpose of allowing the project team to collect qualitative data to add further detail to the lesson observations. The project team could ask questions to clarify reasons for actions within the lesson. For example, if the teacher used the learner response device in a specific way, the project team could ask for explanation. The interviews were considered to be semi-structured, key headings allowed the project team to be flexible and ensured that the teachers had the opportunity to expand on ideas and were able to demonstrate individual examples. It was particularly helpful to have given some thought to the questions, as this helps to be able to cover the breadth of the questions in the allocated time. All interviews were recorded, but teachers were assured of anonymity throughout.

The REVEAL Project team also delivered training to individuals, departments and schools and supported local authority events where Learner Response Systems featured. Teachers welcomed the learning technologies advisers going in to collect research data and observe lessons, knowing that it was not the main purpose of the exercise

to inspect them, but to give practical feedback and guidance on taking the use of the technology forward. The REVEAL Project team developed an observation sheet that was shared with the teachers following each observation. This was enhanced for the third stage of observations as certain issues had become common themes for development, enabling more structured feedback. The model for implementation of the learner response system was also discussed within the second and third set of observations. The observations also allowed the project team to see whether the teacher had the capacity of skills to link the use of the learner response system to the interactive whiteboard. The observations clearly showed that where the teacher is an experienced and effective user of interactive whiteboard authoring tools and digital resources, then s/he is likely to make use of the more complex features and applications with the learner response system.

The research addressed the following key questions:

- What are the opportunities and limitations provided by a learner response system?
- How do teachers use a learner response system to enhance teaching and learning?
- How does a learner response system help teachers to assess pupil progress?
- What are the current limitations for implementing and developing a learner response system and how might they be overcome?

The responses to these research questions have been directly linked to key themes which have emerged from the evidence collated. Each of these themes has been addressed in turn below.

Access and Pupil Involvement

A large proportion of the observations for the REVEAL Project were undertaken in the academic year 2006–2007; most teachers involved had been using the learner response system for less than two years. The learner response system has been introduced to schools in different ways, but it is this same mixture of approaches that occur with a plethora of new technologies. There are examples of the equipment being bought by the headteacher after a commercial demonstration at a conference or trade show. In essence, this can mean that the headteacher has never observed the technology in use in a classroom environment. Equally, this then means that the school has not developed any strategy for implementation and the equipment arrives in school without any forward planning. In almost 100% of schools visited within this project, teachers only have access to one set of 32 devices; this means that different classes can use the devices within one week. In secondary schools, the equipment has been largely purchased by one department, but again there are few examples of how this use will be extended to other areas. The research has identified that the way both the teacher and the pupil are able to access the technology does impact upon the overall success of use.

The REVEAL Project collected evidence from over 130 classroom observations. In primary schools, observations made during the first school visit showed that several teachers had timetabled access to the technology; this meant they could use the devices for one lesson per week. Following the first set of observations, the REVEAL Project team were able to show that where teachers had more regular access to the learner response system and with focus on one particular subject, then it was probable that the pupils would benefit through regular participation. Evidence suggests that the teacher was more likely to prepare his or her classroom materials, rather than using the equipment as an incentive and this would mean the learner response device had been integrated to the planning at some level. It is imperative that the technology is understood as a tool for learning and teaching, rather than the objective of the lesson. The observations showed that whilst teachers often started by using the devices in Mathematics

and Science, during the course of the project and the school visits, this expanded to include other subjects across the curriculum, particularly within the primary school.

Leadership

The data from this research shows that the implementation of the equipment is more successful when a senior leader within the school is involved. This is because there is more potential for a strategy to be developed for the long term aims and goals of using the equipment. It is particularly important that the school leader recognizes how the technology can be used to enhance other activities such as student councils, staff meetings, school open days and parental engagement or consultation. Without clear immediate leadership from when the equipment is purchased and arrives in school, the learner response system can easily become another underused and switched off peripheral device.

Policy and Planning

The issues around policy and planning begin at the point of purchase. The research has shown that schools have typically bought one set of learner response systems for use across the curriculum. However, it also reveals that teachers who make the most progress have regular access to the equipment with focused use with a group of learners. There is little evidence of the use of learner response systems being included within school policies, and at present they are still seen as one of several ICT options. Equally, while some teachers have begun to integrate the technology into their planning, this is primarily on a short term or weekly basis. At the beginning of this project, most teachers were using the technology inconsistently, including for example using activities to reward the pupils for other good work through competitions and other incentives. As part of the developmental work, teachers were encouraged to plan for the use of the learner response system as part of a series of lessons. This helped to develop more focused use and enabled more reflective practice.

Training and Continuing Professional Development

Evidence from this research showed that teachers using the learner response system have typically received training at the time of installation, but this usually involves the commercial provider giving a quick tour of the software. While there is some focus on use and applications within the classroom, teachers comment upon the lack of subject specific training. There are limited examples of one-to-one training, manuals and web support. In most instances, where this does occur, it is during the initial stage of training, rather than as part of continued professional development. The first stage classroom visits within the REVEAL Project demonstrated that the teachers have not considered other training beyond the introductory session. This has resulted in lack of progress with the technology as teachers are not readily aware of how to implement the true potential of the learner response system. This is generally because the teacher can use the technology at an appropriate level and this is acceptable to the pupils.

Teachers within the REVEAL Project were particularly positive about being involved in local authority led projects which facilitated opportunities for both training and creation of resources. However, there is also much evidence to show that advisers and technicians would benefit from training to understand the effective use and application of the learner response system. As yet, there are few examples of collaborative work both within and beyond schools to show how teachers can work together to develop the use of the technology. Teachers welcomed the lesson observations as part of the REVEAL Project as it has meant that they can be shown how to develop their own use of the technology within their own classroom. It is paramount that teachers understand that the

technology can do much more than testing; teachers need to be able to see working examples of the wider applications of the learner response system including understanding of how to develop their questioning skills and how to analyze data both within and beyond the lesson.

Questioning, Dialogue and Discussion

The research from the REVEAL Project shows that teachers need to have a good understanding of how to create effective questions within the classroom to be able to integrate the technology to enhance their own teaching, rather than just using it as a summative assessment tool. In the first phase of observations, there were frequent examples of teachers asking largely closed multiple choice questions requiring factual responses. Evidence from the first set of observations showed that teachers used the pupils' responses to trigger whole class discussion and to explore the range of responses. Initially, there were also a few examples of teachers using the learner response devices to undertake summative tests where the pupils worked individually and the teacher did not address pupil misconceptions; this does little to support or extend the pupil's learning. During the interviews, teachers commented that initial training from the commercial provider when the technology was purchased, encouraged teachers to create their own materials using interactive whiteboard authoring tools, rather than simply asking questions from a previously prepared assessment. This suggests that there is a link between the type of training the teacher receives and the way they subsequently use the technology.

The first set of observations from the REVEAL Project identified few teachers who encouraged pupils to discuss answers with a partner or in a group before agreeing on a single response. However, where this did exist, there was evidence of more dialogue in these classrooms. Classroom observations show that pupils welcome the questions being read aloud, but teachers were also able to support pupils by providing writing frames to help structure classroom discussion. The research recognizes that pupils need time to discuss their ideas with peers, make notes and jot down possible responses before making a response. During the lesson observations, the REVEAL Project team looked for evidence of pupils being given 'thinking time', 'talk time', 'note taking time' or 'writing time.' Furthermore, in order to be able to respond to the teacher's questions, time should be given for the pupils to demonstrate their strategies or reasoning. The questions can also be time limited using the learner response device, i.e. teachers can programme the question template to allow one minute for pupils to make a response. However, evidence from the REVEAL Project showed that teachers actually prefer to be able to make their own judgment about how much time to give the pupils to respond. From the teacher's perspective, it is important to be able to identify the response, to enable the teacher to give immediate feedback. The teacher must also recognize that just because a pupil can respond using the device, does not mean he or she has fully understood and indeed, may have guessed. The teacher must also give some consideration to the pupil's ability to read and interpret the question. Equally, the activity must allow opportunity to extend the learning; throughout the project, the project team worked collaboratively with the teachers to design other types of response, rather than questions requiring a correct answer.

Personalizing Learning, Data and Assessment

At the heart of the learner response system is formative assessment. The more advanced user of the learner response system is able to fully exploit the principles of personalizing learning and Assessment for Learning. This means the teacher uses the evidence of learning within the lesson to inform the next stage of teaching and learning for the pupil. It is paramount that the teacher recognizes that personalizing learning is an ongoing process within and beyond the lesson. While the teacher may have planned the content of the lesson and the main activity, personalizing the process to the individuals is "live progress" within the lesson. Learner response devices are often bought on the premise that they allow the teacher to access the data on individual pupils; however, the observations showed that there is much to be done to ensure that teachers do this to the full extent both within and beyond the lesson. During the REVEAL Project, evidence from the observations showed that teachers were looking at the results to determine correct answers; to show who answered what and sometimes to look at the speed of responses.

Many teachers like using the equipment in "anonymous mode", and questionnaire data shows that over 40% of respondents regularly do this. Pupils also like the fact that they can respond anonymously and do not worry about "getting it wrong". However, evidence from the observations shows that pupils benefit most when they can be identified by the teacher and receive individual feedback. The REVEAL Project team describe this as "identified mode", because while this may be publicly anonymous, the teacher will have pre-determined how to identify the pupils by use of pseudonyms, or more commonly by knowing the number of the pupil's device. Ultimately, teachers involved in the REVEAL Project believed that it was important to establish a classroom ethos where it is commonplace for pupils to share data. Teachers also need to look at questions which allow for different types of response and indeed, some devices currently allow for this. Furthermore, teachers should encourage activity where pupils generate the range of answers as this can demonstrate understanding and interpretation of the question.

Throughout the project, there are few examples of the data being exported to a data analysis programme, however, this is because the data is relatively meaningless whilst it is being used in isolation by only one teacher and others cannot interpret the detail. At present, there is some way to go before learner response devices truly impact on data beyond the lesson. To do this, the device would need to be used by more than a single teacher in one department or to allow for comparative data from a pupil's performance in another curriculum area.

Learner Perspective

Observations showed that learners responded positively to the use of the devices, though it has to be said that at the time of this research project, the "novelty factor" was considered prominent within the classroom as use of the technology was largely embryonic. Pupils find the technology intuitive as they already have access to technologies at home with similar features. Indeed, there is an expectation that people can contribute and "vote" as part of television programmes and other web-based activities and pupils initially view the devices in this way. Pupils welcome the fact that they can work anonymously with the device; they do not have to make a written response and they get immediate feedback; these factors all contribute to removing the fear of failure and encourages participation from all pupils. Evidence from the lesson observations demonstrates that learner response systems can encourage learner interaction. Pupils comment that it can be helpful to discuss their ideas with peers. However, this is an area which needs developing as some teachers are still reluctant to facilitate and structure peer to peer discussion within the lesson. It is because of this that the teacher must recognize the expectations of the learner prior to implementation. Indeed, it is primarily the perspective of the learner which should drive the future development and application of these devices.

Model for Implementation: The Response Technology Pyramid

From the very start of the project, it became apparent that there was no model for successful implementation. Through the research, the team were able to determine that there are different phases of development. These are largely incremental and elements of the later phases suggest that the user will have made some progress through earlier phases. Some users have made progress to more complex use of the technology within a shorter time frame, but this is dependent upon other contributing factors which have been recognized as "preconditions" and appear in the left side of Figure 1.

Within this chapter, there is an outline of the main features of each level of the Response Technology Pyramid; however, the full model gives many more level descriptors for each stage and outlines how teachers can progress from one level to the next. This version is available from the project website.

Response Technology Introductory Phase: Level 1

- To encourage pupil participation within the lesson at the start or on completion of a new module
- Used on an ad hoc basis for quiz type activities, e.g. "Who wants to be a millionaire?" game show type activities.
- The teacher is rarely aware of the individual progress of the pupils using the LRS.
- The data is used to provide a snapshot of the class as a whole.
- The pupils enjoy the lessons as they get the chance to use the learner response system.
- The questions are about factual recall and the activity checks existing knowledge.

Figure 1. Response technology pyramid

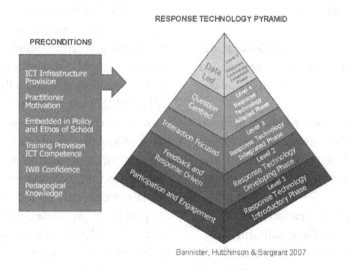

In truth, most pupils have not been challenged by the questions at all and little learning has taken place.

Response Technology Developing Phase: Level 2

- The teacher will make more regular use of the equipment.
- The teacher tends to include the learner response system within their short term plans at classroom level, though there is more work to be done on the long term strategy for effective use.
- The teacher uses the data within the lesson at a basic level to give some feedback to the pupils, and often begins to show the pupils the different ways the data can be explored. For example: looking at "Who answered what?" and "Who answered the fastest?" and giving consideration to the percentage of pupils who gave the same response.
- The teacher may give some opportunities for pupils to discuss answers. However, there will usually be a correct response anticipated.

Response Technology Integrated Phase: Level 3

- The teacher will have integrated the use of the learner response system into classroom planning, knowing when it is appropriate to use the technology.
- The teacher recognizes that the device is just one of the tools that can be used for part of the lesson and for the teacher to assess progress.
- At this stage, the questions will invite opinion or response.
- The teacher considers the range of answers, which in turn highlights misconceptions in knowledge.
- The teacher is able to make use of the data within and beyond the lesson to inform future planning.
- Pupils are familiar with using the equipment on a regular basis and recognize that they need to give some thought to their answers before responding.

Response Technology
Adopted Phase: Level 4

- The teacher will have the confidence to act more spontaneously and make changes to the direction of the lesson, based on the pupil responses.
- The teacher readily creates his or her own materials and while some of the content will be prepared prior to the lesson, the flow of the work will depend upon pupil responses.
- However, because the teacher is likely to be a confident user of the authoring software on the interactive whiteboard, s/he is able to develop ideas to demonstrate pupil examples.

One teacher working with the REVEAL Project identified "learning pit stops" as part of the lesson, where he would use the learner response system to gather how much the pupil's had understood before progressing on to the next activity.

Response Technology
Embedded Phase: Level 5

- The teacher uses the Learner Response System with a seamless approach in the learning and teaching environment.
- The device is used to track individual pupil progression and the data is used to inform both teacher and pupil.
- The teacher will ask questions which allow the pupils to hypothesize around their own ideas with different pupils reaching different conclusions.
- The pupil has individual targets and the data is exported by the teacher to external files to contribute to the overall personalized assessment.

While individual practitioners are making progress with this technology, at present, there are relatively few examples of where the technology has been adopted by more than one department within a school. Furthermore, there are currently only a handful of schools that are committed to all pupils having access to a device in every lesson. In essence, there are strong similarities with the introduction of interactive whiteboards in the late 1990s; those teachers who had regular access, recognized the potential of the technology and soon put demands on the commercial suppliers to provide appropriate and more accessible software which linked to existing resources. Learner response systems are beginning to demand this same approach; the user is dictating the progression and development.

CONCLUSION AND FUTURE RESEARCH DIRECTIONS

This research has been pivotal in helping us to recognize that there was a need to develop a model for effective use of Learner Response Systems. Teachers benefit from continued developmental support and welcome practical feedback and guidance within their own teaching environment. The evidence suggests that teachers will be able to demonstrate greater progress with their use of the learner response technology if it is readily adopted and further developed beyond one single classroom. This is because the data can be used to inform pupil assessment over a longer period and within different subjects. Ultimately, this should impact on pupil attainment and therefore whole school data.

The use of Learner Response Systems is growing and over the next few years manufacturers forecast that an increasing number of schools will purchase devices for classroom use. It is therefore safe to presume that LRSs will feature within educational practice in the foreseeable future, but it will take significant investment for the use of these learning technologies to become mainstreamed.

Commercial suppliers and teachers are considering whether future developments may well lie in the development of learner response software rather than with physical devices. This has the potential to allow LRS tools to be installed on other handheld devices such as netbooks, mobile phones or EDAs (Educational Digital Assistant). While currently the classroom teacher introduces learner response technology through a separate device, ultimately, there is no reason why programs cannot be placed on an existing interface and responses gathered via the internet, network or a wireless connection. The use of a 'virtual handset' could prevent teachers trying to access the single class LRS within the school as software could be placed on the school learning platform or in an ideal world on the pupil's own personal device. At present, this does not happen in practice because of the lack of standardized access to personal handheld devices. While students may have access to their own mobile device, there is work to be done to ensure compatibility between different platforms. Furthermore, the teacher would find it hard to prepare lesson materials without being able to rely on students having access to the same level of functionality from the equipment; this would become an unknown variable and a challenge even to the teacher who is digitally literate.

At present, manufacturers have developed complex LRS software containing a wide range of functions and specialized features. In developing cross platform LRS software, developers would need to consider whether this could have the effect of restricting the possible range of uses and applications. At the moment there are several mobile phone "text" based response systems that contain basic LRS features but lack much of the flexibility and functionality of a dedicated device, features that users rate as valuable.

Current research is exploring the use of text and numerical entry based features of more sophisticated devices. However, there is considerable opportunity to look at a wide scale roll out of the devices across a whole school and the perceived impacts with regular use. There is also the opportunity to explore the development of particular themes such as learner voice, questioning, dialogue and discussion and the analysis of data.

Developing the Model for Implementation

During the REVEAL Project, the research team has challenged some of the current uses of learner response technology. This has involved working with a broad range of teachers to develop and extend existing practice with individual lesson support and feedback. This has led to the development of a model for effective use and implementation of learner response technology: the "Response Technology Pyramid". Ultimately, this will allow teachers, advisers and commercial suppliers to understand how to embed these technologies effectively into the learning and teaching environment. The REVEAL Project has gained considerable momentum both nationally and internationally; it offers a sound platform for future research including the effective use of different and more advanced LRS. The high quality 40-minute television style documentary DVD produced as part of this project includes case studies from across the UK (see www.revealproject.org). It illustrates the ultimate aim of this research and development work is to maximize the achievements of those learners and teachers who have access to the technology both now and in the future.

REFERENCES

Beatty, I. (2004). Transforming student learning with classroom communication systems. *Educause Center for Applied Research, 2004(3)*, 1-13.

Beatty, I. D., Gerace, W. J., Leonard, W. J., & Dufresne, R. J. (2006). Designing effective questions for classroom response system teaching. *American Journal of Physics, 74*(1), 31–39. doi:10.1119/1.2121753

Becta (2007). *Annual review 2007*. Coventry, UK: Becta.

Becta (2007). *Harnessing technology review 2007: Progress and impact of technology in education.* Coventry, UK: Becta.

Becta (2007). *Learning in the 21st Century The case for harnessing technology.* Coventry, UK: Becta.

Black, P., & Wiliam, D. (1998). *Inside the black box: Raising standards through classroom assessment.* London: School of Education, King's College.

Bruff, D. (2007). *Classroom response systems.* Retrieved July 23, 2007, from http://www.vanderbilt.edu/cft/resources/teaching_resources/technology/crs.htlm

Business Balls. (n.d.). *Blooms taxonomy – learning domains.* Retrieved July 25, 2006, from http://www.businessballs.com/bloomstaxonomyoflearningdomains.htlm

Chin, C., Brown, D. E., & Bruce, B. C. (2002). Student-generated questions: A meaningful aspect of learning in science. *International Journal of Science Education, 24*(5), 521–549. doi:10.1080/09500690110095249

Condie, R., Munro, B., Seagraves, L., & Kenesson, S. (2006). *The impact of ICT in schools – a landscape review.* Coventry, UK: Becta.

Cutrim Schmid, E. (2008). Using a voting system in conjunction with interactive whiteboard technology to enhance learning in the English language classroom. *Computers & Education, 50,* 338–356. doi:10.1016/j.compedu.2006.07.001

Department for Education and Skills. (2006). 2020 Vision report of the teaching and learning in 2020 review group. Nottingham, UK: DfES.

Draper, S. W., & Brown, M. I. (2002). *Use of the PRS (Personal Response System) handsets at Glasgow University.* Retrieved May 24, 2006, from http://www.psy.gla.ac.uk/~steve/ilig/interim.htlm

Draper, S. W., & Brown, M. I. (2004). Increasing interactivity in lectures using an electronic voting system. *Journal of Computer Assisted Learning, 20*(2), 81–94. doi:10.1111/j.1365-2729.2004.00074.x

Duncan, D. (2006). Clickers: A new teaching aid with exceptional promise. *Astronomy Education Review, 1*(5), 70–88. doi:10.3847/AER2006005

Gibbs, G., & Simpson, C. (2004). Conditions under which assessment supports students' learning. *Learning and Teaching in Higher Education, 1,* 3–31.

Hargreaves, D. (2004). *Personalising learning: Next steps in working laterally.* Retrieved February 10, 2009, from http://www.ssat-inet.net/resources/publications

Hooper, S., & Rieber, L. P. (1995). Teaching with technology . In Ornstein, A. C. (Ed.), *Teaching: Theory into practice* (pp. 154–170). Needham Heights, MA: Allyn and Bacon.

McCabe, M., Heal, A., & White, A. (2001). The integration of group response systems on teaching and LOLA, the missing link in computer assisted assessment. *Paper presented at the 5th Annual CAA Conference 2001,* Loughborough University, UK.

McTighe, J., & O'Connor, K. (2005). Seven practices for effective learning. *Educational Leadership, 63*(3), 10–17.

Osborne, J., & Hennessy, S. (2003). *Literature review in science education and the role of ICT: Promise, problems and future directions.* Retrieved July 23, 2007, from http://www.nestafuturelab. org/research/lit_reviews.htm#lr6

Oz-TeacherNet. (n.d.). *Revised Bloom's taxonomy.* Retrieved August 21, 2006, from http://rite.ed.qut. edu.au/ozteachernet/index.php?module=Content Express&func=display&ceid=29

Penuel, W. R., Abrahamson, L., & Roschelle, J. (2005). A sociocultural interpretation of the effects of audience response systems in Higher Education . In Banks, D. (Ed.), *Audience response systems in higher education: Applications and cases* (pp. 187–208). Hersey, PA: IGI Global.

Penuel, W. R., Abrahamson, L., & Roschelle, J. (2005). Teaching with student response systems technology: A survey of K-12 teachers. SRI International 2005. Menlo Park, CA

Roschelle, J., Penuel, W. R., & Abrahamson, L. (2004). *Annual meeting of the American educational research association 2004.* San Diego, CA

Sillman, S. E., & McWilliams, L. (2004). Observations on benefits/limitations of an audience response system. *Paper presented at the American Society for Engineering Education Annual Conference and Exposition 2004.* Salt Lake City, USA.

Simpson, V., & Oliver, M. (2005). *Using electronic voting systems in lectures.* Retrieved January 10, 2007, from http://www.ucl.ac.uk/klecturingtecnology/examples/ElectronicVotingSytems.pdf

Stuart, S. A. J., Brown, M. I., & Draper, S. W. (2004). Using an electronic voting system in logic lectures: One practitioner's application. *Journal of Computer Assisted Learning, 20,* 95–102. doi:10.1111/j.1365-2729.2004.00075.x

Thalheimer, W. (2007). *Questioning strategies for audience response systems: How to use questions to maximise learning, engagement and satisfaction.* Retrieved July 20, 2007, from http://www. audienceresponselearning.org/the_report.htlm

Thalheimer, W. (2007). *Learning benefits of classroom 1uestions.* Retrieved July 20, 2007, from http://www.audienceresponselearning.org/ question_benefits.htlm

Ward, D. L. (2005). *The classroom performance system: The overwhelming research results supporting this teacher tool and methodology.* Retrieved January 25, 2005, from http://www. einstruction.com

Wasteney, J. (2004). *The impact of voting systems in the classroom.* Retrieved September 10, 2006, from http://www.naace.org/attachment.asp?attac hmentId=26309&menultemld=8-270K

Section 2
Practice

Part 3
Professional Development

Chapter 11
A Model of Pedagogical Change for the Evaluation of Interactive Whiteboard Practice

Julie Cogill
King's College London, UK

ABSTRACT

This chapter explores how whiteboard pedagogy is constructed from both a theoretical pedagogical perspective and empirical evidence based on interactive whiteboard practice. A brief discussion on what is meant by the terms Pedagogy, Pedagogical Knowledge, Content Knowledge, Curriculum Knowledge and Pedagogical Content Knowledge (Shulman, 1987) is followed by the utilization of established theoretical models of teacher knowledge to form a model of teachers' general pedagogy. An evaluation of IWB practice of 11 teachers in two primary UK schools, over one year, is then presented. Evidence emerging from whiteboard practice is subsequently blended with the model of general pedagogy to construct a theoretical model of pedagogical change subsequent to whiteboard use. Particular whiteboard teaching behaviors are proposed which facilitate greater efficiency and which may extend teachers' existing pedagogical practice or help to transform their teaching. Finally, in the concluding section implications for teachers' professional development in whiteboard practice and future research directions are put forward.

INTRODUCTION

A question which frequently arises is: "What is IWB pedagogy?" Is this pedagogy different from other forms of pedagogy? If so, how does it differ and what are the particular aspects of teaching and learning that relate to the IWB? Since pedagogy itself is not easy to define, this chapter first reflects on what is meant by pedagogy before moving onto teaching practices associated with the IWB. Using a general model of pedagogy and evidence from eleven teachers' use of an IWB over one year, a model of whiteboard pedagogy is constructed. Throughout, the IWB is considered as a tool to provide a catalyst for changing teaching rather than a change factor per se since the stance taken is that

DOI: 10.4018/978-1-61520-715-2.ch011

it is teachers who change teaching, not technology. It is however not always easy for teachers to understand how their teaching has been affected. Some would claim that the whiteboard has not changed their teaching style though an external observer might think otherwise (Cogill, 2008). Using the informed model constructed, I next consider whiteboard practices which may make teaching more efficient or may be considered to extend or transform a teacher's practice (McCormick & Scrimshaw, 2001). With this as a guide, teachers can evaluate their own IWB practice and reflect on ways to extend their pedagogy.

Throughout this chapter the term "whiteboard pedagogy" refers to the act of teaching with the interactive whiteboard through the use of appropriate teaching methods, resources, questioning techniques and the necessary technological skills to foster children's learning. This definition necessarily draws in issues relating to a teacher's knowledge and in particular his or her Pedagogical Knowledge (PK), Content Knowledge (CK), Pedagogical Content Knowledge (PCK) and Curriculum Knowledge (Shulman, 1987). Consequently the term 'whiteboard pedagogy' is used to encompass both pedagogical knowledge and practice. A distinction will be made where appropriate between "whiteboard pedagogical knowledge" and "whiteboard pedagogical practice" if the general term "whiteboard pedagogy" is ambiguous.

BACKGROUND

When whiteboards were first introduced into UK schools in 1998 my interest was roused through a conversation with a secondary mathematics teacher who commented: "The whiteboard changes the way I teach." At the same time I read an observation that while an operating theatre would be unrecognizable from 100 years ago, a classroom might look almost identical. As a result I decided to explore the influence that interactive whiteboards might have. Technology creates some appearance of physical change but what matters are the potential effects the interactive whiteboard has on teachers and learners, often referred to as pedagogical practice.

The empirical evidence on teachers' pedagogical change cited in this chapter is drawn from research on 11 teachers, across one year of IWB use, in two UK primary schools. Pupils involved were aged 5-11. All teachers were competent and experienced in teaching across a range of subjects but new to the whiteboard at the start of the research. I observed each teacher in their classrooms and interviewed each of them once per term, a process that resulted in a total of 33 interviews and 33 observations for subsequent analysis. In addition I interviewed the head teachers of each school at the start and the end of the research year. The theoretical underpinning for analysis of this research, based on grounded theory (Strauss & Corbin, 1998), is supported by Shulman's Framework for teacher knowledge (Shulman, 1987) together with established pedagogical models from a range of literature sources. From these a new model of general pedagogical change is first constructed for the analysis of IWB pedagogy.

WHAT IS PEDAGOGY?

What constitutes pedagogy is not easily defined and appears to be somewhat obscure. Watkins and Mortimer (1999) define it as "any conscious activity by one person designed to enhance the learning of another" (p. 3). Alexander (2003) has his own preferred definition which suggests that pedagogy requires discourse:

Pedagogy is the act of teaching together with its attendant discourse. It is what one needs to know, and the skills one needs to command in order to make and justify the many different kinds of decisions of which teaching is constituted. (p. 3)

Leach and Moon (1999) expand further on what may define pedagogy by describing a Pedagogical Setting as "the practice that a teacher, together with a particular group of learners creates, enacts and experiences" (p. 267). In doing so they suggest that pedagogy is a joint activity in which the learner has an active role. This offers a different perspective from previous definitions offered and draws on the social interaction between teachers and learners. Many other researchers, including for example, Brown and McIntyre (1993), Bruner (1999), Ireson et al. (1999), Loveless (2002) and McNamara (1991), acknowledge that the variables which make up teachers' pedagogy are complex and suggest there are many environmental and personal factors that affect practice: national educational initiatives, the school environment, a teacher's position in the school, previous teaching experience, a teacher's training and a teacher's own experience of learning. Although I will raise these issues briefly during this chapter, the focus is on change in PK, CK and PCK since there is a consensus from those working in the field that teacher knowledge is fundamental to pedagogical practice. By maintaining the focus on teacher knowledge the aim of this chapter is to create a starting point for generalizing IWB pedagogy which is independent of the individual teacher and his or her environment.

Shulman (1987) defines seven categories to provide a framework for teacher knowledge as follows:

1. Content Knowledge
2. General Pedagogical Knowledge, e g., classroom control, using group work
3. Pedagogical Content Knowledge
4. Curriculum Knowledge
5. Knowledge of learners and their characteristics
6. Knowledge of educational contexts e.g., schools and the wider community
7. Knowledge of educational ends, purposes and values

Each of these types of knowledge is worthy of lengthy debate. However, Pedagogical Knowledge (PK) Content Knowledge (CK), Pedagogical Content Knowledge (PCK) and Curriculum Knowledge are those of most interest for this discussion since they form the building blocks of the theoretical model I will explore; first however, we take a brief interlude to explain these types of knowledge.

Shulman (1987) regards Pedagogical Knowledge (PK) as the broad principles and strategies of classroom management and organization that appear to transcend subject matter. Using the work of Brown and McIntyre (1993) and Bruner (1999) Table 1 shows teaching activities which may be considered to reflect PK.

In line with Shulman's definition these teaching activities may apply regardless of the subject matter being taught. Content Knowledge (CK) is the knowledge teachers have of the subject matter they are teaching (Shulman, 1987). McNamara (1991) suggests that knowledge of subject content is essential not only for teaching itself but also for the evaluation of textbooks, computer software and teaching aids. In relation to using ICT, Cox et al. (2003) support these views. They suggest that teachers need to possess relevant CK in order to make appropriate decisions when choosing software. There is a range of views on how teaching experience affects CK. Leach and Moon (1999) consider that CK is changed by teaching practice and in particular, by the resources that may be used in teaching. Prestage and Perks (2000) on the other hand argue that CK is only changed if teachers reflect on their teaching beyond a consideration of simple classroom events. Teachers need to consider their own understanding of the subject if practice is to affect CK. Thus the important aspect in changing CK appears to be how a teacher internally reflects on a teaching experience rather than just the experience itself.

What I wish to explore more deeply however is the relationship between CK and Shulman's categories PK and PCK. Shulman defines Pedagogi-

Table 1. Teaching activities and strategies and qualities of good teachers (Cogill, 2008)

Teaching activity	Strategies and qualities of good teachers
Lesson planning and preparation	Making clear what pupils are to do and achieve
	Considering how planning interacts with the management of classes and lessons
	Managing lesson introductions
	Managing question and answer sessions
Understanding children's learning	Viewing children as imitative learners
	Viewing children as learning from didactic exposure
	Viewing children as thinkers
	Viewing children as managers of their own knowledge
	Judging what can be expected of a pupil
	Helping pupils with difficulties
	Encouraging pupils to raise their expectations
Influencing motivation	Creating a relaxed and enjoyable atmosphere in the classroom
	Presenting work in a way that interests and motivates
	Providing conditions which enable pupils to understand the work
Classroom management	Retaining control in the classroom

cal Content Knowledge (PCK) as the knowledge of how to teach within a particular subject area. It enables teachers to ease the learning for students through use of clear explanations, appropriate analogies and presenting learning in interesting, motivating and even entertaining ways:

Pedagogical content knowledge identifies the distinctive bodies of knowledge for teaching. It represents the blending of content and pedagogy into an understanding of how particular topics, problems or issues are organised, represented, and adapted to the diverse interests and abilities of learners, and presented for instruction. (Shulman, 1987, p. 4)

There is much debate as to how PCK is formed. McNamara (1991) considers that the ability to teach a subject requires more than just an understanding of CK and PK. It also requires an understanding of what happens at their intersection so that it is not the case that CK is simply added to PK but that a teacher

reflecting on classroom practice may create his or her own PCK.

Within the context of IWB practice, however, I consider there are elements of Content Knowledge (CK) across a spectrum of subject areas that require specific subject knowledge from teachers and which are distinct from PCK. This specific knowledge relates to the use of the new range of software resources that teachers will necessarily employ as they adopt the whiteboard. Without the prior CK teachers will not be in a position to make the appropriate choice of such new resources; additionally, use of new resources may also affect teachers' existing CK as they adopt a range of software for teaching particular topics. Consequently, it is important to consider CK in the context of the IWB as an independent entity in its own right rather than subsume CK altogether under the umbrella of PCK.

Curriculum knowledge is knowledge of what should be taught to a particular group of pupils. It requires understanding of children's learning potential, national syllabuses, school planning documents and year group plans. In addition, any examination or testing syllabuses must be taken into account and any local or contextual requirements considered. These "knowledge's": PK, CK, PCK and Curriculum Knowledge will form the foundations of the model for assessing teachers' general pedagogical change.

A THEORETICAL MODEL FOR TEACHERS' PEDAGOGICAL CHANGE

While Shulman (1987) outlines different aspects of teacher knowledge he does not reflect in detail on the interrelationship between them or other influences that may affect teachers' pedagogy (Banks et al., 1999). However from the literature on pedagogy there exists a range of established models and frameworks relating to teachers' professional and pedagogical knowledge and skills:

- Although different terminology is used, Banks et al. (1999) suggest a Venn Diagram representation for PK, CK, PCK and Curriculum Knowledge.
- Prestage and Perks (2000) propose that teachers' beliefs in how children learn, along with their previous teaching and learning experience affect their pedagogy. They also suggest a 3D model for pedagogical change to illustrate the changing nature of teachers' pedagogy.
- Nicholson (1996), emphasizes the effects on pedagogy of "Educational Context" which concerns not only a teacher's current teaching position but the group of pupils being taught, the local community and the educational policy of the country where a teacher is working.
- Alexander (1994) introduces "Observable Practice" as the outcome or effect of a teacher's pedagogical practice and knowledge.

- Cox et al. (2003) provide a framework to investigate change in pedagogy enabled by the affordance of teachers using ICT.

Using these earlier models to take into account the different attributes pertaining to teachers' pedagogy, I have formed a new and more complete model of general pedagogical change as illustrated in Figure 1 and Figure 2. Figure 2 is presented to illustrate the 3 dimensional aspect of this model.

The theoretical model for pedagogical change above aims to demonstrate both the changing nature of teacher knowledge and also the relationship between teachers' beliefs in how students learn, teachers' experience, and the educational context in which they are working. Educational context may be affected not only by the educational institution in which teachers are working but also by the local community and the educational policy of the area or country where they are based. Pedagogical Knowledge, Content Knowledge, Pedagogical Content Knowledge, Curriculum Knowledge and Observable Practice are all strongly influenced by teachers' beliefs and experiences and their educational context. Therefore a teacher's knowledge (shown within the circles) is encompassed by and positioned within the complex intersection of his or her beliefs, practices and teaching context. Although this chapter largely concerns change in teachers' Pedagogical Knowledge, Content Knowledge, Pedagogical Content Knowledge and Curriculum Knowledge following intervention of the IWB, the purpose of this representation is to illustrate that their pedagogy is influenced by all of these variables including their beliefs, experience and educational context, not only teacher knowledge.

At the vertex of the pyramid, formed by connecting the four corners of the base, lies "Teachers' pedagogical change". The purpose of using a 3D model which is illustrated more clearly in Figure 2 is to suggest that there is a constant two-way flow

Figure 1. Theoretical model for teachers' pedagogical change

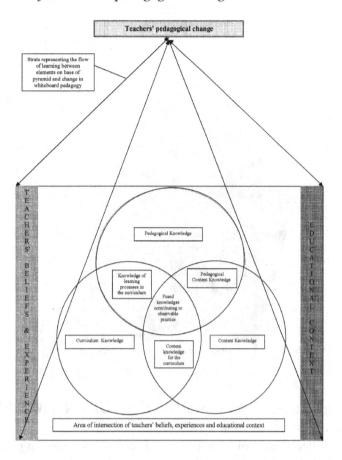

between the base elements: teacher knowledge, teachers' beliefs and experience, educational context and the vertex element: pedagogical change. Through this representation of the two-way process the model also intends to suggest that a teacher's knowledge is dynamic in that it is constantly changing and responding to new events. This theoretical model for teachers' pedagogical change was employed to underpin the analysis of empirical evidence emerging from 11 teachers' IWB pedagogy during their first year of use.

TECHNOLOGICAL PEDAGOGICAL CONTENT KNOWLEDGE (TPCK)

Mishra and Koehler (2006) propose a conceptual framework for ICT which is general in nature rather than specific to IWB technology, but is similarly based on Shulman's formulation of PCK. They argue that effective use of technology requires a complex interplay between content, pedagogy and technology which gives rise to a new knowledge: Technological Pedagogical Content Knowledge (TPCK) (Mishra & Koehler, 2009).

Research conducted by Mishra and Koehler (2006) found that with the right opportunities teachers grew in their capacity to understand the interactions between content, pedagogy and technology, suggesting that their TPCK had developed. They also acknowledge that "no single framework can tell the complete story; no single framework can provide all the answers" (p. 1047). I endorse the TPCK model as providing a good general framework for the integration of technology with pedagogy. However, the concept of TPCK and the

Figure 2. 3d view of "theoretical model for teachers' pedagogical change"

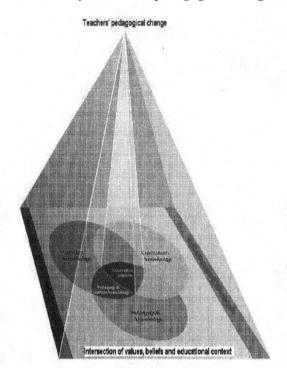

framework proposed applies to all technology and I consider that particular research is required to determine the TPCK for different technologies and their intended pedagogical objectives. I regard the interactive whiteboard as a different pedagogical tool from some other learning technologies in so far as it is a tool that is largely mediated by the teacher. In contrast, if for example a student is undertaking an elearning course or using a webcast, then technology is at the forefront of learning and the student is entirely dependent on how technology frames the learning objectives. In the case of whiteboard technology the teacher is the significant factor in students' learning; the important question is how s/he integrates the technology to involve student interaction in ways that would not otherwise have been possible. I will return to this discussion in relation to IWB technology following an analysis of how I consider IWB practice fits within the pedagogical change model (Figure 1) devised earlier.

EVALUATING IWB PRACTICE

The themes, emerging from analysis of the 33 interviews and observations of classroom practice with the IWB, based on Grounded Theory, were unsurprisingly not entirely in agreement with the model previously presented on general pedagogical change. In particular, differentiating teacher knowledge in whiteboard practice between PK, CK, PCK and Curriculum Knowledge was not straightforward since there is considerable overlap as to which category different elements of practice belong. Consequently, this general theoretical model was used to provide a framework for the analytical themes rather than an attempt to specify how all whiteboard practice slots into PK, CK and PCK. While formalizing the empirical themes it was first considered appropriate to merge Curriculum Knowledge and Content Knowledge (CK) since in the context of whiteboard pedagogy CK requires the necessity to incorporate curriculum knowledge so that teaching is appropriate to the age and ability of the pupils being taught. Second, results reflected the view given earlier that PK is not simply added to CK to create PCK but a teacher reflecting on classroom practice may create his or her own PCK. Consequently, in further discussion Content and Curriculum Knowledge (CCK) is considered as a combined entity in its own right. Similarly PCK was judged to be distinct from PK and CCK since the IWB data suggested that teachers were creating their own PCK often by blending the resource of the whiteboard with their own existing pedagogical practice. The 3 major themes relating to pedagogical change that emerged from empirical evidence subsequent to whiteboard use were:

- Planning, preparation and classroom management: Change in PK
- Selection and use of resources: Change in CCK
- Interactive teaching and understanding children's learning: Change in PCK

PLANNING, PREPARATION AND CLASSROOM MANAGEMENT: CHANGE IN PK

In agreement with Glover and Miller (2001), Smith et al. (2005) and Somekh et al. (2007), I found that the whiteboard ultimately saves time in planning and preparation. Teachers reported that the board gives them "more time to teach". The facility to have materials prepared in advance enables teachers to prepare each lesson "ready to go" rather than spend time writing or drawing diagrams prior to or during the lesson. This capability also makes teaching easier on a minute-by-minute basis which is a consequence of not only having the materials ready beforehand but as cited by teachers, more careful preparation. As one teacher said, "I now know where I'm going next in the lesson" (Cogill, 2008).

Levy (2002) proposes that through the advantage of ICT, teachers are able to share lesson plans more easily. My research evidence suggested that some teachers also share pedagogical ideas to jointly plan their whiteboard lessons and discuss the way classes respond, to consider children's effective learning. It is possible that swapping lesson plans is undertaken purely for efficiency to save additional preparation time, so there appear to be two facets to this dimension of whiteboard use. The first suggests a sharing of pedagogical views which must be of benefit to teachers in changing pedagogical practice. Any advantage gained by just swapping lesson plans depends on how one teacher uses another's lesson; this process might be a stepping stone to self-learning or alternatively a rote "tell me what to do" situation.

The whiteboard may also ease teachers' day-to-day classroom management in other ways: through easier demonstration of concepts and skills; the facility to recap and move between pages so that the class has access to earlier work; drawing on children's own work for learning; or showing a problem on the board before the start of the lesson so that children are immediately occupied. Some teachers feel that the facility to avoid writing too much information down while they are teaching children helps with behavior management. Of equal importance, since the fundamentals of a topic are explained more efficiently if the work is pre-scribed, there may be more time for discussion focusing on effective learning.

In summary, the whiteboard may change PK through generating the potential for more efficient and effective planning and preparation; more time to teach through saving writing time during the lesson; sharing pedagogical views through joint lesson planning; flexible access to work at a later stage and more time for discussion to focus on effective learning. This level of whiteboard practice may create a positive change in teachers' experiences, suggesting that they are learning, with similar positive change reflected in their PK.

SELECTION AND USE OF SOFTWARE RESOURCES: CHANGE IN CCK

Teachers use a wide range of resources with the IWB: the whiteboard's own software, resources they devise themselves, resources from the Internet and interactive software packages. Teachers consider some commercial software resources are not only motivating and exciting but also help children to understand and grasp concepts more easily. Teachers themselves enjoy the learning curve of using new resources since teaching becomes more interesting when they are learning as well. Perhaps not surprisingly, it is those teachers who are more reflective on the content of the software they are experimenting with who enjoy using a wide range of resources to put subject knowledge across.

Nevertheless, over-use of the technology may overwhelm pupils in their learning (Smith et al., 2005). Cogill (2008) found that even good software may result in children becoming bored and unmotivated if overused. More importantly, a very ostentatious presentation may undermine the focus of learning so that children are concentrating on the presentation and waiting for the next dynamic to happen rather than learning. A few teachers may even adopt the whiteboard as a motivating tool for themselves by making the board their own "technology toy" rather than empowering it for children's learning. However, most teachers agree that it is the way software is used and how it is linked to the learning outcomes of the lesson which is significant in teaching practice. Teachers also felt that in the case of large software packages they sometimes required help to understand the learning potential of new resources. Such scrutiny, I argue, indicates a real understanding of the need for relevant whiteboard content which as suggested by McNamara (1991) and Cox et al. (2003) is key to changing CCK.

INTERACTIVITY AND UNDERSTANDING CHILDREN'S LEARNING: CHANGE IN PCK

As Moss et al. (2007) point out, "interactive" does not mean a session of "drag and drop" but requires a link to broader pedagogical aims to enhance children's learning and meaningful verbal interaction. Smith et al. (2005) consider interactivity as reflecting a "socialist, constructivist" view of teaching and learning so that children are enabled through social interaction to (re)construct their own knowledge. Cogill (2008) suggests that: "Interactive teaching involves children in higher level thinking skills and meaningful discussion to promote learning" (p. 129). According to Smith et al. (2005), the whiteboard used with appropriate resources is expected to make interactive teaching easier. Haldane (2007) found that in the early minutes of a science lesson the IWB provided a powerful linking process between a teacher and his or her pupils through verbal, visual and cognitive interaction with images and content displayed on the whiteboard. The technological facility to manipulate images and show animation, similarly triggered interactive learning amongst teachers and pupils. My evidence reflects this view and found that teachers exploit the IWB for interactive learning by:

1. Encouraging children to reflect and think about their learning through the use of appropriate learning software;
2. Enabling children to sometimes become part of the teaching process by leading from the board;
3. Initiating work with the whole class in a creative collaborative process, for example by creating a poem or a diagram;
4. Showing and amending children's own work with the whole class, to foster their learning;
5. Brainstorming a topic and categorizing children's ideas in an ordered way so that

children can see the process of classification unfolding;

6. Enabling children to predict outcomes and then test these predictions;

7. Enabling collaborative problem-solving through the use of appropriate software in which the outcome is either not straightforward, or multi-faceted;

8. Allowing children to prepare resources themselves for presentation to the whole class;

9. Accessing images that children may use to create a story or investigate the meaning of the image;

10. Enabling children's understanding through the use of diagrams or text which may be manipulated or changed in response to children's ideas, potentially creating excitement and a "sense of theatre" (Davison & Pratt, 2003) in the classroom.

This list of 10 possible ways to create an interactive lesson is not definitive nor is it only relevant to whiteboard use. In the hands of a good teacher many other teaching techniques may become "interactive." It is also unlikely that a teacher will act interactively with the whiteboard at every lesson, not least because there are some learning activities which do not necessarily lend themselves to this way of learning. Interactive teaching is, I argue, a mode of teaching which is attributable to a teacher rather than the whiteboard. In other words those teachers who have previously addressed their teaching interactively will reap the benefits of the whiteboard in being able to further these particular teaching skills through greater access to interactive resources. However, for those teachers who have not previously undertaken this style of interactive teaching the introduction of the whiteboard as a teaching tool may provide the catalyst to further these skills. The whiteboard is a tool for teachers but the best whiteboard practice, as some teachers suggest, "enables children to share the whiteboard" so that they become active participants in their learning.

AN INFORMED MODEL FOR TEACHERS' PEDAGOGICAL CHANGE SUBSEQUENT TO IWB INTERVENTION

Through incorporating the empirical results from IWB research with the theoretical model of general pedagogical change discussed earlier (Figure 1), the revised informed model given below was conceived to illustrate potential change in pedagogy subsequent to whiteboard use.

There are several features of this informed model to discuss:

1. At the heart of the model lies the fusion of teacher knowledge that contributes to whiteboard practice stemming from both old and new Pedagogical Knowledge (PK), Content and Curriculum Knowledge (CCK) and Pedagogical Content Knowledge (PCK). I consider that this fusion is core in contributing to change in pedagogical practice and consequently within this informed model the fusion is highlighted to show the particular emphasis of this effect.

2. The background factors: teachers' beliefs, experiences and educational context are factors which influence teachers' learning. However, I found no evidence to suggest that after just one year of whiteboard use teachers had substantially changed their beliefs in how children learn. This is not surprising since such influences are likely to change slowly. Similarly, it may be assumed that within the same time frame the educational context of teaching experience remains substantially static. As these factors appeared to have a less direct influence on pedagogical change over one year, within the informed model (Figure

3) the "flow of learning" lines relating to these background factors are emphasized less strongly than those stemming from the fusion of pedagogical knowledge.

3. Earlier I discussed the struts in the model of general pedagogy as suggesting a constant two-way flow between elements at the base of the pyramid and teachers' pedagogical change. In effect these struts represent teachers' learning. While examining the empirical data I found one teacher, a telling case, who despite having similar beliefs and experience to others and who was working in the same educational context, had developed excellent whiteboard practice while others had not. This particular teacher was very reflective on her practice, enthusiastic to try out new approaches and keen to integrate the whiteboard with her former way of teaching. I concluded that she was a "learning teacher" and that it is a teacher's learning disposition that determines the rate of flow between the fusion of knowledge at the base of the pyramid and change in pedagogy resulting from whiteboard practice situated at the vertex. In contrast a poor learning disposition results in little change in this fusion of knowledge, resulting in minimal change in pedagogical practice. In the "telling case" of this teacher, a positive learning disposition led to a change in pedagogy regardless of external influences such as educational context and her beliefs and previous experience.

4. It remains to address the question of how Figure 3: "The informed model of change and influences on whiteboard pedagogy" is related Technological Pedagogical Content Knowledge (TPCK). Figure 3 considers the affordances of the whiteboard in relation to PK CCK and PCK and how these may affect a teacher's pedagogical practice. In doing so this IWB model has particular relevance for whiteboard use since it has drilled deeply into understanding the pedagogy of IWB

technology. In contrast the Technological Pedagogical Content Knowledge (TPCK) framework is general in nature in so far as it defines the need for understanding the technology relating to PK, CK and PCK but does not define the practice that represents this knowledge for any particular technology, especially IWB technology. The informed IWB model (Figure 3) may be construed as lying at the heart of the TPCK framework in relation to the IWB. What I consider important is the fusion or blending of PK, CCK and PCK with IWB technological knowledge, and this blending gives rise to particular whiteboard pedagogy relating to PK, CCK and PCK. Nevertheless I agree with Mishra and Koehler (2006) that the integration of technology with pedagogy is dynamic in its nature, hence teachers need to have both ownership of the technology they are using and also be aware of its diverse and ever-changing potential.

Assuming that teachers adopting the whiteboard have a basic knowledge of ICT, I propose that this informed model of change with a base derived from pedagogical theory (Figure 3) is appropriate to the examination of whiteboard pedagogical practice. However, any model may never be uniformly applied and teachers do not change consistently, so in the next section levels of pedagogical change are considered to give further insight into teachers' whiteboard practice.

LEVELS OF CHANGE IN PEDAGOGY AS A CONSEQUENCE OF WHITEBOARD USE

Hodgkinson-Williams (2005) proposes that it is necessary to differentiate between "re-presentational" and "generative" use of ICT, terms attributed to Hokanson and Hooper (2000). Re-presentational use is described as the re-pre-

Figure 3. Informed model of change and influences on whiteboard pedagogy incorporating empirical evidence on whiteboard practice

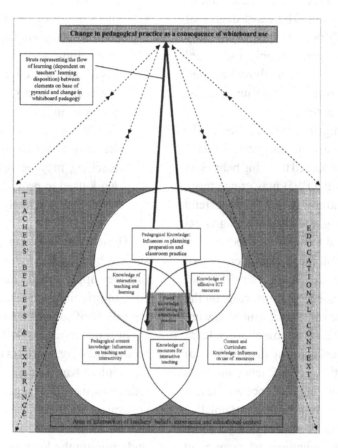

sentation or reproduction of information whereas generative use is explained as having the "capability to generate thought." This distinction appears to fit well with views expressed by McCormick and Scrimshaw (2001) on how ICT may create change in teaching practice. They consider that teachers' existing practice in using ICT may alter by becoming more efficient or effective, extended in some new way or transformed from their earlier practices. I regard making practice more efficient in the context of the whiteboard as closely related to re-presenting teaching. However, use of the IWB to re-present teaching implies not only the facility to create a clear presentation of text and images but also the facility to plan lessons differently and use a wider range of resources. Extending or transforming teaching practice on the other hand

suggests "generative" use or furthering children's higher order discussion and thinking skills through interactive teaching. Nonetheless, these terms need yet further clarification. I have not made use of the term "effective practice" in describing levels of change as my empirical evidence suggests that this is not necessarily synonymous with "efficient practice" in the context of whiteboard practice. Teachers may be working efficiently for themselves, for example, by easing lesson planning but not necessarily effectively for children's learning. Similarly what is meant by "transformed" requires more clarification. It could be argued that teachers' practice can never be "transformed" in so far as a learning teacher is always transforming through responding to changes in circumstance. What is meant by "transforming" in this context is that teachers change their conceptions of teaching and learning to some degree through their use of the interactive whiteboard. The exact degree of change is extremely difficult to quantify for any particular teacher and perhaps only individual teachers themselves can start to analyze the extent of change within their own conceptual understanding of teaching and learning.

Through examining the case studies of 11 teachers' over the course of one year, Table 2 presents a range of whiteboard teaching behaviors that characterize how the IWB may create more efficient pedagogy, and how the IWB may extend or help in transforming a teacher's pedagogical practice and associated teacher knowledge.

I do not suggest that these characteristics of IWB practice are comprehensive, nor do I consider them easily assessed. So much rests on the individual teacher, the context in which they are teaching, a teacher's beliefs in how children learn and his or her individual learning disposition. Of equal importance is the way a teacher interacts with children in class during the process of learning. Nevertheless, by examining the IWB practice of 11 teachers over the course of one year and relating their teaching behaviors to changes in PK, CCK and PCK, Table 2 is given as an initial tool to enable teachers to assess their own IWB practice.

CONCLUSION

The purpose of this chapter is to present a framework for IWB pedagogy based on pedagogical theory and empirical evidence from IWB practice. The model presents whiteboard teaching practices within a framework of Pedagogical Knowledge (PK), Content and Curriculum Knowledge (CCK) and Pedagogical Content Knowledge (PCK). In relation to PK, the IWB has the potential to create change in teaching practice through:

- more efficient and effective lesson preparation;
- the sharing of pedagogical views through joint lesson planning between teachers;
- more time to teach, since writing time saved during the lesson creates greater opportunity to focus on discussion for effective learning;
- flexible access to previous teaching and learning at a later stage so that aspects of teaching may be revisited or pupils' own work used to provide examples of learning for debate and analysis.

These IWB teaching practices apply across subject boundaries and consequently I contend that they apply specifically to PK i.e. the knowledge of principles and strategies of how to teach regardless of subject matter.

In order to assess software resources for effective learning, teachers need good Content and Curriculum Knowledge (CCK) prior to IWB use. Otherwise there is a danger that teachers may adopt software which provides ostentatious presentation but is insubstantial in learning content, thus undermining the learning process. Nevertheless, the IWB presents opportunities to teachers to present learning in a different way; through resources devised by teachers themselves, the board's own software, the Internet, and interactive software packages. In adopting and adapting a range of software resources, teachers are empowered to learn themselves which makes teaching more interesting, and potentially increases teachers' CCK. The use of new resources also provides the challenge of revisiting the learning outcomes of a lesson, and requires teachers to reflect on any new teaching materials adopted to ensure that they both motivate pupils and improve their learning.

Pedagogical Content Knowledge (PCK) is the knowledge of how to teach within a particular subject area so that teaching engages pupils, interests them and enables their understanding. Change in

Table 2. Whiteboard teaching behaviors that may characterize a change in pedagogical practice and a teacher's knowledge (Cogill, 2008)

Efficient whiteboard pedagogy	Extending whiteboard pedagogy	Transforming whiteboard pedagogy
Pedagogical Knowledge: Planning, preparation and classroom management		
sharing lesson plans	adapting others' resources	sharing pedagogy with teachers
preparing lessons in advance	spontaneously answering children's questions	sharing teaching and learning with children
saving writing time in a lesson	using saved writing time for effective discussion	
accessing previous teaching	accessing pupils' learning	
		integrating the board with a teacher's own teaching style effectively
Content and Curriculum Knowledge: Use of resources		
using images and video	searching for a range of appropriate resources	demonstrating more ways of teaching the same thing
using shapes and models from board's software	using tools on the board appropriately	using the board's tools in an innovative way to improve learning
use of some software resources	using software for a specific purpose	teachers learning themselves through use of new resources
		enabling collaborative problem solving through appropriate software
Pedagogical Content Knowledge: Children's learning and interactivity		
children using the board to answer specific questions	children using the board to illustrate their learning	awareness of other children's attention if a child is using the board and extending learning to the whole class
	using the facility to recap on earlier work	children regularly learning from their own work through the IWB
	facilitating relevant discussion	problem solving which involves the whole class
		encouraging children to think and reflect
		whole class creative, collaborative work using the IWB to produce an end product
		enabling children to present results of their own research
		allowing children to become 'a bit of a teacher' through leading from the board

PCK as a consequence of IWB use may lead to interactive teaching since the whiteboard has the potential to provide a linking process or catalyst between teachers and learners. The facility the whiteboard presents for whole class interaction though the manipulation of text and images, the presentation of animation, the potential for whole class activities with a creative outcome, and whole class problem solving, creates greater opportunity for whole class cognitive interaction.

This analysis of IWB practice has implications for teachers' professional development. Teachers need to be informed of what is considered good whiteboard pedagogy and what is mediocre teaching. I suggest that the characteristics noted as extending and transforming practice have value as a useful base for teachers' own self-assessment in their IWB practice. In agreement with Moss et al. (2007) and Smith et al. (2006) I do not regard the whiteboard as a panacea that will automatically produce better teachers or better teaching and learning, but as use of the IWB increases, it will become increasingly important to identify good practice in IWB pedagogy if teachers are to adapt their existing pedagogy appropriately. ICT skills may remain a barrier to the adoption of successful whiteboard practice. Cogill (2003) suggests that teachers who do not feel confident in ICT need specific training, prior to whiteboard adoption, to ensure that they are secure in their handling of basic skills, for example, file handling, word processing, use of the Internet and use of on-screen icons. It is also apparent that the effective use of ICT resources promotes interactive teaching and learning and is thus a significant aspect of whiteboard pedagogy. Teachers should be encouraged to differentiate between good, mediocre and poor software. Moreover, in using ICT teachers need to be able to apply their knowledge to adopt and adapt appropriate software resources (Cox et al., 2003). In the case of large software packages, training is required to enable teachers to appreciate the extent of these ICT resources and how they can be used in the classroom for high-quality interactive teaching and learning. However, the technology of the whiteboard should not undermine the importance of pedagogical practice when developing IWB skills. As teachers become more confident in their ICT skills, I consider that pedagogical practice encompassing PK, CCK and PCK should move to the forefront of professional development in the use of the IWB.

This chapter puts forward an informed model of IWB pedagogy (Figure 3) based on pedagogical theory and empirical evidence from IWB practice, a model which has implications for further research. The model illustrates through PK, CCK and PCK how change may be created in pedagogical practice and teacher knowledge subsequent to whiteboard use. This model may be just a starting point but it raises issues concerning the need for a theoretical pedagogical framework on which future whiteboard research is based. Equally, one of the buzz words within education at the present time is interactivity. The term interactivity, however, in relation to whiteboard use is sometimes misused or poorly defined. Earlier I attempted to cite whiteboard activities that may promote interactive learning. Rigorous research into interactive learning would help to clarify the issue for teachers, who need transparent "goals" in order to become "interactive teachers."

In summary, I propose that a teacher's whiteboard pedagogical practice results from a complex fusion of old and new Pedagogical Knowledge (PK), Content and Curriculum Knowledge (CCK) and Pedagogical Content Knowledge (PCK) which is influenced by a teacher's beliefs, experience, and the school context in which a teacher is working. If positive influencing factors prevail, the IWB changes teachers' pedagogical practice, since it affects their planning, preparation and classroom management (PK), their selection and use of a wider range of resources (CCK) and their ability to teach for interactive learning (PCK). In an age in which teachers are increasingly proficient in their use of ICT, I suggest that teachers' professional development in whiteboard practice should focus strongly on pedagogical as well as technological skills, if the interactive whiteboard is to create more dynamic classrooms through interactive teaching and learning.

REFERENCES

Alexander, R. (1994). Analysing practice. In J. Bourne (Ed.) (1994). Thinking through primary practice (pp. 16-21). London: Routledge.

Alexander, R. (2003). *Still no pedagogy? Principle, pragmatism and compliance in primary education*. Cambridge, MA: University of Cambridge.

Bruner, J. (1999). Folk pedagogies . In Leach, J., & Moon, B. (Eds.), *Learners and pedagogy* (pp. 4–20). London: PCP.

Cogill, J. (2003). The use of the interactive whiteboard in the primary school: Effects on pedagogy . In *ICT Research Bursaries* (pp. 52–55). London: HMSO.

Cogill, J. (2008). *Primary teachers' interactive whiteboard practice across one year: Changes in pedagogy and influencing factors*. Unpublished doctoral thesis, King's College, London.

Cox, M., Webb, M., Abbott, C., Blakeley, B., Beauchamp, A., & Rhodes, V. (2003). *ICT and pedagogy*. Norwich, UK: HMSO.

Davison, I., & Pratt, D. (2003). An investigation into the visual and kinaesthetic affordances of interactive whiteboards . In *ICT Research Bursaries* (pp. 29–33). London: HMSO.

Glover, D., & Miller, D. (2001). Running with technology: The pedagogic impact of the large-scale introduction of interactive whiteboards in one secondary school. *Journal of Industrial Teacher Education, 10*(3), 257–276.

Haldane, M. (2007). Interactivity and the digital whiteboard: Weaving the fabric of learning. *Learning, Media and Technology, 32*(3), 257–270. doi:10.1080/17439880701511107

Hodgkinson-Williams, C. (2005). Revisiting the concept of ICTs as tools. Paper for ITFORUM. Retrieved January 31, 2009, from http:// it.coe.uga.edu/itforum/paper88/Hodgkinson-Williams-2006.pdf

Hokanson, B., & Hooper, S. (2000). Computers as cognitive media: Examining the potential of computers in education. *Computers in Human Behavior, 16*, 537–552. doi:10.1016/S0747-5632(00)00016-9

Levy, P. (2002). *Interactive whiteboards in teaching and learning*. Sheffield: Sheffield University.

Loveless, A. (2002). Professional development with ICT: Looking beyond the technology. *Journal of information technology for Teacher Education, 2*, 117-121.

McCormick, R., & Scrimshaw, P. (2001). Information and communication technology, knowledge and pedagogy. *Education Communication and Information, 1*, 37–57. doi:10.1080/14636310120048047

Mishra, P., & Koehler, M. (2006). Technological pedagogical content knowledge: A framework for teacher knowledge. *Teachers College Record, 108*(6), 1017–1054. doi:10.1111/j.1467-9620.2006.00684.x

Mishra, P., & Koehler, M. (2009). TCPK – *Technological pedagogical content knowledge*. Retrieved May 1, 2009, from http://tpack.org/

Moss, G., Jewitt, C., Lavacic, R., Armstrong, V., Cardini, A., & Castle, F. (2007). *The interactive whiteboards, pedagogy and pupil performance evaluation: An evaluation of the schools whiteboard expansion (SWE) project*. London: Institute of Education.

Nicholson, A. (1996, September). *Can we reveal the inner world of teachers?* Paper presented at the BERA Conference, University of Lancaster, UK.

Prestage, S., & Perks, P. (2000, September). *Subject knowledge: Developing the fourth sense*. Paper presented at the BERA Conference, Cardiff University, UK.

Shulman, L. (1987). Knowledge and teaching: Foundation of the new reform. *Harvard Educational Review, 57*(1), 61–77.

Smith, H., Higgins, S., Wall, K., & Miller, J. (2005). Interactive whiteboards: Boon or bandwagon. A critical review of the literature . *Journal of Computer Assisted Learning, 21*, 91–101. doi:10.1111/j.1365-2729.2005.00117.x

Somekh, B., Haldane, M., Jones, K., Lewin, C., Steadman, S., Scrimshaw, P., et al. (2007). *Evaluation of the primary schools whiteboard expansion project. Report to the Department for Children, Schools and Families UK*. Retrieved January 31, 2009, from http://partners.becta. org.uk/upload-dir/downloads/page_documents/ research/whiteboards_expansion.pdf

Strauss, A., & Corbin, C. (1998). *Basics of qualitative research: Techniques and procedures for developing Grounded theory* (2nd ed.). Thousand Oaks, CA: Sage.

Watkins, C., & Mortimer, P. (1999). Pedagogy: What do we know? In Mortimer, P. (Ed.), *Understanding pedagogy and its impact on teaching* (pp. 1–19). London: Chapman.

Chapter 12
A New Interactive Whiteboard Pedagogy through Transformative Personal Development

Maureen Haldane
Manchester Metropolitan University, UK

ABSTRACT

This chapter examines how teachers acquire proficiency in the use of interactive whiteboards for the enhancement of whole-class teaching. It suggests that teachers are unlikely to make optimal use of the affordances of the technology through preparatory training alone, and that such an expectation could adversely affect the chances of successful implementation. A phased development of teachers' capability is described during which those with initially limited technical skills can begin to explore the pedagogic potential of the interactive whiteboard and then progressively develop their technical skills in tandem with the evolution of their pedagogy. The author proposes a process of Transformative Personal Development (TPD) within which initial expert interventions demonstrate what is ultimately achievable and set the agenda for a more sustained period of collaborative work-based learning.

INTRODUCTION

The chapter aims to identify and describe the professional development critical success factors that underpin the successful implementation of digital interactive whiteboard technologies. It draws heavily on in-depth, government-commissioned evaluations of IWB implementation in England (Somekh et al., 2007) and Scotland (Pearson et al., 2004) in which findings derived from the analysis

of digitally-recorded observed lessons, and interviews with teachers and pupils. These studies reported significant embedding of the technology, at primary and secondary level respectively, and the emergence of a new pedagogy to which pupils responded positively (see also Haldane, 2005a, 2007, 2008). Others drew attention to less successful implementations (Higgins et al., 2005; Moss et al., 2007) where limited use of the affordances of the technology was made, and consequently, the introduction of IWBs resulted in a disappointing impact in the classroom.

DOI: 10.4018/978-1-61520-715-2.ch012

The relative differences in the effective use of the technology reported by different sets of researchers would appear anomalous and this chapter seeks to address this by analyzing the professional learning experiences of teachers who had acquired proficiency in the use of the technology and were making extensive use of its affordances to the apparent benefit of their pupils.

Drawing on research into sustained and collaborative Continuing Professional Development (CPD) provision, and reporting the common factors in the professional learning process from successful interactive whiteboard implementation, the chapter describes a model of provision, grounded in practice, which those currently seeking to maximize the impact of digital interactive whiteboard installations may wish to consider.

BACKGROUND

The value of active, experiential learning as a means of helping teachers to develop the capability to grasp opportunities for innovation that impact positively on learning, has been a live issue for some time, with contributions such as Elliot's (1991) advocacy of action research being particularly influential. However, there is some evidence that, at an operational level, these influences are less embedded in the provision of CPD than might be expected.

For example, in her qualitative study of strategies for teachers' CPD at the school level Cordingley (2008) observes that:

Although heads and teachers were reported to have rated action research very highly, there is no evidence from this report, or from subsequent whole school evaluations (Ofsted, 2006), studies of teachers perceptions of CPD (Hustler, 2003) or meta-studies such as Bolam and Weindling (2006) that their enthusiasm has influenced CPD policies and practices at the whole school level. (p. 5)

Phillips et al. (2004), in a study undertaken on behalf of nine professional bodies (which included the General Teaching Council for England, the custodian of professional standards for teachers) commented on the frustration of the professional bodies at the preponderance of structured learning inputs as the focus for CPD activity. However, they also noted that the professionals themselves were generally happy with this situation. They valued the opportunity to meet and engage with a variety of other professionals of broadly similar backgrounds but with a different set of experiences. Their objective appeared to be the acquisition of relatively discrete inputs of new information that would broaden and update their professional knowledge.

Dissatisfaction, when expressed, related to the nature of the new information input, either because of limited relevance to their practice or because much of it was not new to them. Although such a model of provision was open to the criticism that it provides only surface learning, participants described the impact of the inputs they received in terms of a deeper level of learning that accrued when theory was put into practice at some subsequent date and in the context of their own working environment. The personalization of learning occurred through a process of internalization as newly acquired knowledge was synthesized with their practice.

The scenarios articulated by participants in the study carried out by Phillips et al. suggest that the CPD to which they were exposed was motivated by an objective of continuous and incremental improvement. Knowledge updating, which involved some sharing of experiences and individual and shared reflection, was usually provided via a specific expert-facilitated event that was typically undertaken away from the workplace.

One problem when attempting to evaluate such an approach is that it can be very difficult to identify any audit trail that would demonstrate impact by clearly linking new knowledge inputs to a measurable change in performance, since the expertise applied to any given task is derived from a substantial relevant knowledge base, much of which was pre-existing. The apparently enduring "training" paradigm for CPD described by Phillips et al. appears inconsistent with the apparent heeding, not just by professional bodies but also by the teachers and head teachers involved in participation decisions, of the advocacy of an action learning approach to CPD (Cordingley, 2008).

One possible explanation for this discrepancy is that the Phillips et al. study focused on a relatively continuous change process, i.e. the incremental acquisition and application of new knowledge by reflective practitioners with a substantial existing knowledge base on which to build. This interpretation appears consistent with a longitudinal study reported by Desimone et al. (2002), involving 207 mathematics and science teachers in five American states, who found that professional development activities which focus on very specific instructional practices can increase the adoption of those practices in the classroom. Well-defined and essentially incremental changes in behavior were the desired learning outcome.

Although many teachers may feel exposed to a plethora of changes, for the most part, it is a series of these continuous and incremental change processes with which they are engaging. Whereas Desimone et al. studied the impact of CPD interventions on specific instructional processes, the use of the IWB can potentially influence most of the pedagogic strategies in the teachers' armory. Teachers making successful use of the IWB (Pearson et al., 2004; Somekh et al., 2007) did not typically develop their capability by means of a single training event, subsequent to which they were able immediately to adapt their practice in the light of newly acquired capability. Rather they engaged, at the workplace in a collaborative CPD process, sustained over an extended period, such as that described by Cordingley et al. (2003, 2005).

Re-analyzing the video record of teacher interviews conducted during the above studies

suggested that the reason for this may lie in the order of magnitude of the change process in which they were engaged. It is a relatively complex process, in that two changes are occurring in tandem: the development of new technical skills and the deployment of such skills to effect changes in pedagogy.

While recognizing that all change involves some element of discontinuity the word "discontinuous" is used here to describe a change process which appears, by its nature, rather more complex in character than the more incremental changes described in, for example, the Desimone et al. study cited above. The alternative descriptor "step change" would be misleading because the change is not effected in a single step, but, as will be discussed in more detail below, is more typically effected over an extended period and through a number of relatively small steps.

THE INTERACTIVE WHITEBOARD: A SIGNIFICANT MEDIATING ARTEFACT FOR WHOLE-CLASS TEACHING

A classroom equipped with an interactive whiteboard looks beguilingly similar to ones equipped with a traditional whiteboard and, given the extent to which we are exposed to new media in our daily lives it is easy to underestimate its potential. Imagine for a moment, Miss Smith, a teacher from the late 19th century transported through time to a 2009 classroom not yet equipped with an IWB.

The socio-cultural changes observed might be somewhat bewildering and the curriculum would seem like something from another planet. Some of the content and concepts might appear so alien that they would be difficult for her to grasp as a learner and would probably prove to be impossible for her to deliver as a teacher. However, explaining the technology in this classroom would take only a matter of minutes. The pens with their own supply of ink and the consequent redundancy of ink-wells, or the use of marker pens on an ordinary whiteboard rather than chalk on a blackboard, would seem less than mystifying. However, take our time-traveling teacher next door to an IWB-equipped room and the technology would seem nothing less than miraculous.

Even from a more sanguine 21st century perspective, the escape of the Internet-connected multimedia computer from the IT suite and its functional fusion with the digital image projector to become an instrument for whole class teaching is a significant development. While retaining the facility for the teacher to write or draw, the IWB also enables these teacher-created symbols to be manipulated and integrated with any multimedia learning object that might be displayed on a computer screen. Software can be controlled directly from the board, by means of either a finger or a peripheral device such as an electronic pen according to the type of IWB used, and existing computer software can be integrated with that designed specifically to take advantage of the affordances of this new medium. This increased functionality offers the IWB user considerable advantages in terms of flexibility and variety compared to the use of a computer plus video projector.

As suggested above, when developing a CPD strategy there are two learning curves that need to be followed in tandem:

1. the acquisition of the technical skills needed for mastery of the IWB's functionality and
2. the development of pedagogy so that the full potential of the IWB's functionality for enhancing teaching and learning is realized.

Working in the mid-1990s and examining the pedagogic potential of technologies such as analogue video (that may now seem somewhat archaic) Kozma (1991, 1994) used Salomon's (1979) key characteristics of a learning medium in order to analyze how various mediating artifacts impact on teaching and learning. Table 1 is an extrapolation of the Salomon/Kozma typol-

ogy to help explain the potential impact of the IWB as a mediating artifact that incorporates the functionality of its various predecessors and, in so doing, becomes a whole that is greater than the sum of its parts.

The inclusion of face-to-face teaching via the mediating artifact of a conventional white board in this extrapolated typology alongside the various more complex technologies is because the IWB changes the relationship between the teacher's input and that which is learned via the technology. Prior to the advent of the IWB, the teacher's interaction with a mediating artifact was a much more sequential process. Pupils might be asked to read a few pages from, for example, the manuscript of a play, watch a video or execute certain tasks on a PC. This would then be followed by a period of teacher input and/or teacher/pupil interaction. With the IWB, the face-to-face input and the interaction with the technology proceed in parallel with a fluidity and fluency not possible with previous mediating artifacts. In addition, teachers (or pupils) can still write on the board but there is the extra affordance of being able to superimpose the annotation over whatever image is displayed and to choose to delete, edit or save it.

Of the various media characteristics identified in the Salomon/Kozma typology, cognitive pace and stability are the two which might help explain why the IWB, as a fusion of a number of existing technologies, can be regarded as a discontinuous, as opposed to an evolutionary, change.

Perhaps the most striking illustration of the potential impact of the IWB in terms of cognitive pace lies in the fluency of presentation. When using a conventional white board, the time taken for a teacher to construct a diagram may provide an opportunity for attention to wander and the quality of the graphic produced will be a function both of the teacher's artistic capability and the relative haste with which it is constructed in order to keep the lesson flowing. With the IWB, a click is all that is required to bring up a prepared graphic of a quality more conducive to grasping its sig-

Table 1. Comparison of the key characteristics of learning media

Salomon's 3 Key Characteristics of a Medium	Books [1]	TV/Video [1]	Computers [1]	Conventional white board [2] (using face-to- face teaching strategies)	IWB [2] (a fusion of all existing technologies)
Technology	stable	transient	potential to be highly stable	transient	stability or transience of each "learning object" is controlled by the teacher
Symbol Systems	text, pictures, graphics	simultaneous presentations of visual and auditory symbols	text, graphics, animation, motion video, sound presented in a variety of combinations	words (written and spoken) teacher-generated graphics gesture, body language, tone of voice	combinations of the technologies, the symbol systems and the teacher's interpersonal communication skills come together to support learning
Processing Capabilities	reading	watching and listening	information and procedural processing	reading, watching listening + pupil/teacher interaction	reading, watching listening + pupil interaction with the technology (both physical and cognitive)
Kozma's Notion of Learner Control and Pace	cognitive pace controlled by the learner	cognitive pace not controlled by the learner	cognitive pace controlled by the learner	cognitive pace controlled by the teacher including interaction with learners	cognitive pace controlled by the teacher including pupil/teacher and pupil/ technology interactions

[1]Kozma's (1994) terminology; [2] Author's interpretation of Salomon (1979) descriptors

nificance, which the teacher can begin explaining immediately without the distraction of trying to focus on drawing it carefully. When using an IWB another click can take teacher and learners instantly to a new learning object such as a video clip or a relevant website. The navigational power of the medium is such that the switch from one learning object to the next may be part of the lesson plan or simply an ad hoc response to learner curiosity or spontaneous interaction with the pupils. When compared to a simple video projection of a computer screen, the greater presentational fluency achievable by manipulating the computer via the IWB, the ease of annotation via the electronic pen and other functionalities unique to the IWB, can be quite striking.

Stability and cognitive pace are also relevant when interpreting the impact of various media using constructivist models of learning. When using a stable medium, such as a book, it is the reader's choice whether or not s/he should dwell on the more difficult passages, or perhaps skip back to earlier sections so that a new concept or piece of

information can build on something learned from previous pages. With an IWB, any multimedia object that the teacher chooses to retain is stable. Some objects, such as annotations, either made by the teacher as part of their explanation or in response to a request for clarification arising from pupil interaction, may be retained for revisiting later in the lesson or retained for future use when next the topic is presented, perhaps as a reminder of points that may need particularly careful explanation. The teacher can also choose to retain learners' annotations and use certain saved pages as part of the introduction to subsequent lessons. Where this has been the done, pupils have said that they find it easier to reconnect with previous lessons; "we remember what was being said when we see the bits that we put on the board" commented one eleven-year old pupil (with animated support from his fellow interviewees) during interviews conducted by the author.

The presentational fluency of the medium, and the time saved by not having to write or draw on a conventional white board, may also create more space within the lesson for interaction with pupils to judge learning effectiveness and, if necessary, to find and display information not visible on the board at the time a question is posed.

As discussed above, Kozma (1994) believed the stability of a medium to be a key factor in the learning process. In particular, he considered that the ability to engage in serial, sequential back and forth processing between specific information in a piece of text or between the components of pictures or diagrams, helped to facilitate the construction and elaboration of mental models.

Stability, in the context of an IWB, is a richer attribute than in a single medium, such as text, where the process essentially involves visual scanning and re-scanning parts of a page or pages. When presenting different fragments of information that are intended to be utilized for constructing the learners' mental models the teacher need not rely on the pupils directing their attention to a specific area within a static display. Zooming, color highlighting, dragging fragments of information in order to re-arrange what is displayed or introducing an additional graphical element are among the many affordances that enable attention to be drawn to those "cognitive keys" that help to embed new fragments of knowledge within a learner's mental model.

Where a particular concept may be difficult to grasp, teachers who have no IWB available might offer alternative examples or alternative means of explanation in order to help foster understanding. When using an IWB, the ease with which alternative learning objects can be introduced at the click of a mouse can provide a powerful augmentation of the teacher's explanation.

Kennewell (2005), observing lessons in schools where the technology had been installed but was not yet optimally utilized, found that interactivity was largely confined to pupils responding verbally to teachers' questions, in much the same way as interaction might occur in a class not equipped with the technology. There were also occasions where one pupil would manipulate the technol-

ogy while the rest of the class were apparently passive observers.

Observing and subsequently analyzing digital video recordings of lessons in schools where the technology was more embedded, Haldane (2007) found teachers would often interact verbally while simultaneously manipulating the technology and capturing, by means of annotations, the outcomes of group discourse. Pupils would also be invited to manipulate the technology directly, for example correcting deliberate mistakes, filling in blanks, using "drag and drop" or participating in a simple mini-quiz. Pupil interviews suggested that those observing their peers' efforts were not entirely passive, but remained engaged with the IWB, curious as to the chosen pupil's answer or thinking through how they would have responded in the same situation. An important element of this cognitive interaction, according to pupils' views, is observing the teacher's responses to what is being manipulated on the board; teacher affirmation being conveyed, not only via verbal and non-verbal communication, but also by what s/he chooses to save or change.

In addition to becoming accustomed to utilizing the presentational fluency of the medium to the best advantage of learners, its inherent stability and navigational power enable more experienced users to take advantage of a number of tools at their disposal. These would include presentational alternatives to PowerPoint that are specifically designed with the affordances of the IWB in mind as well as authoring tools for the creation of graphics, animations or simple interactive assessments.

Bruner (1973) suggests that meaning and experiences are ordered and structured by building on a learner's cognitive models (schema) upon which a learner is able to construct unique new ideas and meanings beyond the information that s/he was initially given. Although building on existing teaching and computer literacy capabilities, the relative complexity of the process outlined above may indicate a more sustained period of competence development than could be afforded by a simple two-step CPD process, comprising participation in a training event and then applying the acquired learning at the workplace. A more phased approach to professional development that allows teachers initially to exploit some of the affordances of the technology, and adjust their pedagogy accordingly before progressing further towards full proficiency is examined below.

DEVELOPING IWB SKILLS AND PEDAGOGY

Optimal deployment of IWB affordances for the enhancement of teaching and learning requires the participating teacher to address two elements of competence development simultaneously: the technical skills necessary to manipulate the IWB toolkit fluently, and the evolution of a new pedagogy. Evaluations of successful implementations in the UK (Pearson et al., 2004; Somekh et al., 2007) identified a relatively sustained learning process as suggested above.

The Somekh report was an evaluation of the English Primary Schools Whiteboard Expansion (PSWE) project. Government funding was provided between 2003 and 2004 to support the acquisition and use of interactive whiteboards in primary schools within 21 English Local Education Authorities. The Pearson Report was an evaluation for the Scottish Executive of the impact of IWBs in a new-build secondary school which had been fully equipped with IWBs in every classroom. As a member of both these research teams, the author also had the opportunity to prepare more detailed case studies of four schools (one inner city, one suburban, one in a small market town and one village school in a rural area) participating in the PSWE initiative and to examine very closely the process of teachers' competence development (Haldane, 2008).

In the Scottish IWB evaluation, six teachers agreed to have their lessons observed and digitally recorded so that detailed questions about their IWB usage within their lesson, alongside more general questions concerning their attitudes to the boards, could be asked in subsequent recorded interviews. A further five teachers were interviewed about the boards without a specific lesson being observed. Having sought relevant permissions, additional questions specific to the way teachers acquired IWB skills and how IWBs had affected their pedagogy, were posed. Six recorded focus group discussions were also carried out with pupils from the observed lessons.

In the four PSWE case study schools, two schools received 2x2-day visits and two schools received 3x2-day visits over a two-year period. During each of the 2-day visits, four lessons were observed and recorded using a digital video camera. After each lesson, the teacher was interviewed, as was a small group of pupils who had been involved in that particular lesson; digital audio recordings were made of all the interviews. The same teachers were observed on each visit, in order to address issues of progression in terms of use of the whiteboard. A total of 40x1hour lessons were captured on digital video and 40 teacher and pupil interviews were captured on digital audio recordings.

The value of stability as a characteristic of media used for learning purposes was experienced in a research context during this process. The value for in-depth data analysis of stable digital recordings, both visual and audio, in addition to field notes cannot be overstated. After listening to the teachers' and pupils' responses, it was possible to retrieve the data quickly and to examine and re-examine it with particular reference to identifying significant points on which to focus during subsequent lesson observations. The opportunity subsequently to revisit the record also proved invaluable when analyzing the findings.

When analyzing the data, it was apparent that the process of developing IWB skills and pedagogy was consistent with the findings of Hooper and Reiber (1995), whose research was conducted

Figure 1. A typology of IWB proficiency development

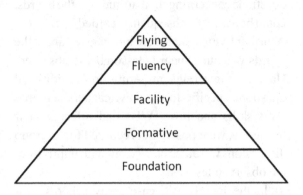

during the adoption of an earlier generation of learning technologies. They observed that teachers tend to progress through a number of reasonably well defined stages in their use of technology, and are able to apply it initially in a somewhat limited way while progressively acquiring the full array of technical skills necessary to realize its full potential.

A similar progressive development of IWB capability was evident, both in the Scottish school and the four PSWE case study schools. Progress is a continuous process, with some individual variation. However, in order to illustrate typical patterns of competence development a 5-phase typology (see Figure 1 and Table 2) was proposed and validated through exposure to experienced IWB users who found it consistent with their own experiences (Somekh et al., 2007; Haldane, 2008).

The expertise of Level 5 practitioners has been likened to a jazz musician's creativity (Haldane, 2005a). They can be seen as exhibiting a level of confidence comparable to the musician's ability to improvise and "go with the flow", deploying a range of notes, scales and rhythms and finding seemingly infinite ways of blending these together. The most expert teachers observed were seen as capable of exhibiting the creativity of a composer

when assembling a lesson and the flair of the conductor when delivering it.

Although external inputs were provided during initial induction, these served a slightly different purpose than that described by respondents to the Phillips (2004) study cited above. That research described a process where surface learning is acquired via some relatively discrete learning event but the knowledge acquired is grasped sufficiently to be applied directly by the learner at their workplace and deeper learning is accomplished through implementation. In the IWB implementations which led to the formulation of the above typology, external expert inputs were followed by a more sustained period of primarily work-based action research and collaborative learning. Although in some instances further direct external expert interventions were provided, the acquisition of "just in time" support, through collaboration with colleagues and via online learning resources or help facilities, were more commonplace. This is consistent with the sustained and collaborative CPD processes reviewed by Cordingley et al. (2003, 2005) which are examined in more detail below.

TRANSFORMATIVE PERSONAL DEVELOPMENT

The teachers whose observed lessons and interviews led to the construction of the above IWB skills and pedagogy typology were describing a relatively sustained developmental process where mastery of the technology and fluency in its application were acquired over a period of some months of work-based, collaborative learning.

As discussed above, action research and sustained, collaborative, situated learning are widely advocated as elements of good practice in CPD, (e.g. Cordingley et al., 2005; Bolam et al., 2005) although it would appear that, in an IWB context, professional development that is an amalgam of

Table 2. IWB proficiency level descriptors

Foundation (Level 1)
At this level teachers are using the interactive whiteboard primarily as a presentation/projection tool for PowerPoint, videos etc. They are most frequently positioned next to the computer itself, using the mouse and keystrokes to manipulate what is seen. They may make forays to the board to write with the electronic pen but if an old whiteboard is still in situ, or a flip chart is available, they are likely to utilize these.
Formative (Level 2)
At this level, teachers are working predominantly from the board, operating the computer functions via the board and beginning to make more use of the simpler IWB functionalities such as the electronic pen and erasing tool. With growing confidence, they are beginning to have interactions with pupils based around board-specific functions and, if useful and appropriate, inviting pupils to utilize the board directly. They are likely to progress to and beyond this level more quickly if no old board or flipchart is available.
Facility (Level 3)
At this level teachers have mastered all the additional functionalities available via the interactive whiteboard and are beginning to use them with greater frequency and facility. They have begun the process of adapting/creating resources and content that utilize, and take specific advantage of, the unique characteristics of the whiteboard. This would include using software tools specifically created for this purpose such as ACTIVstudio for Promethean boards. They are confident with the technology and tools. They feel pleased with how they have creatively adapted and extrapolated their established pedagogy and may feel that they have reached the highest level of IWB capability.
Fluency (Level 4)
At this level teachers find that there are still some new horizons to explore. They continue to broaden their repertoire of tools and techniques and experiment with the unique pedagogic potential of the IWB using high levels of creativity. They are making significant use of functionality such as hyperlinks. They are becoming "hunter-gathers", actively seeking out and harvesting new ideas, new content, new useful Internet sites etc.
Flying (Level 5)
At this level teachers are true virtuoso performers with a wide repertoire of tools techniques and pupil interactions. Their lessons are characterized by the variety of techniques deployed, the fluency with which they move between them and high levels of interaction with pupils. Within well-planned and well-structured sessions they also demonstrate the confidence and ability to adapt and improvise in response to students' signs of interest or difficulty.

all these elements may be a critical success factor. However, some teachers' descriptions of the IWB CPD provision offered to them suggested that it was primarily focused on a training intervention, apparently predicated on the assumption that, on completion, participants would emerge fully equipped with the knowledge and skills necessary to utilize the technology effectively in the classroom. Where there was such an expectation, the subsequent sustained period of collaborative experiential learning was sometimes adopted later at the school level when the actual outcome from initial training did not achieve the desired and expected outcome of being able to deploy all the functionalities of the technology on conclusion of the training input.

This more sustained process appears qualitatively somewhat different from the typical CPD experience described by the participants in the Phillips et al. (2004) study where an external expert source provides some relatively discrete new information for professional updating purposes that is absorbed by the learner and utilized as applicable. The author has found it helpful to use the term "Transformative Personal Development" to distinguish that which appears appropriate in contexts such as IWB implementation from the CPD provision with which teachers may be familiar in other contexts. The term "Personal" was chosen to reflect the personalization of learning that is an implicit element throughout the sustained process of active experimentation at the workplace during which teachers adapt and enhance their own existing pedagogy. The term "Transformative" was chosen because in studies (Pearson et al., 2004; Somekh et al., 2007) where the progressive development of teachers' skills and pedagogy over a sustained period was related to IWB uptake, the impact of the technology on teaching and learning appeared significant both from a teacher and pupil perspective.

During interviews conducted by the author, IWB induction training (which typically begins with a demonstration of the IWB's functionality that requires a high level of technical capability) was likened by one teacher to a magician working through his repertoire of magic tricks. Other teachers suggested that such inductions may prove either daunting or inspirational, the latter outcome being more likely if the performance is both:

a.   described as a demonstration of the "art of the possible" achievable by sustained practice, and
b.   the pedagogic potential of the various affordances of the technology is highlighted and exemplified.

In a broader range of contexts, the impact of CPD processes that are both sustained and collaborative has been examined by Cordingley et al. (2005) by means of an in-depth literature review and analysis. For the purposes of that review, the term "collaborative CPD" referred to programs where there were specific plans for the encouragement and enablement of shared learning and support in which at least two teacher colleagues were engaged. By contrast, the term "individually oriented CPD" was used to describe programs where no such provision had been made. From a sift of 5,500 titles and abstracts and 223 full text reports, 81 studies were identified as relevant to the focus of their study of which 26 were deemed to relate to "individually oriented CPD" and 55 were deemed to focus on "collaborative CPD". Their findings from this literature review reinforced

those from a similar earlier study (Cordingley et al., 2003) which suggested that:

a.   "collaborative CPD" has a positive impact in effecting changes in teaching and learning
b.   there is a relatively low degree of pupil impact and limited evidence of influence on teacher or pupil change found in the studies of "individually oriented CPD".

The use of school-based collaborative learning as a cornerstone of professional development processes is also advocated by Bolam et al. (2005) who propose that the school should seek to function as a learning organization; a "professional learning community" which they define as having the capacity to: "promote and sustain the learning of all professionals in the school community with the collective purpose of enhancing pupil learning" (p iii).

A synthesis and summary of the findings of Phillips et al. (2004), Cordingley et al. (2005) and Bolam et al. (2005) would suggest that:

• Initial external inputs may be absorbed in the first instance at a surface level of learning
• External expert inputs may be delivered on or off-site, although where practicable the former is desirable
• Reflective processes are deployed in order to personalize learning to the context of each participant
• The skills of the teacher as a reflexive practitioner are harnessed in order to embed the learning at a deeper level during the course of its practical application
• A sustained period of collaborative work-based learning has a more positive impact than similar individually oriented provision.

It is not the purpose of this chapter to argue the extent to which sustained and collaborative work-based learning with an action research component could, or should in other circumstances, displace those models of CPD provision where the principal focus is an external expert input such as might be acquired through a short taught course.

However, one obvious factor that differentiates professional development in the use of the IWB from many other CPD experiences, is the fact that there is a significant mediating artifact involved, the affordances of which need to be mastered before they can be fully utilized in order to impact positively on teaching and learning. Previous experience (Hooper & Reiber, 1995) suggests that a more sustained period of professional learning was needed in similar circumstances in the past, and, with new mediating artifacts such as hand-held learner response devices beginning to be deployed, and with new types of physical and virtual learning space being utilized, a similar approach may be desirable in future.

For this reason Transformative Personal Development (TPD) is proposed as a convenient shorthand for the type of professional learning provision suited to such circumstances (see Table 3).

THE IMPORTANCE OF CONSISTENCY OF ACCESS TO THE TECHNOLOGY

The process of achieving excellence in IWB-mediated teaching is somewhat analogous to that of learning to drive a car where the development of skills in manipulating the controls of the vehicle proceeds in tandem with the development of the "road sense" that is also required in order to pass a driving test. In much the same way that a learner-driver is unlikely to develop competence without regular access to a car, likewise teachers' IWB competence is unlikely to flourish without regular access to the mediating artifact itself. However, few schools have the opportunity to equip all rooms with IWBs concurrently and

many have made a limited purchase of one or two boards in the first instance with a view to a rolling programme of installation.

Following the provision of IWB induction training for a group of over 90 secondary level Initial Teacher Training students feedback was elicited on the extent to which they were able to develop their capabilities during a subsequent period of practical teaching experience in schools.

The students reported that in partially equipped secondary schools typical timetabling procedures where both teachers and their students were allocated to a number of different rooms during each working day and each working week, resulted in intermittent and often infrequent access to the technology. Fragmented access militated against competence development by denying opportunities to develop and consolidate new skills and this in turn undermined the motivation to prepare lessons that would make extensive use of the affordances of the IWB (Haldane, 2008). Instances were reported both of students and teachers who had initially been very enthusiastic about the potential of the technology, becoming de-motivated to the point of disillusionment and negativity. This relative lack of consistent access could explain some of the discrepancies between the levels of impact of IWBs in secondary schools (e.g. Moss et al., 2007).

The highly positive feedback on the impact of the IWB from pupils and teachers in the Scottish secondary school that had installations in every classrooms (Pearson et al., 2004) would tend to support the proposition that the less consistent impact sometimes reported at secondary level is not attributable to the IWB being less suited to teaching older pupils but to more mundane logistical issues. In the school that was the subject of the Pearson Report teachers were given laptops so that whatever room they found themselves in all their resources and lesson plans for using the IWB were readily to hand thus further easing the simple practical difficulties encountered by teachers who move around from room to room.

Table 3. Circumstances where a transformative professional development solution is appropriate

CPD		TPD
Emphasis on enhancing capability within an essentially stable or incrementally modified context.	Context (Technology, Learning Environment [physical or virtual], Learning Management)	Emphasis on developing the capability to take full advantage of a distinctively changing context e.g. a new mediating artifact or new learning environment.
New knowledge input plus sharing of current experiences and shared reflection is delivered within the context of an expert-led programme.	Knowledge Construction	After expert-led induction, substantial situated/experiential learning subsequently takes place at the workplace, incrementally over a period, and ideally involving significant collaborative learning alongside colleagues
New Knowledge is acquired which is directly applicable on completion of training	Application of New Knowledge	The construction and application of knowledge occurs simultaneously at the workplace over a period
Continuous Change: Intended Performance Improvements are directed toward excellence as defined by current best practice and/or preparation for new roles and responsibilities.	Change Process	Discontinuous Change: Learning is directed toward excellence in new practice. Discovering/understanding the "art of the possible" may be part of the learning process.

In the English primary schools participating in the Somekh et al. (2007) IWB impact evaluation, classes typically remained in the same room with the same teacher for all or most of the working week. Thus, once their rooms were equipped, each teacher had continuous access to the technology. Lewin et al. (in press) suggest that the more intimate atmosphere of the primary school staff room, typically smaller than its secondary equivalent, may be more conducive to the sharing of experiences, hints and tips, thus enabling collaborative learning to develop more spontaneously.

In secondary, further and higher education, where limited IWB installation is undertaken in the first instance it may seem prudent to design the timetable such that a set of "lead practitioners" have frequent and consistent access to the technology. They are then able to develop and practice their IWB capability to the benefit of their students and with a view to creating a small pool of internal mentors to support those who utilize the technology during subsequent rollout phases.

COLLABORATIVE EXPERIENTIAL LEARNING: EVOLVING A NEW PEDAGOGY WITHIN A "NUCLEAR" COMMUNITY OF PRACTICE (COP)

The in-depth review conducted by Cordingley et al. (2005) and cited above identified within the literature a process of "collaborative CPD" and defined this process as one where specific plans had been developed to encourage and enable shared learning and support.

The government PSWE initiative to support a critical mass of IWB installations in England established just such a structured collaborative professional development process for the local authority officers and consultants who would plan and support the roll-out of the technology to schools (Somekh et al., 2007), but at the school level, the process of sustained collaborative learning that was observed was not specifically planned. In some of its schools, the process adopted exhibited features of a Community of Practice as described by Wenger (1998); in particular, the shared sense of purpose in pursuit of common goals and the informal self-organised nature of the collaboration (as opposed to a more planned and structured collaborative process). The observed practice was consistent with a tentative finding that Cordingley et al. (2005) proposed as a subject for further investigation i.e. that paired or small group collaboration may have greater impact than collaboration within larger groupings.

While there was some sharing of know-how within and beyond institutional boundaries, most of the collaboration observed by the author took place within small (often just two or three), cohesive groups of "close" colleagues (Haldane, 2008). The teachers concerned were "close" (socially) being comfortable about sharing freely their thoughts, ideas, concerns, successes and disappointments and "close" (logistically) with their classrooms being near to each other and/or through sharing of common areas such as staff rooms, dining rooms etc.

If Communities of Practice could be thought of as analogous to extended families, then much of the learning that was taking place in the Scottish school, and more particularly in the four primary case study schools could be likened to a smaller nuclear family. The functioning of these "nuclear" CoPs or "cells" also added support to another tentative conclusion of the Cordingley et al. (2008) study which suggested that active experimentation is a key element in collaborative learning processes that impact positively on the pupil experience. Shared reflections among the members of the nuclear CoPs on their active experimentation with the technology, and the changing pedagogy that it facilitates might then form the subject of dialogue with other colleagues. In most instances, the relationships between the members of the observed nuclear CoPs were relatively symmetrical, in that both/all were at a similar point in their expertise development. However, where the relationship was, at least initially, less symmetrical, for example where one teacher had had the use of the board for longer, or had received more external expert input, the

collaboration still appeared to function effectively and to mutual benefit.

Colleagues would practice together and demonstrate to each other specific functionalities of the IWB and their pedagogic value, thus assembling together a repertoire of IWB skills firmly directed toward improving the student experience. While, when viewed as a whole, this repertoire might appear pedagogically transformative, each individual new skill was invariably an adaptation or extrapolation of a pedagogic device the teacher already used in traditional face-to-face teaching. For example, various functions of the software that "conceal and reveal" words, pictures, or the whole or part of a graphic, provided a number of ways and means of teasing out an answer from the group, offering an engaging alternative to repetitive verbal questioning. While something similar can be achieved by erasing and re-inserting content on a conventional whiteboard, this is a relatively clumsy process which precludes the presentational fluency achievable via the IWB. Similarly, the simple act of writing an incomplete sentence on a conventional white board to prompt interaction with the class can be replaced by a variety of "drag and drop", "conceal-reveal" or multiple choice questions with the option of pupils manipulating the board themselves rather than offering a verbal response. These examples were chosen to illustrate how, even before learning to utilize the more sophisticated affordances of the IWB, teachers, albeit at what might be described as a "surface" level of interaction (Jewitt et al., 2007), are able to focus pupils' attention on those relatively small fragments of knowledge from which more complex constructs can be assembled.

This grounding of new and emergent pedagogy in existing practice, a process the author describes as one of "Pedagogic Exchange" (Haldane, 2007), appears always to start with what one teacher described as "a necessary need-to-know question"; "How can I do on the IWB something similar to but more engaging than what I already do?" The teacher went on to say that this was a necessary

Table 4. IDEA model descriptors

Inquire:	"How can I do this?" A need for skill acquisition and investigation of IWB affordances.
Discover:	often some useful functionality, over and above the simple answer, also emerges.
Explore:	considerations and trials of how the newly discovered skill/s or functionalities of the board can be integrated into existing pedagogy.
Acquire:	new ways of working; synthesizing and embedding IWB skills with an emerging IWB pedagogy.

question because she needed to have a "comfortable starting point". This "inquiry stage" has been commonly described by the vast majority of interviewed IWB novices. Many have gone on to explain that this question is not only used to "get started with the board", but also used as a starting point when they are ready to add new skills to their repertoire. It is the key starting point of a four-stage "IDEA" (Haldane, 2008) sequence of events (see Table 4 and Figure 2) that describes teachers' experiences of mastering some limited sub-set of the affordances of the technology and then gaining some experience of applying it in the classroom before moving on. The "IDEA" model provides a more detailed analysis of the change process through which the evolution of skills and pedagogy described in Figure 1 and Table 2 (above) is affected.

Dialogue between colleagues was common at each stage, often leading to shared experimentation with the same functionalities of the technology. Thus teachers did not tend to move from novice to expert as a consequence of formal induction training, but, stimulated by awareness of the possibilities, progressed step by step, through work-based learning, over a period of time.

When technical skills are managed in a series of personal step-by-step developments, exploring the pedagogic possibilities of each step is far less daunting than feeling that one needs to become a "magician" first in order to leverage improvements in teaching and learning. The "just in time" opportunities to learn provided through "close" (socially and logistically) nuclear CoP relationships enables the "How do I ...?" question to be addressed as it

arises. Depending on when the question arose (and this was quite often when teachers were planning their lessons) some teachers kept "close" to their colleagues via texting, e-mailing or telephoning. In one school, an intranet, that had initially been set up for colleagues to share their IWB resources, was also used by the teachers to support each other during lesson times if a problem arose and leaving their classes was not an option!

In describing their progressive mastery of the technology teachers frequently referred to spending periods of time in a "comfort zone" where their technical skills would not advance significantly. However, what the IDEA model illustrates is that what might seem to be periods of apparent stasis as regards technical skills development, are in fact relatively productive periods where teachers, growing more confident in the skill set that they possess at that point, become engaged in active experimentation, reflecting on the different ways in which they can utilize that skill set for the improvement of the learner experience.

The satisfaction gained from deploying the existing skill set to good effect then provides the incentive to acquire some additional technical skills with a view to exploring the potential for further learning enhancement. Comments made by teachers as regards their interaction with colleagues during this process suggested that the social dynamic helped to stimulate and sustain their progress.

The IDEA model, observed and described above, arose spontaneously within nuclear communities of practice. The teachers concerned were in a situation where there was a high level

Figure 2. The IDEA process: IWB pedagogy emerging over time

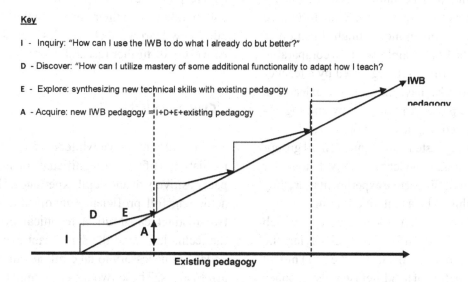

ofmotivation for self-help. They were working on a regular basis in IWB-equipped rooms and their initial induction process had shown them what an expert might be capable of doing, but had not made them fully expert in themselves.

However, when wishing to deploy more actively facilitated interventions, it may be thought helpful to model such an initiative on '"E" above to observed good practice, even if planning an intervention that would be more self-organised in character. Where active support and facilitation is to be offered by a teacher education provider, it is worth noting that a TPD model, as a form of work-based distance learning, lends itself readily to the capture of evidence of achievement for accreditation purposes. A process of collaborative learning, based on active experimentation and shared reflection within nuclear CoPs, can be readily encapsulated in an individual reflective account. Similarly, the generation of IWB lesson plans, and the acquisition or creation of digital learning resources, can form the basis of a portfolio of evidence of successful implementation.

While the support of "close" colleagues plus easy-access to on-line skills tutorials and help facilities are likely to remain the key sources

drawn upon for "just in time" learning, there remains scope for external expert facilitation. Using occasional face-to-face tutorial sessions for performance reviews and personal target setting, can help set the agenda for work-based learning and help keep up momentum and motivation. A more wide-ranging CoP providing opportunities for dialogue with those (other than "close" colleagues) similarly engaged elsewhere could also prove helpful. During a teacher's induction process, the technology, its functionality and the technical skills needed to operate the IWB are likely, understandably, to be the main focus of attention of external expert intervention. However, once teachers have progressed beyond the technical novice stage, it is the pedagogic proficiency of a fluent practitioner that is more inspirational (Haldane, 2005b) and opportunities to observe excellence in practice are valued.

FUTURE RESEARCH DIRECTIONS

Much of the effective collaboration observed by the author was within self-organised nuclear CoPs amongst colleagues with an existing close working relationship and a common need. This raises the question as to how well the Transformative Personal Development model might function in other contexts. For example, would a comparable small action learning set, organised by a teacher education provider, have the same social learning dynamic as a pair or trio of socially and logistically "close" colleagues? Although Cordingley et al. (2005) suggested that planned small groupings of participants can learn effectively together through collaborative active experimentation, they considered this to be a tentative finding.

The author's own work-in-progress, which may make some contribution to clarifying the above issues, involves the use of the TPD model in a pilot evaluation of hand-held learner response devices in a large UK university. Twelve interested pioneers from a cross-section of subject disciplines have access to a pool of 400 devices and are trialing their use in a variety of contexts and environments both on and off campus: from small informal tutor groups to formally presented lectures with 300+ students, from outdoor usage on field trips to large formal committee meetings, from student library inductions to simultaneously occurring cluster meetings with large numbers of external partners.

In addition to "nuclear CoPs" of 2-3 persons, designated by proximity (both discipline and location), other small groupings have tended to form spontaneously, for example, where the nature of particular trials of the devices are similar. The larger CoP of twelve persons meets physically as a group every few weeks, but as a result of some colleagues sharing good ideas, concerns and problems via the blog on a dedicated website, interesting interactions are emerging between the various nuclear CoPs. The members of the larger CoP have been identified as "lead practitioners" should the technology be adopted more widely, either across the university or within particular departments, and they already collaborate on an ad hoc basis, with additional colleagues who have become interested in the potential of hand-held response devices. The nature of nuclear CoP collaborations and their impact on the take-up of other new learning technologies would seem to be worthy of further research.

CONCLUSION

The digital interactive whiteboard is a powerful mediating artifact with significant potential to impact positively on the pupil experience. However, achieving full proficiency involves developing two distinct capabilities; technical mastery of the technology, and the significant evolution of pedagogy necessary to take full advantage of its affordances. These two sets of competences are interdependent and models of CPD provision that provide initial technical skills training, on the assumption that the practical application of these skills will then follow, may therefore prove inappropriate.

Developing technical fluency in parallel with pedagogic fluency in the classroom appears more appropriate than attempting to develop technical and then pedagogic proficiency in serial. While the task of developing full technical proficiency is complex, even for those who already have good ICT literacy, there is evidence that the adaptation of pedagogy can begin when only a relatively limited sub-set of the affordances of the IWB have been mastered.

In order to meet professional learning needs that address the discontinuous change process needed optimally to realize the potential of significant development in learning technology such as the IWB, a process of TPD is proposed. While an initial expert intervention embracing the full functionality of the IWB and illustrating the scope for the enhancement of learner engagement and learning outcomes is seen as part of the TPD process, this intervention is not predicated on the assumption that the majority of participants will, on completion of the intervention, be able to replicate the full repertoire of the expert in question.

Instead, the aim is to provide an aspiration to achieve full proficiency, along with a more basic level of skill, sufficient to launch participants on a sustained period of work-based learning, involving active experimentation with the functionality of the technology and the pedagogic potential that its affordances can help to realize. For implementation of the TPD process, two critical success factors have been identified. Firstly, participants need to be guaranteed access to the technology regularly and frequently in order to hone their technical skills and in order to feel confident that lesson preparation, geared specifically toward utilization of an IWB, is not wasted. Secondly, experience suggests that a sustained process of collaborative learning, based on shared experimentation and reflection within a small group, a "nuclear" community of practice, comprised of, say, just two or three socially and logistically "close" people, provides an effective vehicle for achieving full proficiency.

REFERENCES

Bolam, R., McMahon, A., Stoll, L., Thomas, S., & Wallace, M. (2005). *Creating and sustaining effective professional learning communities.* London: DfES & University of Bristol. Retrieved, February 12, 2009, From http://www.gtce.org.uk/shared/contentlibs/126795/93128/120213/eplc_report.pdf

Bolam, R., & Weidling, D. (2006). *Synthesis of research and evaluation projects concerned with capacity-building through teachers' professional development.* London: GTCE. Retrieved February 12, 2009, From http://www.gtce.org.uk/shared/contentlibs/126795/93128/168771/report.pdf

Cordingley, P. (2008). *Qualitative study of school level strategies for teachers' CPD.* Coventry, UK: Centre for the Use of Research & Evidence in Education.

Cordingley, P., Bell, M., Evans, D., & Firth, A. (2005). *The impact of collaborative CPD on classroom teaching and learning. Review: What do teacher impact data tell us about collaborative CPD?* Retrieved, February 12, 2009, from http://eppi.ioe.ac.uk/cms/LinkClick.aspx?fileticket=trZ0E6NfVy4%3d&tabid=139&mid=960&language=en-US

Cordingley, P., Bell, M., Rundell, B., & Evans, D. (2003). *The impact of collaborative CPD on classroom teaching and learning.* Retrieved, February 12, 2009, from http://eppi.ioe.ac.uk/cms/LinkClick.aspx?fileticket=lvR%2bp8KX%2bRM%3d&tabid=132&mid=758&language=en-US

Desimone, L., Porter, A., Garet, S., Yoon, K., & Birman, B. (2002). Effects of professional development on teacher's instruction: Results from a three-year longitudinal study. *Educational Evaluation and Policy Analysis, 24*(2), 81–112. doi:10.3102/01623737024002081

Elliot, J. (1991). *Action research for educational change. Milton Keynes.* UK: Open University Press.

Haldane, M. (2005a, September). *A typology of interactive whiteboard pedagogies.* Paper presented at the British Educational Research Association Annual Conference, Glamorgan, UK.

Haldane, M. (2005b, September). *Analysing the art of teaching through real-time lesson observation via the medium of the interactive whiteboard.* Paper presented at the British Educational Research Association Annual Conference, Glamorgan, UK.

Haldane, M. (2007). Interactivity and the digital whiteboard: Weaving the fabric of learning. *Journal of Learning Media and Technology, 32*(3), 257–270. doi:10.1080/17439880701511107

Haldane, M. (2008, May). *Developing teachers' effectiveness in the use of interactive whiteboard technology for the enhancement of learning.* Paper presented at IFIP Conference, Charles University, Prague

Higgins, S., Falzon, C., Hall, I., Moseley, D., Smith, F., Smith, H., & Wall, K. (2005). *Embedding ICT in the literacy & numeracy strategies: Final report.* Newcastle, UK: Newcastle University.

Hooper, S., & Reiber, L. P. (1995). Teaching with technology . In Ornstein, A. (Ed.), *Teaching: Theory into practice* (pp. 154–170). Neeham Heights, MA: Allyn & Bacon.

Hustler, D., McNamara, O., Jarvis, J., Londra, M., Campell, A., & Howson, J. (2009). *Teachers' perceptions of continuing professional development.* Nottingham: DfES. Retrieved February 1, 2009, from http://www.dcsf.gov.uk/research/data/uploadfiles/RR429.pdf

Jewitt, C., Moss, G., & Cardini, A. (2007). Pace, interactivity and multimodality in teacher design of texts for IWBs. *Learning, Media and Technology, 32*(3), 302–318. doi:10.1080/17439880701511149

Kennewell, S. (2005, September). *Researching the influence of interactive presentation tools on teachers' pedagogy.* Paper presented at the British Educational Research Association Annual Conference, Glamorgan, UK.

Kozma, R. (1991). Learning with media. *Review of Educational Research, 61,* 179–211.

Kozma, R. (1994). The influence of media on learning: The debate continues. *School Library Media Research, 22*(4). Retrieved, February 12, 2009, From http://www.ala.org/ala/mgrps/divs/aasl/aaslpubsandjournals/slmrb/editorschoiceb/infopower/selectkozmahtml.cfm

Lewin, C., Scrimshaw, P., Somekh, B., & Haldane, M. (in press). The impact of formal and informal professional development opportunities on primary teachers' adoption of interactive whiteboards. *Technology, Pedagogy and Education, 27*(2), 159-170.

Moss, G., Jewitt, C., Levacic, R., Armstrong, V., Cardini, A., & Castle, F. (2007). *The interactive whiteboards, pedagogy and pupil performance evaluation: An evaluation of the schools whiteboard expansion (SWE) project: London Challenge (Research Report RR816).* Annesley, UK: Department for Education and Skills.

Ofsted (2006). *The logical chain: CPD in effective schools.* London: Ofsted.

Pearson, M., Haldane, M., & Somekh, B. (2004). *St. Thomas of Aquin's interactive whiteboard pilot evaluation: Report to the Scottish Executive.* Manchester, UK: Manchester Metropolitan University.

Philips, M., Shane Doheny, S., Hearn, C., & Gilbert, T. (2004). *The impact of continuing professional development.* Bristol, UK: PARN.

Salomon, G. (1979). *Interaction of media, cognition, and learning.* San Francisco: Jossey Bass.

Somekh, B., Haldane, M., Jones, K., Lewin, C., Steadman, S., & Scrimshaw, P. (2007). *Evaluation of the primary schools whiteboard expansion project: Report to the Department for Children, Schools and Families.* Manchester: DCSF.

Vygotsky, L. S. (1978). *Mind in society: The development of higher psychological processes.* Cambridge, MA: Harvard University Press.

Wenger, E. (1998). *Communities of practice: Learning, meaning and identity.* Cambridge, UK: Cambridge University Press.

Chapter 13
First Steps Toward a Model of Interactive Whiteboard Training for Language Teachers

Euline Cutrim Schmid
University of Education Heidelberg, Germany

Estelle Schimmack
Anna-Lindh Primary School, Germany

ABSTRACT

This chapter presents findings of a research project that investigates a model of interactive whiteboard technology training that incorporates a) a "bottom up" approach to teacher professional development in Computer Assisted Language Learning, and b) a pedagogical framework based on a socio-cognitive view of communicative language teaching. The chapter reports on a study conducted with a group of nine English teachers at a secondary school in Germany. Research data were collected via classroom observations, video recordings of IWB training workshops and in depth interviews with the teachers. The research findings shed some light on a) the various competencies that may be required by language teachers who want to exploit the IWB towards a socio-cognitive view of communicative language teaching and b) some principles for the design and implementation of an IWB technology training which would best assist the teachers with achieving this outcome.

INTRODUCTION

Research evidence suggests that the lack of high quality teacher training is a major factor impeding the integration of new technologies in education (Legutke et al., 2007; Hubbard & Levy, 2006). In spite of the growing interest in increasing the amount and quality of in-service technology training programmes, most of the programmes currently provided consist of a series of one-day workshops without appropriate follow-up at the school level. As a result, although teachers tend be become relatively well-informed about the newest approaches in computer assisted learning, they lack a deep understanding of how these new technologies can help them to fulfil their own pedagogical goals. There is thus a need for change in how professional development for technology integration is conducted.

In order to tackle this issue, several innovative approaches to in-service technology training

DOI: 10.4018/978-1-61520-715-2.ch013

have been proposed in the literature. Meskill et al. (2006), for instance, advocate the creation of learning communities through collaboration involving researchers, pre-service and in-service teachers, and Preston et al. (2000) propose the development of online communities of practice as a key means of supporting teaching and action research practices in technology-enhanced classrooms. Most researchers agree on one fact: the training programmes that are most promising are those that support individual teachers' exploration of their current pedagogy, and help identify how the new technologies can support, extend or transform their practice.

This chapter presents research findings of a study that investigates a model of interactive whiteboard technology training that incorporates a) a "bottom up" approach to teacher professional development in CALL, and b) a pedagogical framework based on a socio-cognitive view of communicative language teaching. The project (2008-2011) encompasses seven in-depth longitudinal case studies with English teachers at different levels of technology expertise and teaching experience. Research data are being collected via a variety of ethnographic research instruments, namely classroom observations and field notes, video recordings of school lessons, in-depth interviews and video-triggered reflective dialogues with the teachers. In order to address the purposes of such a study, two research questions were formulated:

1. What are the competencies that English teachers need to acquire in order to use the IWB to develop their practice towards a socio-cognitive view of communicative language teaching?
2. What kind of technical and pedagogical support is mostly needed by them in this process?

This paper discusses findings of a study conducted with a group of nine English teachers at a secondary school in Germany. Three researchers took part in the data gathering, coding and analysis: one university lecturer and two pre-service teachers. In the first stage of the study, we investigated how the teachers in that specific school were using the technology in their English lessons through interviews and classroom observations. In the second stage, we designed and implemented technology training workshops for the English teachers involved in the project. These workshops, which were informed by local pedagogical practice, were designed in response to the specific needs identified in the first stage of the study and offered guidance on how to exploit the potential of IWB technology for English language teaching. This paper presents an in-depth analysis of the process of IWB integration in that context.

THE INTERACTIVE WHITEBOARD IN THE LANGUAGE CLASSROOM

Interactive Whiteboards have become increasingly available in language classrooms across the world. The number of publications dealing with this topic has increased considerably in the last five years. Recent books with focus on ICT and language teaching, which are aimed at practitioners (e.g. Dudeney & Hockly, 2007; Sharma & Barrett, 2007), have dedicated entire sections to the discussion of potential applications of IWB for facilitating classroom language learning. This technology has also stimulated interest in academic research on CALL. A number of recent publications (e.g. Gray et al. 2007, Cutrim Schmid, 2009; Miller & Glover, 2009) present research findings on how the technology is being utilized in language classrooms.

The main pedagogical benefits of adopting IWB technology in the language teaching context are: a) facilitating the integration of new media in the regular language classroom (Cutrim Schmid, 2008a; Gray et al. 2005 and 2007; Walker 2003), b) enhancing the scope of interactivity and learner engagement in the lesson (Cutrim Schmid 2007, 2008b, 2008d; Miller & Glover, 2009), c) supporting the development of so-called "electronic literacies" (Cutrim Schmid, 2009b), and d) meeting the needs of students with diverse learning styles (aural, visual and kinaesthetic) through the use of multiple media (Cutrim Schmid, 2008c; Wall et al., 2004). However, the use of IWBs in language classrooms across the world has also been debated as a potential threat to the principles of communicative language teaching (Cutrim Schmid, 2009a).

Since the advent of communicative language teaching in the 1980s, language teachers have placed increased emphasis on building language proficiency through meaningful use of language in authentic contexts. Current models of second language teaching, as for instance task-based learning (Willis, 1996) and project-based learning (Legutke & Thomas, 1991) view the classroom as a place full of interaction, where learners are actively engaged in negotiating meaning. According to these models, in order to develop communicative competence language learners should have plenty of opportunities to use the target language, mainly through pair and group work, but also in the whole class context. Furthermore, several authors in the CALL field (e.g. Warschauer, 1999) have emphasised the need to exploit technology towards the implementation of a socio-cognitive communicative approach to language teaching, in which the technology is used to support language use in authentic contexts.

A central issue in the concerns expressed by a number of researchers is the question whether the use of IWBs in the language classroom will lead to a return to the whole-class teaching of the last century (Cutrim Schmid, 2009a; Gray et al. 2007; Davies, 2003). Davies (2003), on a website specially aimed for CALL practitioners, advises against the excessive use of presentation technology in the language classroom. He points out: "We live in an age that is obsessed with presentation, and young people have come to expect it, but learning a language is 90% practice following 10% presentation. Good presentation helps, but you learn a language mainly by 'doing it'". Since presentation is usually mainly associated with a transmission model of learning and teacher-centredness, Davies appears to be advising CALL practitioners to avoid using IWB technology as a tool for implementing approaches that do not give the learner enough opportunities to practise the language.

Gray et al. (2007) expressed similar concern regarding IWB use in the language classroom. They conducted research in foreign language IWB-based classrooms in secondary schools in the UK, and their findings have shown a pattern of IWB use, which focused mainly on demonstration by the teacher with little manipulation by the pupils. They concluded that in the context of investigation, teachers' desire to maintain tight control over the linguistic content undermined some of the potential offered by the technology to transform the language classroom. Cutrim Schmid (2008c) also warns against the potential danger of the IWBs being used to support a transmission-oriented teaching approach. Her work analyses the process of multimedia integration in English language classrooms equipped with interactive whiteboards. She points out that since the technology allows a seamless access to multimedia resources, there is "a potential danger of using the technology mainly to give lessons a crisp pace, instead of focusing on making the best pedagogical use of these resources" (p. 1566).

Dudeney (2006) refers to research conducted in British Council centres (Orr, 2006), which reveals that very few of the students surveyed (only three percent) mentioned that they were allowed to use the IWB themselves. He speculates that this might be caused by the fact that teachers with access to IWBs are not receiving the correct training (or not enough of it) and are "finding themselves straight jacketed by the technology, rather like a presenter at a conference can find herself cosseted by PowerPoint" (p. 9). Other studies that investigated teachers' perceptions have also produced similar findings. For example, a survey conducted in a British Council school (Pearson, 2006) shows that although 62.5% of the teachers saw the introduction of IWBs as a positive development, 65% felt that the use of this technology encouraged teacher-centredness.

Since the integration of ICT into pedagogical practice through the use of IWB technology is a relatively new phenomenon in language education, there seems to be a need for the development of models of technology training programmes, which, on the one hand, have a sound theoretical basis, and on the other hand, are informed by the investigation of teachers' pedagogical needs and practice. As the research findings discussed above indicate, special emphasis should be placed on how this technology can be exploited to develop pedagogical practice based on a socio-cognitive view of communicative language teaching, which is in line with the latest developments in language teaching pedagogy.

RESEARCH CONTEXT AND RESEARCH PARTICIPANTS

The School

The school investigated provides high quality teaching in the private sector at primary and secondary levels in Germany. It specializes in education for physically disabled pupils, but it also welcomes children without disabilities. The school is well equipped with information and communication technology hardware. It has more than 300 computers, a high-speed internal network, SMARTBoards in every classroom, and internet access via WLAN. In some classes pupils are also equipped with laptops. The introduction of the IWB technology was part of a larger programme that aimed at encouraging the integration of ICT into the teaching and learning practice in that school. However, the main motivation for

the investment in IWBs by this school was the possibility of saving and printing what was written on the board, as this is very beneficial for the severely handicapped pupils who have problems taking notes or are unable to write. The school used a "total-solution" approach, in which chalkboards in most classrooms were removed and replaced by SMARTBoards.

The decisions regarding the purchase and installation of IWBs in that school were mainly made by the school administration and ICT co-ordinators, who did not implement a structured training programme for their staff. Although the teachers received initial training, in which they were introduced to the basic functions of the IWBs, they were not provided with further training to upgrade their skills. As it will be seen later on, this top-down approach to decision-making and the lack of appropriate technology training had a negative impact on teachers' perceptions of the added value of using the IWB technology in their teaching.

All nine participants are English as a Foreign Language (EFL) teachers at the secondary level; two are male and seven female. They are aged between thirty and fifty years, their teaching experience ranges from three to twenty-five years and their levels of media literacy also varies, ranging from basic to intermediate. All teachers participating in the study employ a communicative approach to language teaching. Since the overall pedagogical framework underlying our research is also based on the main principles of the communicative approach, we thought that this school would suit well as a research site for our project.

Research Process

Initial Interviews

At the initial stage of the project, we conducted in-depth, semi-structured individual interviews with the teachers, which lasted approximately twenty minutes. The questions covered four different areas, namely the teacher profile, the experience with IWB technology, the training and technical support previously received, and the perceived impact of the IWB use on their teaching.

Classroom Observation and Field Notes

The interviews were followed by four weeks of classroom observation. All in all, 37 lessons were observed by the three researchers, and field notes were taken on how and for which pedagogical purposes the IWB was used. These field notes were later used as a resource for the design of the teacher training workshops.

Teacher Training

During the teacher training period five training sessions were held. Each session lasted two hours and they were attended by a small group of the teachers each time. The main researcher wrote field notes after each session. One of the workshops was video recorded and the data fully transcribed for detailed analysis.

Final Interviews

The main objective of these individual interviews was to receive feedback on the training sessions. We wanted to find out what the teachers gained, what they found particularly useful and interesting, and what they would like to suggest for future training sessions. The teachers were also asked whether their attitudes or use of the IWB had changed since the training sessions and about their visions regarding the kind of training they would need in the future. Again, the interviews were recorded and fully transcribed.

Feedback for the Participating Teachers

The project was rounded off by providing the participating teachers with some feedback on our

views regarding how the technology was being used in that school and some recommendations for future development. The teachers also received a CD-ROM with suggestions of activities, parts of the video-recorded workshop, and a handout with ideas on how to further exploit the IWB technology for English teaching.

Data Analysis

Therefore, a range of data-collection instruments and techniques were used in order to attempt to maximize reliability through triangulation. Although all sources of data contributed to the findings, due to space limitations, the data discussed in this article are drawn mainly from interviews with the teachers.

Interactive Whiteboard Use

The teachers were at a very early stage of their professional development as IWB users. Although the school had been using IWBs for about three years at the beginning of the project, their level of IWB technology expertise was still considerably low. Three of them used the IWB only as a substitute for the chalkboard, i.e., as a mere writing space, and four of them also used it as a display medium for showing videos, images, animations and Web sites. All teachers lacked knowledge of the basic IWB software tools, such as: annotation tools, handwriting recognition, spotlight, blind, screen capture, text editor, library of ready-made images/animations, and so on.

When inquired about the impact of the use of IWB technology on their teaching practice, all teachers responded that they did not perceive the IWB as a tool enhancing their teaching considerably. They did point out some benefits, such as: immediate access to the Internet, and seamless access to digital images and audio files, but they also highlighted that the same gains could be achieved with a simple computer-projector setup. Most teachers stated that the main changes that had occurred were related to the learners' use of the technology. They pointed out, for instance, that the availability of this technology raised pupils' motivation to do presentations, since they could draw on a great variety of multimedia resources.

All teachers mentioned the possibility of saving their annotations for future use as the main advantage offered by the technology. However, they also expressed their frustration for having access to an expensive piece of technology without being trained to use it to its full potential. In the initial interviews, they explained that they did not only lack the skills to utilize the technology to its full potential, but they were also "not aware of many of the possible applications" of the technology. Although they believed in its potential, which would justify the enormous financial investment made by their school, they could not imagine how else they could use it. Two teachers stated:

Teacher 1: That's the problem: I cannot imagine what else we could do. If the imagination were there, I would have liked to go into it and profit from it, but so far ... I don't see what else I could do.

Teacher 2: It's like having a Porsche in the backyard and you only drive on the first gear, you think you could do so much with it, but you don't know how to do it.

These findings indicate that the teachers had little knowledge of how to exploit the technology to enhance their practice. Although they had full access to the technology, their use was restricted by what they felt was a low level of skill in using the IWB tools and their limited knowledge of ICT in general. The teachers also pointed out that the "trial and error" approach that they had been using so far was not effective in enhancing their understanding of the technology and its potential applications.

Considering the teachers' interest in exploiting the technology towards a learner-centred approach

to language teaching, this study had a twofold purpose: a) to identify competencies, pedagogical strategies and principles of material design, and b) to conceptualize and implement an IWB technology training programme, which would best assist the teachers with achieving this outcome. In what follows, we will present some research findings, which shed some light on these issues. The first section discusses the main competencies teachers need to develop in order to exploit the potential of the IWB technology, and section two presents and discusses research findings which indicate teachers' preferred ways of acquiring and developing these new competencies.

New Competencies Related to the Use of IWB Technology

Migrating from Old to New Technologies

The research findings indicate that one of the main barriers for the integration of the IWB technology in that school was teachers' reluctance to migrate from old to new technologies. As already pointed out earlier, most teachers used the IWB in much the same way as a traditional blackboard, i.e. to annotate grammar rules, grammar exercises, vocabulary items, and mind maps. They also used the IWB to display worksheets, which were either scanned documents or MS Word files. These worksheets contained mainly fill-in-the-gaps vocabulary or grammar exercises. They were sometimes completed as a whole class activity directly on the board, or pupils were given printed versions to work on individually before annotating their answers on the IWB. However, for these activities, the teachers made very little use of the wide range of multimodal resources provided by the technology, such as special annotation tools (e.g. shapes, lines), the variety of colour, fonts, images, and so on. Therefore, most of the materials projected on the whiteboard followed the same design principles of the print-based resources the teachers used before the installation of IWBs in their classrooms.

As they tried to use the new technology (IWB) in the mode of the old technology (blackboard), the teachers also faced some challenges. For instance, eight teachers mentioned the fact that the whiteboard provided less space for presenting information in comparison to blackboards. According to these teachers, the change from blackboards to whiteboards limited their possibilities of presenting information in the form of mind maps, diagrams, and drawings. In the following interview extract, one teacher comments on this limitation:

Teacher: Well, as a means of the connection to the internet, this is really a very useful device. As a writing system it is not always satisfactory. Because very often you lack room. For instance, you want to do a mind map, a network, and then it's really too small to develop everything you would want to connect. So there are limits to it.

The following teacher expressed the same view. She explained how the blackboard design facilitated the realization of her pedagogical goals, since she could display a complete diagram, vocabulary corner and annotations all at once, without the need to scroll up/down or move to another page.

Teacher: If you're reading a novel and you want to present a board diagram, you want to develop it. The board is too small for that. I really need the blackboard with the vocabulary on one side, the middle part for the main body of the diagram and annotations on the right. And the interactive whiteboard is too small for that. You always have to turn the pages to go on.

Because of the size and layout, the IWB would not support the same kind of display described by the teacher. Later in the interview, the teacher pointed out that turning to another page would not have the same effect, as the "all at once" access, which was supported by the chalkboard, provided the pupils with some scaffolding, which would not have been possible otherwise.

Two teachers also commented on some advantages of the overhead projector over the IWB. In spite of the fact that the interactive whiteboard eliminates the need for the overhead projector, some teachers mentioned that they would still welcome this "old technology" into their classrooms because of the ease of creating transparencies in comparison to scanning images on a computer. One teacher referred to the difficulties involved in scanning the materials she had designed as print documents in order to be able to use it with the IWB. She then asked me about a technology that would allow her to display images directly from a book or sheet onto an IWB.

In order to facilitate the teachers' migration to the new technology, the initial part of the training programme focused on helping them to exploit the IWB to implement the same pedagogical activities they carried out with the previous technology they had at their disposal and in similar formats. Regarding the effective use of the writing space provided by the IWB screen, for instance, a key competency to be acquired by these teachers involved the ability to explore the wide range of multimodal resources provided by the technology. For instance, the limited writing space could be compensated by one of the features of the IWB software, which enables the creation and annotation of unlimited flipchart pages. Furthermore, other IWB software tools, such as: handwriting recognition, colour, font size and annotation tools could be used to improve the organization, clarity of presentation and readability of the text displayed on the IWB. The handwriting recognition tool, for instance, can be used to save some space, as typewritten text is generally clearer than handwriting and therefore more readable in smaller fonts. The lack of space could also be compensated for by the use of hyperlinks to images, word definitions or diagrams, which can be activated or ignored depending of the learners' needs and interests.

Another competency that we thought may assist these teachers in better exploiting the multimodal potential of the IWB is the knowledge of how to enhance the functionality of this technology through the use of peripheral hardware and software. Regarding the construction of mind maps, for instance, the lack of writing space on the IWB could be compensated for by the use of multimodal concept mapping software. The display of print based images on the whiteboard can be done with the use of visualizers or digital cameras in combination with an IWB. These topics were hence dealt with in the training sessions, which were provided to the teachers as part of the research project. However, an issue that was raised during the workshops was the extra financial investment that would be required and the question whether the school would be willing to make this investment.

As a result of being forced to change from old to new technologies without the provision of appropriate support, these teachers experienced several challenges, not only at the technical, but also at the pedagogical level. As the research findings indicate, two consequences of this are teachers' resistance to the technology and their limited use of its potential. In the next section, we discuss how the teachers' view of the technology as supporting teacher-centred approaches also contributed to their resistance to technology use and integration into their teaching. Consequently, a central theme of the training programme was to explore the use of the IWB as a tool to enhance collaborative learning and learner participation during the lessons.

From a Teacher-Centred to a Learner-Centred Approach to Technology Use

It has been pointed out in the literature that there is a tendency for educators to use new technologies to replicate traditional practice. In terms of IWB use more specifically, several researchers have discussed the different phases that teachers often go through in the process of integrating IWB technology into the curriculum; the first phase being replication and the subsequent ones are concerned with transformation (Walker, 2003; Miller & Glover, 2009).

However, an issue that has not been discussed in sufficient depth in the literature is the argument that technology use may sometimes represent a step backwards in pedagogical terms. This may happen, for instance, when teachers want to integrate a new technology into their teaching, but they do not have enough technical skills to do so or because the technology is not advanced enough to support specific approaches (see Fullan, 2001 for further explanation of "implementation dip"). In these situations, teachers may compromise the quality of the teaching in favour of the technology. Although our study does not allow us to determine whether the teachers experienced such a phenomenon, since our investigation only started after IWBs had been in use for three years, interview findings indicate that most teachers were concerned that the greater emphasis on whole class teaching would make their lessons more teacher-centred, which would mean taking a step backwards in their teaching.

In the following interview extract, a teacher comments on some of the benefits offered by IWBs. He cites the use of the Internet in whole-class mode as a possible benefit. However, he also admits that the pedagogical activities he has implemented so far have mainly focused on the use of the IWB as a presentation tool for the learners to receive information and not so much as a "work tool":

Teacher: It's also... you can use it again, if you want to do something with the Internet... because it's easier if one can see at the same time, this is what we do... But it's still a lot of ... too much showing... not enough working with it!

The seamless access to a great variety of resources offered by the IWB technology was also seen by the teachers as a factor that may encourage teacher-centredness in that context. Although the teachers acknowledged the potential pedagogical benefits of this feature of the technology, they also pointed out that the ease of access to multimedia resources may have led to the adoption of a show-and-tell teaching style in some of their lessons. One of the teachers pointed out that the act of switching back and forth between the abundant resources she had at her disposal, might have been detrimental to those pupils with concentration problems, who were sometimes exposed to too many stimuli and were not given enough time to "digest" or interact cognitively with those stimuli:

Teacher: So I have a picture: a burger, and then I can show them. And that's really practical because you can open up pages where you write and open up the picture at the same time. Just switch to it again, maybe you have a word document at the same time and everything has the right size, so you can jump to and through. I think maybe it's not good for every pupil because those who have concentration problems can't follow you sometimes, if you're too fast.

Some teachers also pointed out that the use of IWB technology raised new issues for classroom management. Some teachers expressed some concern regarding the one-at-a-time nature of IWB-based activities. In the following extract, a teacher comments on this issue. She points out that the increased focus on whole class interaction mediated by the IWB might have a negative impact on pupils' engagement with learning tasks:

Teacher: well ... sometimes maybe it's too easy for them. When we have, for example, the information gap exercise, one of them is working (on the board) and the others just have a look.

These findings suggested at least three competencies that these teachers needed to develop in order to be able to use the technology to promote

a learner-centred pedagogy. Firstly, they needed to learn how to design IWB materials which support opportunities for learner interaction with the whiteboard and with the learning content. Secondly, they needed to develop strategies for managing IWB-based activities in a way that *all* learners are provided with opportunities to become actively involved in the learning process. Finally, they needed to be able to coherently integrate various multimedia resources in their IWB-based lessons, by considering issues of pace, cognitive load and learners' active processing of these materials.

Therefore, another important component of the training programme was the development of criteria for designing and evaluating electronic flipcharts. As mentioned in the previous section, most of the electronic materials used by the teachers contained only text and followed the same design principles of print-based resources. Therefore, the first step was to teach them how to add visual, audio and tactile input to their flipchart pages (e.g. embedding of audio, image and video files). The second step focused on how to make use of IWB software tools to add elements of physical and cognitive interactivity to their materials (e.g. drag and drop, hide and reveal tools, point and click programming). Finally, special emphasis was placed on how to design materials that create space for pupils' contributions and ideas in order to allow adequate room for learner experimentation and discovery. Some of these strategies include opportunities to redirect instruction and/or content based on learner feedback, and the inclusion of open-ended questions. During the workshops we also stressed the key role played by the kind of classroom interaction that takes place around the interactive whiteboard – i.e. what the teacher does with the content displayed or how she interacts with it on the board.

The analysis of final interview data shows that the teachers found this component of the training programme especially useful, as it allowed them to look at the whiteboard from a different angle or perspective. In fact, a few teachers pointed out that they had started to experiment with the various strategies learnt during the workshops to create electronic flipcharts that supported learner active participation. When asked about the possible benefits she gained from the training sessions, one of the teachers replied that the materials and activities used during the workshop "reminded her of a different way of working in the classroom".

Transitioning from Print-Based to Digital Materials

Another key competency for exploiting the potential of IWB technology, which was often mentioned by the teachers in the interviews, was the ability to find and evaluate ready-made digital materials, which can be used in connection with the IWB. Most teachers admitted that they lacked these abilities and that this may have affected negatively their level of technology adoption. As one teacher points out:

Teacher: I'd like to find a better and more efficient access to useful sites and material. This is often still just a matter of looking around and by chance you find something.

When asked about her learning needs regarding IWB use, this teacher highlighted her interest in developing strategies for finding ready-made electronic materials. She admits that the 'trial and error' approach she has been using so far has not been effective enough, as it is unstructured, highly uncertain and time-consuming. Therefore, one of the aims of the training programme was to provide teachers with resources (e.g. software, electronic flipcharts, videos and animations), links to useful websites and search strategies for finding relevant and useful material on the Internet.

The research findings indicate that the discussion and sharing of information regarding electronic resources was the component of the technology training that was mostly valued by the teachers. As the teachers moved from a print-based to an electronic environment, they needed to find or create new sets of resources, but with very little time in their hands. As one of the teachers pointed out:

Teacher: It's a matter of time. It's really...when you gave that session on the different designs you can use I felt that's really a great idea, but then again you don't do it because there are so many other things that keep you up and you would really have to sit down for half a day or a day whatever and dedicate it to this sort of business. The other question is also, is it really worth investing so much time into it?

Researcher: Yeah. So what do you think?

Teacher: When I feel the result is one chart maybe, that I can use for five minutes in my lesson and I have spent maybe two or three hours designing it, then it's not really the right relation. (laughing)

In this extract, the teacher refers to the various ideas for the design of interactive flipcharts, which were presented during the workshops. In spite of her enthusiasm for all these design options, she highlights the difficulties associated with finding the time to dedicate to the preparation of these materials. Our research findings have shown that, as a result of this problem, several teachers lost motivation to use the technology or opted for using uncomplicated adaptations of their print-based materials (e.g. by scanning worksheets). This issue was taken into account in the design of the IWB training programme and a considerable amount of time and effort was devoted to searching for educational electronic resources, which could be relevant and useful to that specific group of teachers. Apart from the work with Internet-based resources and other more general commercial software, we also introduced the teachers to some electronic resources that accompany the textbooks used by them. Most of the teachers were not aware of these resources and consequently did not use them.

One of the aims of the training programme was to help teachers to develop an understanding of the IWB as a platform for integrating different types of ICT in the classroom. A key assumption underlying the conceptualization and implementation of the training programme was the idea that the main added value of an IWB does not come from the hardware itself, and not even from the software that accompanies it, but mainly from the wide range of electronic resources that can be used in connection with this technology. Therefore, it became especially important to provide teachers with suggestions of ready-made materials and links to useful Internet sites where they could find extra information and materials.

This first section has focused on teachers' perceptions regarding what they would like or needed to learn and on how their views were incorporated into the conceptualization of the training programme. The following section focuses on teachers' perceptions of their preferred ways of learning about technology and how they would like to be trained.

TEACHERS' PREFERRED WAYS OF LEARNING ABOUT IWB TECHNOLOGY

When asked about their own ideas of what constitutes effective training, the teachers highlighted three factors, which they find especially relevant, namely focus on their immediate pedagogical needs, gradual learning through practice and continuous technical and pedagogical support.

Focusing on Teachers' Immediate Pedagogical Needs

In the interviews, all teachers emphasised the importance of working with contextualized examples of technology use, as they had a special interest

in learning how the IWBs could enhance their teaching and not only what they could do with the technology. The teachers attributed special value to the trainer's consideration of their prior knowledge regarding how languages should be taught and pointed out that their immediate pedagogical needs should serve as the starting point for the technology training. Most teachers criticized the structure and content of the technology training sessions that had been provided by their institution because of their limited focus on pedagogy. They especially highlighted the fact that they were not subject-specific, which meant that the trainers did not provide them with ideas for using the technology to enhance language teaching, in particular. As one of the teachers pointed out:

Teacher: They can't really help me with what I need for languages.

Our research findings have shown that the teachers saw the need for the IWB training to be not only rooted in solid language learning theory, but also based on the investigation of their practice and their specific pedagogical needs. According to them, this approach would be more effective in allowing them to develop a more accurate and objective evaluation of the added value of the technology. For instance, if they want to teach vocabulary in a way that maximizes retention, how could the IWB assist them in achieving this purpose? Teachers also valued the use of concrete examples of complete lessons (or phases), and the discussion of how the IWB can be integrated into these lessons in a way that enhances teaching and learning.

As pointed out earlier in this chapter, the conceptualization of the training programme was based on the observation of 37 lessons taught by the nine teachers involved in the project. Therefore, contextualized examples of technology use, which were directly taken from the observed lessons, could be incorporated into the training sessions. In one of the workshops, we took two lessons that had been observed during the first stage of the project as the basis for the IWB-based activities presented. The lessons in question focused on the topic "homelessness" and the teacher used the interactive whiteboard in several stages. For instance, in the introduction stage, she used the whiteboard to display digital images of homeless people, which were added to an MS Word document. She also used a MS Word document for vocabulary work, which was designed in the form of a hide and reveal exercise. For this activity, she utilized the "trick" of hiding the definitions of words by changing their font colour to white in order to play a memory game. She also used the IWB to display students' writing (in MS Word format) so that it could be analyzed and edited by the whole class.

As it can be seen, the lesson contains elements of a communicative approach, and the teacher made use of effective strategies to integrate new technologies into her teaching. In the examples described above, she used ICT to provide visual support, enhance interactivity and incorporate collaborative learning into her teaching. This was mainly done through the use of MS Word, which was a type of software which she was familiar with on a small screen; and the transition to operating this on the large whiteboard was the next step in her development as a CALL practitioner. The teacher had thus not started to experiment with other types of software and functions which were specifically designed for IWBs; as for instance, the Smartboard Notebook software. Therefore, one of the aims of this specific workshop was to demonstrate other ways of using the IWB, in combination with other types of software, to support the design and implementation of the same lesson in question. Indeed, one of the issues discussed in the workshop was the fact that the use of MS Word documents in combination with the IWB may lead to little exploitation of the touch-sensitiveness of the whiteboard, as the operation of MS Word is more easily done directly from the computer.

The research findings indicate that the teachers especially valued this approach, as they could visualize more clearly how their practice could be supported and enhanced with the use of IWB technology. In the following interview extract, the teacher had been asked about her preferred ways of learning about the IWB. She then points out:

Researcher: So you think teacher trainers should go and see what the teachers are doing?

Teacher: Yes, for example, when you came to my lesson where I did that thing with the...

Researcher: Homeless?

Teacher: Homeless, yes exactly. And you had some more ideas what I could have made and I think that was good, that was helpful.

The use of contextualized examples based on whole lessons, with clear structure and pedagogical goals, was also especially useful for discussing the "place" of IWB technology in the language teaching classroom. Research has shown (e.g. Hennessy et al., 2007) that teachers, especially in early stages of technology integration, tend to "over generalize" the use of IWB technology to all stages of the lesson. Therefore, an important competency to be developed by IWB users is the ability to make the right judgement regarding when to use the technology and when not to use it. The discussion of complete lessons, which involve not only IWB-based activities, but also other types of pedagogical activities, can help teachers to grasp a better understanding of the strengths and limitations of this technology. As already discussed in section 6.1.2, one of the main interests of the teachers participating in this study was to find the right balance of technology use, as they feared that the whiteboard could "dominate" their lessons.

Therefore, one of the objectives of the IWB training programme was to raise teachers' awareness to the importance of retaining essential aspects of language teaching methodology, such as role plays, pair work, handling real objects, miming activity and so on. The use of various types of media and interaction patterns was considered important, as it allows teachers to cater for different learning styles and to provide learners with various opportunities for language practice.

The other workshops offered during the training programme, however, had a different focus and structure. Instead of concentrating on one lesson (or teaching unit), they were organized around a theme (e.g. Irish history and culture) and examples of IWB-based activities were developed and implemented. The main learning focus was on how to use the tools offered by the Smart Notebook software to design electronic flipcharts, which allow room for learner active participation during a lesson. Therefore, these workshops did not contain the same degree of contextualization and connection to teachers' practice as the one describe above.

In spite of teachers' overall positive evaluation of the training programme, the analysis of final interviews indicates that the workshops did not impact the teachers' pedagogical use of the IWB significantly. In fact, when asked about their learning experiences and competency development during and after the implementation of the workshops, most teachers mainly referred to the various "tricks" (e.g. hide and reveal, colour effect, point and click programming) that had been taught, without a clear reference to how these "effects" could enhance their teaching. The following quote is representative of these comments:

Researcher: So, what did you gain from the workshops?

Teacher: Well, there were certain things, like focussing on certain areas, you know, that was relatively simple, but it was quite good/impressive, like when you darken bits of the text and you can focus on certain bits. Or another thing that I can

remember was when you had words disappear, where you had this box and you could put words in and other words wouldn't go in (magic box).

It is reasonable to conclude that the structure of most workshops, without a clear contextualization of the learning materials may have contributed to the teachers' relatively superficial understanding of the potential of the technology. The analyses of field notes and video recorded data also indicate that there was a pattern of performativity (Warschauer et al., 2004) in most sessions, i.e. "the tendency to focus on the completion of technology tasks as an end in themselves, without considering their relationship to relevant teaching and learning goals". Therefore, our research findings indicate that our initial goal to implement a training programme around a specific pedagogical framework, i.e. the socio-cognitive approach to communicative language teaching, was not fully realized because of the misplaced focus on technological tools rather than on teaching and learning goals, which characterized at least most of the workshops.

Gradual Learning through Practice and Continuous Support

The teachers in our study also stated a preference for training programmes, which include hands-on practice sessions in their design. According to them, a series of demonstrations would not be enough to encourage and/or enable them to use the IWB in their lessons. The teachers criticized the format of the IWB training sessions that had been organized by the school, because the participants had not been provided with enough opportunities for hands-on experimentation with the technology. They also added that the self-training approach they had used so far had not been effective in developing their skills and in motivating them to use the technology during their lessons. It is important to highlight that, in the absence of a well-structured training programme, these teachers attended technology courses on top of their regular workload, and their overall process of technology learning was not integrated into their normal duties.

In fact, all teachers pointed out in the interviews that, due to the lack of extra time, their lessons had become the main context for experimenting with the IWB and for trying out their newly acquired skills. However, they also emphasised that they were not comfortable with this approach due to two main factors: the exposure of their lack of skills in front of their technology-savvy pupils and the pressure to fulfil their curriculum requirements. As a result, most teachers opted for postponing the use of the technology, until they felt confident and skilled enough to try using the IWB in their classes. These findings are in line with those obtained by other studies (e.g. Gray et al., 2007), which have shown that teachers will normally only try out what they are confident they can cope with. The findings by Moss et al. (2007) also indicate that teachers who do not feel confident in using IWBs are less likely to progress, since they do not use the board regularly enough to significantly extend their own practice.

The inclusion of practice exercises and opportunities for direct manipulation of the IWB during the workshops was seen by the teachers as one of the most positive features of the training programme. This can be seen in the following extract:

Teacher: Well, the first thing I remember was the session with you when we were a really small group, 2 or 3 or 4 persons, and then you had really the chance to come to the front and try it out and if it doesn't work there is someone right at this moment when I need it, to tell me, okay that was the wrong thing, and you have to do it like this.

In this part of the interview, the teacher had been asked to express her views about the most appropriate ways of learning about the pedagogical use of IWB technology. The teacher then highlights

the importance of hands-on practice and illustrates this by referring to her own experience during one of the workshops provided as part of this study. This quote shows that this teacher especially valued the feedback she obtained from the trainer, as she tried out her newly acquired knowledge. According to her, this kind of approach allowed her to obtain feedback and input "at the moment when she needed it".

Our decision to design the IWB training programme around a specific pedagogical framework, i.e. the socio-cognitive approach to communicative language teaching, was seen by the teachers as appropriate, because it facilitated the exploration and strengthening of the link between pedagogy and technology. However, an even closer connection to pedagogy was advocated by the teachers. While recognizing the benefits of training sessions or workshops, the teachers also stressed the importance of adding a component of "continuous pedagogical and technical support" to any IWB training programme. According to them, this support, which could be provided by an external trainer or internal "multiplier" (i.e. one of their colleagues), would allow them to improve their skills in a way that is more realistic and thus more sustainable. Most teachers stated that the training workshops often overwhelmed them with a huge amount of information and resources, which they found difficult to "digest" and assimilate. Although these training sessions fired them with initial enthusiasm, this tended to fade away, as the teachers faced the challenges of having to apply these new skills without further technical and pedagogical support. All teachers stated a preference for training programmes which involve some kind of practical training that is directly connected to their teaching. In the following interview extract, the teacher describes the kind of support she would expect from an "ideal trainer":

Teacher: You could go to the lessons and see what the teachers do, how they manage, and afterwards you have your own ideas, additional ideas and you can talk about that, so that we [teachers] have this small snowball and afterwards we get something bigger.

This teacher highlights the importance of contextualization, i.e. technology training that is embedded in the work teachers actually do. She then compares the work of the teacher trainer to the one of a consultant, who picks up the teachers where they are and works together with them to develop their knowledge and skills further. By using a snowball metaphor, she also draws attention to the importance of providing teachers with enough opportunities for gradual accumulation of knowledge and experience within their constraints of time and energy. This quote also illustrates a common view among the teachers that, during technology training, the best learning opportunities are created when teachers themselves are able to request technical and/or pedagogical support for implementing a specific pedagogical activity with the use of the technology.

Research on IWB use and training (e.g. Moss et al., 2007) has shown that most of the technology training programmes available to teachers tend to have the technology and its tools as the main points of departure. Our research findings, however, indicate that this approach does not lead to a substantial competency development, as teachers typically desire a close connection to their pedagogical practice and needs in order to be able to fully benefit from a technology training programme. This becomes especially relevant if we consider that the effective integration of the IWB into teaching involves not only the adaptation to a new tool, but also concurrent changes in pedagogical practice.

CONCLUSION

The research findings discussed here are part of a larger research project that investigates a model of interactive whiteboard technology training that incorporates a) a "bottom up" approach to teacher professional development in CALL, and b) a pedagogical framework based on a socio-cognitive view of communicative teaching. This chapter reports on a study conducted with a group of nine English teachers at a secondary school in Germany. The main aims of the study were the identification of competencies that may be required by language teachers who want to exploit the IWB towards a socio-cognitive view of communicative language teaching and the development of principles for the design and implementation of an IWB technology training which would best assist the teachers with achieving this outcome.

The main competencies identified and discussed in this chapter are:

- designing IWB materials, which support opportunities for learner interaction with the whiteboard and with the learning content
- managing IWB-based activities in a way that ALL learners are provided with opportunities to become actively involved in the learning process
- coherently integrating various multimedia resources in IWB-based lessons by considering issues of pace, cognitive load and learners' active processing of these materials
- enhancing the functionality of the IWB through the use of peripheral hardware and software, and
- finding and evaluating ready-made digital materials, which can be used in connection with the IWB.

The presentation of this study has also shown the complexities of the issues involved in embracing the IWB technology in an educational context. The teachers' low technological expertise, in spite of a three-year access to the IWB, confirms what has been found in previous studies and widely discussed in the literature, namely that equipping schools with hardware and software without appropriate investment in high quality training does not guarantee that the technology will be successfully integrated into the curriculum. The analysis of teachers' understandings of what constitutes a "high quality training" has also shown that they would like "top-down" training programmes, in which mainly the technological aspects are addressed in one-day workshops, to be replaced by "bottom-up" programmes, in which they are supported in refining their pedagogical practice when adopting the IWB in collaboration with experienced teacher trainers or colleagues. Our research findings are in line with most of the existing literature, which suggests that teachers benefit mostly from IWB technology training that:

- has a sound theoretical basis and a clear pedagogical framework
- focuses on teachers' immediate pedagogical needs
- uses contextualized examples of technology use
- provides teachers with enough opportunities for gradual accumulation of knowledge and experience within their constraints of time and energy.
- is embedded in the work teachers actually do

The analysis of teachers' perceptions presented in this chapter points towards the importance of designing IWB training programmes which are rooted in solid language learning theories and based on the investigation of teachers' pedagogical practice and their specific pedagogical needs. These findings provide the first steps towards the development a competency model of IWB technology-supported language teaching and a model of IWB training which are being further investigated and developed throughout the research project.

ACKNOWLEDGMENT

We are extremely grateful to the teachers who devoted their time and energy to our investigation. This research project is funded by a grant from the University of Education Heidelberg.

REFERENCES

Cutrim Schmid, E. (2007). Enhancing performance knowledge and self-esteem in classroom language learning: The potential of the ACTIVote system component of interactive whiteboard Technology. *System*, *35*, 119–133. doi:10.1016/j.system.2007.01.001

Cutrim Schmid, E. (2008a). Interactive whiteboards and the normalisation of CALL. In R. de Cassia, V. Morriott & P. L. Torres (Eds.), Handbook of research on e-Learning methodologies for language acquisition. Hershey, PA: IGI Global.

Cutrim Schmid, E. (2008b). Using a voting system in conjunction with interactive whiteboard technology to enhance learning in the English language classroom. *Computers & Education*, *50*, 338–356. doi:10.1016/j.compedu.2006.07.001

Cutrim Schmid, E. (2008c). Potential pedagogical benefits and drawbacks of multimedia use in the English language classroom equipped with interactive whiteboard technology. *Computers & Education*, *51*(4), 1553–1568. doi:10.1016/j.compedu.2008.02.005

Cutrim Schmid, E. (2008d). Facilitating whole-class collaborative learning in the English language classroom: The potential of interactive Whiteboard Technology. In A. Müller-Hartmann & M. Schocker-v. Ditfurth (Eds.), Aufgabenorientiertes Lernen und Lehren mit Medien: Ansätze, Erfahrungen, Perspektiven in der Fremdsprachendidaktik (pp. 325-335). Frankfurt am Main, Germany: Peter Lang.

Cutrim Schmid, E. (2009a). The pedagogical potential of interactive whiteboards 2.0 . In Thomas, M. (Ed.), *Handbook of research on web 2.0 and second language learning*. Hershey, PA: IGI Global.

Cutrim Schmid, E. (2009b). *Interactive whiteboard technology in the language classroom: Exploring new pedagogical opportunities*. Mueller, Germany: VDM Verlag Dr.

Davies, G. (2003).*Computer-assisted language learning: Where are we now and where are we going?* Retrieved June 8, 2005, from http://www.nestafuturelab.org/viewpoint/learn23.htm

Dudeney, G. (2006). Interactive, quite bored. IATEFL CALL Review, Summer, pp. 8-10.

Dudeney, G., & Hockly, N. (2007). *How to teach English with technology*. London: Longman.

Fullan, M. (2001). *Leading in a Culture of Change*. San Francisco: Jossey Bass.

Gray, G., Hagger-Vaughan, L., Pilkington, R., & Tomkins, S. (2005). The pros and cons of interactive whiteboards in relation to the key stage 3 strategies and framework. *Language Learning Journal, 32*, 38–44. doi:10.1080/09571730585200171

Gray, G., Hagger-Vaughan, L., Pilkington, R., & Tomkins, S. (2007). Integrating ICT into classroom practice in modern foreign language teaching in England: Making room for teachers' voices. *European Journal of Teacher Education, 30*(4), 407–429. doi:10.1080/02619760701664193

Hubbard, P., & Levy, M. (2006). *Teacher education in CALL*. Amsterdam, The Netherlands: John Benjamins.

Legutke, M., & Thomas, H. (1991). *Process and experience in the language classroom*. London: Longman.

Legutke, M., Mueller-Hartmann, A., & Schocker v.Ditfurth, M. (2007). Preparing teachers for technology-supported English language teaching. In J. Cummins & C. Davison (Eds.), *Kluwer handbook on English language teaching* (pp. 1125-1138). New York: Springer.

Meskill, C., Anthony, N., Hilliker, S., Tseng, C., & You, J. (2007). Expert-novice teacher mentoring in language learning technology . In Hubbard, P., & Levy, M. (Eds.), *Research in CALL teacher education* (pp. 283–29). Amsterdam, The Netherlands: John Benjamins.

Miller, D., & Glover, D. (2009). Interactive whiteboards in the Web 2.0 Classroom . In Thomas, M. (Ed.), *Handbook of research on web 2.0 and second language learning*. Hershey, PA: IGI Global.

Moss, G., Carrey, J., Levaaic, R., Armstrong, V., Cardini, A., & Castle, F., (2007). *The interactive whiteboards pedagogy and pupil performance evaluation: An evaluation of the schools whiteboard expansion (SWE) project: London Challenge*. Institute of Education: University of London.

Orr, M. (2006, May). *Interactive Whiteboards – the difference that makes the difference? Learners speak their minds*. Paper presented at Learning Technologies in the Language Classroom: A step closer to the future, University of Cyprus.

Preston, C., Cox, M., & Cox, K. (2000). *Teachers as innovators in learning: What motivates teachers to use ICT*. London: Teacher Training Agency/MirandaNet/Oracle/Compaq.

Sharma, P., & Barrett, B. (2007). *Blended learning*. London: Macmillan.

Walker, R. (2003). Interactive whiteboards in the MFL classroom. *TELL & CALL, 3*, 14–16.

Wall, K., Higgins, S., & Smith, H. (2005). "The visual helps me understand the complicated things": Pupils' views of teaching and learning with interactive whiteboards . *British Journal of Educational Technology, 36*(5), 851–867. doi:10.1111/j.1467-8535.2005.00508.x

Warschauer, M. (1999). *Electronic literacies: Language, culture, and power in online education.* Mahwah, NJ: Lawrence Erlbaum.

Warschauer, M., Grant, D., Del Real, G., & Rousseau, M. (2004). Promoting academic literacy with technology: Successful laptop programs in K-12 schools. *System, 32*(4), 525–537. doi:10.1016/j.system.2004.09.010

Warschauer, M., & Meskill, C. (2000). Technology and second language learning . In Rosenthal, J. (Ed.), *Handbook of undergraduate second language education* (pp. 303–318). Mahwah, NJ: Lawrence Erlbaum.

Part 4
Teacher Perspectives

Chapter 14
Using Interactive Whiteboards to Teach Grammar in the MFL Classroom:
A Learner's Perspective

Barbara Bettsworth
Lancaster Girls' Grammar School, UK

ABSTRACT

The purpose of this study was to examine, from the pupil's perspective, how effective the interactive whiteboard is in promoting understanding and retention of specific grammar points in the Modern Foreign Languages classroom within the secondary school sector. Fifty-eight pupils, in two parallel teaching groups, participated in the study over an eight-week period at a secondary school in the UK. The lessons were delivered entirely from the IWB, using a wide range of interactive features. Pupils completed a questionnaire designed to assess their perceptions of language learning before and after the study. In addition, six pupils from each of the groups were interviewed in more detail. The results of the questionnaires and interviews indicated a strong preference for IWB enhanced lessons, particularly where these related visual features of the IWB to elements of language. The results will inform future training within the languages department, and then within other teaching areas at the school.

THE CONTEXT OF THE PROJECT

Interacting with the IWB would appear to have considerable impact on learning in the classroom. Lopez (2006) talks of technology in the classroom as emphasizing "students constructing meaning based on a high degree of interactivity" (p. 1) and it is the process of this collective construction of meaning which is at the heart of this study. Many proponents advocate that students must be allowed to use IWBs (Kennewell, 2001), yet the issue, as always, is how such interaction is to be managed effectively by the teacher such that the whole class is involved in the action happening on the board. It is undoubtedly true that "pupils' active involvement with the board during whole-class teaching reduces the pace of the lesson and can cause boredom" (Smith, 2001, cited in Smith et al., 2005), yet pupils want to interact physically with the board and it would appear that the class as a whole continues

DOI: 10.4018/978-1-61520-715-2.ch014

to engage with the activity, even if vicariously. Kennewell and Beauchamp (2007) in their study of primary schools note, "One teacher saw the 'hands-on' interaction as very valuable for the selected student, but also thought that all the other students were cognitively engaged in the same task" (p. 230). Miller, Glover and Averis (2008) approach this issue in the context of the Mathematics classroom, describing the pedagogy as "at the board, on the desk, in the head" (p. 11). The triangular approach they highlight in the mathematics classroom also has significant implications for the language classroom. However, the dilemma for the language teacher is how to ensure that the work happening at a pupil's desk level can generate meaningful communication in the target language. Miller, Glover, Averis and Door (2005) make specific reference to the use of the IWB in the modern languages classroom from the trainee teacher's point of view, but there has been relatively little research into the pupils' experiences. Pupils say they enjoy coming up to the board to use the pen and there would appear to be positive benefits in affording pupils this control over the lesson. Kennewell (2001) suggests that pupil involvement of this sort is a more effective use of the technology: "In this scenario, the IWB assumes the role of cognitive tool for the learner rather than communication aid for the teacher" (p. 5). At the beginning and the conclusion of this study, pupils' perceptions of their personal involvement in the lesson and in the learning process were recorded and analysed.

THE TECHNOLOGY INFRASTRUCTURE

Lancaster Girls' Grammar School in the UK is a selective state school with a specialist designation in languages and technology. There has been considerable investment in IWBs over the past five years such that every classroom is now equipped with a data projector, a teacher's laptop and a Promethean Activboard running Activstudio Professional Edition V2 or V3. Usage of this equipment varies widely among teachers and the prevalent tendency is to use it as little more than a projection system for presentation software, an issue highlighted by Miller et al. (2005) when assessing the training needs of trainee teachers.

Issues of classroom management need further consideration so that trainees do not fall into the trap of using the IAW as just another form of illustration but consider all elements of group structure, classroom layout, exercise and textbook use, behaviour management and gender issues to maximise pupil involvement and learning. (Miller et al., 2005, p.4)

However, within the Modern Foreign Languages, the Mathematics and the History departments there has been a concerted effort to exploit the interactivity of the whiteboard and to adopt an experimental approach to this new technology. Teachers across all subjects are constantly seeking ways to enhance the learning experience in the classroom and the consensus is that IWBs may have a significant role to play in this. The pupils are highly receptive to innovative teaching and seem to respond particularly well to creative tasks where they have an element of freedom to explore beyond the prescribed content of the curriculum. The pupils are also at the top end of the ability spectrum and the level of motivation is particularly high.

THE RATIONALE

Within language lessons there often appears to be significant disparity between pupils' understanding of grammar during the actual lesson and their subsequent incorporation of that grammar into their written work, whether tested specifically under exam-conditions or in work of a more creative nature where the grammar point happens to arise. Certain features of the IWB may address this issue. It is widely acknowledged that IWBs positively influence motivation, but the issue of motivation is only one aspect of a much more complex picture. The focus of this study was to examine whether IWB enhanced lessons (i.e. those in which the IWB is a central feature in delivery, support and practice) facilitate comprehension of new language and if this is indeed the case, then whether such enhanced comprehension will automatically result in improved retention and recall.

THE TEACHING AND LEARNING AIMS AND OBJECTIVES OF THE PROJECT

The pupils who took part in this study are in their third year of learning French. The aim of the series of lessons was to introduce pupils to the imperfect tense in French (formation and usage) and to show pupils when to use the imperfect and the perfect tenses. The sequence began with revision of the formation of the perfect tense, particularly where choice of auxiliary is concerned, and the agreement of the past participle. By the end of the project, pupils would be able to speak and to write accurately about an imaginary or real event in the past, using the perfect and imperfect tenses correctly, justifying and explaining their choice of tense. They would be able to compare what they used to do at primary school with what they now do at secondary school and describe something they had done in the past on a holiday or similar event. In addition, pupils would be able to examine critically their peers' work, evaluating the quality of language used and assessing the overall accuracy of tenses used.

A typical approach in communicative language teaching involves the presentation and practice model, in which the structure of the lesson moves from demonstration by the teacher to guided practice by the pupils to a final emancipation activity, in which pupils have the chance to practise the language acquired in a controlled context. However, within this structure there is often scant opportunity for pupils to analyse the elements of language that they are learning. Repetition of key vocabulary or of a particular structure rarely affords the opportunity for engaging explicitly with the language, comparing and contrasting with one's own language or other languages being learned. The IWB, while providing excellent visual support during the presentation and practices phases, also appears to encourage another level of engagement. During the study, pupils could often be observed discussing what they were seeing, sometimes in the target language, sometimes in English, sometimes at partner level and on occasions as part of a wider, whole-class discussion. One pupil commented that because of the large visual display, it felt as if they were creating the structures and rules of grammar "real-time". This was no longer presentation of rules to be memorised but rather a deeper level of analysis and exploration of how the language actually works.

KEY FEATURES OF THE PROJECT

During the first lesson, and before encountering the imperfect tense, pupils agreed together on assigning colours to the range of tenses with which they were already familiar: green for the present tense; blue for the infinitive; red for the past and orange for the future. These colours were used consistently throughout the study, and as the pupils began to understand the difference between the perfect and imperfect tenses, the colour red came to be either straight, representing a single action, or wavy, representing a continuous action. The vast majority of pupils chose to mirror this colour coding in their own notes even though not specifically asked to do so. Pupils then demanded consistency in flipcharts and black text was labelled unacceptable, unhelpful and even inferior, although it later became a useful way of testing their recall of the tenses. Some pupils even asked if they could use coloured pens in their assessments.

The ability to move text around on the IWB in full view of the whole class is one of the features which pupils say they appreciate most. Whether the focus is re-ordering words in a sentence, categorising words or phrases or demonstrating specific features of word-order in the target language, the reaction of the pupils is unanimous. Watching elements of language move on screen helps them to concentrate and makes them question what they are seeing in a way that does not appear to happen with static, printed text.

One example of this ability to move text was when pupils were presented with the step-by-step rules in English for forming the imperfect tense in French, but the steps were not in the right sequence. Two pupils came up to the IWB to drag the steps into the correct sequence. What was striking was the total concentration from the rest of the class, and this was the case in both teaching groups. Pupils raised their hands when they disagreed with the decisions being made by the two pupils at the IWB. The two pupils did not ask for help from their peers, but instead they looked to see how many hands were raised, and then revised their previous decision, with only minimal discussion between the two of them. The focus and silent response of all pupils was remarkable. When the two pupils and the class as a whole were happy with the sequence of the steps, the screen was then blanked with the blind tool and the sequence revealed one step at a time in response to prompting from the pupils. The activity was repeated several weeks later and the pupils responded confidently, whether they had been physically manipulating the text on the IWB or observing the process.

A similar activity involved creating time-lines on the IWB, in order to demonstrate the different uses of the imperfect and perfect tenses. Pupils seemed happy with the idea that the timeline worked from left to right, with the past on the left,

the present straight ahead and the future on the right. They were then presented with a selection of events to drag onto the right area of the time-line. Once again, this created much discussion as the pupils sought to sequence events. Individuals volunteered to come out to the board to drag a particular event to its place, and then they justified their choice as other individuals questioned their decisions. With this particular activity, the pupils were required to watch the action on the IWB before then making their own versions of the time-line.

It is symptomatic of this particular cohort that many hesitate to put pen to paper until they are confident that they are right. They are often quick to point out mistakes or shortcomings in their peers but many of the pupils were quick to praise the provisionality of the IWB as a possible solution to this tension. In the words of Annie, "it makes it clearer as you can change things". When questioned further, Annie suggested that it was more reassuring to be able to write on the IWB, knowing that it was easy to undo, change, or highlight an answer. She mentioned that in another subject the pupils sometimes worked in small groups, recording their thoughts with pen on traditional flipchart paper. The pupils felt that the IWB was a much more reassuring medium in which to work as they often had time to self correct their work before presenting it to the class or even during the presentation phase.

Probably the most useful of all new activities trialled with these classes during the study was one involving a whole-class approach to the marking of homework. Six samples at random of a written homework were scanned and incorporated into a flipchart. Pupils were intrigued to see a genuine homework displayed on the IWB. Under normal circumstances, pupils would only ever see their own homework and occasionally that of the pupil sitting next to them, yet here was a chance to see six different examples of homework written by their peers. Levy (2002) describes the benefits of a whole-class viewing of an individual's work,

"Students appreciate having the opportunity to use the IW to show their work to others in the class, and some consider that it helps them to articulate their ideas and give explanations" (Levy, 2002, N.P.). This was certainly corroborated during this activity. There was initially a certain element of trepidation. The homework samples were presented anonymously, and several pupils seemed anxious in case their homework was the next to be subjected to peer scrutiny. Pupils volunteered to come up to the IWB and highlight the verbs used in the homework as a non-threatening, purely statistical exercise. Another pupil would then volunteer to come up to the IWB and annotate the homework, using the red pen, identifying two things she liked about the homework. Pupils appreciated this chance to be affirmative rather than critical. A third pupil then volunteered to suggest how the homework might be improved next time. Some pupils felt threatened by the potential for peer criticism and kept quiet if their homework appeared. Others were less worried and commented on the positive benefits of such an approach: "That's mine. I shouldn't have made that mistake in the first line – why didn't I see it in my book?" (Emma).

The collective marking of the samples gave pupils a very clear understanding of what was required on this sort of task. The good points they were identifying corresponded for the most part to higher-level requirements of the National Curriculum. Pupils were encouraged to decide for themselves what the criteria for a good mark should be, and only occasionally did the teacher intervene to point out elements that had been overlooked. Consequently, the impact of the lesson was a collective, shared appreciation of an individual's work. Every pupil had the opportunity to be involved in this process, and it was interesting to see that those who rarely contribute in class were happy to give their input. "I like to discuss homework with the whole class because you get more responses and suggestions for improvement" (Alice).

By displaying a text on the IWB that the pupils also have in front of them in a smaller version, a dual-focus is created. Pupils constantly have to compare and contrast the work they are doing on a personal level with the collective text on display. This appears to encourage a critical eye and promotes an element of questioning beyond what might be expected from reading the text in the textbook alone. This was evident when a key text containing many examples of the imperfect tense was scanned and displayed on the IWB. Pupils had the same text in their textbooks, and were given a reading task in pairs namely to count how many examples of the imperfect tense there were in the text.

Simultaneously, two pupils approached the board to highlight all the examples of the imperfect tense on the IWB. Seeing the examples gradually highlighted on the IWB promoted much discussion in the pairs who were reading. There was agreement and disagreement with the pair working at the board; pupils debated with each other whether they had missed an example; pupils prepared to suggest what the pair at the board had missed. What might otherwise have been a standard, individual reading comprehension became a whole-class experience infused with heated debate. The process of switching attention rapidly from a small printed text at desk level, to a large-scale version on the IWB being annotated real-time appeared to generate considerable engagement from all pupils.

The sheer size of the display on an IWB provides a compelling focal point for the classroom. Beyond the obviously visual focus, it implies all students physically facing the front. As so much of the lesson is happening on the board, pupils tend to watch this unique focal point in the classroom. There is something inherently attractive about the impact of the IWB in gaining this total attention. This is evident to an observer as well as to the pupils themselves. A colleague observing a lesson commented on how every single pupil was engaged in a rapid-response flashcard presentation where key words were appearing on the screen and then disappearing. Similarly, two of the pupils who were interviewed as part of the study were keen to point out that in the IWB enhanced lessons, every pupil had to focus on the same area. "I think it gives a focus for the class" (Antonia); "it gives a centre of attention for everybody" (Sarah); "a place where everybody can concentrate" (Annie). They felt that this was significantly different from lessons where the focal point was an individual text-book, or a physical experiment for a small group. They said they appreciated the whole-class moving forward together in their exploration of a particular structure. When asked to describe lessons in which the IWB was not used, they said, "we act less as a class and more on our own" (Jess). Without being able to suggest why, the pupils were adamant that the IWB increases participation: "I feel more involved" (Antonia); "it involves everyone" (Alice).

The implications of this single focal point are many: in terms of lesson planning, it implies more whole-class teaching, while at the same time relating this to the individual pupil; in terms of the seating of pupils in the classroom, it requires attention to the physical layout of the room; of particular importance to the languages teacher is whether such a focus implies less verbal interaction, less communication, less speaking practice. It is clear that as with so many new technologies the power of the IWB lies entirely in the hands of the teacher.

Although the vast majority of the pupils who took part in the study were enthusiastic about the IWB, a few remained detached. One in particular felt disappointed by some of the IWB activities, "Alternatively, Miss, you could just buy a good grammar book and learn it yourself" (Mary). When questioned further, Mary expressed occasional frustration with the IWB enhanced lessons. She felt that they slowed down the learning process and although she enjoyed the lessons, she did not necessarily need to go through certain steps in order to learn the content of the lesson. Another pupil

voiced similar concerns. "I'm one of those boring people who reads it and remembers it" (Sophie). These two pupils are at the top end of the ability spectrum and are both very able linguists. Their reactions suggest a case for researching IWB enhanced lessons with high-achievers. Much research has been done on the IWB's impact on learners with specific learning difficulties and as a motivational tool in lower-achievers, but there has been little specific research on the IWB's appeal to the upper-end of the ability spectrum. It is acknowledged that the IWB has a central role in teaching visual, audio and kinaesthetic learners (VAK), but in this particular cohort, there are clearly those who prefer to elide some or all of the VAK steps. In the context of languages, the instant availability of authentic texts and video via Internet is one example of the IWB's potential to tackle the high-ability learner's needs. Further research is needed on the IWB's specific role in Modern Languages teaching and learning – in the current climate of falling numbers opting for languages and their perceived difficulty as compared with other subjects, could IWBs be a key element in addressing this issue?

EVALUATION AND ASSESSMENT CRITERIA USED

From the outset, the pupils' impressions and reactions were seen as being crucial. The pupils completed a detailed questionnaire designed to assess their current impressions of language learning, their perceived learning style and their general attitude towards learning French. The questionnaire was divided into three main sections: closed questions to assess pupil's attitude to their French lessons; open questions to find out which particular activities pupils appreciated most in their lessons; and specific grammar questions to test pupils' ability to manipulate a range of common tenses. Consequently, the initial questionnaire generated a broad understanding of the pupils' perceptions. This was compared with the results from the same questionnaire conducted at the end of the study, after sixteen lessons delivered over an eight-week period. The purpose of the study was to examine how the pupils relate to the wide range of interactive features afforded by the IWB. The key question was whether the pupils had the impression that colour, image, movement and other features had an appreciable impact on their learning.

The initial questionnaire began with closed questions such as "Did you learn French at primary school?", "Do you enjoy learning French?" and "Are you likely to continue with French next year?" (i.e. continuing with French out of choice, beyond the compulsory curriculum). Across the whole cohort, 67% said they enjoyed learning French and 52% said they hoped to continue to study French. In the second section, pupils responded to a range of open questions such as "What are your favourite activities in the French classroom?", "Which IWB activities help you to understand French?" and "How far do you think you will go with your French?" Pupils' responses varied widely, but the pupils were almost unanimous in their appreciation of the IWB. Many of them favourably compared the use of IWB in French with other subjects, and they commented on the fact that the predominant use of the IWB in other subjects rarely went beyond that of a display mechanism. Favourite activities were those in which pupils had a real reason for communicating in the language and had the opportunity to interview their peers in a genuine way, finding out things they really wanted to know. At this early stage in the project, some pupils included IWB activities in their list of favourites, but the range of activities listed was rather limited. The third section of the questionnaire revealed that over 90% of the pupils could manipulate the present tense accurately, almost 80% could give examples of the perfect tense accurately, and only 12% could attempt the imperfect or the conditional (which was only to be expected at this stage).

After sixteen IWB enhanced lessons, the pupils were given exactly the same questionnaire. The number of pupils who said they enjoyed French had risen to just over 75% and the number hoping to continue to study French had also risen, this time to 60%, a figure which was subsequently confirmed by the pupils' final option choices for GCSE. In the second section, the responses were significantly biased towards IWB activities. Those who had previously commented on their enjoyment of communicative activities were now enthusiastic about "watching it all happen on the IWB" (Sophie). Many of them were particularly positive about linking colours to tenses and then seeing these tenses form on the IWB for all to see. Similarly, many were keen to mark more of their own work collectively on the IWB, using highlighters and coded marking. Pupils said they enjoyed coming out to the IWB to manipulate language on screen, but equally enjoyed watching their peers engaged in this sort of activity. The third section of the questionnaire revealed that all of the pupils could now manipulate the present tense accurately, with nearly 90% manipulating the prefect tense with precision and a similar number demonstrating success on the imperfect tense. A small number had managed to work out for themselves how to form the conditional and were keen to share this new knowledge with the entire cohort.

In addition to the questionnaire, six pupils were interviewed and their responses recorded and transcribed. The interviews gave the pupils the opportunity to explain in more detail some of their answers in the questionnaire and to explore the implications of their reflections. They were keen to suggest other ways in which the IWB could be used in their lessons, such as the use of slates to enable more rapid interaction with the IWB from their desks.

THE FUTURE IMPLICATIONS OF THE PROJECT

Having examined the concept of IWB enhanced lessons for French grammar within this particular institution, the next step is to explore the effectiveness of the IWB in the teaching and learning of other aspects of the language. The principles examined here may well apply to other year groups at different stages in their language learning, and they may also be of importance to groups of different abilities. If the techniques and interactive features of the IWB are applied to the teaching of literature with advanced pupils, for example, then there is increased potential for sharing of good practice with other subjects such as English or History. Many pupils commented on how the one thing they felt was missing from the experience was the ability to be able to interact instantly with the IWB from their desks. "I would prefer it if everybody had a mini interactive whiteboard" (Jessica) "we should all get personal laptops or little whiteboards that are connected to the IWB" (Sophie). The suggestion from the pupils went beyond a single Activslate in the classroom. They felt that opportunities for multiple individual interactions with the IWB would be the next step.

The IWB promotes a sense of shared experience and shared ownership of the lesson. It might be expected that pupils would be less than enthusiastic when individuals are invited to the board to manipulate text physically in front of the class. What was striking in this study, however, was the extent to which such activity encouraged the spectators to discuss and debate in smaller groups, not just in terms of spotting mistakes but also in reacting to the demonstration in front of them and speculating about the next step, or suggesting alternatives. There was an evident shift from being a spectator to participation. Whether the demonstrator was an outgoing, lively member of the class or a shy, hesitant member, the overall reaction of the class was the same. The atmosphere was that of a supportive, together, group-experience. When encountering a new structure there was a whole-class exploration of the ideas and possibilities. Pupils maintained a high level of concentration and their instinct was to watch and comment. At times, they were allowed to voice these comments to the whole class and at times, their comments and reactions were limited to discussion in small groups or pairs. The latter seemed to promote a greater depth of discussion, with possibly more honesty of reaction. Though no pupils voiced it per se, the number of pupils who described themselves as confident about their understanding of French at the end of the study was significantly higher than at the beginning of the study. Though the focus was on two specific tenses, many of the pupils commented that their overall understanding of grammar had improved.

Overall, the lessons involved more whole-class teaching than usual and this generated an unexpected depth of discussion and debate. Pupils spent more time in each lesson discussing and debating how the language works; this is a very different approach from the demonstration and practice type of lesson. On many occasions, a significant number of pupils deduced the rules collectively from examples in a text. This was good for the cohesion of the group and pupils were quick to note that they felt as if they were interacting more with a wider group of people: "it makes the lesson more vocal and social" (Antonia); "it involves the whole class" (Sarah). One hopes that this whole-class interaction will have a specific, measurable and long-lasting impact on the retention of the grammar points learned in the course of the study. It is already clear that the pupils are unanimous in their appreciation of the IWB enhanced lessons and that the majority gain more of an insight into the language as a result. As a direct consequence of this intensive period of IWB delivered lessons, the pupils said they felt more confident with French, more involved in the lessons and more open to exploring complex grammar points. The enthusiasm demonstrated by the pupils may develop into a greater commitment to the study of languages at a higher level.

REFERENCES

Kennewell, S. (2001). Interactive whiteboards – yet another solution looking for a problem to solve? *Information Technology in Teacher Education, 39*, 3-6. Retrieved February 15, 2009, from http://www.itte.org.uk/newsletters/itte_nl_39.pdf

Kennewell, S., & Beauchamp, G. (2007). The features of interactive whiteboards and their influence on learning. *Learning, Media and Technology, 32*(3), 227–241. doi:10.1080/17439880701511073

Levy, P. (2002). *Interactive whiteboards in learning and teaching in two Sheffield schools: A developmental study*. Retrieved February 15, 2009, from http://dis.shef.ac.uk/eirg/projects/wboards.htm

Lopez, O. (2006). *Lighting the flame of learning for English language learners through the use of interactive whiteboard technology*. Retrieved February 15, 2009, from www.prometheanworld.com/upload/pdf/WP_ELL_20081201075615.pdf

Miller, D., Glover, D., & Averis, D. (2004). *Motivation: The contribution of interactive whiteboards to teaching and learning in mathematics*. Retrieved February 15, 2009, from http://cerme4.crm.es/Papers%20definitius/9/Miller-Glover-Averis.pdf

Miller, D., Glover, D., & Averis, D. (2008). *Enabling enhanced mathematics teaching with interactive whiteboards*. Retrieved February 15, 2009, from http://www.keele.ac.uk/depts/ed/iaw/docs/ncetmreport/ncetmreport.pdf

Miller, D., Glover, D., Averis, D., & Door, V. (2005). *From technology to professional development: How can the use of an interactive whiteboard in initial teacher education change the nature of teaching and learning in secondary mathematics and modern languages?* Report made to the Teacher Training Agency. London: Training and Development agency. Retrieved February 15, 2009, from http://www.ttrb.ac.uk/attachments/0d65acf3-488a-4fca-8536-918d6dafd694.pdf

Smith, H. J., Higgins, S., Wall, K., & Miller, J. (2005). Interactive whiteboards: Boon or bandwagon? A critical review of the literature . *Journal of Computer Assisted Learning, 21*, 91–101. doi:10.1111/j.1365-2729.2005.00117.x

Chapter 15
Technology Shaping a Democratic Classroom:
The Livingstone Case Study

Brenda Lim-Fong
University of British Columbia, Canada

Rebecca Robins
David Livingstone Elementary School, Canada

ABSTRACT

This chapter presents a case study of how the educational potential of interactive whiteboards spread from one teacher to her staff, the district and subsequently to other teachers in a province in Canada. This initiative is unique because of the "bottom up" nature of teachers coming together and sharing their expertise and experience with interactive whiteboards, which in turn inspired other teachers. Over a number of years, Livingstone staff have observed, discussed and documented multiple ways in which IWBs support teaching and learning. These findings have been adopted and improved as the staff collaborate and change their authoritarian style to a more student-directed classroom. This case outlines the power and potential of this type of collaborative, bottom up approach among teachers and university educators rather than the more common "top down" approach typically identified with administrators requiring teachers to use interactive whiteboards.

INTRODUCTION

Over the past fifty years, teaching practice and principles have shifted from an emphasis on reproducing knowledge by rote learning to transforming knowledge via meaningful experiences (Cairncross & Mannion, 2001). Of the many forms of technology that are available for use by teachers with their students in the classroom, interactive whiteboards

have demonstrated considerable potential in helping to meet the needs of students with diverse learning styles and to engage students during the learning process (Beeland, 2002; Glover, Miller, Averis & Door, 2005; Smith, Higgins, Wall & Miller, 2005). Allowing for collective viewing, interactive whiteboards have permitted teachers and students to interact with technology in a manner that has not been previously possible (Glover et al., 2005). The technology has permitted a multimodal approach that allows participants to move beyond language

DOI: 10.4018/978-1-61520-715-2.ch015

barriers or abstract content by presenting a variety of means including color, image, sound, spatial and kinaesthetic modalities for students to make meaning (Jewitt, Moss & Cardini, 2007). Integrating elements of text, graphics, sound, video, and the capability of the user to physically interact with the objects on the screen, the IWB has offered an innovative approach to teaching and learning interactively.

Designed for whole-group interactive teaching (Glover & Miller, 2001), the IWB generates a level of excitement, attraction, and interest in learning (Glover, Miller, Averis & Door, 2007) for a generation of techno-savvy learners. The ability of the user to actively engage with moving objects on the screen and to use dedicated software harnesses a power of technology and provides access to a variety of presentational techniques that is unlike the traditional method of presenting information by simply standing at the board (Glover et al., 2005). Moreover, unlike traditional board work, a record of the notes, annotations, and student comments can be saved and retrieved for future reference.

CASE STUDY RATIONALE

Teachers at David Livingstone Elementary School in East Vancouver, Canada, have gradually been adding SMART Boards (SBs), one type of interactive whiteboard, to each classroom as staff have identified the potential of these IWBs to enhance lessons and their educational community. This chapter is a case study of the Livingstone School community and outlines how the educational potential of IWBs spread from one teacher to her staff, the district and subsequently to other teachers in our province.

Educators are familiar with the pattern of the introduction of a new initiative and then the subsequent mandatory implementation often required by our school boards. Although many new initiatives are educationally sound and will benefit students, teachers may feel pressure of an increased workload as they are required to change existing practices to accommodate the initiative. Unlike previous case studies done in the United Kingdom (Glover et al., 2005; Smith, Higgins, Wall & Miller, 2005; Cogill, 2002) where a technology mandate for its schools and an influx of financial support from the government enabled the implementation of IWBs, the Livingstone case is unique in that it was through professional and personal interests that Livingstone teachers came together and shared a common excitement and vision in order to attain IWBs for all of the classrooms in the school. Through an inquiry process involving teachers from Livingstone and from other district schools, several educators from the University of British Columbia and a researcher from the British Columbia Teacher's Federation, the teachers came to understand the significant potential of IWBs to enhance lessons within their immediate educational environment and subsequently worked with teachers from other districts throughout the province. We believe it is through the "bottom up" nature of this initiative that an exciting and collaborative teaching and learning environment has been created for teachers and students. This process compares favorably with other initiatives that are typically mandated by school or district administrators using a "top down" approach.

CONTEXT AND TECHNOLOGY INFRASTRUCTURE

For over five years, teachers at David Livingstone Elementary School have expressed a keen interest in the innovative technology of IWBs and have been using them in their classrooms. The introduction of IWBs began in 2002 when a teacher at the school received an email about a grant programme for obtaining free IWBs and subsequently applied to the SMARTer Kids Foundation. The proposal was accepted and consequently the school received two IWBs plus a paid trip to Calgary, Alberta, for one week of professional development during the summer months. A condition of the grant was that the new boards be used in the grade five classrooms during the first year and then passed onto the grade six teachers for the following year. At the end of this year, the teacher who had applied for the initial grant was reluctant to give up her board as she had transitioned to using it in nearly every lesson. At this time, her IWB functioned similar to a whiteboard with the multi-colored pens but the ability to save the lessons for the next day or print off the digital notes for certain students who might have been away or struggled with writing was a significant support in creating continuity from one day to the next. She successfully appealed to the School Parents' Association to purchase one more board that could remain in her classroom. Although her initial use of the IWB was relatively simplistic, it already offered features that enhanced traditional lessons. While her colleagues at Livingstone school appeared to share an enthusiasm and passion for IWB use in their classrooms with their students, its use remained limited. It took several years for some of the teachers to gradually develop confidence and conviction that IWB technology would lead to long term student and teacher gains for teaching and learning. The two boards from the grant that stayed in the school were rarely turned on in the second year, as the teachers who were given an IWB had not received any professional development and generally were not so interested in adopting new technology. The original teacher continued to use hers and her students would talk about the boards in their other classes. In the third year, a teacher with a one year contract arrived. He was enthusiastic about the use of new technologies. He talked to the staff about how he was able to use the IWB to capitalize on more "teachable moments" by finding up-to-date information on the internet and projecting it to the entire class. When additional funding was made available to the school, Livingstone staff surprisingly voted to purchase three additional IWBs in lieu of other educational equipment or textbooks. The value of IWB permeated the rest of the school staff through praise from students and the small group of teachers using them. Consequently IWB use eventually captured the interest of the remaining staff. With technology being quite prevalent in the homes of the students, teachers wanted to build on these skills and explore the educational potential further.

During the 2005 school year, Livingstone staff became involved in a year-long professional development program which entailed working with teachers in the nearby high school plus district support staff. This program drew upon a framework called "Appreciative Inquiry" (Proudfoot, 2006) whereby the schools identified strategies and school-generated initiatives that were working well in terms of encouraging student learning and increased student involvement in the school communities. After numerous interviews with parents, educational staff, and students, IWBs emerged as a powerful tool for learning and increased engagement. Next, the schools met to decide how they could add more resources to enhance any initiatives that were identified. Both schools approached SMART Technologies for a grant to purchase more boards at a substantial price discount. Consequently, Livingstone was able to acquire six more IWBs.

As of 2007, every classroom at Livingstone has an IWB. The staff were excited by the observed increase in student interest, motivation, and interaction. Teachers informally shared views with one another about how more children seemed to be volunteering to contribute ideas and to come up to the front of the room and answer questions. In a follow-up to the earlier Appreciative Inquiry, the Associate Dean of Education at the University of British Columbia was approached by Livingstone staff to help them investigate the effects of IWB use in classrooms. In the fall of 2007, an Inquiry Group consisting of a group of teachers from Livingstone and another district school, several educators from the University of British Columbia, and a researcher from the British Columbia's Teacher's Federation, was created to document and explore teacher-derived observations and questions about how interactive whiteboards were influencing teaching and learning in their classrooms.

THE LIVINGSTONE INQUIRY GROUP

Nearly half of Livingstone's teaching body came together voluntarily over monthly dinners in the staffroom to discuss the effects of IWBs on the classrooms. While all Livingstone teachers were invited to join, half accepted. This group included: two primary teachers, two intermediate teachers, a resource teacher, teacher-librarian, one teacher from another school who did not have a board yet and the school principal. At present, the Inquiry group has grown to include two additional Livingstone teachers as well as one teacher from another school interested in the professional discussions and topics of the group.

Some initial areas of inquiry for the group included:

- Can IWBs support active learning in the classroom?
- If teachers deliver their lessons using IWBs, can this model meet the needs of more learners better than the more traditional approach of using a blackboard? If so, how?
- How do video clips affect learning?
- How does using the IWB allow people to collaborate?

During the discussions, natural partnerships emerged among teachers of similar interests. For example, the two primary teachers focused on their shifting pedagogy from a teacher-directed approach to more of a collaborative learning-together structure. Moreover, an intermediate and

resource teacher who team-taught some subjects focused on how IWBs could support diverse learners. In each meeting, participants shared stories that exemplified educational advantages and how their pedagogy was shifting. Working with this group were external facilitators, including two university faculty members, one research assistant and a teacher's union researcher. These facilitators were valuable in terms of meeting one-on-one with teachers to develop a focus area. During the monthly group meetings, they also guided the group with key questions, such as "how has your practice changed?" and "how is this improving student learning?", questions that helped the conversation to delve deeper into what exactly was working. To help explore the inquiry topics, some teachers observed each other's lessons and discussed how the interactive whiteboards were being used and to record what exactly the students were doing while the lesson was being taught. Others surveyed their students to better understand what the children found most valuable.

A very collaborative community was created among the participating teachers. For example, using their IWB, teachers from different grades identified strategies and whole units that were working well and placed these materials on a school network. These materials became available to the teachers whereupon they adapted them to support their own curriculum. The facilitators created a members-only wiki space where teachers could record their observations and the facilitators could respond. Key themes emerged from the Inquiry Group that the teachers shared with all their colleagues and staff within the district. The meetings were so useful for the members that it was continued in 2008-2009 and will resume in 2009-2010. As previously mentioned not only have additional members joined the group, but original questions and interests have also evolved and expanded in order to explore an issue with greater depth.

In 2008, Livingstone requested and received the distinction of becoming Vancouver's only technology inquiry school. This meant that all the staff agreed to use IWBs while continuing to investigate other technologies like video and digital cameras to enhance lessons. Certain teachers who were less comfortable with technology were initially apprehensive but not resistant. A key to these initiatives was to provide continuing professional development opportunities to be mentored by fellow staff. Teachers also continue to be engaged in a thoughtful examination regarding how technology can be used to support student learning and teacher effectiveness, in terms of preparation and lesson delivery. Using technology has become a part of a larger school goal which is to create more opportunities for active learning, meaning the lessons have interactive components. To provide a cohesive learning community, David Livingstone School has maintained the IWBs in all its classrooms, from kindergarten to grade seven, and recently installed one in the library, music room, district gifted classes, all resource rooms and the staffroom. It was noted in the Inquiry group that teachers tried to describe projects they were working on and software features they were using during lunch in the staffroom. In response to this teacher interest for an informal demonstration space, an IWB was installed in the staffroom. An unexpected use was that aides of special needs students began booking the staffroom to work on projects and the teacher with our community school team used the board to review lessons more deeply with students who needed extra support.

As other schools within the Vancouver area add IWBs to their classroom, the district has referred teachers and administrators to Livingstone for consultations. So many requests came in that the teacher who received the original grant for an IWB has taken on the job of SMART Board Mentor one day per week. The teacher now offers professional development workshops by traveling to schools to work one-on-one with teachers to build up their skill level or to deliver an example lesson in another teacher's classroom to better demonstrate the potentials of the technology.

Members of the Inquiry group decided to offer two types of workshops on their own time for district teachers. The first are free, monthly SMART cafes which are intended to be a place for teachers from across the district to share lessons, ask questions and discussion classroom applications. Each meeting is attended by twenty-five to forty teachers depending on the preset topic.

Initially for the café, Livingstone staff created a one-hour workshop that showcased primary and intermediate applications with twenty minutes allocated for questions at the end. In 2008-2009, other teachers outside of the Inquiry group were encouraged to bring examples from their classrooms to share. To further support this collaborative environment in 2009-2010, five other schools have agreed to host a café at their school with Livingstone's support. Topics have included subject areas like Mathematics and English, supporting learners with special needs and student presentations. Feedback from these monthly cafes has been very positive and many teachers attend regularly.

The second workshop is done less frequently and provides an introduction to SMART Board technology. These workshops are offered two to three times a year and are for schools considering acquiring a board for the first time. Teachers and administrators from a variety of local school districts, as well as parents representing their parent association attend the workshop. Inquiry Group members feel the workshop is different from the product demonstration offered by the local suppliers as it showcases how IWBs meet the needs of diverse learners and support multimodal lessons. It can be described in fact as a type of vision workshop.

One result of the workshops was that educators from around the province started to ask if the Inquiry Group would offer additional workshops in their area. Accordingly two day Summer Institutes were offered twice in the summer of 2008 by the Inquiry members and a total of approximately 75 participants attended. The 2009 Summer Institute anticipates about 60 teachers will attend. The design of the Institute is such that the participants begin by learning the basic functions of an IWB and the corresponding software and progress to developing their own lessons that they can take back to their school. A portion of each Institute focuses on how the educational pedagogy is shifting for members of the Inquiry group and presents some of the key findings emerging from the Inquiry process to date.

A simplified version of the Institute workshop was offered in October 2008 for teachers during a province–wide professional development day. 100 educators from around British Columbia attended. Inquiry group members recommended the SMART cafes to those teachers in the Vancouver region wanting to continue their professional development in this area.

Key Findings from the Inquiry Group

Some key findings are emerging from the Inquiry Group that are documenting how experienced teachers have changed, principally in terms of how they design and deliver their lessons as well as document changes in student learning and behaviour in their classrooms.

Increased Student Engagement

As documented in the research literature (Higgins, Beauchamp & Miller, 2007; Glover, Miller, Averis & Door, 2005), Inquiry Group members discovered that IWBs support student engagement. These teachers have observed more on-task behavior as students attend to instructions better. For example one kindergarten teacher said:

I can introduce a math lesson on the SMART Board and I do not have to worry that some of my students are missing the demonstration. The screen is large allowing everyone to see what I am teaching. Also my students are raising their hands to participate and are following along. When I

hand out the math manipulatives, I see that more students are on–task because they understand what to do independently.

Increased Confidence

Several Inquiry participants have reflected on their students' greater willingness and confidence to participate in classroom lessons and discussion. As one teacher stated during an Inquiry Group meeting:

We feel that the SBs enhance the students' learning in several ways. Students and struggling students in particular seem to take risks. The use of SB technology in daily lessons seems to increase their confidence in volunteering answers, oral presentations and research skills. Many who would never get up in front of the class now volunteer to use the SB technology to showcase their understanding. There seems to be a willingness to make mistakes and not feel ashamed. In fact these students will continue to stand at the SB and try to problem solve rather than wanting to escape back to their desks. We surmise this confidence may come from experience with computer and video games that requires them to try again and again until they get it right. This routine seems to transfer to classroom learning with technology.

Using Visuals to Support Student Learning

Livingstone teachers have found that using video clips and moving images to extend ideas in text can significantly increase students' comprehension, connections to the material and recall. This finding is particularly useful when working with students who struggle with academic learning. For example, in a language art class of grade 6/7 students whose reading comprehension skills were at about a grade 2/3 level, the class was reading *The Composition* by Antonio Skarmeta and Alfonso Ruano which explores the realities of a family living in a country with a non-democratic government. They were discussing the text when one student, with a severe learning disability, said, "We need to watch the video clip on North Korea that we saw last year because some students did not see it and it will help them understand some of the conditions in countries with dictators". The teachers only then recalled actually showing this five-minute video clip about ten months early. As video clips help students to understand concepts at a deeper level, Livingstone teachers are introducing more sophisticated topics; at the intermediate grades this includes modern day child labour, civil rights, the Industrial Revolution and the First World War. Using our English subject block, we are selecting these sophisticated themes that will build a solid foundation for our students when they study high school topics.

Using a 'Guided Viewing' Technique for Video Clips

Another grade six/seven teacher used a technique she learned in the Inquiry Group that we call "guided viewing" to watch the film, *Gandhi*, as an introduction to her world religion unit. As they watched the movie, the teacher frequently paused to explain some of the history and add background knowledge that helped the students to better contextualise the events. This film was watched over a period of one week. The IWB software was used to record notes as significant events unfolded. Each viewing session alternated between the film and the note-taking handout. Students connected so deeply with the story that parents explained how their children retold the story over the dinner table. Other students extended the class discussions by explaining how their family was influenced by Gandhi's teachings in their home country and some of the students while part of a school babysitting service entertained the grade 1 and 2 students by recounting the greatness of the man. The teacher-librarian

had many requests from students of all ages to borrow books on Gandhi. Our school culture was bolstered as the students continued conversations around peace and civil rights. Four months later following the recommendation of the Inquiry Group, the teacher asked the students to mindmap everything they remembered about Gandhi on a blank piece of paper. The retention was impressive. On her wiki page, she documented how the students described most of the significant events but went further by explaining their significance. Many students explained sophisticated concepts about colonisation, non-violent protests and the potential for a united India. Even students with designated learning disabilities created detailed mind maps.

As we do not always have time to use the "guided viewing" technique to watch feature length films or documentaries, teachers have been looking for shorter video clips that bring the curriculum to life. As part of a pilot project, the district has given Livingstone a license to view video clips via the Discovery Education site. In the fall of 2008, the grade 7 social studies teacher told us how video clips were making an impact on her students' grades. During the fall term three units were studied, two on ancient peoples and one on the discovery of the Ice Man. One student received a failing grade on the tests for the first two units. The final unit was supported heavily with videos from the Discovery site. This student achieved a B average on this test. When asked at a parent–teacher conference about how she accounted for this difference in achievement, the student explained how the videos helped her to understand what her textbook was trying to explain. The student also explained that she remembered the unit better because of the narrative format of the videos: "I remember facts better when I can watch videos too. Studying from the textbook is hard for me". It is a powerful moment when a student identifies how her teachers can better support her learning. Though searching for appropriate videos can be time consuming, Livingstone teachers are looking for more opportunities to link these clips to their every day lessons.

Collaboration

The teacher-librarian began documenting the many levels of collaboration that she has observed both within the school and externally and the Inquiry Group expanded on her observations.

Student–Student

Each term, most teachers assign a project where students must demonstrate their knowledge using the IWB. Sometimes partnerships are purposefully created as older students are assigned to work with younger students or more technology savvy students assist beginners. At times, one student will demonstrate a design element or software feature to their friend and a small gathering may form around the IWB as other students want to learn.

Student–Teacher

Students become partners in the learning as their ideas or questions can become a feature of a lesson. Teachers can use a search engine to find images that build upon the contributions of their students. Before IWBs, a teacher would have to delay some ideas until she could get a book from the library that would illustrate the answer. Information is now more accessible and transferable.

In addition students can be a valuable resource in helping teachers to navigate the features of the software. Students often show teachers different short-cuts. For example, one primary teacher explained how her students taught her to erase a larger portion of the board by drawing a circle around it and tapping the centre. These types of interactions can democratize the classroom and the teacher can become a member of the learning community rather than the sage.

Teacher–Teacher

The Inquiry Group has given the teachers an opportunity to meet and have professional discussions that are a rarity during the normal teaching day. These strengthened relationships help us to come together to better teach our students. More collaborative lessons are being planned. Teachers have in some cases developed networks where they connect with job-alike teachers in other schools and districts, sometimes through school district structures and sometimes through teacher union structures. Together teachers deliver lessons each contributing their unique strengths. We have become accustomed to teaching in tandem. The unusual nature of how collaborative the Inquiry teachers have become was particularly evident with the addition of new staff in September 2008. The teacher-librarian had a class visiting the library to begin a research project. As the new primary teacher was giving instructions to her class, the teacher-librarian interjected that she could demonstrate this on the IWB. Though the new teacher was not upset, she was surprised to have a colleague spontaneously join her teaching mid-lesson. After the teacher-librarian said, "I just became so accustomed to work in a team; I did not realize it would be foreign to her". Also a new intermediate teacher was reluctant to use lessons from the shared drive to teach his Industrial Revolution unit. He was used to building his lessons himself. The Inquiry teachers explained that if each teacher builds a section of a larger unit then they can adapt each others' lessons for their own students and reduce preparation. Collaborative teaching creates a superior and cohesive learning environment for our students as teachers are learning from each other and designing carefully thought out lessons that incorporate the strengths of the group.

Our passion for rich lessons that are supported by the SMART Board is being communicated to teachers around the province through our workshops but also the committees that the Inquiry members sit on. The teacher-librarian has made many valuable connections with colleagues within the teacher-librarian organizations, and the various technology committees she attends. She invites people to come to Livingstone to see how our educational model is changing.

Teacher–Administrator

Being a part of the Inquiry Group has given the principal a voice as an educational leader. Rather than discussing test scores and behaviour issues, more pedagogical discussions are occurring both within and separate from the Inquiry Group. The principal quickly recognized the benefits of IWBs for his teachers and students and advocated on behalf of our work for greater funding and support. Strong relationships have been fostered and teachers see him as part of the team. In fact, he plans to deliver some lessons in 2009 that will introduce the students to the concept of the Knowledge Revolution as an extension of their study of the Industrial Revolution. He is a key figure in our collaborative practices. Administrators from other schools have asked how he has achieved such a cohesive staff. He has prepared a document in response that outlines how he has supported this teacher-driven, IWB initiative. Some of his recommendations include:

- providing one-on-one or small group mentorship
- allowing staff to learn at their own pace and give time to practice in between learning new information
- respecting the effort of the staff by providing some in-school time for professional development
- Good technical support is essential.

Unit Planning

Some teachers believed that teaching using the IWB changed the way lesson preparation oc-

curred. In some instances, this was because of searching on-line for information and resources. In other cases, it involved the use of different media such as short video clips or the production of an educational game electronically rather than as a hard copy. In some ways preparation post-IWB may have involved extra time, but there was also a longer-term payoff such as making the lessons available in an electronic format such that they can be shared among teachers and used in subsequent years.

Although teachers initially used the IWB as a whiteboard and created lessons designed to last for only one or two days, during the summer of 2008, one Inquiry member used the IWB software to design a unit with multiple chapters that would last a full term and other members have begun to develop the digital unit plans and are adding their own layers to the initial design. Consequently, the Inquiry Group is beginning to discuss the components that make a good digital unit. These components include:

Title Page

An initial page that outlines all the chapters and reminds the students what we have studied before and where we are going next. An important design element is to illustrate each chapter with an icon that can support the students who organize information visually.

Prior Knowledge Pages

At the beginning of a chapter, teachers are trying to include a page that helps students to examine their previous beliefs and knowledge of the topic. We have found that a page that is image-based, interactive and generates discussion is the most beneficial and can be used as a vehicle to introduce new vocabulary. For example, in the First World War unit, students were asked to brainstorm reasons countries go to war. Then students were asked to reflect on Canada's role in global conflict over the past 100 years. Other prior knowledge pages have included sorting pictures into harmful and helpful categories, matching vocabulary with definitions and looking at an image with guiding questions to ascertain the events or mood.

Information Pages

Though we use textbooks at the intermediate grades, some of our students have difficulty with text at their grade level. Moreover, teachers sometimes want to explore certain topics more deeply than the textbook. With teacher-created information pages, we can adjust the text to the reading level of our students. The layout of these pages is carefully designed. Each digital page can be printed off on one page with a readable sized font for students to follow and build notes. With the text on the left hand, there is a large space on the right hand side of the page to be used for class note taking. Our students enjoy learning new information in narratives and we try to find individuals who were key figures during the time of our topic. Embedded within or beside the text are still images or links to maps that are integral to the topic. In addition, as often as possible, the page contains multiple links to video and radio clips that illustrate the topic. Video clips with a more narrative nature are easier for the students to understand. If more than one information page is needed to develop a topic, all pages are created on the same color background to create unity.

Questions

At the end of each chapter, students must answer a deep thinking question. These questions usually do not have a right or wrong answer but can be argued from each side. For example in the First World War unit, the chapter on the assassination of Franz Ferdinand ends with the question "Is Serbia, the country, responsible for starting the war?" After discussing their point of view with a partner, the students must write their names in the Yes or No column. These types of questions help the students to synthesize the information from the chapter and help the teacher to assess if all the students understand the content based on the sophistication of their reasoning.

Review

An interactive review that uses the crossword, sort or quiz features, included in the IWB software, concludes each chapter. Sometimes the students will build the review for their class members using the information learned or the teacher may have prebuilt it. Some classes divide into teams to create a competitive atmosphere, while others do the review collaboratively. The students look forward to the review and it can serve as a practice for a written test.

Discussions and Projects

While some units are now presented in a digital format, all teachers continue to include written components, discussions and hands-on projects. Using the IWB is only one component of our lessons. We make the distinction that IWBs are not being used for the sake of technology but support our multifaceted program. IWBs are a mode of curriculum delivery that is only as effective as the teacher who designs the lesson.

Students as Teachers

Student presentations are rich learning experiences for the presenters but often not so much for the audience. This is particularly true for the work of academically struggling students. Their poster projects can be awkward and unorganized and a PowerPoint presentation probably does not engage their peers. When we began assigning student projects and reviews on the IWB software, we were surprised with how our students used many of our teaching techniques. They adopted our language of instruction and created opportunities for their peers to predict, participate and question. In short, they engaged the audience to such a profound extent that the other students were learning. Our students were becoming teachers. This revelation first happened when one student asked her classmates, "Who would like to come up and slide Sweden into the right position on the map?" All the hands went up. It was a heart-racing moment. The teacher had not expected the students to imitate her. Teacher expectations have shifted and our students are now assigned to create an interactive review of a previous day's math lesson and at times create presentations that are essential in teaching the curriculum. There is a partnership in education. During the inquiry group, a teacher stated that:

The SB is a powerful learning experience to show students that teachers are not omnipotent. We model lifelong learning and show how to access information. Unexpectedly, we have created a democratic globally inclusive approach to learning. Students and teachers combine our knowledge to create new understanding with support of technology. Often students become the experts of many of the special skills to make technology work. They are recommending to us how to do things more efficiently on the SB and computer. The student is becoming the teacher.

IMPLICATIONS FOR TEACHING AND LEARNING

Knowledge can be represented and communicated in a number of ways. The classroom does not consist of a homogeneous group of students but is comprised of students with various modes of learning and multiple intelligences. No single instructional strategy will be equally effective for all students (Tobias, 1982). The use of the IWB presents an additional means of presenting information with the intent of promoting conditions for meaningful learning by drawing in and involving

as many students as possible in the process. Interactive teaching is where teachers integrate into their plans, their knowledge of pupils and evaluate means for appropriate student input within set parameters (Cooper & McIntyre, 1994). If deep learning is to be promoted, then teaching practices should actively engage the user in carrying out tasks (Cairncross et al., 2001) and allow them to apply new knowledge to other situations. Students no longer need to crowd around one computer to view instructions or watch a projected image on a screen where they are unable to see what the teacher is doing. Students can be engaged in discussions where students are prompted to think critically rather than reproduce ideas that the instructor conveys.

Teaching effectively requires a reflective practice to ensure that learning is holistic, personalized, engaging, and relevant. It entails enabling learners to expand or modify knowledge often in situations involving collaboration, scaffolding and intervention when needed. Teachers must be reflective, flexible, responsive and supportive of students and their needs while they discover learning in their new technology-enhanced environments. Effective IWB use entails teachers having a transformed pedagogy and deeper understanding of the full potential of technology when implemented appropriately.

The Livingstone case study is an example of how the interactive whiteboard has become more than a resource in the classroom but is used as an integral element that maximizes the value of interactions and matches teaching to the learning needs (Glover, Miller & Averis, 2005). Digital technologies connect to the world that today's students live in. They build bridges and improve communication and collaboration. The stronger the connection you make, the better the learning is. If teachers create learning experiences in school that are separate from the real world and isolate separate bits of content too much, the students will see no relevance to what they are learning.

CONCLUSION

There is great optimism that the effective integration of technology in the classroom will improve the classroom environment and ultimately the learning experience. However, the potential benefits of technology must be considered along with the goals for learning knowledge, skills and attitudes that will enable students to be life-long learners. Teachers must be challenged to develop an integrated and meaningful approach to teaching. Teachers are critical agents in mediating quality interactions, experiences and student needs.

The description of this Inquiry Group represents a unique community that has initiated an ongoing process of inquiry as a form of collaborative professional development. It has also resulted in other supports including whole group facilitation, individual project support, and supporting participation in workshops and presentations. While the fundamental educational philosophy of the teachers has not changed, significant changes in pedagogical approaches are evident in improved students' engagement, retention and output.

REFERENCES

Beeland, W., Jr. (2002). Student engagement, visual learning and technology: Can interactive whiteboards help? *Action Research Exchange, 1*(1). Retrieved October 15, 2007, from http://chiron.valdosta.edu/are/Artmanscrpt/vol1no1/beeland_am.pdf

Cairncross, S., & Mannion, M. (2001). Interactive multimedia and learning: Realizing the benefits. *Innovations in Education and Teaching International, 38*(2), 156–164. doi:10.1080/14703290110035428

Cogill, J. (2002). *How is the interactive whiteboard being used in the primary school and how does this affect teachers and teaching?* Retrieved October 11, 2007, from http://www.virtuallearning.org.uk/whiteboards/IFS_Interactive_whiteboards_in_the_primary_school.pdf

Cooper, P., & McIntyre, D. (1994). Patterns of interaction between teachers' and students' classroom thinking, and their implications for the provision of learning opportunities. *Teaching and Teacher Education, 10*(6), 633–646. doi:10.1016/0742-051X(94)90031-0

Glover, D., & Miller, D. (2001). Running with technology: The pedagogic impact of the large-scale introduction of interactive whiteboards in one secondary school. *Technology, Pedagogy and Education, 10*(3), 257–276. doi:10.1080/14759390100200115

Glover, D., Miller, D., Averis, D., & Door, V. (2005). The interactive whiteboard: A literature survey. *Technology, Pedagogy and Education, 14*(2), 155–170. doi:10.1080/14759390500200199

Glover, D., Miller, D., Averis, D., & Door, V. (2007). The evolution of an effective pedagogy for teachers using the interactive whiteboard in mathematics and modern languages: An empirical analysis from the secondary sector. *Learning, Media and Technology, 32*(1), 5–20. doi:10.1080/17439880601141146

Higgins, S., Beauchamp, G., & Miller, D. (2007). Reviewing the literature on interactive whiteboards. *Learning, Media and Technology, 32*(3), 213–225. doi:10.1080/17439880701511040

Jewitt, C., Moss, G., & Cardini, A. (2007). Pace, interactivity and multimodality in teachers' design of texts for interactive whiteboards in the secondary school classroom. *Learning, Media and Technology, 32*(3), 303–317. doi:10.1080/17439880701511149

Proudfoot, S. (2006). Using action research to promote collaborative participation. *BC Educational Leadership Research*, *6*, 1–6.

Smith, H., Higgins, S., Wall, K., & Miller, J. (2005). Interactive whiteboards: Boon or bandwagon? A critical review of the literature. *Journal of Computer Assisted Learning*, *21*(2), 91–101. doi:10.1111/j.1365-2729.2005.00117.x

Tobias, S. (1982). When do instructional methods make a difference? *Educational Researcher*, *11*(4), 4–9.

Chapter 16
IWBs as Support for Technology–Related Projects in EFL Education in Brazil

Doris de Almeida Soares

Brazilian Naval Academy & Pontifical Catholic University of Rio de Janeiro, Brazil

ABSTRACT

This chapter describes the use of interactive whiteboards (IWBs) in two collaborative projects developed with 12 English as a Foreign Language students, aged 10-12, in a school in Rio de Janeiro, Brazil. Data were collected by asking the students to complete two questionnaires which assessed a) their views on the newly introduced technology and b) their opinion on the projects vis-à-vis the support the IWB offered. Critical reflection on the teacher's practice was also considered. The data suggests that the students see the board as enhancing motivation for learning and that it can be useful in learner-centered contexts, provided that teachers revisit their practices and give their students more autonomy in class.

INTRODUCTION

The use of IWB technology has spread worldwide. Notwithstanding, some educators are still suspicious of its benefits either because they imagine this technology might dictate the design of the lesson at the expense of pedagogical principles (Goodison, 2003, p. 565) or for fear that the board, by ensuring that practitioners teach from the front of the class, may reinforce the role of the teacher as a lecturer to the detriment of the learner's autonomy (Hall & Higgins, 2005, p.112). Upon recognizing the

importance of critically assessing the value of the IWB, this case study contributes to the discussions in this book by offering a snapshot of what it was like for my 12 students, aged 10-12, to experiment with this technology as an aid for two collaborative projects carried out in a language school in Rio de Janeiro, Brazil, in 2007.

This chapter begins with an overview of this institution, focusing on its long tradition of using computer technology in the curriculum. Next, it describes the shift to IWB technology in 2007. Having set the scene, the activities which make up this case study and the issues they gave rise to are described and analyzed. This is followed by a discussion of

DOI: 10.4018/978-1-61520-715-2.ch016

the participants' views on the impact of the IWB on the lessons and its potential for fostering collaborative projects. Finally, the learning outcomes for my students are presented.

THE INSTITUTION

Our school was founded in Rio de Janeiro in 1934 as a cultural integration centre between Brazil and the United Kingdom. Since then, the institution has opened branches in Rio de Janeiro, and more recently, in other states, and has a total of 45,000 students and 600 teachers distributed in 40 branches across the country.

The basic teaching procedures are standardized and the teachers are advised to follow the lesson plans provided by the institution. The main aim of instruction is to enable students to use the language for communication in meaningful tasks that mirror real life contexts. As the lessons are student-centered, we are encouraged to observe our students' learning styles and to reflect upon what works best for each group. Therefore, there is room for the customization of the lesson plans. Ideally, we expect to find a relaxed classroom atmosphere where peer learning and teaching is fostered. Regarding resources and infrastructure, investment in information technology dates back to the mid-1990s, when the institution foresaw the potential of computers for educational purposes. Therefore, to understand how the participants in this study reacted to the integration of the IWBs in the curriculum in 2007, it is important to understand how computers became part of our teaching routine back in the 1990s.

FIRST WINDS OF CHANGE

Concerning education technology, this institution has been at the vanguard since the mid-90s when computer laboratories were installed in all branches to provide students with digital self-access language learning activities. Later on, in 1998, every classroom in every branch was equipped with a computer connected to a 33" television set. This provided teachers with instant access to a large number of in-house materials such as PowerPoint presentations to present, practice and recycle language, an image bank, and weekly newsflash presentations designed to bring the real world into the classroom and to stimulate discussion. Later on, Flash media games and animations were included and all computers gained Internet access.

The students welcomed the changes and enjoyed having less book-based activities since a lot of those were replaced by more attractive and dynamic PowerPoint slides which integrated text, audio and animation. Some traditional activities such as fill in the blanks, or match the columns for example, were adapted to be done orally or were turned into game-like activities. Consequently, students did not have to write much in class. Thus, one of the aims for introducing technology into the curriculum had been achieved: increasing the number of opportunities for spoken activities.

From the teachers' point of view, adapting to this new reality was initially a major challenge. Such challenges existed, firstly, because we needed to develop new technical skills, and secondly because we needed to incorporate the new technology into our teaching routines. The former was tackled by means of providing teacher training, mainly to enable the staff to play audio CDs and to run PowerPoint presentations. The latter, however, was more of an individual enterprise as we received little instruction on how to conduct the presentations in a student-centered manner. Therefore, after some initial insecurity, we started experimenting with different techniques in order to utilize the digital resources so as to foster spoken interaction among students. We then shared the results with our peers. In addition, by observing the way in-house materials had been built, we learnt how to design our own.

However, as we were newcomers to technology, there were some issues we had to deal with in our daily practices. For example, although most materials were of high quality, the presentations which were text heavy, or had too much animation and/or sound, actually hindered the learning experience – each successful presentation was met by a round of applause as we often had to wait for an answer to appear or for the text to stabilize, which seemed to take up class time and annoy students. Moreover, requiring students to spend long periods focusing on the screen (sometimes for up to half the class) no matter how varied the task seemed to be counter-productive as students felt bored and tired.

We eventually came to understand that we had been carried away by the possibilities offered by technology and had sometimes exaggerated its use. This led to the revamping of activities and to the design of shorter and more sober materials which could effectively aid the teaching and learning process. We also understood how important it was to strike a balance between technology-based activities (i.e. PowerPoint presentations) and traditional practices (i.e. book-based activities, using cards, realia and flashcards, for example) to keep students alert and on task in a dynamic classroom atmosphere.

In the long run, teachers became more aware of the advantages of having a computer in the classroom and of its pitfalls, and developed strategies to avoid them. Students in turn viewed technology as part of the curriculum, a differential that other languages schools could not afford at that time. It was in this context that IWB technology was introduced into the curriculum in 2007.

IWBS in the Curriculum

In October 2006, the institution decided to introduce Promethean Interactive Whiteboards as substitutes for the technology we had been using for almost a decade. The rationale for purchasing a total of 400 boards was based on existing evidence that this technology promotes more intensive interaction and collaboration among students (Cutrim Schmid, 2006), thus stimulating conversation and participation in the target language. In addition, it is believed that the possibility of creating visually appealing materials which integrate different media assist teachers in bringing the outside world into the classroom, especially as "the Internet can be accessed 'as and when' it is needed to find information – thus helping to 'situate' learning in today's world" (Somekh & Haldane, 2006, n.p.). This is supposed to make lessons more relevant to students and to have a positive effect on the learners' concentration and attention (Wall, Higgins & Smith, 2005). As a consequence, learning is made easier and more motivating, thus raising students' interest in the learning experience.

To certify that we understood this rationale, training occurred on two occasions: in December 2006, to present the board, giving us a preview of what it would be like to work with it in the following year, and on the day before the school term began, in February 2007, when we were trained to use the basic tools and watched demonstrations on how to integrate the in-house flipcharts into the old lesson plans. Informal conversation revealed that despite our fear of not being able to use the board properly and thus risking exposure in front of our students, we were also eager to learn to produce our own flipcharts as we were enchanted by the demonstrations we had seen. Therefore, after having used the board on a daily basis for a month, I started to create my own materials. The next challenge was to avoid getting carried away by the "wow" effect (i.e. projecting course book materials onto the screen unnecessarily, using the board for every stage of the lesson, focusing on what was on the board for long periods, etc.). That would mean repeating our early practices of the 1990s, apart from making the lessons teacher/technology-centered.

It was important to understand that teachers should not allow the technology to take over the lessons. Though I was aware of this it did not exempt me from experiencing new difficulties, probably because "history tends to suggest that whenever a new technology is introduced into society, our first inclination is to use it to replicate the traditional technology it has been designed to replace" (Burden, 2002, p. 2). Therefore, I soon realized I was basically using the board to reproduce my teaching practice with PowerPoint. Upon reflecting on this issue, I tried to do things differently by inviting my younger students to decide on which crayon to write with or to choose from different backgrounds for our flipchart pages, for example. More mature students were also allowed to share short YouTube videos they enjoyed. This was always preceded by a brief oral presentation which either explained why the presenter liked the video or discussed its content. These were simple actions which were innovative in the sense that they called for more direct student participation in the design of the lessons. This reflection also triggered my desire to learn more about the way my students perceived the use of the board and its potential as a tool for allowing more collaboration in class. This process gave rise to the case study which I will now describe.

THE CASE STUDY

In the second term of 2007, the institution invited me and nine teachers from other branches to participate in a class twinning project to promote interaction between groups of students of all levels/ages and to experiment with the use of podcasting. Among the suggested activities, there was a collaborative story creation task based on a set of three photos chosen by the Academic Department. Our guidelines for the project were as follows: On day 1 of the project, the teacher was supposed to use an institutional flipchart to introduce the project. This defined the term podcast and activated the students' knowledge of the topic by asking a) if they had ever listened to/

produced a podcast and b) where one could listen to them. Next, it introduced the theme narratives by referring students to a children's story podcasting site and by asking them to consider what makes a story interesting. On day 2, Class A was supposed to choose one of the photos available, create the introduction to their story and record it using an MP3 player. The teacher would then have to upload this file to the school's Internet page. On day 3, Class B would then continue the story using another photo from the set provided. This would be uploaded and on day 4, Class A would listen to it to provide an appropriate ending. Each teacher could decide whether to involve all the students in a group of their choice or to choose volunteers to participate. Moreover, we could either produce/record the podcast in class or set it as homework. I chose to involve all 12 of my students, who worked in pairs and trios during our regular class time.

Although the institutional project was supposed to end on day 4, I decided to use it as a starting point for another collaborative task: the design of our end-of-term project. Therefore, this case study analyses data from two inter-related short term projects, both developed with 12 upper middle-class beginner students (six boys and six girls), aged 10-12, who shared a similar socio-cultural background. Project 1 (the podcasting project, which was developed during three classes) fostered collaboration among my students, in the north zone of Rio de Janeiro city, and a twin group, in the south zone of Rio de Janeiro city. Project 2, (an end-of-term project, which was developed during two classes) encompassed Project 1 and other pieces of work produced and assembled together on flipchart pages by my students. For this study, two questionnaires were devised. Questionnaire 1, administered on the day before Project 1 was launched, collected the participants' views on the impact of IWB technology on the lessons vis-à-vis our previous technology and aimed at helping me understand how my students assessed IWB technology. Questionnaire 2, administered at the end of Project 2, collected students' opinions about our projects vis-à-vis the support provided by the IWB. I also kept a journal to reflect upon the uses of the board in our project-related activities.[1]

The Teacher's View on the Use of IWB

The analysis provided in this section derives from my reflections on the use of the IWB a) to present and develop Project 1 and b) to assemble Project 2. Upon revisiting what had occurred in class, I identified four issues which I thought were of interest. To present them, I will first describe the procedure which relates to each of them and then proceed with the discussion.

The first issue which I believe to be of interest, especially for those who are unfamiliar with the use of education technology, is the use of flipcharts to enhance the teaching and leaning process. To introduce podcasting to our students, we were supposed to use the institutional flipchart. The first page showed a man sitting in front of a microphone and a laptop. On the bottom we read the words "pod" and "cast" written inside two distinct circles that when clicked on revealed the items "portable on demand" and "broadcast".

Despite being visually attractive, the definition "portable on demand broadcast" would not help my students realize what podcasting was. Therefore, I decided to only exploit the photo, eliciting what they could see, what the man was doing and so on. Next, instead of showing them the definition and moving on to the following flipchart pages[1], I decided to shift the focus from the board to my own MP3 player, encouraging the students to find out who had a player, what they used it for, if they had ever recorded their voices on it and so on. Only after having listened to their experiences did I explain what podcasting was and I then showed them an example from the Internet. Finally, I told them about the project and showed them the set of photos to choose from.

The rationale for using the flipchart differently from what had been suggested was based on my awareness that, as with any other piece of technology, the board is there to help us teach better. In fact, I believe we must resist the temptation to use it for every step of our lessons or as the only available resource. As Haldane (2007) rightly points out "[I]t is the user of the board who chooses whether or not to take full advantage of the digital whiteboard's interactive potential" (pp. 258-259). In adapting the material, I tried to make the most of the technology to suit my teaching needs, which in this example meant spending less time focusing on the board to allow for more interaction.

The second issue to discuss is the potential for the board resources to save the teacher's material preparation time or as pointed out in Questionnaire 1, "to make the teacher's life easier", and to make the lessons more engaging for the learners. The Project 1 Day 2 activity was devised as a response to my students' reactions to the photos sent by the department. Student 2 said it would be difficult for him to create a story using any of those photos while Student 4 and Student 7 asked if it would be possible to change the photos. I replied it was not possible as the twin class had received the same set. Therefore, I built a flipchart page to provide them with some guidance using a brainstorming activity.

Ten minutes before our class started I pasted the photo they had selected (a young girl working on a laptop and a woman sitting next to her) on the flipchart and added the following question: what kind of information do we need to start a story based on the photo? I wrote some possibilities (the characters' names, where they were, what they were doing and the relationship between them) and hid those by using the bucket tool to paint the background the same color as my answers. In class, the students discussed the question in pairs/trios. After eliciting their contributions, I asked Student 2 to come to the board and paint the background to reveal my answers. Then, we compared those prompts to theirs. Only then did the students start to work on their introductions collaboratively, using the prompts as a guide. This activity exemplifies how practical and fast it is to design a flipchart with an element of surprise (i.e. the answers being magically revealed by the student). It also suggests how this technology can be exploited in a learner-centered way to provide input for a writing activity while fostering communication and collaboration in the target language. Because the board was only used as initial support for the activity, the students were soon free to focus their attention on the creation of the stories and thus on language production.

It is also worth mentioning that by letting the students decide which photo to use I wished to help them create a sense of ownership of the photo-story. In retrospect, I do believe that this activity could have been personalized by encouraging students to bring digital photos of their own to class. Once uploaded, the photos could have been shown to the students, who could then have discussed which ones to use in their stories. This would probably have been another step forward in extending collaboration and involving learners in the design of the lessons.

The third issue worth considering is the potential of the board to support collaboration. On Project 1 Day 2, five stories were created by my students, who worked in pairs and trios. However, some felt their stories needed improvement and did not wish to include them in the podcast project. Therefore, only three stories (*My Friend's Going to Travel*, *A Girl's Dream* and *Once Upon a Time*) were inserted in the project. After some technical problems with the school's Internet page, these were uploaded and played to the whole group during a subsequent lesson.

The board was useful as support for this phase of Project 1 as it provided easy real-time access to the podcast Internet page, thus enabling its participants to follow one another's progress. Regarding this possibility, I observed that my students felt so curious to learn about what other groups were producing that they asked me to play the inter-mediate level's podcasts (twin classes describing their cities to each other). In this respect, the board supported the development of an asynchronous language project for a real audience outside the classroom walls and collaboration between students who were physically separated. Eventually, during one of our visits to the podcasting site, we found that only *A Girl's Dream* had been continued by the twin class, where only two students joined the project. As a consequence, I decided to work with the *A Girl's Dream* authors outside class time. On Project 1 Day 4, I played the recording and asked them to transcribe it so that they could write their ending on their own. This was checked and later recorded and uploaded. Finally, it was played to the whole group so that they could check on their classmates' creation. Although the project had officially ended, I felt the need to extend it by providing the learners with an opportunity to make their work on story telling public while interacting with the board more autonomously. This is where Project 2 begins.

On Project 2 Day 1, I ended the class by saying that for the next two classes we would have the opportunity to collaborate on preparing flipchart pages to present their stories to parents during our graduation ceremony. I asked them to choose the materials they wanted to include for homework. For those who did not record the podcast or whose stories were not continued by the twin class, I suggested working on them. Alternatively, they could also choose one of the narratives we had written during the semester and type it onto the flipchart page. Next, I photographed my students with their podcasting project partners.

Before Project 2 Day 2, I uploaded each photo and embedded their recordings so that *A Girl's Dream* parts 1-3 were assembled together. On Project 2 Days 2 and 3 I set aside half the class time to let the children collaboratively design and organize the flipchart pages on their own, providing help and suggestions only upon request.

This activity seemed to provide the students with opportunities to make collective decisions on how to present their work while experimenting with the resources to create a flipchart of their own. Although the participants switched to their L1 at times, I felt we were finally heading towards the use of the board as support for self-expression. This tends to be in line with the so-called transformation stage, when there is a re-appraisal of the role and potential of the technology to support pupils who are "actively involved, and accredited, with the production of resources via the board" (Burden, 2002, p. 9). This evidence was confirmed by the analysis of Questionnaire 2, answered at the end of Project 2.

The Students' View on the IWB

The day before introducing Project 1, I set aside 15 minutes of class time to ask my students to recall the lessons they had had so far and answer Questionnaire 1, which consisted of ten questions, divided into three parts. Part 1 required the participants to express their views on a) being called to the board, b) the way the board had affected the pace of the lessons and their motivation to learn, and c) the board as a tool to facilitate learning. Part 2 focused on a comparison between the lessons with the computer and TV arrangement and the lessons with the IWB. Part 3 provided a list of board activities (i.e. drawing, writing and so on) for them to choose from, according to their preferences.

At this point, it is relevant to point out that the participants had been studying in our school since 2006, which meant that computer technology had already been part of their routine for a year when the boards where introduced. This may explain why some participants, as we shall see, did not assess the use of the IWB as having a major impact on their learning. In addition, as the participants were children, it was sometimes difficult for them to justify their answers. These were issues which were accounted for during the analysis, which is presented hereafter.

As regards Part 1, being called to the board was something eight students always appreciated, although the adjectives used to justify their answers were vague. The participants described this activity as "cool" (4 students), "different" (1 student), "very interesting" (1 student) and "interactive" (2 students). When asked about what they meant by interactive, these students explained that it had to do with standing up and walking up to the board in order to use it. Two students reported enjoying the opportunity to answer questions and to express themselves while another said it made learning easier for her. This may mean that they perceived it as allowing for more room for student participation in the lessons due to the board. Only one student justified not enjoying using the board because of his poor handwriting.

Concerning pace, ten students believed it made the class feel faster. Those who were able to justify their answers[2] said that "the board made students and teacher's lives easier" (Student 12) and that "certain activities could be done faster" (Student 10). This is true as regards homework correction. For example, I often had the key ready on a flipchart page before the lesson started. To check it, I used to invite a student to come to the board to gradually reveal the answers as we checked them orally. This saved time as I did not have to write the answers on the board on the spot. Perhaps this also added to their perception of the lessons as being "more dynamic" (2 students) and "more fun" (2 students) because of the games we played on the board (2 students) or because "the things shown on the board were interesting" (Student 7). However, two students felt there was no change in pace because the lessons had always been fun for them.

Motivation was higher for nine students while eleven felt they were learning more easily. However, only a few participants were able to say why they thought so. To them, the lessons were "different" (1 student) and "the IWB facilitated understanding of the subject as the teacher could

Table 1. Students' preferred activities

SAMPLE ACTIVITY	HOW MANY STUDENTS ENJOYED IT
Drawing	9
Changing flipchart background	7
Writing	5
Showing photos to the class	5
Showing videos to the class	5
Playing audio for the class	4
Recording themselves	4
Coloring	4
Hiding and revealing objects	2

go back to the flipchart pages where the student had questions" (2 students). This finding corroborates Haldane's claim (2007) that IWBs make it possible for teachers to "respond spontaneously to curiosity or miscomprehension by retrieving content from previous lessons, accessing unused content on the teacher's computer or by accessing the Internet" (p. 265). Three students also mentioned the combination of Internet access and the board's resources as reasons for enhanced learning. Notwithstanding, three students felt no difference in motivation either because they saw the board as just another tool in the classroom, and consequently, "it did not interfere with performance" (2 students) or considered the activities in the book already motivating (1 student).

In Part 2, when asked to rate the lessons using the IWB as very different, somewhat different or not different from the previous ones, five believed them to be very different as "the classroom looked more modern" (2 students). Besides, "the teacher did not have to walk back and forth in the classroom" (i.e. from the computer/TV set to the white board and vice-versa), as stated by Student 7. In addition, "the felt tip pens did not last long, which made reading from the whiteboard more difficult, wasting class time" (Student 6). In fact, when this happened, students often complained as we had to rewrite the word/sentence with another pen or go to the office to get a new one. For the

seven students who perceived the lessons to be somewhat different, one of the reasons was that "the IWB was larger than the TV screen," so they could see the content better (2 students).

Aspects such as the room décor, the way teachers moved around in the classroom or the size of the board, which had never occurred to me, seemed to be relevant to the students, but perhaps the most interesting finding refers to the fact that five students perceived the lessons to be somewhat different because in the past they were not used to being invited to write on the white board (3 students) or to use the computer (2 students). Since writing in class in our context was supposed to be kept to a minimum and asking students to write on the board seemed old-fashioned, teachers preferred to do those tasks themselves. However, this practice changed with the introduction of the IWB as the technology allowed for much more interactivity than just writing on a board with a felt tip pen or clicking the mouse to control PowerPoint slides, as Table 1 illustrates.

Since this was a children's class, drawing and changing backgrounds were popular activities, especially among the girls, who really enjoyed doodling and often asked to be allowed to do so when they had finished their tasks or a few minutes before our class started/ended. Giving the flipchart pages a personal touch was also popular as students enjoyed writing their names

Table 2. Contrasting both projects

STATEMENT	NUMBER OF ANSWERS	
	Project 1	Project 2
I liked the project	11	12
I disliked the project	1	0
It was fun	9	10
It was different	9	10
I liked working in collaboration with my peers	9	10
The project helped me to learn better	6	6
It's boring to use the board	0	0
I could not use the board the way I wanted to	0	2
It was difficult to use the board	0	0
The group did not use my ideas	0	0
I would like to have another project	11	11
Other reasons for liking/disliking the project	0	0

or messages to their classmates along with simple drawings and pictures from the resources library. These were often saved at their request. Another popular activity was sharing YouTube videos and song clips.

This desire to bring something of their own to the lessons is in line with the idea that:

Learners must engage with the teaching in some meaningful manner, bringing something of themselves to the exchange and not merely acting as passive recipients of preformed information. We conceive of interactivity as demanding a degree of active participation by learners who contribute to the development of collective understanding. (Tanner, Jones, Kennewell & Beauchamp, 2005, p. 722)

Although this concept in education is not new, curricular constraints, for instance, may prevent teachers from incorporating it into their practice. Nevertheless, this can be achieved by developing projects as part of the curriculum, as we shall discuss shortly.

The Students' View on the Projects

Questionnaire 2 Part 1 focused on Project 1 while Part 2 focused on Project 2. Both parts contained similar questions. Firstly, these required the participants to state whether they enjoyed working on the projects or not. To support their answers, they were asked to choose the statements they agreed with from a list (see Table 2). Secondly, they were asked if using the IWB made the project activities more interesting, and finally, if they would like to have similar projects in the future. In general terms, participants viewed this as a positive experience and demonstrated a desire to repeat it. Table 2 presents an overview of Questionnaire 2 statements and my students' choices.

The analysis indicated that the majority enjoyed both projects, although Project 2 was ranked a little higher. Moreover, ten students wanted to do other projects with the board in the future and half the group felt the projects had a positive effect on their learning, which confirmed their initial view of the board as making learning easier for them. Project 1 was interpreted positively, and even though some students opted not to record their stories, only one participant reported disliking it, as his story was not continued by the twin class. Although that was not a big issue for most students, I believe teachers who develop collaborative projects should make sure everybody's work is valued. In fact, this was one of the worries that motivated the development of Project 2: to make sure all the students had the opportunity to share their stories with a real audience.

In my group, working collaboratively was something the participants enjoyed in both projects, as Table 2 illustrates. This data matched my lesson observations as I felt the participants were actively involved throughout the different stages of this project. Student 3, for example, revealed that she found the idea so interesting that she asked her regular school teacher to devise a similar podcasting project.

In relation to the value the students placed on fun and variety, the data in Questionnaire 2 mirrors that of Questionnaire 1. These elements were also referred to when providing the reasons for seeing the board as a resource that made the projects more interesting. Data collected on this issue was categorized according to the aspect of the technology that seemed to emerge from the participants' answers[3]. Therefore, the following categories were identified:

1) The pleasure the students derived from using the board:
   ◦ Student 1/Sudent 2 "It's fun."
   ◦ Student 4: "It's fun to have projects on it."
   ◦ Student 7: "Using the board is very nice."
   ◦ Student 9: "We are eager to use it."
   ◦ Student 11: "The board makes the projects fun, cool and creative."
2) Its visual appeal:
   ◦ Student 6: "It's interesting and attractive."
3) Its variety of resources:
   ◦ Student 3: "There are many more activities we can do on the board."

4) Its interactive nature:
   ◦ Student 5: "We can see podcasts from other students, from other places."
5) Its impact on learning:
   ◦ Student 10: "The projects helped me to learn."
6) Its support for the project:
   ◦ Student 7: "It is easier to access the podcasts."
   ◦ Student 8: "The podcasting project was clearer because of the board."

Those quotes seem to highlight some of the features offered by the board and to provide evidence to support the view that using IWB technology is beneficial for the development of class projects with young language learners.

CONCLUSION

This case study provided both the participants and myself as teacher with an opportunity to assess the introduction of IWB technology in our lessons and to reflect upon our practices. My students seemed to be aware of the changes that the IWB brought to our routine and to consider them as learning facilitators. The chance they had to be more active and to collaborate with one another because of the board, especially as regards Project 2, was also highly valued. Therefore, from the students' perspective, the benefits of using the IWB seemed to be more related to enhancing motivation and learning and to making the lessons a more enjoyable event.

From my perspective, I initially faced the challenge of bridging the gap between my expertise as regards the use of computers in a learner-centered context and my own lack of sound knowledge of the new possibilities IWB technology provided. Therefore, this case study offered me the opportunity to go beyond the training I had received, and actually learn more about the board as a pedagogic tool. At this point, it is worth mentioning Rudd (2007), who states that:

when there is a willingness on the behalf of teachers to create an interactive environment at the classroom level, and when this interacts with experience and understanding of the affordances of the technology's interactive components, we are likely to see better and more dynamic interactions with IWBs. (p. 7)

This quote relates to the learning process I underwent in that it tells us that in order to make the most of technology, we should embark upon a reflective journey. Being a teacher who is in line with the Vygotskyan ideas that learning takes place through social interaction, I felt the need to find ways to use the board to enhance that among my students. This search was facilitated by my technology background as I had been there before and knew, to a certain extent, what pitfalls to avoid as regards the introduction of technology in the teaching context.

However, finding the right balance between using technology and having your students as the centre of the learning process may be harder for some practitioners, especially those newcomers to technology. As the literature reveals, there are a large number of institutions that tend to acquire IWB technology without having a clear idea of how it can be used as an aid to teaching in their specific context. In such cases, the electronic board is used mostly as a simple presentational tool with learners being largely passive (Burden, 2002, p. 8). In those contexts, I believe it is advisable to first attend to pedagogic issues such as the social theories of learning, or the communicative approaches to teaching languages, for example, before expecting the staff to use the board to its fullest.

Ultimately, it is the practitioner's teaching beliefs that will pave the way for them to explore the interactive potential of the board. One aid in this exploration is the assessment of existing literature on IWBs. This knowledge is perhaps as important as knowing how to use a whiteboard properly, for instance. Consequently, teachers should reflect on the pedagogic issues related to this technology while searching for best practices. In my personal search, I came to understand that I should try to encourage my students to take a more active role in our lessons, not only by manipulating the tools, as we had been trained to do, but also by contributing to the curriculum with their own topics and materials as much as possible. These are some of the lessons I have learned through this case study and that I have tried to put into practice in my current position at the Brazilian Naval Academy, where, under my supervision, 17 English teachers are presently facing the challenge of moving from a chalk and talk tradition to the electronic boards.

REFERENCES

Burden, K. (2002, June). *Learning from the bottom up – the contribution of school based practice and research in the effective use of interactive whiteboards for the FE/HE sector*. Paper presented at LSDA, Making an Impact Regionally Conference, Doncaster, UK. Retrieved December 10, 2008, from www.lsda.org.uk/files/lsda/regions/8_Bio_KBurden.pdf

Cutrim Schmid, E. (2006). Investigating the use of interactive whiteboard technology in the language classroom through the lens of a critical theory of technology. *Computer Assisted Language Learning*, *19*(1), 47–62. doi:10.1080/09588220600804012

Goodison, T. (2003). Integrating ICT in the classroom: A case study of two contrasting lessons. *British Journal of Educational Technology*, *34*(5), 549–566. doi:10.1046/j.0007-1013.2003.00350.x

Haldane, M. (2007). Interactivity and the digital whiteboard: Weaving the fabric of learning. *Learning, Media and Technology*, 32(3), 257-270. Retrieved 10 December, 2008, from http://www. soton.ac.uk/~pgce/ict/NewPGCE/pdfs%20IWBs/ Interactivity%20and%20the%20digital%20 whiteboard%20weaving%20a%20fabric%20 of%20learning.pdf

Hall, I., & Higgins, S. (2005). Primary school students' perceptions of interactive whiteboards.

Journal of Computer Assisted Learning. *21*, 102–117. Retrieved 10 December, 2008, from http:// www.soton.ac.uk/~pgce/ict/NewPGCE/pdfs%20 IWBs/Primary%20School%20children's%20 perceptions%20of%20IWBs.pdf

Rudd, T. (2007). *Interactive whiteboards in the classroom*. Bristol, UK: Futurelab. Retrieved 10 December, 2008, from http://www.futurelab.org. uk/resources/documents/other/whiteboards_report.pdf

Somekh, B., & Haldane, M. (2006, June). *How can interactive whiteboards contribute to pedagogic change? Learning from case studies in English primary schools*. Paper presented at Imagining the Future for ICT and Education Conference. Ålesund, Norway. Retrieved December 10, 2008, from http://ifip35.inf.elte.hu/alesund/?q=node/155

Tanner, H., Jones, S., Kennewell, S., & Beauchamp, G. (2005). Interactive whole class teaching and interactive white boards. In P. Clarkson, A. Downton, D. Gronn, M. Horne, A. McDonough, R. Pierce & A. Roche (Eds.), *Building connections: Research, theory and practice, Proceedings of the 28th annual conference of the Mathematics Education Research Group of Australasia* (pp. 720-727). Melbourne, Australia: MERGA. Retrieved 10 December, 2008, from http://www. merga.net.au/documents/RP832005.pdf

Wall, K., Higgins, S., & Smith, H. (2005). The visual helps me understand the complicated things: Pupils' views of teaching and learning with interactive whiteboards. *British Journal of Educational Technology, 36*(5), 851–867. Retrieved December 10, 2008, from http://www. soton.ac.uk/~pgce/ict/NewPGCE/pdfs%20IWBs/ The%20visual%20helps%20me%20understand%20complicated%20things%20pupils%20 views%20IWBs.pdf

ENDNOTES

[1] The second page contained pictures of people looking at a large painting, probably at a museum, a radio, and a girl listening to an MP3 player to elicit where we can listen to podcasts. The third page asked students to answer the following questions, "Have you ever listed to / produced a podcast? What was it about?".

[2] Some students reported not knowing how to express their feelings in words. Others included more than one reason to justify a single answer.

[3] Student 12 did not justify his answers.

Chapter 17
Documenting Teachers' and Students' Experiences with Interactive Whiteboards in Ireland:
Key Findings from an Irish Pilot Project

Miriam Judge
Dublin City University, Ireland

ABSTRACT

This case study discusses the key findings from a pilot Interactive Whiteboard Project in Ireland which ran from 2005 to 2007. Eight primary and secondary schools were involved. The project exemplifies a bottom-up initiative as it was neither government funded nor supported. Findings indicate that Interactive Whiteboards were well received and utilized by teachers and students whose views on the benefits of IWBs reveal strong correlations. Despite a lack of national policy guidance and funding for this technology in Ireland, IWBs are becoming increasingly popular. However, there is a danger that this policy vacuum will create its own problems as schools increasingly rely on IWB suppliers for advice and direction on how to proceed. It may also have digital divide implications as more affluent schools are better able to fund this technology.

BACKGROUND AND CONTEXT

This case study will discuss the key findings from a pilot Interactive Whiteboard Project in Ireland which ran from 2005 to 2007. This pilot, involving eight Dublin schools, is an interesting example of a bottom-up-initiative as it was neither government funded nor supported. Instead Cláir Bhána Idirghníomhacha (Gaelic for Interactive Whiteboard Project) or the CBI project as it is known locally, was initiated by an ICT education advisor based in the Drumcondra Education Centre in Dublin. Although all 275 local schools were invited to participate in the project, only 8 responded with expressions of interest, which was somewhat disappointing. However, this lack of response probably tells its own story about the lack of appetite and enthusiasm among many teachers for school-based ICT and its attendant change implications.

DOI: 10.4018/978-1-61520-715-2.ch017

During the 1990s, Ireland embarked on an ambitious program to computerize all schools. Under its "Schools IT 2000 – A Policy framework for the New Millennium" initiative, a sum of €51 million was allocated to investment in ICT for schools over the period 1997-2000. Since then, however, despite the roaring Celtic Tiger economy, now defunct, ICT in schools has suffered as a result of both underfunding and a lack of guidance when it comes to national policy in this key area. Consequently the quality of ICT provision in schools in the aftermath of "Schools IT 2000" has come to depend largely on the enthusiasm of a dedicated staff member who has ICT expertise and motivational skills to inspire others, the committed school principal prepared to prioritize ICT development, and parents with sufficient wealth to fund the purchase of up-to-date technology. Unfortunately, this has led to the uneven development of ICT across schools nationally and a situation where Cuban's (1986, p. 5) "exhilaration/ scientific/credibility/disappointment" innovation cycle is very much in evidence.

Given this situation, it is easy to understand why a mere 3% of schools contacted volunteered to participate in the pilot IWB project. It also helps to explain why, when compared to our nearest neighbors, the UK, who already had national strategies in place to endorse this technology (Higgins et. al., 2007), Ireland was behind the curve when it came to the deployment of IWBs. Effectively, a lack of policy direction and leadership in relation to educational ICT meant that an awareness of this relatively new technology had yet to register at a national level.

Undeterred, the ICT advisor put a small team together to drive the project comprising himself as project manager, two teachers from each of the 8 schools, a researcher from a local university and two project sponsors, Computer Education Society of Ireland the Computer Society of Ireland. These sponsors funded the purchase of one interactive whiteboard per school, a data projector and associated software.

The eight schools comprised three primary schools, three second level schools, one GaelScoil (i.e. an all Irish-speaking Primary School) and a secondary school for deaf girls. Two of the schools were located in disadvantaged communities while two other schools were located in affluent city suburbs. Three different board types – Promethean, SmartBoard and Hitachi were distributed among the schools. These were chosen because they represented the three major IWB board manufacturers at the time. The Promethean boards were placed in the three mainstream primary schools while the Smart and Hitachi models were distributed across the remaining schools. Each school agreed to dedicate two teachers to the project who committed to take part in training and use the board for the bulk of their teaching. This was achieved by replacing the main blackboard with an IWB. Participants were also required to attend regular project meetings hosted by the ICT advisor who initiated the project and who managed its dedicated website and discussion forum (http:// www.cbiproject.net). These meetings took place three times per term and provided networking and professional development opportunities for the project participants.

PROJECT RATIONALE, AIMS AND OBJECTIVES

The rationale behind the project was straightforward. Acutely aware of the substantial investment and support at policy level for IWBs in the UK (Kitchen et al., 2006), the local ICT advisor realized the Irish education system was falling behind as the potential of IWB Technology as a teaching and learning tool had yet to enter national policy discourse. Although he tried to get national policy makers to support the development of a pilot project, he found little support for or interest in IWBs. Hence Cláir Bhána Idirghníomhacha, a low key, locally driven, bottom-up initiative was born.

The overarching aim of the project was twofold. Firstly, it aimed to investigate the effectiveness of using IWBs in the classroom; secondly, it aimed to provide support and assistance to other schools outside the project interested in installing them.

THE RESEARCH AND EVALUATION FRAMEWORK

In recognition of the exploratory nature of the pilot project, the research design, orientation and perspective of the researcher was predominantly qualitative. Of the five qualitative research traditions identified by Cresswell (1998), a case study methodology as advocated by Merriman (1998), Stake (1995) and Yin (1994) was deemed the most appropriate. Using a phenomenological research perspective (Maykurt & Morehouse, 1994; Patton, 2002) within a case study methodology framework, the researcher employed a combination of data-gathering tools to support the research design including in-depth research interviews, focus groups, classroom observations and student surveys. This research framework and subsequent research questions were shaped by findings which emerged from exploratory research interviews conducted with teachers towards the end of the pilot's first year, 2005/2006, and the findings from the publicly available literature on IWBs compiled mainly in the UK by Smith (2001), Glover and Miller (2002), Levy (2002), Kennewell and Morgan (2003), Cogill (2003), The Review Project (2004) and Becta (2005).

Among the more interesting findings of the early research data was the extent to which teachers clearly enjoyed using this new technology. Given the often contested nature of teachers' relationships with new technology (Cuban, 1993; Judge, 2003, 2004; Knuffer, 1993; Veen, 1993) this was surprising and deemed worthy of further investigation by the researcher who felt it was important to look beyond the lure of this technology and ask: "What is it about the IWB that appears to have captured the imagination of teachers so much?" Another noteworthy, early research finding was teachers expressed preference for the IWB over the dedicated computer room. This "emic" (Stake, 1995) issue as raised by participants themselves and which had not featured in any of the aforementioned UK studies seemed to warrant further investigation. Given the paucity of studies investigating student experiences with IWBs, the work of Wall et al. (2005) excepted, the research brief was expanded to include students' perceptions of this technology.

Thus based on the initial research interviews and literature review a number of research questions were identified. These guided the second phase of the research process encompassing the period 2006/2007 when the researcher, supported by a research fellowship from Dublin City University (DCU), worked full-time on the project. From the perspective of the theme of this publication, the most relevant of these questions were:

- What do teachers and students think about interactive whiteboards and what benefits, if any, do they bring to the classroom environment?
- Can parallels be drawn with the experiences of UK teachers who were early adopters of this technology as a result of national policy interventions?
- Is the interactive whiteboard primarily a teaching tool – more of benefit to teachers than learners?
- Why do teachers in Ireland appear to favor the IWB over the dedicated computer room?
- Is this technology changing teachers' professional practices in any way and, if so, how is this manifesting itself in the classroom?

Given the qualitative nature of the study and the limited amount of research resources relative to the scale of the project, (i.e. one researcher who was required to work across 8 schools), the breadth of this research investigation was inevitably circumscribed. Therefore, it was deemed beyond the scope of this study to include any comparative study on the performance of the different board types. Furthermore, due to the newness of the technology in the Irish context, it was decided that this pilot project would not have been sufficiently developed to allow meaningful findings to be drawn from a learning measurement point of view. Instead, in true phenomenological style, it was decided that research attention would focus exclusively on uncovering how useful participants perceived the technology to be through an in-depth examination of their thoughts, words and actions.

In all, the researcher conducted 87 classroom observations of IWBs in use across the 8 schools. Classroom visits lasted on average 30-45 minutes. Individual interviews were conducted with 10 of the 12 teachers originally interviewed in 2005/2006 and focus groups comprising a further 43 teachers were also conducted. They were interviewed on the basis that, in most schools, many teachers had commenced using the IWB once they saw how the initial project's teachers were using them and how positively they viewed them. Both individual and focus group interviews lasted approximately 40 minutes.

Student focus group interviews involving a total of 86 students in seven schools were also conducted. The youngest students interviewed were third class primary school pupils (average age 9) while the oldest were final year secondary school students (average age 18). Both teacher and student interviews were conducted using a structured interview format. All interviews were recorded and subsequently fully transcribed and thematically analyzed.

KEY OUTCOMES AND FINDINGS

An analysis of the triangulated research data revealed that a number of positive indicators emerged from the pilot project. Crucially, findings indicate that IWBs have been well received and utilized by teachers with attendant benefits on student and teacher motivation and enjoyment, ICT integration and teachers' professional practices and development. Although all participants were encouraged to discuss any difficulties they had encountered with IWBs, few issues were raised apart from occasional references to calibration issues, the problematic quality of penmanship when using the digital pen and sunlight interference on bright days. However, these were dismissed as minor inconveniences rather than major drawbacks. Nonetheless, one major downside which emerged related to the amount of time required for lesson preparation. Teachers expressed concern that many of their colleagues would be unwilling to invest this extra preparation time. This was viewed as an obstacle which could potentially stymie the further development of IWBs in their schools and elsewhere if IWB penetration increased.

Of the 13 teachers who participated in the classroom observation sessions, 10 were in their second year of IWB use while three were using IWBs for the first time. The researcher's analysis of the observation data revealed that teachers' use of the technology could be classified along a continuum of IWB use (Becta, 2005). The three novice users plus one teacher from the more experienced cohort used the IWB in accordance with the "supported didactic" (p. 4) mode. Four teachers were operating in the "interactive" mode while the remaining five teachers had reached the "enhanced interactive" stage. Classroom lessons observed ranged from phonetic lessons for four-year- olds, to math lessons for deaf teenagers using the onboard software and tools, and social geography lessons aimed at senior cycle secondary students. Most teachers used a variety of both self-created materials and internet-related resources to engage their students and were quite adept at exploiting the board's interactive capabilities to increase student participation through the use of drag and drop, hide and reveal, highlighting and matching words and numbers techniques.

The study also revealed that interest in using IWBs extended beyond the initial cohort of teachers formally associated with the project to include other staff members in each school including a number of teachers who, up to this point, were self-confessed technophobes. Furthermore, the student research data indicates that enthusiasm for this technology is not just a teacher phenomenon but that it also extends to students whose views on the benefits of IWBs reveal strong correlations with those of their teachers. Unsurprisingly perhaps, the research also shows that Irish teachers' views on the benefits of IWB technology closely matched those of their UK counterparts. The key outcomes and findings are described

More Varied, Creative and Engaging Classrooms

Teachers reported that the use of the IWB led to greater variation in how subjects were taught and more creativity in how lessons were conducted resulting in more engaged, more involved and more motivated students. Most teachers considered that this technology was helping to modernize teaching and the classroom environment by, as one teacher said: "bringing teaching into the 21st century". The challenge of managing a classroom environment brimful of digital natives (Prensky, 2001) loomed large in the consciousness of many interviewees, despite the more recent contested nature of the assumptions underpinning the digital natives thesis. As argued by Bennett, Maton and Kervin (2008), the uncritical acceptance of this concept in popular culture has created a form of "academic moral panic" based on the unproven but widely accepted assumption that there now

exists a new generation of students so in tune with technology that they even learn differently from previous generations.

Nonetheless, many teachers in this study viewed the IWB as an important tool which allowed them to engage more effectively with a generation of technology-savvy children immersed in a digital and media-saturated world. Teachers were particularly enthusiastic about the board's visual and interactive capabilities. This was summed up by one secondary teacher teaching second year students who said: "The visual dimension to it is great because it helps their imagination and stimulates them more and, for History especially, it really allows you to let History come alive". Similarly, a teacher of 10-year-olds in a disadvantaged primary school commented: "I think the IWB makes the classroom a lot more interesting and more engaging for the students because they can actually come up to the board and do things, so you can actually get them involved in the lesson - so they can see they have a part to play in it as well."

These sentiments were shared by their students who reported that lessons with the IWB were more fun, more interactive and more interesting, requiring more involvement by students in the learning process. Some students spoke about how learning with the IWB was like "learning in 3D" because the board made subjects come alive and enhanced subjects so that they became more interactive. Students also mentioned how the use of color and sound made it easier for them to learn and how diagrams and pictures enhanced their learning and made many lessons less confusing and easier to understand. The very static nature of much classroom-based learning where the board or the textbook or just the teacher talking was centre stage now appeared to be changing as this more dynamic and interactive form of teaching and learning took hold. As one special needs student who had seen a significant increase in her geography grades since her teacher had commenced using the IWB commented: "it makes things easier for me to learn because it describes everything in detail and shows diagrams and puts them in motion."

Improved Student Concentration Levels

Teachers reported that student concentration levels and attention spans increased when using the IWB. Most teachers believed that the highly visual and interactive nature of the IWB was responsible for this along with the increased freedom that the IWB brought to classroom learning, particularly when allied to Internet access.

Inevitably, because lessons with the IWB were seen to be more interesting, more fun and more interactive, students naturally enough reported that they now paid more attention in class and that the IWB helped them to concentrate more, as these 9-year-olds revealed:

Q. Why do you think you pay more attention?

S1: I think it's more interesting, so it's kind of easier to pay attention because it's really interesting and you can get to the point really quicker.

S2: And it's more fun because if you have the blackboard it's only the teacher doing the work. On the IWB the children get to do it as well not just the teacher.

S3: Yeah everyone can join in the lesson, everyone can use it and as Ronan (i.e. S1- not his real name) said it's more interesting because you can put things together better – I used to hate math before but now I'm getting way better at it because I used to be way behind all the time. -- Focus Group Interview (3ʳᵈ class primary pupils)

Compared to books, or working on the normal board, or listening to the teacher, students felt that the boredom factor associated with much classroom learning was reduced. Primary pupils reported how the IWB made subjects such as History and Geography (which they often found boring) more stimulating while making more difficult subjects such as Math and Science easier to understand.

Benefits for Multisensory Learners and Less Academic Students

While teachers believed that all students benefited from having an IWB in the classroom, the benefits for visual and kinesthetic learners were particularly emphasized. The versatility of IWBs in classroom settings meant that teaching could now be more easily conducted to accommodate varying learning styles. Teachers believed that the technology also brought significant benefits for academically weaker students, helped largely by the visual dimension and the medium's interactive capabilities. One teacher teaching a class of 14-year-olds said:

I teach a very weak class and, on the basis of my experience, I would say the types of learners that benefit most from the IWB are: the students for whom text is very heavy; the student who learns visually or who can understand the world through images; the student for whom the classroom is tough and whose attention span is low. -- Secondary Teacher

There is a striking similarity in this teacher's observations and the views of a group of 11 and 12-year-olds from a primary school who argued that, while the IWB was good for all learners, it was particularly good for those students "who don't listen much in class" when using the normal board, or for "students that find it hard to concentrate", or who need "loads of images to get it into their heads." In other words, just like their teachers, students understood the added value of this technology for the more visual learners among them. As one student bluntly said: "It gets stuck in your head when you can see it."

More Organized, Focused and Productive Classrooms

Teachers reported that since they began using IWBs, their lessons became more organized and more focused. This meant they were able to get through material faster leading to an increase in classroom productivity from both an efficiency and effectiveness perspective. This was largely attributed to the amount of pre-planning required to organize lessons to ensure the board was utilized to its full potential. As one teacher said: "you can't really wing it on an IWB - you need to have everything organized and ready beforehand".

The efficiency gains in classroom learning that teachers highlighted were also noted by their students who found that they now covered more material in class because everything was typed up and prepared in advance.

Q. So why do you think you get more covered in class when you use the IWB?

S1 I think it's because there's no time wasted writing up all the notes on the board or calling everything out and things like that.

S2: It's much quicker because she can just explain it and then get everyone to take it down, it takes just a few minutes to take it down, but if she was calling it out we would probably keep saying, "Miss how do you spell that or can you say that again" whereas it's just quicker to take it down from the IWB. -- Focus Group Interview (2nd year secondary students)

The labor saving benefits of the technology were also noted. In one primary school students commented on how their teacher "saves all her IWB material on her teacher folder" on the school computer system and how they could access this material when they went to the computer room to revise that material.

Improved Lesson Planning

All teachers reported that the IWB had enhanced lesson planning as they were now preparing more. Although many teachers reported spending three hours a night or more on preparation, they felt that the benefits in terms of more interactive classrooms, more involved and engaged students, and an overall improved pedagogical environment, justified the extra effort involved.

Well it gives you a lot of satisfaction as a teacher that you might spend hours doing something but when you actually come in and see that the kids really appreciate it and they are engaged in it – you feel a great deal of satisfaction from it – it's like well I didn't waste my time and this is definitely worthwhile and they are really learning from it. -- Primary Teacher

The extra effort invested in planning was noted by their students who commented that, when using the IWB, their teachers were more organized and knew "exactly what they wanted to do". Because students could see the amount of work the teacher put into lessons from image capturing to the presentation of neatly typed up chapter summaries and notes, to the fact that "she downloads everything onto her USB key", or "emails her lessons from home to the school computer", students felt "I really should listen to this because the teacher has gone to all this trouble."

Increased Teacher Motivation and Enjoyment

Most teachers reported that the IWB had increased their work motivation and enjoyment. This is largely attributable to the amount of creativity they could now bring to lesson planning and delivery in everyday classrooms. It would seem that when students enjoy what's happening in the IWB classroom, it further motivates teachers, leading to mutual benefits for both parties.

I don't mind the extra preparation time because I enjoy it myself and if it makes teaching and learning easier I prefer that. I just love to see the look on their faces and they are so interested and they can be involved so much more. -- Secondary Teacher

Students also felt that the fun element which they associated with IWBs in the classroom was not solely their preserve. They could see that teachers also enjoyed working with this technology, not least because it made their job more interesting and, in some cases, easier; but probably most importantly because they could see that "the kids are enjoying it too" and in the process, "the teacher was learning new stuff too".

A Change in Teacher Thinking

It would seem that the IWB is challenging teachers' thinking about how they teach. Teachers revealed how the technology was "challenging them" to think of different ways of learning and different ways of doing things to involve students more. Teachers who had been teaching a long time reported how the IWB had added a new excitement and freshness to their teaching as they tried to incorporate more visuals, more animation and more educational games into their lessons.

What's interesting about all of these developments when merged together – i.e. more time invested in preparation, more motivated teachers, and the change in how teachers now think about teaching their subjects, is the overall change that this is having – not only on classroom learning and activity, but also on the dynamics of that environment. Some teachers felt that the IWB led to more group work in the classroom and a reduction in the amount of bookwork as the IWB and the internet combined opened up a whole new world of exciting possibilities for children's learning.

There was also a new awareness that teachers were on a journey of learning with their students and this notion of being co-learners in the educa-tional process came across quite strongly. Teachers spoke about how this technology was democratizing the classroom in terms of involving students and giving them a say in how lessons should proceed. In one primary school, a self-confessed technophobe who "had never wanted anything to do with computers", informed the researcher how, having taught for 20 years, she saw herself as "very much a traditional teacher in the talk and chalk mode and who was very teacher-directed in terms of her teaching style". But, the interactive whiteboard, she said, had broadened her perspective on teaching. She explained how the IWB now facilitates her pupils to determine what goes on in the classroom when something that has captured their imagination arises:

We are no longer stuck within the perimeters of our textbooks. Whereas you might have an idea of going one direction they might take you in another direction. Let's take something very simple like a lesson on clouds - that could develop into something on the rain forest, or indigenous tribes or saving the planet. So we ended up then having a kind of rain forest day. So it's that kind of thing, you end up going in a direction that catches their attention and you get far, far more feedback from the children as a result.

Similarly, a secondary teacher commented:

I think one of the first things to recognize is that with this technology, teachers and students are on a journey together and the authoritative model won't work. If you still wish to be at the top of the room running everything and being dogmatic, forget it. It's much more a context where there is exchange. Ok there's still a teacher in the room, alright, but it's a journey together and they too have something important to contribute to that. So the balance of power does have to change and you have to be comfortable around that shifting balance of power.

Better ICT Integration

All teachers reported that the presence of an IWB in the classroom led to better and more meaningful ICT integration. Teachers were unanimous in their view that the permanent presence of an IWB in their classroom was a far more useful device for increasing ICT integration in their teaching compared to using a dedicated computer room. This is because teachers feel that access to computer labs is restricted, either through timetabling or resource constraints, which in turn limits the amount of time ICT can be realistically deployed in everyday teaching and learning:

I prefer the IWB because it's much better for integrating technology into your teaching. I used to use the computer lab once a week or once a fortnight for teaching, but I don't think much more often than that unless we were doing a particular project which I wanted to get finished. But I use the IWB in all of my classes now. -- Secondary Teacher

Despite the fact that one of the key reasons cited by most schools for becoming involved with the IWB project was attributed to a supportive ICT culture, when one scratched the surface, a much more challenging and complex picture of ICT provision in most schools emerged. The ICT co-ordinators, particularly in the more disadvantaged schools, spoke about how their computer systems were creaking at the seams; of the struggle to maintain and keep old machines in good running order, and the limitations of the software you could realistically deploy on Windows 98 machines. In some respects, it can be argued that they were the lucky ones because at least they were managing to keep their machines running, unlike another school where one teacher said:

Realistically computers in schools are a joke; they are not maintained, there's viruses on them, the drives are getting damaged, the disks are get-

ting damaged and it's the same for every school throughout the country. That's why I would choose an IWB in every classroom over a computer lab in a school any day. -- Primary Teacher

Judged in this context and against this backdrop, it's easy to understand why, when asked if they had to choose one above the other which they would choose and why, teachers unanimously responded the "Interactive Whiteboard". This was not only because they felt it was a much more intuitive pedagogic device, but also because it offered a real technological alternative to the nightmare of the computer room where no professional technical support system exists.

Like their teachers, most students indicated a distinct preference for learning with an IWB in their classroom rather than spending more time in the computer room. Of all the findings in this study, this was probably the most surprising, as this was the one area where one expected students' views to diverge from those of the teachers. Yet they did not, and the sophistication of their responses on this issue was most revealing.

Unlike their teachers, the students did not get bogged down in the technical difficulties of the computer room (although some students mentioned these obstacles), but rather they took the discourse to another level where they discussed primarily the pedagogical impediments to learning that the computer room presented for them. That is not to say that children disliked going to the computer room – on the contrary, virtually every student interviewed revealed that they absolutely loved going there – but when asked why, most responded, Neil Postman (1995) style, by saying that they liked it because "it was a break from class"; "it was something different" and they could "play games" when they went there. When the children were asked how much they felt they learned from playing those games, most indicated that they were actually learning very little. One nine-year-old said: "I feel it's better when you learn in the classroom with the interactive whiteboard because the class is for learning and the computer room is just for playing games." Another group of twelve-year-olds similarly expressed their views:

Q. But do you not think you would be better off spending more time in the computer room using the computers than using the IWB in the classroom?

S2: No.

Q. Why do you say that?

S2: Because it's just looking up stuff

S3: Yes and it doesn't really teach you things - like on the IWB she [the teacher] teaches us math on it and other subjects.

S2: And they're easier to learn on the board.

S3: Yes and sometimes it gets real boring in the computer room if you sit there for long. -- Focus Group Interview (6th class primary pupils)

This apparent disconnect between classroom learning and the way in which computer rooms are used probably largely explains why most students in this study felt that classroom learning with the IWB was a preferable learning environment to working in the computer room. It may also indicate, as discussed earlier, that those who question the universality of the digital natives thesis may have a point. Many young people may be less adept at computers than we adults and educators think. Perhaps this also partly explains why many students in this study viewed the IWB classroom as a more effective and efficient way of learning. Some students indicated that they found learning with computers confusing and it was hard to convince them of one of the more often cited benefits of computers in learning i.e. the ability to learn at one's own pace. On the contrary, they argued

that this could mean some students would get left behind as the more academic students progressed. They saw many benefits to whole class learning such as the pressure to keep up with one's peers, the comfort in knowing that "I'm not the only one struggling with this topic" as it became clear from the teacher's questioning of the class that other students were also experiencing difficulties, and the fact that, as one 10-year-old said: "If you're stuck on a sum the whole class can help you with it on the IWB."

Student responses seem to indicate that they, like their teachers, frequently find the dedicated computer room a "difficult learning environment". The students in this study at least seemed to find comfort in the communal learning experience; in the traditional notion of everyone moving more or less at the same pace as they learn and they had a measured appreciation of the crucial role that the teacher plays in the learning environment. This was probably best summed up by a group of final year 18-year–old students who argued that: "Learning from the interactive whiteboard is better than learning from the computer because the teacher explains and simplifies things on the interactive whiteboard and so you understand them more."

IMPLICATIONS

In December 2007, the Drumcondra Education Centre hosted a forum for Irish education policy makers on interactive whiteboards at which the research findings from this pilot project and from the then recently published report on the "Evaluation of the Primary Schools Whiteboard Expansion Project" (Somekh et al., 2007), were presented. Despite the evidence from both studies that IWBs clearly have a role to play in the 21st century classroom, Irish policy makers have stayed silent. Nonetheless, the bottom-up movement initiated by the ICT advisor continues to gather pace as schools continue to invest in this technology through their own fundraising efforts. It would seem that schools and teachers are voting with their feet and installing these systems anyhow. In 2008, 35% of schools in the Drumcondra Education Centre's catchment area were using IWBs, up from 15% in 2007. Nationally, figures from FutureSource Consulting (2008) reveal that in 2008, 16% of all Irish classrooms had an IWB. They predict that by 2009 classroom penetration will reach 32%, rising to 44% in 2010, and reaching more than one in two by 2011.

This trend, in a jurisdiction where there is no policy or financial support for IWB implementation, suggests that the presence of IWBs in Irish classrooms may have more to do with the technology's inherent "pull" characteristics, unlike the UK situation where the "push" model of penetration was deployed. Nonetheless, despite radically different deployment models, it is interesting, based on this pilot study, to note how closely matched the experiences of teachers with IWBs in both nations appear to be. This would suggest, despite many differences in our education systems and cultures, that many of the conclusions drawn from the UK experience to date (where they are well ahead of other countries in their deployment of interactive whiteboards), may in fact be relevant to other educational cultures and systems.

Disappointingly, however, in the absence of any national policy support for IWBs in Irish schools, it looks as though IWBs will be introduced on a piecemeal basis and in an ad-hoc manner. Worryingly, it looks as though, for the foreseeable future, the board manufacturers and suppliers rather than educators will drive IWB implementation in Ireland and shape the educational agenda in this arena. In the absence of any national support and guidelines on the role of IWBs in the classroom, schools will turn to the board suppliers for advice on how to proceed, especially as they come under increasing pressure from parents and others to adopt this technology.

However, if the right policy guidance is not put in place to support the procurement, installation

and training and development needs of teachers, there is a real danger that the many challenges associated with IWB technology use may not be adequately addressed in Irish schools. More recent UK research has revealed the complexity of the proliferation of IWBs in schools. Research by Somekh et al. (2007) has shown that extensive use of interactive whiteboards for teaching has made good technical support a necessity rather than an option for all schools. Smith et al. (2006) have argued that, while an IWB may be technically interactive it may not be used interactively and therefore can lead to more didactic teaching which allows teachers to teach in a traditional manner "with the central focus of a board, but with the excitement of media-rich content that doesn't interfere with their existing pedagogy" (Heppell, 2004, p. 8). Moss et al. (2007) have shown that actual usage of IWBs can vary across both teachers and subject areas and that increased pupil motivation in the IWB classroom may be short-lived. It is clear that as Irish schools continue to scale up their investment in IWBs, they will need guidance in addressing these issues. Such guidance is unlikely to come from IWB manufacturers and suppliers.

There is also the added challenge that if schools have to fund these boards from their own limited resources (as is currently the case), a new digital divide will emerge. Schools located in more affluent communities will find it easier to fund IWBs than less affluent schools. This digital divide was already evident in the pilot project where the two schools located in well-off leafy suburbs were planning to buy more IWBs at the end of the pilot; while the less well-off schools, while equally enthusiastic about doing so, could not foresee it happening in the immediate future.

CONCLUSION

This chapter has discussed the key findings and issues that emerged from the Irish IWB pilot based on a qualitative study of the project's implementation and teachers' and pupils' perceptions of the technology. Although the number of schools involved was small, they represented a good mix of different school types. From the outset, the study had a number of key objectives that aimed to assess the impact of the technology on teachers and pupils; to examine how closely the experiences of Irish teachers with IWBs matched those of their UK counterparts; and to ascertain how the technology was changing teachers' professional practices. The research found that both teachers and students viewed the technology favorably and that IWBs enhanced the overall classroom environment as well as impacting teachers' professional practices in a positive manner. It also revealed that the experiences of Irish teachers with IWBs closely matched the experiences of UK teachers despite the fact that the policy response to this technology in both countries has been radically different.

When the pilot project commenced, the ICT advisor responsible for initiating it hoped that it would act as a spur and encourage Irish policy makers to take a lead in supporting the introduction of IWBs into schools. However, to date, this has not happened and it now seems unlikely to happen given the severity of the global recession and its adverse impact on Ireland. Already ICT spending in education has been cut - so much so that even the ICT advisory service itself was terminated in June 2008. In these straitened times, it is easy for governments to argue that IWBs are a luxury they simply cannot afford and to dismiss them, either publicly or privately, as just an expensive, electronic version of chalk and talk. However, as this case study and studies elsewhere have shown, IWBs are viewed positively by both teachers and students and are seen as devices which enhance the classroom environment as well as having a positive impact on teachers' professional practices. By virtue of their pull characteristics, they can also act as a hook for attracting those ICT "laggards" (Rogers, 1995) which lurk in every school

to actually seriously engage with technology in the classroom for the very first time, a development which can only be welcomed. Although an assessment of learning attainment was beyond the scope of this research, concurrent research by Somekh et al. (2007) clearly demonstrates that where teachers have permanent access to IWBs for at least two years, attainment gains can be achieved. Assessed in this context, the question must therefore be asked: are IWBs a luxury which Irish policy makers simply cannot afford to ignore?

REFERENCES

Becta (2005). *How can the use of an interactive whiteboard enhance the nature of teaching and learning in secondary mathematics and modern foreign languages: ICT Research Bursaries.* Retrieved October 21, 2005, from http://www.becta.org.uk

Bennett, S., Matton, K., & Kervin, L. (2008). The 'digital natives' debate: A critical review of the evidence. *British Journal of Educational Technology, 39*(5), 775–786. doi:10.1111/j.1467-8535.2007.00793.x

Cogill, J. (2003). *The uses of interactive whiteboards in the primary school: Effects on pedagogy.* Coventry, UK: Becta.

Cresswell, J. (1998). *Qualitative inquiry and research design: Choosing among five traditions.* California, USA: Sage Publications.

Cuban, L. (1986). *Teachers and machines: The classroom use of technology since 1920.* New York: Teachers College Press.

Cuban, L. (1993). Computers meet classroom: Classroom wins. *Teachers College Record, 95*(2), 185–210.

Futuresource Consulting. (2008). *Interactive displays quarterly insight: State of the market report.* Retrieved February 12, 2009, from http://www.futuresource-consulting.com/reports.htm

Glover, D., & Miller, D. (2002). The interactive whiteboard as a force for pedagogic change: The experience of five elementary schools in an English education authority. *Information Technology in Childhood Education Annual, 1,* 5–19.

Heppell, S. (2004). *Interactive whiteboards are useful stepping stones to other technologies* (interviewed by George Cole), *TES Online, 8.* Retrieved July 10, 2009, from https://tslwspr02.www.tes.co.uk/article.aspx?storycode=2047323

Higgins, S., Beauchamp, B., & Miller, D. (2007). Reviewing the literature on interactive whiteboards. *Learning, Media and Technology, 32*(3), 213–225. doi:10.1080/17439880701511040

Hull University. (2004). *The review project.* Retrieved August 25, 2005, from http://www.thereviewproject.org

Judge, M. (2003). *Wired for learning in Ireland final evaluation report.* Ireland: Dublin City University.

Judge, M. (2004). The wired for learning project in Ireland. A classic tale of technology, school culture and the problem of change. In P. Isaias, P. Kommers & M. McPherson (Eds.), *Proceedings of the IADIS International Conference, 1* (pp. 226-234). e-Society 2004, Avila, Spain.

Kennewell, S., & Morgan, A. (2003). *Student teachers' experiences and attitudes towards using interactive whiteboards in the teaching and learning of young Children.* Paper presented at the IFIP Working Groups 3.5 Conference: Young Children and Learning Technologies. University of Western Sydney, Australia.

Kitchen, S., Butt, S., & Mackenzies, H. (2006). *Evaluation of curriculum online: Emerging findings from the third survey of schools.* Report for National Centre for Social Research. Retrieved July 10, 2009, from http://www.becta.org.uk/page_documents/research/curriculum_

Knuffer, N. (1993). Teachers and educational computing: Changing roles and changing pedagogy. In R. Muffoletto & N. Knuffer N. (Eds.), Computers in education: Social, political and historical perspectives, 1(1), 163-179.

Levy, P. (2002). *Interactive whiteboards in learning and teaching in two Sheffield schools: A developmental study.* Sheffield Department of Information Studies, University of Sheffield.

Maykut, P., & Morehouse, R. (1994). *Beginning qualitative research: A philosophic and practical guide.* London: Falmer Press.

Merriman, S. B. (1998). *Case study research in education: A qualitative approach.* San Francisco: Josey-Bass.

Moss, G., Jewitt, C., Levaãiç, R., Armstrong, V., Cardini, A., & Castle, F. (2007). The interactive whiteboards, pedagogy and pupil performance evaluation: An evaluation of the Schools Whiteboard Expansion (SWE) Project. DfES Research Report 816. London: DfES.

Patton, M. Q. (2002). *Qualitative research and evaluation methods* (3rd ed.). London: Sage Publications.

Postman, N., & Knopf, A. A. (1997). *The end of education.* New York: Knopf.

Prensky, N. (2001). *Digital natives, digital immigrants.* Retrieved October 16, 2007, from http://www.marcprensky.com/writing

Rogers, E. M. (1995). *Diffusion of innovations.* New York: Macmillan Publishing Company.

Smith, F., Hardman, F., & Higgins, S. (2006). The impact of interactive whiteboards on teacher-pupil interaction in the national literacy and numeracy strategies. *British Educational Research Journal, 32*(2), 443–457. doi:10.1080/01411920600635452

Smith, H. (2001). *SmartBoard evaluation: Final report, Kent NGfL*. Retrieved August 15, 2005, from http://www/tented.org.uk/ngfl/whiteboards/report.html

Somekh, B., & Haldane, M. (2007). *Evaluation of the primary schools whiteboard expansion project*. London: Department for Education and Skills.

Stake, R. E. (1995). *The art of case study research*. California, USA: Sage Publications.

Veen, W. (1993). The role of beliefs in the use of information technology: Implications for teacher education, or teaching the right thing at the right time. *Journal of Information Technology for Teacher Education, 2*(2), 139–153.

Wall, K., & Higgins, S., & Smith. (2005). 'The visual helps me understand the complicated things': Pupil views of teaching and learning with interactive whiteboards. *British Journal of Educational Technology, 36*(5), 851–867. doi:10.1111/j.1467-8535.2005.00508.x

Yin, R. (1994). *Case study research: Design and methods*. California, USA: Sage Publications.

Afterword
Magic Wand or Museum Piece?
The Future of the Interactive Whiteboard in Education

Stephen Bax
University of Bedfordshire, UK

ABSTRACT

This chapter looks at the processes by which a technology such as the interactive whiteboard can become "normalized" in our practice, in other words how it can reach the stage when it is used seamlessly and almost invisibly in our everyday pedagogy. After briefly reviewing the literature on the concept of normalization, and the ways in which a technology can reach that stage, the chapter argues that the IWB is not yet fully normalized in education, but the indications are that it might be some way through the process. It then draws on the work of the other contributors to the volume as a whole in order to identify some of the key factors which might contribute to the normalization of the IWB. It concludes with some recommendations for research and development for those seeking the normalization of the IWB in future.

*The key to making the IWB work for you is to take tried and tested teaching strategies and resources as your starting point, then **wave that whiteboard wand** over them to transform them into dynamic and interactive resources. (Evans et al., 2009, p.188; my emphasis)*

If we are to believe the above quotation, the interactive whiteboard is magical in its transformative capabilities, its sorcery requiring a minimum of human effort in order to impact on learning.

This magical power has also been witnessed by others. According to McLean in *The Guardian* newspaper, the IWB is a worker of miracles, "not only allowing young students access to the curriculum but also *simultaneously teaching them the English language*" (McLean, 2006, p.7; my emphasis). Teachers, in this formulation, will be redundant very soon. The IWB will simply do our teaching for us while we lie on the nearest beach.

Or will it? In sharp contrast with those who see the IWB as an educational magical wand, others are starkly negative. Dudeney (2006, p. 10), while attracted to some of the IWB's features in language education, considers that it will never play a significant role in most language classes, partly because it is "an elite tool, or an impossible goal for the great majority". Equally doubtful, Thornbury transforms the IWB acronym in order to damn it as an "Interactive White Elephant" (2007), implying likewise that it is doomed to failure, to end up as a dusty museum piece. Many classroom teachers are also skeptical, as exemplified by this quotation from a teacher's blog:

I am not ... a big fan of interactive whiteboards and remain to be convinced of their importance to teaching and learning. I believe interactive whiteboards are only so popular in schools because they tend to reinforce traditional teacher led modes of learning. The teacher in front of a class leading the lesson with a visual aid is what we have been doing since schooling began. Teacher active - pupils passive ...

I can see mileage in using a large visual display at the beginnings and ends of lessons to briefly introduce or consolidate the learning and also for fostering open ended discussion of pictorial sources. But can't this be done much more cheaply and just as effectively with an internet ready laptop and a digital projector?

Why spend oodles of money on an expensive board which offers perhaps at best a presentation tool, a reveal tool and a quiz builder? (Walker, 2006)

So as we conclude this volume and look to the future it is timely to pose the questions: will the IWB be an educational magic wand, or will it instead end up as an expensive museum piece? Who is likely to be proven right in this debate? In what ways can the contributions to this volume shed light on the possible future impact of IWB technology on education?

ORGANIZATION OF THIS CHAPTER

Since it is impossible at the moment to predict the future of the IWB with any certainty I cite the opposing viewpoints above not so much to decide between them as to illustrate the wider point which this chapter seeks to make, namely that the ways in which such debates over technology are commonly presented reflects a polarized and rather blinkered understanding of how technological innovations operate in society in general and in education in particular. To put it another way, as we seek to understand the possible future role of the IWB in education I propose that we need to adopt a perspective on technological innovation in education which is rather more complex and nuanced, and to my mind more satisfactory as a model of how technologies operate in life and in education, than the models which implicitly underpin the polarized viewpoints exemplified above.

One of my aims in approaching the debate in this way is to help us to move towards a more robust and accurate understanding of how technologies such as the IWB actually operate and can potentially operate in education. I will start by looking at sociotechnical innovation in the broadest sense, alluding briefly to what we know so far about how we interact with new technologies, and then in the later stages of the chapter I will consider how this might help us to understand the particular case of the IWB. In that later section I am fortunate in being able to draw on the many varied and insightful chapters in this volume as a whole, in order to reflect on how the IWB might perhaps impact on education in the years to come.

NORMALIZATION REVISITED

The background to my approach derives from arguments I advanced some years ago concerning what I termed the "normalization" of technology

(Bax, 2003), by which I meant the stage when a technology, be it an everyday one such as a watch or a fork, or a pedagogical one such as a textbook or pen, can become after time relatively invisible in our daily use, so seamlessly is it employed in our everyday practice. This stage of relative "invisibility" or normalization is when – I argued – a technology is at its most useful, having gone through various intermediate stages when it is not yet normalized, including what I termed the excessive "awe" stage, when it is felt to be perfect for every possible use (as in the McLean quotation above), or the excessive "fear" stage when the technology is felt to be somehow dangerous or at best useless (as in those quotations above which condemn the IWB out of hand). Having perhaps passed through these and other stages, a technology can then sometimes reach the normalization stage, when it has found its proper place and therefore become relatively invisible and most useful.

To express this in more formal terms, the underlying hypothesis relating to the concept of normalization can be set out as follows:

A technology has reached its fullest possible effectiveness when it has arrived at the stage of "normalization", namely when it is invisible, used automatically and without our being consciously aware of its role.

Since my original article in 2003 (and also Chambers & Bax, 2007; Bax, 2008) this concept of normalization has been cited and addressed in a variety of discussions concerning the role of technology in education (e.g. Jung, 2005; Levy & Stockwell, 2006; Hansson, 2008; Allford & Pachler, 2007; Lamy & Hampel, 2007; Spencer-Oatey, 2007; Davies, Walker, Rendall & Hewer, 2009). The concept is seen by those who cite it as potentially useful for teachers seeking a better understanding of their relationship with technologies. For example it has been seen as useful for language teachers:

we believe that working towards normalization is a useful, practical strategy. Language teachers are very much working within a complex system of opportunity and constraint. Normalization then becomes a process of understanding the infrastructure, the support networks, and the materials, and working effectively within them. (Levy & Stockwell, 2006, p. 234)

Other writers apply the concept to related technologies such as interactive whiteboards themselves (Cutrim Schmid, 2008), distance learning and autonomy (O'Dowd, 2007), and even to more general analysis of methodologies and pedagogies (Farmer, 2006).

To my mind the concept of normalization can prove useful also in our discussion on the possible future place of the IWB in education since it allows us to frame a number of salient questions, such as: to what extent is the IWB currently "normalized" in education? If it is not currently normalized, could the IWB in future attain full normalization in education, in its current form or in some modified form? How, if we choose to do so, might we speed up the process of normalization?

We will return later to consider these and other issues relating to the possible normalization of the IWB in education, but first it is important to understand in further detail what normalization entails and how a technology can reach that stage.

TOWARDS NORMALIZATION

I have suggested elsewhere (Bax, 2003, 2007, in preparation) that the progress towards normalization, in very general terms, can be characterized broadly in diagrammatic form as in Figure 1.

We take the end point of normalization, at the right of the diagram, to be the stage when we use the technology without considering it even to be a technology, when it is invisible. We

Figure 1. Towards the normalization of a technology

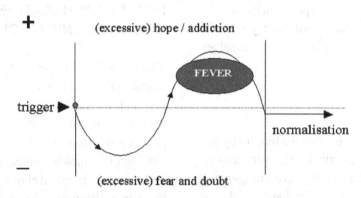

use it without our being consciously aware of its value to us, as when we put our spectacles on our nose in the morning or our shoes on our feet. The diagram aims to illustrate in broad terms some of the stages which a technology typically goes through before reaching that normalization stage. Research on the impact of innovations in general (Rogers, 1995; Bax, 2003; Chambers & Bax, 2006) suggests that we can characterize some typical stages as follows.

Early Adopters

A few users adopt the technology out of curiosity or obsession. Most of us are not "early adopters", or else we are not early adopters with every technology, but a few people will obsessively buy any new technology which arrives on the market. Such users are rather pejoratively treated as "geeks" or "anoraks" but they serve a crucial function as trendsetters, and also in effect fund future development of the technologies in question. In terms of the diagram in Figure 1, they often act as the "trigger" for the average user, as indicated on the left of the diagram. We see someone with a new gadget and this triggers our own interest.

Try Once

People try it out but reject it because of early problems. They cannot see its value. They are

skeptical or uncertain. Frequently, after the first flush of enthusiasm, our interest dips. We try the gadget once but we are not convinced. The new technology does not seem to add anything of "relative advantage" (Rogers, 1995) to our lives or work.

Fear

At this point we are often excessively nervous of the technology and its possible impact on our cozy patterns of activity. With many innovations scare stories begin to circulate which cause users to be nervous. When microwave ovens were introduced there were rumors that they could spread cancer ("Don't be fooled by the scare stories", 2009). With mobile phones there have been constant rumors of brain damage or testicular cancer. Concerning the search engine Google, it was recently alleged in a daily newspaper that "[t]he digital age *is destroying us* by ruining our ability to concentrate" (Appleyard, 2008, n.p.). In the diagram this is indicated by the dip in confidence, the uncertainty of the new.

Try Again

Sometimes such fears can kill off a new technology completely, but often we see others using the new technology and we gradually start to believe that it can indeed help us in one way or other, either in practical ways or else simply to help us to fit in with the fashion or the crowd. We try it again. We see its "relative advantage" for ourselves (Rogers, 1995).

Awe

In the normalizing process we also frequently encounter a stage of high enthusiasm, even passion, the stage at which we start to have *exaggerated* expectations of what the technology can do for us. It will change our lives. If it is educational technology, it will allow us, as teachers, to spend more time relaxing while our students are soaking up education on their own from the IWB.

Normalizing and Normalization

Gradually we realize (perhaps subconsciously) that we were excessive in our fear and no less excessive in our awe, and at this point the technology starts to take a more normal place in our work or daily activity. We start to see it as a natural part of our lives or activity, not the centre of what we do, but a useful tool, in its place, alongside other useful tools. It comes to be seen as something normal. The technology is so integrated into our lives that it becomes invisible – "normalized".

This informal characterization of a typical process should not lead us to assume that normalization always happens, nor that it always happens in this order or in these ways, but I suggest that this is a useful general characterization of a process which successful technologies and innovations of various kinds frequently go through. I have described it here in fairly straightforward, unsophisticated terms, so it is now appropriate to look in greater depth at the theoretical background to the concept itself and processes involved in normalization, and then to see how this can help us to understand where the IWB might figure in education in future.

A THEORETICAL FRAMEWORK FOR NORMALISATION: SOCIOTECHNICAL CHANGE

The danger of a diagrammatic representation such as that in Figure 1 is that it might be taken to imply a straightforward and linear movement towards normalization of a kind which rarely occurs in practice. It is important to bear in mind, then, that although a technology might go through some or all of the stages identified above, it might go through them in a different order, it might omit some of them, and or it might not ever reach normalization. Furthermore, although this diagram represents some stages by which a technology might achieve normalization, a second danger of such a representation is that it might also oversimplify the *reasons why* a technology might succeed in normalizing. As we now turn to consider the factors which underlie sociotechnical innovation in general, it is therefore important to treat the process of normalization as highly complex, involving a potentially wide variety of factors.

We have already hinted, in the characterization above, at some of the reasons why a technology such as the IWB might catch on and become normalized in education. We noted the role of "early adopters", the point about "relative advantage" (meaning that we will only use a new technology if it adds something significant to what we do already), the role of fashion, and so on. This alerts us immediately to the fact that the reasons why a new technology becomes normalized can be many and varied; as I said, it is therefore important to avoid reductionism in our attempt at explanation, but unfortunately many writers do not do so. For example, many popular debates, when conceptualizing the broad relationship between technology and society in such simplistic terms, typically base their analyses on variants of what I have termed the "single agent" or "sole agent" fallacy (Bax, 2003). It is often supposed, for example, that single inventors "cause" technological change by themselves, or that particular inventions are in themselves the main agents of change (Bijker, 1997). Of course in a few cases single inventors have had unusual impacts, or particular inventions have caused change in themselves, but for the most part sociotechnical change or normalization is far more complex than these formulations imply, and results from numerous interconnected factors working together in subtle and often intricate ways, rather than from any single factor or agent (Pacey, 1983).

This is to call for a more complex conception of sociotechnical change than is commonplace in popular and even some academic debates, a conception which perforce sees technological change as resulting from an intricate interplay of social, historical, economic and political forces, rather than from any one or two causes in isolation. In arguing for a more complex view of the relationship between technology and society I align myself with Bijker's broadly constructivist approach (Bijker, 1997), which in turn fits with what Mercer and Fisher (1997) have called a "neo-Vygotskian" perspective as a means of understanding the place of technology in education, with in its emphasis on the social and cultural as opposed to the merely technical.

As I have argued more recently (Bax, in preparation) seeing normalization in these terms requires us to take into account a range of wider social and cultural forces which might be bear on the individual user of a technology. It requires us to conceive of the teacher using the IWB, for example, not as operating in a vacuum, deciding by his or her own volition whether or not to use the IWB for the next lesson, but as a social actor enveloped in and profoundly influenced by a mesh of wider cultural and human forces. This broad sociocultural perspective is consonant also with Pacey's work which emphasizes the need to examine "technology practice", which includes the sociocultural dimension, as opposed to simply the "technical" dimensions (Pacey 1983). It is also consonant with research into other aspects

of technology in education, typified by positions such as this:

a sociocultural approach to online research encourages educators to look at technology, not as an independent force that shapes and determines how learners carry out a learning task, but rather as a part of a complex mesh of factors which go to making up any particular learning context. (O'Dowd 2007, pp. 32-3; my emphasis)

When considering the future of the IWB in education, then, my discussion will draw on this broadly social constructivist perspective which in effect stands against simplistic "single agent" explanations of sociotechnical change. In this regard Bijker makes the important point that:

[a] central adage for this research is that one should never take the meaning of a technical artifact or technological system as residing in the technology itself. Instead, one must study how technologies are shaped and acquire their meanings in the heterogeneity of social interactions. (Bijker, 1997, p. 6)

This is another way of saying that it is a mistake to attribute sociotechnical change to any signal agent, such as "the technology itself", since to do so would be to fall into the "single agent" fallacy. Bijker then goes on to describe the debate between what he calls "internalists" as opposed to "contextualists". The first group of theorists tend, in Bijker's view, to believe that "we can understand the development of a technology only if we start with an understanding of the technology in all its minute details" (Bijker, 1997, p. 10). Here too I align myself with Bijker on the opposite side of the debate, as a contextualist, supporting the contrary view that:

the economic, social, political, and scientific context of a technology is as important to its develop-

ment as are its technical design characteristics. (Bijker, 1997, p. 10)

For our debate concerning the IWB, therefore, this warns us against suggesting that the mere attributes of the IWB in themselves will be the main or sole factors in the technology's eventual success or failure. Furthermore, it will be clear from this that I see dangers in any approach which seeks to explain sociotechnical change in terms of a sole agent, be that sole agent the technology itself or its creator, or anything else in isolation. Such views are in my view dangerously simplistic, since they run the risk of ignoring other factors which can potentially be of significance. To reinforce the point, Bijker in his analysis (1997) offers detailed discussion of three technologies as a means of showing just how complex and multifaceted the factors behind sociotechnical change can be, namely the bicycle, bakelite and the electric bulb, and demonstrates through close analysis of their histories the complexity of their progress towards normalization (as I would call it) and the wide range of social, economic and other factors involved in that process. This can act as a warning, so that when we consider how technologies such as the IWB can become normalized in education we must do so from a perspective which allows us to take account of as wide a range of social and other factors as possible, not focusing too narrowly on the features of IWBs in themselves, or on any other single aspects of the technology or its use.

To put this another way, when we ask ourselves how a technology such as the IWB can become normalized, it is advisable to seek to answer that question in terms of a broad range of factors as opposed to a narrower set. This derives from the awareness that, historically, as Pacey (1983), pointed out some time ago, sociotechnical change always comes about as the result of a number of interconnected factors, social and cultural as well as technical, and this in turn is to set the debate on normalization within a resolutely social

constructivist neo-Vygotskian "contextualist" framework.

The consequence of this is that we should wherever possible eschew simplistic explanatory statements or predictions. These include those which we quoted at the start of this chapter, which might suggest simplistically that the IWB, for example, or any other technology, will fail simply because it is too expensive, or too elitist. We must equally be suspicious of the opposing view, that the IWB will succeed simply because it is "interactive" or "easy to use". To offer such views is, I suggest, to fall too easily into the simplistic "single agent" mode of thinking. It is important that we should go beyond this if we are to understand fully how any technology such as the IWB can operate in education, and how it might or might not have a useful future impact on learning.

This general view of normalization as a process which results from a complex interplay of factors, social and other, was already part of my original formulation of the concept (Bax, 2003), but drawing now on discussions such as Bijker's, as well on the wider literature on sociotechnical change seen in its social and cultural context, including the work of those authors cited above, we can now begin to appreciate in even greater detail how a proper understanding of normalization and its processes can help us to understand where the IWB might be going in future.

WHAT DOES THIS MEAN FOR THE IWB?

We are therefore now in a position to review the ways in which the other contributors in this volume have assisted us in understanding the possible normalization of the IWB, but before doing so it may be helpful to summarize my arguments so far. I have suggested that when we consider a technology such as the IWB and how it might become normalized in our lives or in our educational work, we can expect to see it following a typical path perhaps starting with skepticism on the part of users, then moving to excessive fear mingled with exaggerated awe at its possibilities, and then perhaps settling into a pattern of use which is natural and relatively invisible or normalized. That was the thrust of the diagram in Figure 1 and the discussion which followed. I then argued for the importance of seeing the interplay of forces leading to normalization as a complex and intricate one, as a process occurring within a complexity of social and cultural forces, which means we should resist the lure of any more reductionist approaches which might tend to oversimplify how and why technologies succeed or fail. I stressed the importance of avoiding the "sole agent" fallacy, which is so common in discussions of technology, and the importance of taking a broader and nuanced view which includes a wide range of social and cultural factors in our analysis.

THE IWB AND NORMALISATION

Is the IWB normalized in education at the moment? Normalization operates differently and at different rates in different contexts, of course, so at any one moment a technology such as the IWB might be normalized in one school or in one organization or in one country but not in another. However, the very fact that we have in front of us a volume on the IWB in education, meaning that sufficient numbers of stakeholders from around the world see a need and a value in such a volume, suggests in itself that the IWB is not yet typically normalized in many areas of education, and that this volume has a part to play in that process. A number of contributors in earlier chapters have pointed to an element of skepticism and doubt among users, typical of an early stage in a normalization process. In Chapter 2, for example, Moss and Jewitt note that recent large-scale research into the effectiveness of the IWB has been cautious about the resulting

educational benefits, noting that "uptake has not necessarily changed teaching in the ways that were anticipated". Others too have cited skepticism from various quarters.

By contrast, awe and passion are also evident: although no-one in this volume has been unwise enough to characterize the IWB as a magic wand, almost all have highlighted the value of the IWB in various educational domains. Bettsworth (Chapter 15) reports on "unanimous" enthusiasm among pupils in her study. Hennessy, Deaney and Tooley (Chapter 7) report on the "meteoric rise" in the popularity of the IWB; Higgins (Chapter 6) cites teachers and students as being "overwhelmingly positive" about the IWB. In short, the general thrust of the volume is that this technology does have a potentially positive role to play in education. However, the fact that this needs to be said at all indicates that normalization of the IWB is not yet the norm. It suggests again that in terms of the diagram in Figure 1, we are probably in the middle of it, some of us skeptics and doubters, others in the throes of passion, and others still undecided.

WHAT MIGHT HELP THE NORMALIZATION OF THE IWB IN EDUCATION?

From this point of time onwards, there is of course no guarantee that the IWB will in fact ever become normalized in many or even most educational settings. That will depend on a host of factors including the economic, social, political, and scientific dimensions which I referred to above. This volume does, however, offer us many useful insights into some of the key elements which might assist the process of the normalization of the IWB, so as we try to look into the future of this technology it is useful to review some of the factors which contributors to the volume have considered to be most significant.

Pedagogy and the Teacher

In this regard it is noteworthy, from the outset, that many chapters in this volume focus on pedagogy, on the teacher and on teacher training. Early in the volume, Gray in Chapter 5 makes use of a set of examples to illustrate the ways in which teachers can "meet their own immediate concerns in the situated reality of their classrooms". Hennessy, Deaney and Tooley examine pedagogy in a science context in Chapter 7, while Miller and Glover in Chapter 8 focus on maths pedagogy. Swan, Kratcoski, Schenker and van 't Hooft in Chapter 9 explore in some detail teachers' practice, looking at how teachers' use of the IWB can impact on students' reading, language arts and mathematics. These discussions of pedagogy and the teacher are continued in Chapter 11 when Cogill focuses usefully on "teacher's whiteboard pedagogical practice", and unpacks some of the aspects of that knowledge as central factors which underlie teachers' practice. Teacher development is a focus of Chapter 12, where Haldane considers "Transformative Personal Development" (TPD) as a means of improving IWB use. Still in the area of pedagogy, but this time discussing training, Cutrim Schmid and Schimmack in Chapter 13 note that "the lack of high quality teacher training is a major factor impeding the integration of new technologies in education".

This focus on pedagogy and the teacher is then further emphasized in Part IV which looks at teacher perspectives. Lim-Fong and Robins, for example, in their fascinating discussion in Chapter 14 of the Livingstone Inquiry Group, focus on how teachers "came to understand the significant potential of these IWBs to enhance lessons within their immediate educational environment".

This strong focus on pedagogy and the teacher, evident throughout the volume, fits well in fact with Miller and Glover's comprehensive survey of the literature on IWB use in Chapter 1, in which they chart the use of the IWB since its introduction into UK schools, and note the central role of the teacher in the possible normalization of the IWB: "the IWB will only be of lasting significance in enhancing student attainment if teachers are prepared to change their teaching approaches into a more interactive mode".

This is surely true. Pedagogy, the teacher, and therefore teacher development and training are of course crucial, given the obvious centrality of the teacher in most educational settings, so the amount of attention devoted to teachers, to pedagogy and to teacher training and development in the chapters and case studies in this volume reflect the importance of this dimension. However, it would be a mistake to assume from this that the IWB will simply reach normalization if we pay all or most of our attention to the teacher. We need to recognize that the teacher is but one agent in the process, and furthermore that the teacher is an actor on a wider social stage - indeed contributions by the writers cited above and by others in the volume repeatedly make it clear that if we wish for the normalization of the IWB it would be an error to devote our attention exclusively to teachers' attitudes, practice and training.

Pupils

For one thing, that would be to ignore the pupils. One need only read Bettsworth's vivid account of pupils using the IWB in what I consider a normalized way, almost oblivious of their teacher, to see the huge role that pupils' attitudes and practices play and will play in the normalization process:

Two pupils came up to the IWB to drag the steps into the correct sequence. What was striking was the total concentration from the rest of the class, and this was the case in both teaching groups. Pupils raised their hands when they disagreed with the decisions being made by the two pupils at the IWB. The two pupils did not ask for help from their peers, but instead they looked to see how many hands were raised, and then revised their previous decision, with only minimal discus-

sion between the two of them. The focus and silent response of all pupils was remarkable.

One general point to be drawn from this is that no matter how far the IWB is normalized in the teacher's practice, it will only be effective if and when it is normalized in the learner's practice also. Just as teachers need to adapt their attitudes and practices to a new technology, learners do too, and we ignore this fact at our peril.

Administration, Policy and Power

Another important factor in normalization is the attitude of the school as a whole, and of the wider school system, and in particular the attitude of those in power. At times technologies can be imposed in educational settings in a top-down manner in a flush of enthusiasm, but without the appropriate planning and understanding of the ecology of the setting (Tudor, 2001, 2003), in ways doomed to failure. In Chapter 10 Bannister, Hutchinson and Sargeant, discussing learner response systems, give an illuminating description of just how this can operate:

There are examples of the equipment being bought by the headteacher after a commercial demonstration at a conference or trade show. In essence, this can mean that the headteacher has never observed the technology in use in the classroom environment. Equally, this then means that the school has not developed any strategy for implementation and the equipment arrives in school without any forward planning.

The assumption underlying this headteacher's action appears to be that simply buying the equipment will be enough to make it effective, thereby once again falling into the "single agent" trap and ignoring the host of pedagogical, social, human and other factors which normalization requires. By contrast, supportive and enlightened management can make a genuine difference. The same authors found from their study that:

the implementation of the equipment is more successful when a senior leader within the school is involved. This is because there is more potential for a strategy to be developed for the long term aims and goals of using the equipment.

This again serves to make the wider point that it is not the teacher alone, nor even the teacher and the pupils, who will necessarily be the sole or main determining factor as to whether a technology is normalized in education, since the attitude and behavior of those "higher up the chain" can also be crucial. However, I would go further, and argue that if we are to understand how the IWB or any other technology is to become normalized in education or in wider society, we need also to consider the role of larger social and cultural forces, far beyond the school walls, as they impact on users. Teachers, pupils and headteachers do not exist in a vacuum but are subject to wider societal attitudes, forces and pressures just like anyone else. A crucial factor here of course can be aspects of government policy; Moss and Jewitt in Chapter 2 make the key point that those in power are frequently too hasty in their approach to implementation, and often have too ambitious expectations about quick returns on investment.

This dimension is alluded to by several of the other authors in this volume, among them Gray and Higgins, who demonstrate the way in which educational factors (such as the National Literacy and Numeracy strategies in the UK, and the emphasis on whole class teaching) can operate with political forces and indeed with economic strategies in the process of sociotechnical change, but Higgins' finding that despite much investment and planning "the impact in terms of students' attainment on national tests was very small and short-lived" must surely give all policy makers pause for thought, and cause us furthermore to agree with Moss and Jewitt that those in power need, amongst other things, to identify more "modest objectives", and perhaps more besides.

CONCLUSION: WHERE NEXT?

The central thrust of this chapter has been that, since research into innovation and sociotechnical change in general shows the crucial importance of taking into account a wide range of factors, including social, cultural, political, economic and psychological matters, we will only be able to predict the future of the IWB in education with any success if we insist on adopting such broader perspectives in our analysis and discussion. The other authors in this volume have shed important light on some of the central factors involved in the possible normalization of the IWB, including the pedagogy, teacher, teacher development, pupils' attitudes and behaviors, the role of management and policy and others, some of which I have alluded to above. However, in order for us to obtain a fully rounded picture of how the IWB might become normalized in future, I suggest that our next step could be to address four further issues in our research and practice, here framed as four questions:

Are We Planning Appropriately for Sociotechnical Change as Regards the IWB?

Numerous of the previous chapters, for example Moss and Jewitt, have suggested that policy makers and planners have not always planned and prepared appropriately for the use of the IWB in education, and many of those planners seem to have adopted narrow "single agency" approach, as I noted above. Higgins proposes in the light of his comprehensive study that: "embedding new or developing technologies in education needs a pedagogical design phase as well as a technological one".

This implies, rightly in my view, that too frequently those who plan for the use of the IWB have tended to focus too narrowly on the technology, and do not take sufficient account of the full range of issues involved in normalization. These include the pedagogical areas which Higgins mentions, but in my view policy makers also frequently neglect many other relevant social and cultural issues of crucial importance in normalization. In short, planners and policy makers, if they are to plan for a normalized IWB in education, need to have a far greater awareness of how the processes of sociotechnical change operate and of the complexity and long-term nature of the process, and they then need to tailor their promises, strategies and investments accordingly.

Are We Taking a Too Optimistic and Too Short-Term View of the Impact of the IWB?

Several contributors to this volume cite examples of excessive optimism in the use of the IWB, and an exaggerated expectation of immediate or speedy impact or change. History shows, however, that the normalization of a major technology is frequently a long, slow and unpredictable process, so we need to expect and plan with medium- and longer-term vision, as well as with caution. I would echo Gray's suggestion, for example, that a longitudinal study of teachers' use of the IWB would be beneficial, since a shorter term study is unlikely to tell us much about genuine sustained impact. In this regard the extensive research described in Higgins' chapter is also salutary, since it warns us not to expect massive impacts all at once. We need constantly to remember that the process of normalization is a long series of small steps rather than a giant leap, and to be prepared for that.

Have We Taken Full Account of all the Social and Cultural Factors which Bear on the Possible Normalization of the IWB?

In my view the profession has so far neglected to consider some of the social and cultural dimensions of IWB use, without which our picture is incomplete. Tudor (2001, 2003) has warned against taking a too "technical" view of educational change, and argued instead for a more "ecological" approach, and in light of this I would propose the need for more qualitative and ethnographic research into the particular contexts of use of the IWB around the world. The chapter offered in this volume by Lim-Fong and Roberts gives a rich insight into the daily lives of teachers, for instance, and I suggest we need more studies of this kind to flesh out the details of the particular social and cultural factors which impact on the normalization of the IWB. We recall Bijker's emphasis on "the economic, social, political, and scientific context of a technology" (Bijker, 1997, p.10) and on the fact that "technologies are shaped and acquire their meanings *in the heterogeneity of social interactions*" (Bijker, 1997, p. 6; my emphasis). We might also consider in greater depth the emotional and affective dimensions (McCarthy & Wright, 2004) of our and our pupils' use of the IWB. This is to argue for a more sustained analysis of the local and the particular, including the relatively neglected pupils, their perceptions and modes of use, and to call for a program of research, probably in ethnographic mode, into the ways in which different cultural groups in different socio-economic environments make use of the IWB, so as to allow us to see (as we cannot currently see) to what extent success or failure depends on these factors.

Could the IWB Evolve into Something Else?

In our calmer moments none of us would claim, of course, that the IWB is a magic wand. Perhaps one day decades hence we will indeed walk through a dim museum corridor and glimpse a lonely IWB gathering dust alongside the record player and video machine. However, I suggest that it is unlikely that the whole of IWB technology will now simply disappear; it is far more likely that it will evolve, perhaps converging with other

technologies by taking on functions previously reserved for separate different devices (cf. Jenkins, 2006).

The teacher whose blog we quoted at the start of this chapter wondered why the functions of the IWB could not be carried out more cheaply with "an internet ready laptop and a digital projector" (Walker, 2006), but we might equally anticipate that the IWB could eventually combine all the functions of a laptop, a traditional whiteboard and more besides. We might also expect, with Higgins (Chapter 6), that "[t]he stage after this is perhaps the development of multi-user, multi-touch environments" which aligns with Bettsworth's call for more "individualized interactions" (Chapter 15).

Given Bannister, Hutchinson and Sargeant's chapter on learner response systems (Chapter 10), it is therefore surely possible that the IWB might combine with such interactive systems to provide a technology which is even more interactive and individualized than anything currently available, perhaps a "hybrid IWB" or something with a new name altogether. And so long as such a device succeeds in putting the learner and learning first, and therefore putting itself in the background, I suggest that it might well succeed in eventually becoming the norm in our classrooms, as normal and as normalized in the education of the future as the pen and pencil are today.

REFERENCES

Allford, D., & Pachler, N. (2007). *Language, autonomy and the new learning environments*. Bern, Switzerland: Peter Lang.

Appleyard, B. (2008). *Stoooopid ... why the Google generation isn't as smart as it thinks*. *The Sunday Times*, July 20. Retrieved June 10, 2009, from http://technology.timesonline.co.uk/

Bax, S. (2003). CALL – past, present and future. *System, 31*(1), 13-28.

Bax, S. (2008, August). *Bridges, chopsticks and shoelaces: 'Normalising' computers and computer technologies in language classrooms.* Paper presented at the WorldCALL conference, Fukuoka, Japan.

Bax, S. (in preparation). *The normalisation of technology in language education.*

Bijker, W. (1997). *Of bicycles bakelites, and bulbs: Towards a theory of sociotechnical change.* Cambridge, MA: MIT Press.

Chambers, A., & Bax, S. (2006). Making CALL work: Towards normalisation. *System, 34,* 465–479.

Cutrim Schmid, E. (2008). Interactive whiteboards and the normalization of CALL. In R. Marriott & P. Torres (Eds.), *Handbook of research on E-Learning methodologies for language acquisition* (pp. 69-83). Hershey, PA: IGI Global.

Davies, G., Walker, R., Rendall, H., & Hewer, S. (2009). Introduction to computer assisted language learning (CALL). In G. Davies (Ed.), *Information and communications technology for language teachers (ICT4LT).* Slough: Thames Valley University. Retrieved June 24, 2009, from http://www.ict4lt.org/en/en_mod1-4.htm

Dudeney, G. (2006). Interactive, quite bored. *IATEFL CALL Review,* Summer, 8-10.

Evans, C., Midgley, A., Rigby, P., Warham, L., & Woolnough, P. (2009). *Teaching English: Developing as a reflective secondary teacher.* London: Sage.

Farmer, F. (2006). *Professionalism in ELT.* Mexico: Plaza y Valdes.

Hansson, T. (Ed.). (2008). *Handbook of research on digital information technologies: Innovations, methods and ethical issues.* Hershey, PA: IGI Global.

Jenkins, H. (2006). *Convergence culture.* New York: New York University Press.

Jung, U. (2005). CALL: past, present and future — a bibliometric approach. *ReCALL, 17,* 4-17.

Lamy, M., & Hampel, R. (2007). Online communication for language learning and teaching. Basingstoke, UK: Palgrave Macmillan.

Levy, M., & Stockwell, G. (2006). *CALL dimensions: Options and issues in computer assisted language learning.* Mahwah, NJ: Lawrence Erlbaum Associates.

McLean, H. (2006). How to give lessons a real talking point. *Educ@guardian,* June 20, p. 7.

Mercer, N., & Fisher, E. (1997). The importance of talk. In R. Wegerif & P. Scrimshaw (Eds.), *Computers and talk in the primary classroom* (pp. 13-21). Clevedon, UK: Multilingual Matters.

O'Dowd, R. (2007). *Online intercultural exchange: An introduction for foreign language teachers.* Clevedon, UK: Multilingual Matters.

Pacey, A. (1983). *The culture of technology.* Cambridge, MA.: MIT Press.

Rogers, E. (1995). *Diffusion of innovations* (4th ed.). New York: Free Press.

Spencer-Oatey, H. (2007). *E-Learning initiatives in China: Pedagogy, policy and culture.* Hong Kong, China: Hong Kong University Press.

Thornbury, S. (2007, June). *Plenary address.* Paper presented at the Cutting Edges conference, University of Canterbury, UK.

Triggs, J. (2009). "Don't be fooled by the scare stories". *Daily Express,* February 10. Retrieved February 10, 2009, from http://www.express.co.uk/posts/view/84174/Don't-be-fooled-by-the-scare-stories

Tudor, I. (2001). *The dynamics of the language classroom.* Cambridge, UK: Cambridge University Press.

Tudor, I. (2003). Learning to live with complexity: Towards an ecological perspective on language teaching, *System*, *31*, 1-12.

Walker, A. (2006). Blog posting, June 14, 2006. Retrieved June 10, 2009, from http://education-forum.ipbhost.com

Compilation of References

Abrahamson, D. (2003). Embodied spatial articulation: A gesture perspective on student negotiation between kinaesthetic schemas and epistemic forms in learning mathematics. In D. E. McDougall & J. A. Ross (Eds.), *Proceedings of the 26th Annual Meeting of the International Group for the Psychology of Mathematics Education, 2*, (pp. 791-797).

Alexander, R. (1994). Analysing practice. In J. Bourne (Ed.) (1994). Thinking through primary practice (pp. 16-21). London: Routledge.

Alexander, R. (2000). *Culture and pedagogy: International comparisons in primary education*. Malden, MA: Blackwell Publishers.

Alexander, R. (2003). *Still no pedagogy? Principle, pragmatism and compliance in primary education*. Cambridge, MA: University of Cambridge.

Alexander, R. (2008). *Towards dialogic teaching: Rethinking classroom talk*. Thirsk, UK: Dialogos.

Allen, J. (2004). Getting interactive. *Secondary Education, 29*(6), 243–247.

Armstrong, V., & Curran, S. (2006). Developing a collaborative mode of research using digital video. *Computers & Education, 46*(3), 336–347. doi:10.1016/j.compedu.2005.11.015

Armstrong, V., Barnes, S., Sutherland, R., Curran, C., Mills, S., & Thompson, I. (2005). Collaborative research methodology for investigating teaching and learning: The use of interactive whiteboard technology. *Educational Review, 57*(4), 457–469. doi:10.1080/00131910500279551

Austin, N. (2003, January 7). Mighty white. *The Guardian*. Retrieved November 10, 2008, from http://education.guardian.o.uk/elearning/story/0,869705,00.html

Baker, J. (2007). SmartBoard in the music classroom. *Music Educators Journal, 93*(5), 18–19. doi:10.1177/002743210709300504

Ball, B. (2003). Teaching and learning mathematics with an interactive whiteboard. *Micromath, 19*(1), 4–7.

Banner, G., & Rayner, S. (2002). Learning language and learning style: Principles, process and practice. *Language Learning Journal, 21*, 37–44. doi:10.1080/09571730085200091

Barber, D. (2008). Learning and teaching with interactive whiteboards. *British Journal of Educational Technology, 39*(3), 570. doi:10.1111/j.1467-8535.2008.00855_12.x

Bax, S. (2006). Interactive whiteboards: Watch this space. *California Law Review*, (Summer): 5–7.

Bayliss, T., & Collins, L. (2007). *Invigorating teaching with interactive whiteboards: Case Studies 7-10*. Teaching Geography, Geographical Association.

Beastall, L. (2006). Enchanting a disenchanted child: Revolutionizing the means of education using information technology and e-learning. *British Journal of Sociology of Education, 27*(1), 97–110. doi:10.1080/01425690500376758

Beatty, I. (2004). Transforming student learning with classroom communication systems. *Educause Center for Applied Research, 2004(3)*, 1-13.

Beatty, I. D., Gerace, W. J., Leonard, W. J., & Dufresne, R. J. (2006). Designing effective questions for classroom response system teaching. *American Journal of Physics, 74*(1), 31–39. doi:10.1119/1.2121753

Beauchamp, G. (2004). Teacher use of the interactive whiteboard in primary schools: Towards an effective transition framework. *Technology, Pedagogy and Education, 13*(3), 327–348. doi:10.1080/14759390400200186

Beauchamp, G., & Parkinson, J. (2005). Beyond the 'wow' factor: Developing interactivity with the interactive whiteboard. *The School Science Review, 86*, 316.

Beauchamp, G., & Parkinson, J. (2008). Pupils' attitudes towards school science as they transfer from an ICT-rich primary school to a secondary school with fewer ICT resources: Does ICT matter? *Education and Information Technologies, 13*(2), 103–118. doi:10.1007/s10639-007-9053-5

Beck, R. (2003). *What are learning objects?* Center for International Education, University of Wisconsin-Milwaukee. Retrieved November 10, 2007, from http://www.uwm.edu/Dept/CIE/AOP/LObib.html

Becta (2003). *What the research says about interactive whiteboards.* Retrieved February 22, 2009, from http://partners.becta.org.uk/page_documents/research/wtrs_whiteboards.pdf

Becta (2003a). *Primary Schools – ICT and Standards: An analysis of national data from Ofsted and QCA.* Coventry, UK: Becta.

Becta (2003b). *Secondary Schools – ICT and Standards: An analysis of national data from Ofsted and QCA.* Coventry, UK: Becta.

Becta (2004). *Getting the most from your interactive whiteboard: A guide for secondary schools.* Coventry, UK: Becta. Retrieved December 8, 2008, from http://foi.becta.org.uk/content_files/corporate/resources/foi/archived_publications/getting_most_whiteboard_secondary.pdf

Becta (2004). Getting the most from your interactive whiteboard: A guide for secondary schools. Coventry: Becta. Retrieved February 22, 2009, from http://foi.becta.org.uk/content_files/corporate/resources/foi/archived_publications/getting_most_whiteboard_secondary.pdf

Becta (2004a). *Getting the most from your interactive whiteboard: A guide for secondary schools.* Coventry, UK: Becta.

Becta (2004b). *Planning to purchase an interactive whiteboard.* Retrieved June 15, 2009, from http://www.becta.org.uk/leas/leas.cfm?section=6_2&id=3160

Becta (2005). *How can the use of an interactive whiteboard enhance the nature of teaching and learning in secondary mathematics and modern foreign languages: ICT Research Bursaries.* Retrieved October 21, 2005, from http://www.becta.org.uk

Becta (2007). *Annual review 2007.* Coventry, UK: Becta.

Becta (2007). *Harnessing technology review 2007: Progress and impact of technology in education.* Coventry, UK: Becta.

Becta (2007). *Learning in the 21st Century The case for harnessing technology.* Coventry, UK: Becta.

Becta. (2008). *Harnessing Technology: Next Generation Learning 2008-14.* Coventry, UK: Becta.

Beeland, W. D. (2002). Student engagement, visual learning and technology: Can interactive whiteboards help? *Action Research Exchange, 1*(1). Retrieved June 15, 2009, from http://chiron.valdosta.edu/are/Artmanscrpt/vol1no1/beeland_am.pdf

Bell, M. A. (2001). Update to survey of use of interactive electronic whiteboard in instruction. Retrieved February 22, 2009, from http://www.shsu.edu/~lis_mah/documents/updateboardindex.htm

Bell, M. A. (2002). Why use an interactive whiteboard? A baker's dozen reasons! *Teachers Net Gazette 3*(1). Retrieved June 15, 2009, from http://teachers.net/gazette/JAN02/mabel.html

Bennett, S., Matton, K., & Kervin, L. (2008). The 'digital natives' debate: A critical review of the evidence. *Brit-*

ish Journal of Educational Technology, 39(5), 775–786. doi:10.1111/j.1467-8535.2007.00793.x

Birmingham, P., Davies, C., & Greiffenhagen, C. (2002). Turn to face the bard: Making sense of the three way interactions between teacher, pupils and technology in the classroom. *Education Communication and Information, 2*(2-3), 139–161. doi:10.1080/1463631021000025330

Black, P., & Wiliam, D. (1998). *Inside the black box: Raising standards through classroom assessment.* London: School of Education, King's College.

Blamires, M. (2004). Virtual learning or real learning? In Hayes, D. (Ed.), *The RoutledgeFalmer guide to key debates in education.* London: Routledge.

Blane, D. (2003). The whiteboard's a whizz! *Times Educational Supplement.* Retrieved June 15, 2009, from http://www.tes.co.uk/article.aspx?storycode=383940

Blanton, B., & Helms-Breazeale, R. (2000). Gains in self-efficacy: Using SMART board interactive whiteboard technology in special education classrooms. Retrieved February 22, 2009, from http://smarterkids.org/research/paper2.asp

Blanton, P. (2008). Using interactive whiteboard to enhance student learning. *The Physics Teacher, 46*(3), 188–189. doi:10.1119/1.2840991

Blatchford, P. (2005). A Multi-method approach to the study of school class size differences. *International Journal of Social Research Methodology, 8*(3), 195–205. doi:10.1080/13645570500154675

Bloom, B. S. (1956). *Taxonomy of educational objectives.* Boston: Pearson Education. reprinted 1984

Boag-Munro, G. (2005). 'The naming of cats is a difficult matter' – how far are government and teachers using the same words to talk about educational concepts? In J. Satterthwaite & E. Atkinson (Eds.), Discourses of education in the age of new imperialism (pp. 131-150). Stoke on Trent, UK: Trentham Books.

Bolam, R., & Weidling, D. (2006). *Synthesis of research and evaluation projects concerned with capacity-building through teachers' professional development.* London:

GTCE. Retrieved February 12, 2009, From http://www.gtce.org.uk/shared/contentlibs/126795/93128/168771/report.pdf

Bolam, R., McMahon, A., Stoll, L., Thomas, S., & Wallace, M. (2005). *Creating and sustaining effective professional learning communities.* London: DfES & University of Bristol. Retrieved, February 12, 2009, From http://www.gtce.org.uk/shared/contentlibs/126795/93128/120213/eplc_report.pdf

Bourne, J., & Jewitt, C. (2003). Orchestrating debate: A multimodal analysis of classroom interaction. *Reading, 37*(2), 64-72.

Bozhuizen, H. P. A., & Wopereis, I. G. J. H. (2003). Pedagogic benchmarks for information and communications technology in teacher education. *Technology, Pedagogy and Education, 12*(1), 149–159. doi:10.1080/14759390300200150

Bransford, J. D., Brown, A. L., & Cocking, R. R. (1999). *How people learn: Brain, mind, experience and school.* Washington, DC, USA: National Academy Press.

Branzburg, J. (2008). The whiteboard revolution. *Technology & Learning, 28*(9), 44. Retrieved February 22, 2009, from http://www.wright.edu/~marguerite.veres/SmartWorkshop/whiteboardinfo.pdf

Brown, S. (2004). *Interactive whiteboards in education. TechLearn Briefing.* UK: JISC Technologies Centre, Joint Information Systems Committee.

Bruff, D. (2007). *Classroom response systems.* Retrieved July 23, 2007, from http://www.vanderbilt.edu/cft/resources/teaching_resources/technology/crs.htlm

Bruner, J. (1999). Folk pedagogies. In Leach, J., & Moon, B. (Eds.), *Learners and pedagogy* (pp. 4–20). London: PCP.

Bruton, S. (2005). Task-based language learning: For the state secondary FL classroom? *Language Learning Journal, 31*, 55–68. doi:10.1080/09571730585200091

Buckinghamshire, L. E. A. (2002). *Developing the use of interactive whiteboards.* Retrieved 22, February 2009, from http://www.bucksict.org.uk/Effective/Whiteboards. htm

Burden, K. *(2002)*. Learning from the bottom up – the contribution of school based practice and research in the effective use of interactive whiteboards for the FE/HE sector. Learning and Skills Research – Making an Impact Regionally Conference. *The Earth Centre: Doncaster.*

Burden, K. (2002, June). *Learning from the bottom up – the contribution of school based practice and research in the effective use of interactive whiteboards for the FE/HE sector.* Paper presented at LSDA, Making an Impact Regionally Conference, Doncaster, UK. Retrieved December 10, 2008, from www.lsda.org.uk/files/lsda/ regions/8_Bio_KBurden.pdf

Burns, C., & Myhill, D. (2004). Interactive or inactive? A consideration of the nature of interaction in whole class teaching. *Cambridge Journal of Education, 34*(1), 35–49. doi:10.1080/0305764042000183115

Business Balls. (n.d.). *Blooms taxonomy – learning domains.* Retrieved July 25, 2006, from http://www. businessballs.com/bloomstaxonomyoflearningdomains. htlm

Cairncross, S., & Mannion, M. (2001). Interactive multimedia and learning: Realizing the benefits. *Innovations in Education and Teaching International, 38*(2), 156–164. doi:10.1080/14703290110035428

Canterbury Christ Church University College (Faculty Learning Technology Team). (2003). *Briefing paper on the application of interactive whiteboards to learning and teaching.* Canterbury Christ Church University College, Learning and Teaching Enhancement Unit. Retrieved February 22, 2009, from http://www.canterbury.ac.uk/support/learning-teaching-enhancement-unit/publications/ FLT-briefing-notes/interactive-whiteboards-briefing-note-non-cccuc.pdf

Carr, L. (1999). Bringing lessons to life. *Managing Schools Today, 9*(1), 14.

Charalambous, K., & Karagiorgi, Y. (2002). Information and communications technology in-service training for teachers: Cyprus in perspective. *Tech-nology, Pedagogy and Education, 11*(2), 197–215. doi:10.1080/14759390200200132

Chiappe, A., Yasbley, S., & Yadira, R. (2007). Toward an instructional design model based on learning objects. [Boston: Springer.]. *Educational Technology Research and Development, 55,* 671–668. doi:10.1007/s11423-007-9059-0

Chin, C., Brown, D. E., & Bruce, B. C. (2002). Student-generated questions: A meaningful aspect of learning in science. *International Journal of Science Education, 24*(5), 521–549. doi:10.1080/09500690110095249

Chinnappan, M., & Thomas, M. (2003). Teachers' function schemas and their role in modelling. *Mathematics Education Research Journal, 15*(2), 151–170.

Clark, R. E., & Sugrue, B. M. (1991). Research on instructional media, 1978-1988. In Anglin, G. J. (Ed.), *Instructional technology: Past, present, and future* (pp. 327–343). Englewood, Colorado, USA: Libraries Unlimited.

Cleaves, A., & Toplis, R. (2008). Pre-service science teachers and ICT: Communities of practice? *Research in Science & Technological Education, 26*(2), 203–213. doi:10.1080/02635140802037344

Clemens, A., Moore, T., & Nelson, B. (2001) Math Intervention. *SMART Project Research Report.* Retrieved November 17, 2008, from http://www.smarterkids.org

Cobb, P., & Yackel, E. (1996). Constructivist, emergent and socio-cultural perspectives in the context of developmental research. *Educational Psychologist, 31*(3/4), 175–190. doi:10.1207/s15326985ep3103&4_3

Cogill, J. (2002). *How is the interactive whiteboard being used in the primary school and how does this affect teachers and teaching?* Retrieved October 11, 2007, from http://www.virtuallearning.org.uk/whiteboards/IFS_Interactive_whiteboards_in_the_primary_school.pdf

Cogill, J. (2003). The use of the interactive whiteboard in the primary school: Effects on pedagogy. In *ICT Research Bursaries* (pp. 52–55). London: HMSO.

Cogill, J. (2008). *Primary teachers' interactive white-board practice across one year: Changes in pedagogy and influencing factors.* Unpublished doctoral thesis, King's College, London.

Condie, R., Munro, B., Seagraves, L., & Kenesson, S. (2006). *The impact of ICT in schools – a landscape review.* Coventry, UK: Becta.

Conlon, T. (2004). A failure of delivery: The United Kingdom's new opportunities fund programme of teacher training in information and communications technology. *Journal of In-service Education, 30*(1), 115–139. doi:10.1080/13674580400200286

Cooper, P., & McIntyre, D. (1994). Patterns of interaction between teachers' and students' classroom thinking, and their implications for the provision of learning opportunities. *Teaching and Teacher Education, 10*(6), 633–646. doi:10.1016/0742-051X(94)90031-0

Cordingley, P. (2008). *Qualitative study of school level strategies for teachers' CPD.* Coventry, UK: Centre for the Use of Research & Evidence in Education.

Cordingley, P., Bell, M., Evans, D., & Firth, A. (2005). *The impact of collaborative CPD on classroom teaching and learning. Review: What do teacher impact data tell us about collaborative CPD?* Retrieved, February 12, 2009, from http://eppi.ioe.ac.uk/cms/LinkClick.aspx?fileticket=trZ0E6NfVy4%3d&tabid=139&mid=960&language=en-US

Cordingley, P., Bell, M., Rundell, B., & Evans, D. (2003). *The impact of collaborative CPD on classroom teaching and learning.* Retrieved, February 12, 2009, from http://eppi.ioe.ac.uk/cms/LinkClick.aspx?fileticket=lvR%2bp8KX%2bRM%3d&tabid=132&mid=758&language=en-US

Coupal, L. V. (2004). Constructivist learning theory and human capital theory: Shifting political and educational frameworks for teachers ICT professional development. *British Journal of Educational Technology, 35*(5), 587–596. doi:10.1111/j.0007-1013.2004.00415.x

Cox, M., Abbott, C., Webb, M., Blakeley, B., Beauchamp, T., & Rhodes, V. (2003a). *ICT and attainment: A review of the research literature. A report to the DfES.* Coventry, UK: Becta.

Cox, M., Webb, M., Abbott, C., Blakeley, B., Beauchamp, A., & Rhodes, V. (2003). *ICT and pedagogy.* Norwich, UK: HMSO.

Cox, M., Webb, M., Abbott, C., Blakeley, B., Beauchamp, T., & Rhodes, V. (2003b). *ICT and pedagogy: A review of the research literature. A report to the DfES.* Coventry, UK: Becta.

Cresswell, J. (1998). *Qualitative inquiry and research design: Choosing among five traditions.* California, USA: Sage Publications.

Crook, C. (2008). *Web 2.0 technologies for learning: The current landscape – opportunities, challenges and tensions.* Coventry, UK: Becta.

Crowne, S. (2008). 'Next generation learning' – promoting the benefits of technology in schools and FE. *Education Journal, 109,* 10.

Cuban, L. (1986). *Teachers and machines: The classroom use of technology since 1920.* New York: Teachers College Press.

Cuban, L. (1993). Computers meet classroom: Classroom wins. *Teachers College Record, 95*(2), 185–210.

Cuban, L. (2001). *Oversold and underused: Computers in the classroom.* Cambridge, MA: Harvard University Press.

Cuckle, P., & Clarke, S. (2003). Secondary school teacher mentors and student teachers views on the value of information and communications technology in teaching. *Technology, Pedagogy and Education, 12*(3), 377–391. doi:10.1080/14759390300200168

Cuthell, J. (2006). Tools for transformation: The impact of interactive whiteboards in a range of contexts. In Crawford, C. (Eds.), *Proceedings of society for information technology and teacher education international conference 2006* (pp. 1491–1497). Chesapeake, VA: AACE.

Cuthell, J. P. (2003). Interactive whiteboards: New tools, new pedagogies, new learning? Retrieved February 22, 2009, from http://www.virtuallearning.org. uk/2003research/whiteboards_survey.doc

Cuthell, J. P. (2004). Can technology transform teaching and learning? The impact of interactive whiteboards. In J. Price, D. Willis, N. Davis & J. Willis (Eds.), *Proceedings of SITE 2004*. Norfolk, VA: Association for the Advancement of Computing in Education.

Cuthell, J. P. (2005). The impact of interactive whiteboards on teaching, learning, and attainment. [Phoenix, AZ: AACE.]. *Proceedings of SITE, 2005*, 1353–1355.

Cuthell, J. P. (2005a). The Impact of interactive whiteboards on teaching, learning and attainment. In J. Price, D. Willis, N. Davis & J. Willis (Eds.), *Proceedings of SITE 2005* (pp. 1353-1355). Norfolk, VA: Association for the Advancement of Computing in Education.

Cuthell, J. P. (2005b). Seeing the meaning. The impact of interactive whiteboards on teaching and learning. In *Proceedings of WCCE 05*, Stellenbosch, South Africa.

Cuthell, J. P. (2006). Steering the supertanker: Transforming teaching and learning through the use of ICT computers in schools. *Technology Applications in Education, 23*(1-2), 99–110.

Cuthell, J. P. (2007). Ambassadors for ACTIVlearning. In R. Carlsen, K. McFerrin, J. Price, R. Weber & D. A. Willis (Eds.), *Proceedings of SITE 2007* (pp. 1443–1499) Norfolk, VA: Association for the Advancement of Computing in Education.

Cuthell, J., & Preston, C. (2007). An interactivist e-community of practice using Web 2:00 tools. In C. Crawford et al. (Eds.), *Proceedings of Society for Information Technology and Teacher Education International Conference* 2007 (pp. 2316-2325). Chesapeake, VA: AACE.

Cutrim Schmid, E. (2006). Investigating the use of interactive whiteboard technology in the language classroom through the lens of a critical theory of technology. *Computer Assisted Language Learning, 19*(1), 47–62. doi:10.1080/09588220600804012

Cutrim Schmid, E. (2007). Enhancing performance knowledge and self-esteem in classroom language learning: The potential of the ACTIVote system component of interactive whiteboard Technology. *System, 35*, 119–133. doi:10.1016/j.system.2007.01.001

Cutrim Schmid, E. (2008). Using a voting system in conjunction with interactive whiteboard technology to enhance learning in the English language classroom. *Computers & Education, 50*, 338–356. doi:10.1016/j.compedu.2006.07.001

Cutrim Schmid, E. (2008). Using a voting system in conjunction with interactive whiteboard technology to enhance learning in the English language classroom. *Computers & Education, 50*(1), 338–356. doi:10.1016/j.compedu.2006.07.001

Cutrim Schmid, E. (2008a). Interactive whiteboards and the normalisation of CALL. In R. de Cassia, V. Morriott & P. L. Torres (Eds.), Handbook of research on e-Learning methodologies for language acquisition. Hershey, PA: IGI Global.

Cutrim Schmid, E. (2008b). Potential pedagogical benefits and drawbacks of multimedia use in the English language classroom equipped with interactive whiteboard technology. *Computers & Education, 51*(4), 1553–1568. doi:10.1016/j.compedu.2008.02.005

Cutrim Schmid, E. (2008d). Facilitating whole-class collaborative learning in the English language classroom: The potential of interactive Whiteboard Technology. In A. Müller-Hartmann & M. Schocker-v. Ditfurth (Eds.), Aufgabenorientiertes Lernen und Lehren mit Medien: Ansätze, Erfahrungen, Perspektiven in der Fremdsprachendidaktik (pp. 325-335). Frankfurt am Main, Germany: Peter Lang.

Cutrim Schmid, E. (2009a). The pedagogical potential of interactive whiteboards 2.0. In Thomas, M. (Ed.), *Handbook of research on web 2.0 and second language learning*. Hershey, PA: IGI Global.

Cutrim Schmid, E. (2009b). *Interactive whiteboard technology in the language classroom: Exploring new pedagogical opportunities*. Mueller, Germany: VDM Verlag Dr.

Damcott, D., Landato, J., & Marsh, C. (2000). *Report on the use of the SMART board interactive whiteboard in physical science.* Retrieved February 15, 2008, from www.smarterkids.org.

Damcott, D., Landato, J., & Marsh, C. (2000). *Report on the use of the SMART board interactive whiteboard in physical science.* Retrieved February 22, 2009, from http://smarterkids.org/research/paper3.asp

Davies, G. (2003). *Computer-assisted language learning: Where are we now and where are we going?* Retrieved June 8, 2005, from http://www.nestafuturelab.org/viewpoint/learn23.htm

Davies, G., & Rendall, H. (2004). *ICT4LT module 1:4. Introduction to computer assisted language learning (CALL).* Retrieved January 29, 2004 from http://www.ict4lt.org/en/en_mod1-4.htm

Davis, B., & Simmt, E. (2003). Understanding learning systems: Mathematics education and complexity science. *Journal for Research in Mathematics Education, 34*(2), 137–167.

Davison, I., & Pratt, D. (2003). An investigation into the visual and kinaesthetic affordances of interactive whiteboards. In *ICT Research Bursaries* (pp. 29–33). London: HMSO.

Davison, I., & Pratt, D. (2003). *An investigation into the visual and kinaesthetic affordances of interactive whiteboards. Research Bursary Reports.* Coventry, UK: Becta.

Davison, I., & Pratt, D. (2003). *An investigation into the visual and kinaesthetic affordances of interactive whiteboards. Report made to Becta.* Retrieved February 22, 2009, from http://publications.teachernet.gov.uk/eOrderingDownload/DfES-0791-2003.pdf#page=31

Deaney, R., Ruthven, K., & Hennessy, S. (2006). Teachers' developing 'practical theories' of the contribution of information and communication technologies to subject teaching and learning: an analysis of cases from English secondary schools. *British Educational Research Journal, 32*(3), 459–480. doi:10.1080/01411920600635460

Department for Education and Employment. (1998a). *The national literacy strategy: A framework for teaching.* London: HMSO.

Department for Education and Employment. (1998b). *Initial teacher training national curriculum for the use of information and communication technology in subject teaching. Circular 4/98, Annex B.* Department for Education and Employment.

Department for Education and Skills. (2003). *Excellence and enjoyment: A strategy for primary schools.* London: Department for Education and Skills. Retrieved October 28, 2008, from http://www.standards.dfes.gov.uk/primary/publications/literacy/63553/pns_excell_enjoy037703v2.pdf

Department for Education and Skills. (2006). 2020 Vision report of the teaching and learning in 2020 review group. Nottingham, UK: DfES.

Desimone, L., Porter, A., Garet, S., Yoon, K., & Birman, B. (2002). Effects of professional development on teacher's instruction: Results from a three-year longitudinal study. *Educational Evaluation and Policy Analysis, 24*(2), 81–112. doi:10.3102/01623737024002081

DfEE. (1998a). Circular 4/98 teaching: high status, high standards. London: DfEE

DfEE. (1998b). Initial teacher training National Curriculum for the use of information and communications technology in subject teaching. DfEE Circular 4/98, Annexe B. London: DfEE.

DfES (2001). *NGfL Pathfinders: Preliminary report on the roll out of the NGfL programme in ten Pathfinder LEAs.* NGfL Research and Evaluation Series Number 2.

DfES (2003). *Fulfilling the potential.* Policy statement on ICT signed by Charles Clarke.

DfES (2003). *The key stage 3 national strategy. Framework for teaching modern languages: Years 7, 8 and 9.* London: DfES.

DfES. (2001). The key stage 3 national strategy. London: DfES.

DfES. (2002). Transforming the way we learn: A vision for the future of ICT in schools. DfES Report No: 0008/2002. London: DfES.

DfES. (2004). *Interactive whiteboards - frequently asked questions.* Retrieved June 15, 2009, from http://www.dfes.gov.uk/ictinschools/ict_active/factfile.cfm?articleid=511

DfES. (2005). Harnessing technology: Transforming learning and children's services. London: DfES.

DfES. (2007). Teaching and learning in 2020 Review. DfES Report No: 6856/2007. London: DfES.

Dhindsa, H. S., & Emran, S. H. (2006, March). Use of the interactive whiteboard in constructivist teaching for higher student achievement. *Proceedings of the Second Annual Conference for the Middle East Teachers of Science, Mathematics, and Computing* (pp. 175-188). Abu Dhabi, UAE: METSMaC

Dillenbourg, P., & Traum, D. (2006). Sharing solutions: Persistence and grounding in multimodal collaborative problem solving. *Journal of the Learning Sciences, 15*(1), 121–151. doi:10.1207/s15327809jls1501_9

Draper, S. W., & Brown, M. I. (2002). *Use of the PRS (Personal Response System) handsets at Glasgow University.* Retrieved May 24, 2006, from http://www.psy.gla.ac.uk/~steve/ilig/interim.htlm

Draper, S. W., & Brown, M. I. (2004). Increasing interactivity in lectures using an electronic voting system. *Journal of Computer Assisted Learning, 20*(2), 81–94. doi:10.1111/j.1365-2729.2004.00074.x

Driessen, G., Smit, F., & Sleegers, P. (2005). Parental involvement and educational achievement. *British Educational Research Journal, 31*(4), 509–532. doi:10.1080/01411920500148713

Dudeney, G. (2006). Interactive, quite bored. IATEFL CALL Review, Summer, pp. 8-10.

Dudeney, G., & Hockley, N. (2007). *How to teach English with technology.* Harlow, UK: Pearson Longman.

Duncan, D. (2006). Clickers: A new teaching aid with exceptional promise. *Astronomy Education Review, 1*(5), 70–88. doi:10.3847/AER2006005

Ekhami, L. (2002). The power of interactive whiteboards. *School Library Media Activities Monthly, 18*(8), 35–38.

Elliot, J. (1991). *Action research for educational change. Milton Keynes.* UK: Open University Press.

Ernest, P. (1994). The impact of beliefs on the teaching of mathematics. In Bloomfield, A., & Harries, T. (Eds.), *Teaching and learning mathematics.* Derby, UK: Association of Teachers of Mathematics.

Ernest, P. (1994). The impact of beliefs on the teaching of mathematics. In A. Bloomfield, & T. Harries (Eds.) (1994), Teaching and Learning Mathematics (pp. 62-72). Derby, UK: Association of Teachers of Mathematics.

Ertmer, P., Addison, P., Lane, M., Ross, E., & Woods, D. (1999). Examining teachers' beliefs about the role of technology in the elementary classroom. *Journal of Research on Computing in Education, 32*(1), 54–72.

Field, K. (Ed.). (2000). *Issues in modern foreign languages teaching.* Cambridge, MA: Cambridge University Press.

Fisher, T. (2006). Educational transformation: Is it, like 'beauty', in the eye of the beholder, or will we know it when we see it? *Education and Information Technologies, 11*(3-4), 293–303. doi:10.1007/s10639-006-9009-1

Fry, J. M., & Hin, M. K. T. (2006). Peer coaching with interactive wireless technology between student teachers: Satisfaction with role and communication. *Interactive Learning Environments, 14*(3), 193–204. doi:10.1080/10494820600852969

Fullan, M. (2001). *Leading in a Culture of Change.* San Francisco: Jossey Bass.

Futuresource Consulting. (2008). *Interactive displays quarterly insight: State of the market report.* Retrieved February 12, 2009, from http://www.futuresource-consulting.com/reports.htm

Galàn, J. G., & Blanco, S. M. (2004). Design of educational web pages. *European Journal of Teacher Education, 27*(1), 99–103. doi:10.1080/0261976042000211793

Galton, M., Hargreaves, L., Comber, C., Wall, D., & Pell, A. (1999). *Inside the primary classroom: 20 Years On.* London: Routledge.

Ganalouli, D., Murphy, C., & Gardner, J. (2004). Teachers perceptions of the effectiveness of ICT-competence training. *Computers & Education, 43*(1-2), 63–79. doi:10.1016/j.compedu.2003.12.005

Gardner, H. (1991). *The unschooled mind: How children think and how schools should teach.* New York: Basic Books Inc.

Gee, J., & Green, J. (1998). Discourse analysis, learning, and social practice: A methodological study. *Review of Research in Education, 23*(1), 119–169. doi:10.3102/0091732X023001119

Gerard, F., Greene, M., & Widener, J. (1999). *Using SMART board in foreign language classes.* Paper presented at Society for Information Technology & Teacher Education International Conference, San Antonio, TX.

Gibbs, G., & Simpson, C. (2004). Conditions under which assessment supports students' learning. *Learning and Teaching in Higher Education, 1,* 3–31.

Gibson, I. (2001). At the intersection of technology and pedagogy: considering styles of teaching and learning. *Journal of Information Technology for Teacher Education, 10*(1-2), 37–60.

Gill, C. (2000). *Improving MFL learning through ICT. Dunstable & Dublin.* Ireland: Folens Limited.

Gillen, J., Kleine Staarman, J., Littleton, K., Mercer, N., & Twiner, A. (2007). A 'learning revolution'? Investigating pedagogic practice around interactive whiteboards in British primary schools. *Learning, Media and Technology, 32*(3), 243–256. doi:10.1080/17439880701511099

Gillen, J., Kleine Staarman, J., Littleton, K., Mercer, N., & Twiner, A. (2007). A 'learning revolution'? Investigating pedagogic practice around interactive whiteboards in British primary classrooms. *Learning, Media and Technol-*

ogy, 32(3), 243–256. doi:10.1080/17439880701511099

Gillen, J., Littleton, K., Twiner, A., Kleine Staarman, J., & Mercer, N. (2008). Using the interactive whiteboard to resource continuity and support multimodal teaching in a primary science classroom. *Journal of Computer Assisted Learning, 24*(4), 348–358. doi:10.1111/j.1365-2729.2007.00269.x

Gillespie, R. (1991). *Manufacturing knowledge: A history of the Hawthorne experiments.* Cambridge, UK: Cambridge University Press.

Glover, D., & Coleman, M. (2005). School climate, culture and ethos: interchangeable or distinctive concepts? *Journal of In-service Education, 31*(2), 251–272. doi:10.1080/13674580500200359

Glover, D., & Miller, D. (2001). Running with technology: The pedagogic impact of the large-scale introduction of interactive whiteboards in one secondary school. *Technology, Pedagogy and Education, 10*(3), 257–276. doi:10.1080/14759390100200115

Glover, D., & Miller, D. (2001b, October). *Missioners, tentatives and luddites: Leadership challenges for school and classroom posed by the introduction of interactive whiteboards into schools in the UK.* Paper presented at the British Educational Management and Administration Society conference, Newport Pagnell, UK.

Glover, D., & Miller, D. (2002). Running with technology: The impact of the large-scale introduction of interactive whiteboards in one secondary school. *Journal of Information Technology for Teacher Education, 10*(3), 257–276.

Glover, D., & Miller, D. (2002). The interactive whiteboard as a force for pedagogic change: The experience of five elementary schools in an English education authority. *Information Technology in Childhood Education Annual, 1,* 5–19.

Glover, D., & Miller, D. (2005). Leadership implications of using interactive whiteboards: linking technology and pedagogy in the management of change. *Management in Education, 18*(5), 27–30. doi:10.1177/089202060501800506

Glover, D., & Miller, D. (2007). Leading changed classroom culture: The impact of interactive whiteboards. *Management in Education, 21*(3), 21–24. doi:10.1177/0892020607079988

Glover, D., & Miller, D. (in press). Optimising the use of interactive whiteboards: An application of developmental work research (DWR). *Journal of In-service Education.*

Glover, D., & Miller, D. J. (2002). Running with technology: The pedagogic impact of the large-scale introduction of interactive whiteboards in one secondary school. *Journal of Information Technology for Teacher Education, 10*(3), 257–278.

Glover, D., & Miller, D. J. (2002). The introduction of unteractive whiteboards into schools in the United Kingdom: Leaders, led, and the management of pedagogic and technological change. *International Electronic Journal for Leadership in Learning, 6*(24), University of Calgary Press. Retrieved June 15, 2009, from http://www.ucalgary.ca/~iejll/volume6/glover.html

Glover, D., & Miller, D. J. (2003). Players in the Management of Change: introducing interactive whiteboards into schools. *Management in Education, 17*(1), 20–23. doi:10.1177/0892020603017001070101

Glover, D., Miller, D., & Averis, D. (2003). The impact of interactive whiteboards on classroom practice: Examples drawn from the teaching of mathematics in secondary schools in England. *The Mathematics Education into the 21st Century Project: Proceedings of the International Conference The Decidable and the Undecidable in Mathematics Education* (pp.181-5). Brno, Czech Republic.

Glover, D., Miller, D., & Averis, D. (2004). Panacea or prop: The role of the interactive whiteboard in improving teaching effectiveness. Paper presented at the Tenth International Congress of Mathematics Education, July 4-11, Copenhagen, Denmark.

Glover, D., Miller, D., & Averis, D. (2004). Panacea or prop: The role of the interactive whiteboard in improving teaching effectiveness. In *Tenth International Congress of Mathematics Education*, Copenhagen. Retrieved February 22, 2009, from http://www.icme-organisers.dk/tsg15/Glover_et_al.pdf

Glover, D., Miller, D., Averis, D., & Door, V. (2005). The interactive whiteboard: A literature survey. *Technology, Pedagogy and Education, 14*(2), 155–170. doi:10.1080/14759390500200199

Glover, D., Miller, D., Averis, D., & Door, V. (2007). The evolution of an effective pedagogy for teachers using the interactive whiteboard in mathematics and modern languages: An empirical analysis from the secondary sector. *Learning, Media and Technology, 32*(1), 5–20. doi:10.1080/17439880601141146

Goodison, T. (2003). Integrating ICT in the classroom: A case study of two contrasting lessons. *British Journal of Educational Technology, 34*(5), 549–566. doi:10.1046/j.0007-1013.2003.00350.x

Goodison, T. A. (2002). *Looking in classrooms* (8th ed.). New York: Addison Wesley.

Graham, K. (2003). *Switching on switched-off children: Does the Promethean ACTIVboard promote lesson participation among switched-off children?* Retrieved June 15, 2009, from http://www.virtuallearning.org.uk/2003research/Switching_Switched_Off.doc

Gray, C., Hagger-Vaughan, L., Pilkington, R., & Tomkins, S. (2005). The pros and cons of interactive whiteboards in relation to the key stage 3 strategy and framework. *Language Learning Journal, 32*, 38–44. doi:10.1080/09571730585200171

Gray, C., Pilkington, R., Hagger-Vaughan, L., & Tomkins, S. (2007). Integrating ICT into classroom practice in modern foreign language teaching in England: Making room for teachers' voices. *European Journal of Teacher Education, 30*(4), 407–429. doi:10.1080/02619760701664193

Gray, C., Pilkington, R., Hagger-Vaughan, L., & Tomkins, S. A. (2007). Integrating ICT into classroom practice in modern foreign language teaching in England: Making room for teachers voices. *European Journal of Teacher Education, 30*(4), 407–429. doi:10.1080/02619760701664193

Gray, G., Hagger-Vaughan, L., Pilkington, R., & Tomkins, S. (2005). The pros and cons of interactive whiteboards in relation to the key stage 3 strategies and framework. *Language Learning Journal, 32*, 38–44. doi:10.1080/09571730585200171

Gray, G., Hagger-Vaughan, L., Pilkington, R., & Tomkins, S. (2005). The pros and cons of interactive whiteboards in relation to the key stage 3 strategies and framework. *Language Learning Journal, 32*(1), 38–44. doi:10.1080/09571730585200171

Gray, G., Hagger-Vaughan, L., Pilkington, R., & Tomkins, S. (2007). Integrating ICT into classroom practice in modern foreign language teaching in England: Making room for teachers' voices. *European Journal of Teacher Education, 30*(4), 407–429. doi:10.1080/02619760701664193

Greenfield, S. (2006). How will we nurture minds of the future? *Times Educational Supplement,* (4684): 21.

Greiffenhagen, C. (2000). *Interactive whiteboards in mathematics education: Possibilities and dangers.* Paper presented at the working group on The Use of Technology in Mathematics Education held at the 9th International Congress on Mathematical Education, Tokyo, Japan.

Greiffenhagen, C. (2002). *Out of the office into the school: Electronic whiteboards for education.* Retrieved February 22, 2009, from ftp://ftp.comlab.ox.ac.uk/pub/Documents/techreports/TR-16-00.pdf

Haldane, M. (2003). Real-time lesson observation: Using technology in teacher training to learn about technology in the classroom. *Learning and Teaching in Action, 2*(3), 15–18.

Haldane, M. (2005). *A typology of interactive whiteboard pedagogies.* Paper presented at the British Educational Research Association Conference, Glamorgan, UK.

Haldane, M. (2005b, September). *Analysing the art of teaching through real-time lesson observation via the medium of the interactive whiteboard.* Paper presented at the British Educational Research Association Annual Conference, Glamorgan, UK.

Haldane, M. (2007). Interactivity and the digital whiteboard: Weaving the fabric of learning. *Learning,*

Media and Technology, 32(3), 257-270. Retrieved 10 December, 2008, from http://www.soton.ac.uk/~pgce/ict/NewPGCE/pdfs%20IWBs/Interactivity%20and%20the%20digital%20whiteboard%20weaving%20a%20fabric%20of%20learning.pdf

Haldane, M. (2007). Interactivity and the digital whiteboard: Weaving the fabric of learning. *Journal of Learning Media and Technology, 32*(3), 257–270. doi:10.1080/17439880701511107

Haldane, M. (2008, May). *Developing teachers' effectiveness in the use of interactive whiteboard technology for the enhancement of learning.* Paper presented at IFIP Conference, Charles University, Prague

Haldane, M., & Somekh, B. (2005). *A typology of interactive whiteboard pedagogies.* Paper presented at BERA 2005, University of Glamorgan, UK.

Hall, I., & Higgins, S. (2005). Primary school students' perceptions of interactive whiteboards. *Journal of Computer Assisted Learning, 21*, 102–117. doi:10.1111/j.1365-2729.2005.00118.x

Hall, I., & Higgins, S. (2005). Primary school students' perceptions of interactive whiteboards. *Journal of Computer Assisted Learning, 21*, 102–117. doi:10.1111/j.1365-2729.2005.00118.x

Hall, K., Collins, J., Benjamin, S., Nind, M., & Sheehy, K. (2004). SATurated models of pupildom: assessment and inclusion/exclusion. *British Educational Research Journal, 30*(6), 801–817. doi:10.1080/0141192042000279512

Hannele, N. (2003). Towards a learning society in Finland: Information and communications technology in teacher education. *Technology, Pedagogy and Education, 12*(1), 85–103. doi:10.1080/14759390300200147

Hardman, F., Smith, F., & Wall, K. (2003). 'Interactive whole class teaching' in the National Literacy Strategy. *Cambridge Journal of Education, 33*(2), 197–215. doi:10.1080/03057640302043

Hargreaves, D. (2004). *Personalising learning: Next steps in working laterally.* Retrieved February 10, 2009, from http://www.ssat-inet.net/resources/publications

Hargreaves, L., Moyles, J., Merry, R., Paterson, F., Pell, A., & Esarte-Sarries, V. (2003). How do primary school teachers define and implement 'interactive teaching' in the national literacy strategy in England. *Research Papers in Education, 18*(3), 217–236. doi:10.1080/0267152032000107301

Harris, V. (1998). Making boys make progress. *Language Learning Journal, 18*, 56–62. doi:10.1080/09571739885200271

Harrison, C., Comber, C., Fisher, T., Haw, K., Lewin, C., & Lunzer, E. (2002). *ImpaCT2: The impact of information and communication technologies on pupil learning and attainment. A report to the DfES. ICT in Schools Research and Evaluation Series No 7.* Coventry, UK: Becta.

Harrison, C., Comber, C., Fisher, T., Haw, K., Lewin, C., Lunzer, E., et al. (2002). ImpaCT2. The impact of information and communication technologies on pupil learning and attainment. (ICT in Schools Research and Evaluation Series No. 7). London: DfES/BECTA.

Hedge, T. (2000). *Teaching and learning in the language classroom.* Oxford, UK: Oxford University Press.

Heilbronn, R. (2004). The national strategy for key stage 3 and its application to modern foreign language teaching. *Language Learning Journal, 30*, 42–49. doi:10.1080/09571730485200221

Hennessey, S., Deaney, R., & Ruthven, K. (2006). Situated expertise in integrating use of multimedia simulation into secondary science teaching. *International Journal of Science Education, 28*(7), 701–732. doi:10.1080/09500690500404656

Hennessey, S., Wishart, J., & Whitelock, D. (2007). Pedagogical approaches for technology-integrated science teaching. *Computers & Education, 48*(1), 137–152. doi:10.1016/j.compedu.2006.02.004

Hennessy, S. (2008). *Interactivity means more activity for students.* ESRC. Retrieved June 15, 2009, from http://www.esrcsocietytoday.ac.uk/ESRCInfoCentre/PO/releases/2008/september/whitebo ard.aspx

Hennessy, S., & Deaney, R. (2005-2007). *T-MEDIA: Exploring teacher mediation of subject learning with ICT: A multimedia approach.* ESRC-funded project: RES-000-23-0825.

Hennessy, S., & Deaney, R. (2006, September). *Integrating multiple teacher and researcher perspectives through video analysis of pedagogic approaches to using projection technologies.* Paper presented at British Educational Research Association conference, Warwick, UK.

Hennessy, S., & Deaney, R. (2007). *Teacher mediation of subject learning with ICT: A multimedia approach (T-MEDIA).* Retrieved June 15, 2009, from http://www.educ.cam.ac.uk/research/projects/istl/T-MEDIA_Fin_Rep_Main.pdf

Hennessy, S., & Deaney, R. (2009a). 'Intermediate theory' building: Integrating multiple teacher and researcher perspectives through in-depth video analysis of pedagogic strategies. *Teachers College Record, 111*(7), 1753–1795.

Hennessy, S., & Deaney, R. (2009b). The impact of collaborative video analysis by practitioners and researchers upon pedagogical thinking and practice: A follow-up study. *Teachers and Teaching: Theory and Practice, 15*(5), 617–638.

Hennessy, S., Deaney, R., & Ruthven, K. (2006). Situated expertise in integrating use of multimedia simulation into secondary science teaching. *International Journal of Science Education, 28*(7), 701–732. doi:10.1080/09500690500404656

Hennessy, S., Deaney, R., Ruthven, K., & Winterbottom, M. (2007). Pedagogical strategies for using the interactive whiteboard to foster learner participation in school science. *Learning, Media and Technology, 32*(3), 283–301. doi:10.1080/17439880701511131

Hennessy, S., Wishart, J., Whitelock, D., Deaney, R., Brawn, R., & la Velle, L. (2007). Pedagogical approaches for technology-integrated science teaching. *Computers & Education, 48*(1), 137–152. doi:10.1016/j.compedu.2006.02.004

Heppell, S. (2004). *Interactive whiteboards are useful stepping stones to other technologies* (interviewed by George Cole), *TES Online, 8*. Retrieved July 10,

2009, from https://tslwspr02.www.tes.co.uk/article.aspx?storycode=2047323

Higgins, S. Clark. J., Falzon. C., Hall, I., Hardman, F., Miller, J., Moseley, D., Smith, F., & Wall, K. (2005). *Embedding ICT in the literacy and numeracy strategies: Final report April 2005.* Newcastle Upon Tyne, UK: Newcastle University. Retrieved June 15, 2009, from http://www.staff.ucsm.ac.uk/rpotter/ict/research/univ_newcastle_evaluation_whitebo ards.pdf

Higgins, S., & Moseley, D. (2001). Teachers' thinking about ICT and learning: Beliefs and outcomes. *Teacher Development, 5*(2), 191–210. doi:10.1080/13664530100200138

Higgins, S., Beauchamp, B., & Miller, D. (2007). Reviewing the literature on interactive whiteboards. *Learning, Media and Technology, 32*(3), 213–225. doi:10.1080/17439880701511040

Higgins, S., Beauchamp, G., & Miller, D. (2007). Reviewing the literature on interactive whiteboards. *Learning, Media and Technology, 32*(3), 213–225. doi:10.1080/17439880701511040

Higgins, S., Clark, J., Falzon, C., Hall, I., Hardman, F., & Miller, J. (2005). *Embedding ICT in the literacy and numeracy strategies: Final Report.* Newcastle Upon Tyne, UK: Newcastle University.

Hinostroza, J. E., & Mellar, H. (2001). Pedagogy embedded in educational software design: Report of a case study. *Computers & Education, 37*(1), 27–40. doi:10.1016/S0360-1315(01)00032-X

Hodge, S., & Anderson, B. (2007). Teaching and learning with an interactive whiteboard: A teacher's journey. *Learning, Media and Technology, 32*(3), 271–282. doi:10.1080/17439880701511123

Hodgkinson-Williams, C. (2005). Revisiting the concept of ICTs as tools. Paper for ITFORUM. Retrieved January 31, 2009, from http://it.coe.uga.edu/itforum/paper88/Hodgkinson-Williams-2006.pdf

Hokanson, B., & Hooper, S. (2000). Computers as cognitive media: Examining the potential of computers in education. *Computers in Human Behavior, 16*, 537–552. doi:10.1016/S0747-5632(00)00016-9

Hooper, S., & Rieber, L. P. (1995). Teaching with technology. In Ornstein, A. C. (Ed.), *Teaching: Theory into practice* (pp. 154–170). Needham Heights, MA: Allyn and Bacon.

Hubbard, P., & Levy, M. (2006). *Teacher education in CALL.* Amsterdam, The Netherlands: John Benjamins.

Hughes, M., & Longman, D. (2005). *Interactive digital display boards and class teaching: Interactive or just another epidiascope.* Paper presented at BERA 2005, University of Glamorgan, UK.

Hull University. (2004). *The review project.* Retrieved August 25, 2005, from http://www. thereviewproject.org

Hustler, D., McNamara, O., Jarvis, J., Londra, M., Campell, A., & Howson, J. (2009). *Teachers' perceptions of continuing professional development.* Nottingham: DfES. Retrieved February 1, 2009, from http://www.dcsf.gov.uk/research/data/uploadfiles/RR429.pdf

Iding, M. (2000). Is seeing believing? Features of effective multimedia for learning science. International. *Journal of Instructive Media, 27*(4), 403–416.

Ilomaki, L., Jaakkola, T., Lakkala, M., Nirhamo, L., Nurmi, S., Paavola, S., et al. (2003). *Principles, models and examples of designing learning objects (LOs). Pedagogical guidelines in CELEBRATE. Working paper for the European Commission, CELEBRATE Project, IST-2001-35188.* Retrieved 9 February 2009, from http://www.helsinki.fi/science/networkedlearning/texts/principlesforlos.pdf.

Ilomaki, L., Lakkala, M., & Paavola, S. (2006). Case studies of learning objects used in school settings. *Learning, Media and Technology, 31*(3), 249–267. doi:10.1080/17439880600893291

International Certificate Conference (2003). *The impact of information and communications technologies on the teaching of foreign languages and on the role of teachers of foreign languages. A report commissioned by the Directorate General of Education & Culture.* Retrieved February 26, 2004, from http://icc-europe.com/ICT_in_FLT_Final_Report_Jan2003/ICT_in_FLT_in_Europe.pdf

Ireson, J., Mortimore, P., & Hallam, S. (2002). What do we know about effective pedagogy? In Moon, B., Shelton Mayes, A., & Hutchinson, S. (Eds.), *Teaching, learning and the curriculum in secondary school: A reader* (pp. 64–69). London, New York: Open University/Routledge Falmer.

Jamerson, J. (2002). *Helping all children learn: Action research project*. Retrieved February 22, 2009, from http://smarterkids.org/research/paper15.asp

James, M., & Brown, S. (2005). Grasping the TLRP nettle: Preliminary analysis and some enduring issues surrounding the improvement of learning outcomes. *Curriculum Journal*, *16*(1), 7–30. doi:10.1080/0958517042000336782

Jewitt, C. (2002). The move from page to screen: the multimodal reshaping of school English. *Journal of Visual Communication*, *1*(2), 171–196. doi:10.1177/147035720200100203

Jewitt, C., Moss, G., & Cardini, A. (2007). Pace, interactivity and multimodality in teacher design of texts for IWBs. *Learning, Media and Technology*, *32*(3), 302–318. doi:10.1080/17439880701511149

Jewitt, C., Moss, J., & Cardini, A. (2007). Pace, interactivity and multimodality in teachers' design of texts for interactive whiteboards in the secondary school classroom. *Learning, Media and Technology*, *32*(3), 303–317. doi:10.1080/17439880701511149

John, P., & Sutherland, R. (2005). Affordance, opportunity and the pedagogical implications of ICT. *Educational Review*, *57*(4), 405–413. doi:10.1080/00131910500278256

Jonassen, D. (2000). *Computers as mindtools for schools: Engaging critical thinking* (2nd ed.). New Jersey, USA: Prentice Hall.

Jones, A. (2004). *A review of the research literature on barriers to the uptake of ICT by teachers*. Coventry, UK: Becta.

Jones, B., & Jones, G. (2001). *Boys' performance in modern foreign languages. Listening to learners*. London: CILT.

Jones, J., & Coffey, S. (2006). Modern foreign languages 5-11: A guide for teachers. London: David Fulton.

Jones, S., & Tanner, H. (2002). Teacher's interpretations of effective whole class interactive teaching in secondary mathematics classrooms. *Educational Studies*, *28*(3), 265–274. doi:10.1080/0305569022000003717

Journal of Computer Assisted Learning. *21*, 102–117. Retrieved 10 December, 2008, from http://www.soton.ac.uk/~pgce/ict/NewPGCE/pdfs%20IWBs/Primary%20School%20children's%20perceptions%20of%20IWBs.pdf

Judge, M. (2003). *Wired for learning in Ireland final evaluation report*. Ireland: Dublin City University.

Judge, M. (2004). The wired for learning project in Ireland. A classic tale of technology, school culture and the problem of change. In P. Isaias, P. Kommers & M. McPherson (Eds.), *Proceedings of the IADIS International Conference, 1* (pp. 226-234). e-Society 2004, Avila, Spain.

Kaptelinin, V. (1997). Activity theory: Implications for Human-Computer Interaction. In Nardi, B. A. (Ed.), *Context and consciousness: Activity theory and Human-Computer Interaction*. Boston: MIT Press.

Kemeny, H. (2004). *Review of some literature and classroom research into IWB use in primary schools*. Unpublished paper produced for the "IWB pedagogy and pupil performance project".

Kemeny, H. (2005). *Transforming learning? Interactive whiteboards in the primary classroom: Case studies from a London school*. Paper included in the proceedings of the CRPP Transforming Pedagogy Conference, NIE June 2005.

Kendon, A. (2000). Language and gesture: Unity or duality. In McNeill, D. (Ed.), *Language and gesture* (pp. 47–63). Cambridge, UK: Cambridge University Press.

Kennewell, S. (2001). Interactive whiteboards – yet another solution looking for a problem to solve? *Information Technology in Teacher Education*, *39*, 3-6. Retrieved February 15, 2009, from http://www.itte.org.uk/newsletters/itte_nl_39.pdf

Kennewell, S. (2004). Researching the influence of interactive presentation tools on teacher pedagogy. Paper presented at BERA.

Kennewell, S. (2006). *Reflections on the interactive whiteboard phenomenon: A synthesis of research from the UK Swansea School of Education.* Australia: The Australian Association for Research in Education.

Kennewell, S., & Beauchamp, G. (2007). The features of interactive whiteboards and their influence on learning. *Learning, Media and Technology, 32*(3), 227–241. doi:10.1080/17439880701511073

Kennewell, S., & Morgan, A. (2003). *Student teachers experiences and attitudes towards using interactive whiteboards in the teaching and learning of young children.* Paper presented to Young Children and Learning Technologies Conference. Australia: Australian Computer Society Parramatta.

Kennewell, S., Beauchamp, G., Jones, S., & Norman, N. Parkinson, J., Tanner, H., et al. (2008). *The use of ICT to improve learning and attainment through interactive teaching: Full research report.* Economic and Social Research Council end of award report. RES-139-25-0167-A. Retrieved October 20, 2008, from http://www.esrcsocietytoday.ac.uk/ESRCInfoCentre/ViewOutputPage.aspx?data=v9XrjLJ6xhGKkb12HPJ7W5ye0b9qtr8%2fqVQxkan2L1TIciduxIHf6agYU3K1R1Cc1XeShX2F5UjcyVTLWid0cK3oi%2bu3Y8Y1%2fejJYVW6gMQ%3d&xu=0&isAwardHolder=&isProfiled=&AwardHolderID=&Sector=

Kennewell, S., Parkinson, J., & Tanner, H. (Eds.). (2003). *Learning to teach ICT in the secondary school.* London: RoutledgeFalmer.

Kennewell, S., Tanner, H., Jones, S., & Beauchamp, G. (2008). Analysing the use of interactive technology to implement interactive teaching. *Journal of Computer Assisted Learning, 24*(1), 61-73(13).

Kent, M. (2006). Our journey into whiteboard hell. *Times Educational Supplement,* (4703): 40.

Kirschner, P., & Davis, N. (2003). Pedagogic benchmarks for information and communications technology in

teacher education. *Technology, Pedagogy and Education, 12*(1), 125–147. doi:10.1080/14759390300200149

Kirschner, P., & Selinger, M. (2003). The state of affairs of teacher education with respect to information and communications technology. *Technology, Pedagogy and Education, 12*(1), 5–17. doi:10.1080/14759390300200143

Kitchen, S., Butt, S., & Mackenzies, H. (2006). *Evaluation of curriculum online: Emerging findings from the third survey of schools.* Report for National Centre for Social Research. Retrieved July 10, 2009, from http://www.becta.org.uk/page_documents/research/curriculum_

Kitchen, S., Mackenzie, H., Butt, S., & Finch, S. (2006). *Evaluation of Curriculum Online report of the third survey of schools.* London: National Centre for Social Research.

Knight, P., Pennant, J., & Piggott, J. (2004). What does it mean to 'Use the interactive whiteboard' in the daily mathematics lesson? *MicroMath, 20*(2), 14–16.

Knuffer, N. (1993). Teachers and educational computing: Changing roles and changing pedagogy. In R. Muffoletto & N. Knuffer N. (Eds.), Computers in education: Social, political and historical perspectives, 1(1), 163-179.

Kounin, J. S. (1970). *Discipline and group management in classrooms.* New York: Holt, Rinehart & Winston.

Kozma, R. (1991). Learning with media. *Review of Educational Research, 61,* 179–211.

Kozma, R. (1994). The influence of media on learning: The debate continues. *School Library Media Research, 22*(4). Retrieved, February 12, 2009, From http://www.ala.org/ala/mgrps/divs/aasl/aaslpubsandjournals/slmrb/editorschoiceb/infopower/selectkozmahtml.cfm

Latane, B. (2002). Focused interactive learning: a tool for active class discussion. *Teaching of Psychology, 29*(1), 10–16. doi:10.1207/S15328023TOP2901_03

Latham, P. (2002). *Teaching and learning primary mathematics: The impact of interactive whiteboards.* North Islington Education Action Zone: BEAM research papers. Retrieved October 13, 2008, from http://www.beam.co.uk/pdfs/RES03.pdf

Laurillard, D. (1997). *The TELL consortium – formative evaluation report*. Hull, UK: University of Hull. Retrieved January 29, 2004, from http://www.hull.ac.uk/cti/tell/eval.htm

Laurillard, D. (2002). *Rethinking university teaching: A conversational framework for the effective use of learning technologies* (2nd ed.). London: RoutledgeFalmer.

Law, N. (2004). Teachers and teaching innovations in a connected world. In Brown, A., & Davis, N. (Eds.), *World yearbook of education 2004: Digital technology, communities and education* (pp. 145–163). London: RoutledgeFalmer.

Lawes, S. (2000). Why learn a foreign language? In Field, K. (Ed.), *Issues in modern foreign languages teaching* (pp. 41–51). Cambridge, MA: Cambridge University Press.

LeDuff, R. (2004). Enhancing biology instruction via multimedia presentations. In C. Crawford et al. (Eds.), *Proceedings of the Society for Information Technology and Teacher Education International Conference 2004* (pp. 4693-4695). Chesapeake, VA: AACE. Retrieved October 8, 2007 from http://www.edcompass.de/NR/rdonlyres/B65DEF10-F8F0-40A3-B91A-A892BED75292/0/LeDuff_Jan04.pdf

Lee, J. C. (2007). *Using infrared (IR) light pens and the Wii Remote, it is possible to create very low-cost multipoint interactive whiteboards and multi-point tablet displays*. Retrieved April 10, 2009, from http://www.youtube.com/watch?v=5s5EvhHy7eQ

Legutke, M., & Thomas, H. (1991). *Process and experience in the language classroom*. London: Longman.

Legutke, M., Mueller-Hartmann, A., & Schocker v.Ditfurth, M. (2007). Preparing teachers for technology-supported English language teaching. In J. Cummins & C. Davison (Eds.), *Kluwer handbook on English language teaching* (pp. 1125-1138). New York: Springer.

Levy, P. (2002). *Interactive whiteboards in learning and teaching in two Sheffield schools: A developmental study*. Sheffield Department of Information Studies, University of Sheffield.

Levy, P. (2002). *Interactive whiteboards in teaching and learning*. Sheffield: Sheffield University.

Lewin, C., Scrimshaw, P., Somekh, B., & Haldane, M. (in press). The impact of formal and informal professional development opportunities on primary teachers' adoption of interactive whiteboards. *Technology, Pedagogy and Education, 27*(2), 159-170.

Lewin, C., Somekh, B., & Steadman, S. (2008). Embedding interactive whiteboards in teaching and learning: The process of change in pedagogic practice. *Education and Information Technologies, 13*(4), 291–303. doi:10.1007/s10639-008-9070-z

Lightbown, P. M. (2003). Second language acquisition research in the classroom/second language acquisition research from the classroom. *Language Learning Journal, 28*, 4–13. doi:10.1080/09571730385200151

Ligorio, M. B. (2001). Integrating communication formats; synchronous versus asynchronous and text based versus visual. *Computers & Education, 37*(2), 103–125. doi:10.1016/S0360-1315(01)00039-2

Littleton, K., Twiner, A., & Gillen, J. (in press). Instruction as orchestration: Multimodal connection building with the interactive whiteboard. *Pedagogies: An International Journal, 5*(4).

Lloyd, M., & McRobbie, C. (2005). The whole approach: An investigation of a school-based practicum model of teacher professional development in ICT. *Journal of Educational Computing Research, 32*(4), 341–351. doi:10.2190/623G-MT8A-VC17-R1TA

Lodge, A. (2000). Higher Education. In Green, S. (Ed.), *New perspectives on teaching and learning modern languages* (pp. 105–123). Clevedon, UK: Multilingual Matters Ltd.

Lopez, O. (2006). *Lighting the flame of learning for English language learners through the use of interactive whiteboard technology*. Retrieved February 15, 2009, from www.prometheanworld.com/upload/pdf/WP_ELL_20081201075615.pdf

Loveless, A. (2002). Professional development with ICT: Looking beyond the technology. *Journal of information technology for Teacher Education, 2*, 117-121.

Loveless, A., DeVoogd, G. L., & Bohlin, R. M. (2001). Something old, something new... Is Pedagogy affected by ICT? In Loveless, A., & Ellis, V. (Eds.), *ICT Pedagogy and the curriculum: Subject to change* (pp. 63–83). London: RoutledgeFalmer.

Lyle, J. (2003). Stimulated recall: a report on its use in naturalistic research. *British Educational Research Journal, 29*(6), 861–878. doi:10.1080/0141192032000137349

Mayer, R. E. (2001). *Multimedia learning*. New York: Cambridge University Press.

Maykut, P., & Morehouse, R. (1994). *Beginning qualitative research: A philosophic and practical guide*. London: Falmer Press.

McCabe, M., Heal, A., & White, A. (2001). The integration of group response systems on teaching and LOLA, the missing link in computer assisted assessment. *Paper presented at the 5th Annual CAA Conference 2001*, Loughborough University, UK.

McCarney, J. (2004). Effective models of staff development in ICT. *European Journal of Teacher Education, 27*(1), 61–72. doi:10.1080/0261976042000211801

McCormick, R., & Scrimshaw, P. (2001). Information and communication technology, knowledge and pedagogy. *Education Communication and Information, 1*, 37–57. doi:10.1080/14636310120048047

McCormick, R., & Scrimshaw, P. (2001). Information and communications technology, knowledge and pedagogy. *Education Communication and Information, 1*, 37–57. doi:10.1080/14636310120048047

McTighe, J., & O'Connor, K. (2005). Seven practices for effective learning. *Educational Leadership, 63*(3), 10–17.

Mercer, N., & Littleton, K. (2007). *Dialogue and the development of children's thinking: A sociocultural approach*. London, New York: Routledge.

Merriman, S. B. (1998). *Case study research in education: A qualitative approach*. San Francisco: Josey-Bass.

Meskill, C., Anthony, N., Hilliker, S., Tseng, C., & You, J. (2007). Expert-novice teacher mentoring in language learning technology. In Hubbard, P., & Levy, M. (Eds.), *Research in CALL teacher education* (pp. 283–29). Amsterdam, The Netherlands: John Benjamins.

Miller, D. (2003). Developing interactive whiteboard activity. *Micromath, 19*(3), 33–35.

Miller, D. J., Averis, D., & Glover, D. (2008). *Professional development for teachers of mathematics using interactive whiteboards: Report to National Centre for Excellence in Teaching Mathematics. Keele*. Staffordshire, UK: Keele University.

Miller, D. J., Averis, D., Door, D., & Glover, D. C. (2005). *How can the use of an interactive whiteboard enhance the nature of teaching and learning in secondary mathematics and modern foreign languages?* Retrieved February 15, 2008, from http://www.becta.org.uk/page_documents/research/bursaries05/interactive_whiteboard.pdf

Miller, D. J., Glover, D. C., & Averis, D. (2004). *Enhancing mathematics teaching through new technology: The use of the interactive whiteboard*. Retrieved February 15, 2008, from http://www.keele.ac.uk/depts/ed/IWB/nuffield.htm

Miller, D. J., Glover, D., & Averis, D. (2006). *Interactive whiteboard evaluation for the secondary national strategy: Developing the use of interactive whiteboards in mathematics. Final Report for the Secondary National Strategy*. Retrieved February 15, 2008, from http://www.standards.dfes.gov.uk/keystage3/downloads/ma_IWB_eval_rpt.pdf

Miller, D. J., Glover, D., & Averis, D. (2008). *Enabling enhanced mathematics teaching: Final Report for the National Centre for Excellence in the Teaching of Mathematics*. Retrieved February 22, 2009, from http://www.keele.ac.uk/depts/ed/iaw/docs/ncetmreport/ncetmreport.pdf

Miller, D., & Glover, D. (2002). The interactive whiteboard as a force for pedagogic change: The experience of five elementary schools in an English education authority. *Information Technology in Childhood Education, 1,* 5–19.

Miller, D., & Glover, D. (2004). *Enhancing mathematics teaching through new technology: The use of the interactive whiteboard. Summary of a report made to the Nuffield Foundation on completion of a funded two-year project* (April 2002-March 2004). Retrieved June 15, 2009, from http://www.keele.ac.uk/depts/ed/iaw/nuffield. htm, downloadable file at: http://www.keele.ac.uk/depts/ed/iaw/docs/NuffieldReport.pdf

Miller, D., & Glover, D. (2004). Enhancing mathematics teaching through new technology: The use of the interactive whiteboard, Summary of a report made to the Nuffield Foundation on completion of a funded two year project (April 2002–March 2004).

Miller, D., & Glover, D. (2006a). *Interactive whiteboard evaluation for the secondary national strategy: Developing the use of interactive whiteboards in mathematics, Final Report for the Secondary National Strategy.* Retrieved February 22, 2009, from http://nationalstrategies. standards.dcsf.gov.uk/node/97754

Miller, D., & Glover, D. (2006b). *Enhanced secondary mathematics teaching: Gesture and the interactive whiteboard.* Keele University BERA: Warwick. Retrieved February 22, 2009, from http://www.keele.ac.uk/depts/ed/iaw/docs/Bera06Enhanced%20secondary%20maths%20and%20gesture.pdf

Miller, D., & Glover, D. (2007). Into the unknown: The professional development induction experience of secondary mathematics teachers using interactive whiteboard technology. *Learning, Media and Technology, 32*(3), 319–331. doi:10.1080/17439880701511156

Miller, D., & Glover, D. (2009). Interactive whiteboards in the Web 2.0 Classroom. In Thomas, M. (Ed.), *Handbook of research on web 2.0 and second language learning.* Hershey, PA: IGI Global.

Miller, D., Averis, D., Door, V., & Glover, D. (2005a). *How can the use of an interactive whiteboard enhance the nature of teaching and learning in secondary math-*

ematics and modern foreign languages? Report made to Becta. Retrieved February 22, 2009, from http://partners. becta.org.uk/upload-dir/downloads/page_documents/research/bursaries05/interactive_whiteboard.pdf

Miller, D., Averis, D., Door, V., & Glover, D. (2005b). *From technology to professional development: How can the use of an interactive whiteboard in initial teacher education change the nature of teaching and learning in secondary mathematics and modern languages?* Training and Development agency, London. Report made to the Teacher Training Agency. Retrieved February 22, 2009, from http://www.ttrb.ac.uk/attachments/0d65acf3-488a-4fca-8536-918d6dafd694.pdf

Miller, D., Glover, D., & Averis, D. (2003, March). *Exposure: The introduction of interactive whiteboard technology to secondary school mathematics teachers in training.* Paper presented at CERME3: Third Conference of the European Society for Research in Mathematics Education, Bellaria, Italy.

Miller, D., Glover, D., & Averis, D. (2004). *Motivation: The contribution of interactive whiteboards to teaching and learning in mathematics.* Retrieved February 15, 2009, from http://cerme4.crm.es/Papers%20definitius/9/Miller-Glover-Averis.pdf

Miller, D., Glover, D., & Averis, D. (2004). *Panacea or prop: the role of the interactive whiteboard in improving teaching effectiveness.* Paper presented at the Tenth International Congress of Mathematics Education, Copenhagen. Retrieved June 15, 2009, from http://www. icme-organisers.dk/tsg15/Glover_et_al.pdf

Miller, D., Glover, D., & Averis, D. (2005). Presentation and pedagogy: The effective use of interactive whiteboards in mathematics lessons. In D. Hewitt & A. Noyes (Eds.), *Proceedings of the sixth British congress of mathematics education* (pp. 105-112). Coventry, UK: University of Warwick.

Miller, D., Glover, D., & Averis, D. (2005). Presentation and pedagogy: The effective use of interactive whiteboards in mathematics lessons. In D. Hewitt & A. Noyes (Eds), *Proceedings of the sixth British Congress of Mathematics Education held at the University of Warwick*, pp.

105-112. Retrieved February 22, 2009, from http://www. bsrlm.org.uk/IPs/ip25-1/BSRLM-IP-25-1-14.pdf

Miller, D., Glover, D., & Averis, D. (2008). *Enabling enhanced mathematics teaching with interactive whiteboards.* Retrieved February 15, 2009, from http://www. keele.ac.uk/depts/ed/iaw/docs/ncetmreport/ncetmreport. pdf

Miller, D., Glover, D., Averis, D., & Door, V. (2005). *From technology to professional development: How can the use of an interactive whiteboard in initial teacher education change the nature of teaching and learning in secondary mathematics and modern languages?* Report made to the Teacher Training Agency. London: Training and Development agency. Retrieved February 15, 2009, from http://www.ttrb.ac.uk/attachments/0d65acf3-488a-4fca-8536-918d6dafd694.pdf

Mishra, P., & Koehler, M. (2006). Technological pedagogical content knowledge: A framework for teacher knowledge. *Teachers College Record, 108*(6), 1017–1054. doi:10.1111/j.1467-9620.2006.00684.x

Mishra, P., & Koehler, M. (2009). TCPK – *Technological pedagogical content knowledge.* Retrieved May 1, 2009, from http://tpack.org/

Mitchell, R. (2000). Research, inspection and teacher education: The quest for a consensus on effective MFLs pedagogy. *Links (New York, N.Y.), 21,* 5–12.

Moss, G. (2003). Analysing literacy events: Mapping gendered configurations of readers, texts and contexts. In Goodman, S., Lillis, T., Maybin, J., & Mercer, N. (Eds.), *Language, literacy and education: A reader* (pp. 123–137). London: Trentham Books.

Moss, G., Carey, J., Levaãiç, R., Armstrong, V., Cardini, A., & Castle, F. (2007). The interactive whiteboards, pedagogy and pupil performance evaluation: An evaluation of the schools whiteboard expansion (SWE) project: London challenge. School of Education and Policy Studies, Institute of Education, University of London, Research Report 816.

Moss, G., Carrey, J., Levaaic, R., Armstrong, V., Cardini, A., & Castle, F., (2007). *The interactive whiteboards pedagogy and pupil performance evaluation: An evaluation of the schools whiteboard expansion (SWE) project: London Challenge.* Institute of Education: University of London.

Mroz, M. A., Smith, F., & Hardman, F. (2000). The discourse of the literacy hour. *Cambridge Journal of Education, 30*(3), 379–390. doi:10.1080/03057640020004513

Muijs, D., & Reynolds, D. (2001). *Effective teaching: Evidence and practice.* London: Paul Chapman Publishing.

Munn, P., & Lloyd, G. (2005). Exclusion and excluded pupils. *British Educational Research Journal, 31*(2), 205–221. doi:10.1080/0141192052000340215

Murphy, J. F., Jain, N. L., Spooner, S. A., Hassan, S. W., Schnase, J. L., & Metcalfe, E. S. (1995). Use of an interactive electronic whiteboard to teach clinical cardiology decision analysis to medical students. *Journal of the American College of Cardiology, 25*(2), 238A. doi:10.1016/0735-1097(95)92448-E

Myers, H. (2003). *Case study 5: The Ashcombe School, Language College. Information and Communications Technology for Language Teaching (ICT4LT) Module 3:1. Managing a multimedia language centre.* Retrieved 26 February, 2004, from http://www.ict4lt.org/en/ en_mod3.1.htm

Nachimias, R., Mioduser, D., & Forkosh-Baruch, A. (2008). Innovative pedagogical practices using technology: The curriculum perspective. In Voogt, J., & Knezek, G. (Eds.), *International handbook of information technology in primary and secondary schools* (pp. 163–179). Guildford, UK: Springer Science. doi:10.1007/978-0-387-73315-9_10

Nicholson, A. (1996, September). *Can we reveal the inner world of teachers?* Paper presented at the BERA Conference, University of Lancaster, UK.

Nonis, A., & O'Bannon, B. (2001). *Technology and teacher preparation: Creating learning environments for increasing student involvement and creativity.* Retrieved February 22, 2009, from http://smarterkids.org/ research/paper11.asp

Noss, R., & Pachler, N. (1999). The challenge of new technologies: Doing old things in a new way or doing new things? In Mortimore, P. (Ed.), *Understanding Pedagogy and its impact on learning*. London: Paul Chapman.

Nystrand, M., & Gamoran, A. (1991). Student engagement: When recitation becomes conversation. In Waxman, H. C., & Walberg, H. J. (Eds.), *Effective teaching: Current research*. Berkley, CA: McCutchan.

Office for Standards in Education. (2002). *ICT in schools: the effect of government initiatives. Secondary modern foreign languages (HMI 706)*. London: Her Majesty's Inspectorate.

Office for Standards in Education. (2003). *Modern foreign languages (MFL). Progress and improving boys' achievement in modern foreign languages*. Ofsted subject reports conference series 2002/2003 (HMI 1641). London: Her Majesty's Inspectorate.

Office for Standards in Education. (2004). *ICT in schools – the impact of government initiatives. Secondary modern foreign languages. HMI 2191*. London: Her Majesty's Inspectorate.

Office for Standards in Education. (2005). *Embedding ICT in schools – a dual evaluation exercise*. London: Office for Standards in Education.

Ofsted (2004). *ICT in schools: The impact of government initiatives five years on*. London: Ofsted.

Ofsted (2006). *The logical chain: CPD in effective schools*. London: Ofsted.

Ofsted, (2005). *The annual report of her majesty's chief inspector of schools*. London: Ofsted.

Olive, J. (2002). Computer tools for interactive mathematical activity in elementary schools. *International Journal of Computers for Mathematical Learning, 5*, 241–262. doi:10.1023/A:1009813723928

Ollin, R. (2005). Professionals, poachers or street-level bureaucrats: government policy, teaching identities and constructive subversions. In J. Satterthwaite & E. Atkinson (Eds.), Discourses of education in the age of new imperialism (pp. 151-162). Stoke on Trent, UK: Trentham Books.

Orr, M. (2006, May). *Interactive Whiteboards – the difference that makes the difference? Learners speak their minds*. Paper presented at Learning Technologies in the Language Classroom: A step closer to the future, University of Cyprus.

Osborne, J., & Hennessy, S. (2003). *Literature review in science education and the role of ICT: Promise, problems and future directions*. Retrieved July 23, 2007, from http://www.nestafuturelab.org/research/lit_reviews.htm#lr6

Oz-TeacherNet. (n.d.). *Revised Bloom's taxonomy*. Retrieved August 21, 2006, from http://rite.ed.qut.edu.au/ozteachernet/index.php?module=ContentExpress&func=display&ceid=29

Painter, D. D., Whiting, E., & Wolters, B. (2005). The use of an interactive whiteboard in promoting interactive teaching and learning. *VSTE Journal, 19*(2), 31–40.

Parry, J. (2004). Pupil authors and teacher innovators. *European Journal of Teacher Education, 27*(1), 83–98. doi:10.1080/0261976042000211810

Passey, D. (2002). *ICT and school management: A review of selected literature. Lancaster University*. Retrieved February 22, 2009, from http://partners.becta.org.uk/page_documents/research/ict_sm.pdf

Passey, D. (2006). Technology enhancing learning: Analysing uses of information and communication technologies by primary and secondary school pupils with learning frameworks. *Curriculum Journal, 17*(2), 139–166. doi:10.1080/09585170600792761

Patton, M. Q. (2002). *Qualitative research and evaluation methods* (3rd ed.). London: Sage Publications.

Pawson, R., & Tilley, N. (1997). *Realistic evaluation*. Thousand Oaks, CA: Sage.

Pearson, J. (2003). Information and communications technologies and teacher education in Australia. *Technology, Pedagogy and Education, 12*(1), 39–58. doi:10.1080/14759390300200145

Pearson, M., Haldane, M., & Somekh, B. (2004). *St. Thomas of Aquin's interactive whiteboard pilot evaluation: Report to the Scottish Executive.* Manchester, UK: Manchester Metropolitan University.

Penuel, W. R., Abrahamson, L., & Roschelle, J. (2005). A sociocultural interpretation of the effects of audience response systems in Higher Education. In Banks, D. (Ed.), *Audience response systems in higher education: Applications and cases* (pp. 187–208). Hersey, PA: IGI Global.

Penuel, W. R., Abrahamson, L., & Roschelle, J. (2005). Teaching with student response systems technology: A survey of K-12 teachers. SRI International 2005. Menlo Park, CA

Petrou, M., Kerawalla, L., & Scanlon, E. (2009). *The talk Factory software: Scaffolding students' argumentation around an interactive whiteboard in primary school science. Paper submitted to the Computer Supported Collaborative Learning conference.* Greece: Rhodes.

Philips, M., Shane Doheny, S., Hearn, C., & Gilbert, T. (2004). *The impact of continuing professional development.* Bristol, UK: PARN.

Pilkington, R., & Gray, C. (2004). Embedding ICT in the modern foreign language curriculum: pedagogy into practice. In Cook, J. (Ed.), *Research proceedings of ALT-C 2004. Blue skies and pragmatism* (pp. 270–283). Exeter, UK: ALT-C.

Pinar, W. (2005). Curriculum studies and the politics of educational reform. In J. Satterthwaite & E. Atkinson (Eds.), Discourses of education in the age of new imperialism (pp. 25-46). Stoke on Trent, UK: Trentham Books.

Pittard, V., Bannister, P., & Dunn, J. (2003). The big pICTure: The impact of ICT on attainment, motivation and learning. London: DfES

Polyzou, A. (2005). Growth in teachers knowledge while learning to teach with multimedia: What has been learned from concrete educational experiences? *Technology, Pedagogy and Education, 14*(2), 205–223. doi:10.1080/14759390500200202

Postman, N., & Knopf, A. A. (1997). *The end of education.* New York: Knopf.

Powell, A., Francisco, J., & Maher, C. (2003). An analytical model for studying the development of learners' mathematical ideas and reasoning using videotape data. *The Journal of Mathematical Behavior, 22,* 405–435. doi:10.1016/j.jmathb.2003.09.002

Prensky, M. (2001). Digital natives, digital immigrants. *On the Horizon, 9*(5). Retrieved July 10, 2009, from http://www.marcprensky.com/writing/Prensky%20-%20Digital%20Natives,%20Digital%20Immigrants%20-%20Part1.pdf

Prensky, N. (2001). *Digital natives, digital immigrants.* Retrieved October 16, 2007, from http://www.marcprensky.com/writing

Prestage, S., & Perks, P. (2000, September). *Subject knowledge: Developing the fourth sense.* Paper presented at the BERA Conference, Cardiff University, UK.

Preston, C., & Mowbray, L. (2008). Use of SMART Boards for teaching, learning and assessment in kindergarten science. *Teaching Science - the Journal of the Australian Science Teachers Association, 54*(2), 50-53.

Preston, C., Cox, M., & Cox, K. (2000). *Teachers as innovators in learning: What motivates teachers to use ICT.* London: Teacher Training Agency/MirandaNet/Oracle/Compaq.

Proudfoot, S. (2006). Using action research to promote collaborative participation. *BC Educational Leadership Research, 6,* 1–6.

Radford, L. (2003). Gestures, speech and the sprouting of signs: a semiotic-cultural approach to students' types of generalisation. *Mathematical Thinking and Learning, 5*(1), 37–70. doi:10.1207/S15327833MTL0501_02

Reedy, G. B. (2008). PowerPoint, interactive whiteboards, and the visual culture of technology in schools. *Technology, Pedagogy and Education, 17*(2), 143–152. doi:10.1080/14759390802098623

Reedy, L. (2005). A whiteboard success story. *Media & Methods, 41*(6), 17.

Rex, L., Steadman, S., & Graciano, M. (2006). Researching the complexity of classroom interaction. In Green, J., Camilli, G., & Elmore, P. (Eds.), *Handbook of complementary methods for research in education.* Washington, DC, USA: American Educational Research Association.

Reynolds, D., & Farrell, S. (1996). *Worlds apart? A review of international surveys of educational achievement involving England.* London: HMSO.

Reynolds, D., & Muijs, D. (1999). The effective teaching of mathematics: A review of research. *School Leadership & Management, 19*(3), 273–288. doi:10.1080/13632439969032

Richardson, A. (2002). Effective questioning in teaching mathematics using an interactive whiteboard. *Micromath, 18*(2), 8–12.

Robison, S. (2000). Math classes for the 21st century. *Media and Methods, 36*(4), 10–11.

Rogers, E. M. (1995). *Diffusion of innovations.* New York: Macmillan Publishing Company.

Rogoff, B. (1995). Observing sociocultural activity on three planes: Participatory appropriation, guided participation, and apprenticeship. In Wertsch, J. V., Del Rio, P., & Alvarez, A. (Eds.), *Sociocultural studies of mind* (pp. 139–164). Cambridge, MA: Cambridge University Press.

Roschelle, J., Penuel, W. R., & Abrahamson, L. (2004). *Annual meeting of the American educational research association 2004.* San Diego, CA

Roythorne, P. (2006). ABC or ICT. *Times Educational Supplement,* (4691): 5.

Rudd, T. (2007). *Interactive whiteboards in the classroom.* Bristol, UK: Futurelab. Retrieved 10 December, 2008, from http://www.futurelab.org.uk/resources/documents/other/whiteboards_report.pdf

Sakoda, J. M., Cohen, B. H., & Beall, G. (1954). Tests of significance for a series of statistical tests. *Psychological Bulletin, 51,* 172–175. doi:10.1037/h0059991

Salomon, G. (1979). *Interaction of media, cognition, and learning.* San Francisco: Jossey Bass.

Sawyer, R. (2004). Creative teaching: Collaborative discussion as disciplined improvisation. *Educational Researcher, 33*(2), 12–20. doi:10.3102/0013189X033002012

Scanlon, E., Jones, A., & Waycott, J. (2005). Using a PDA as a learning or workplace tool. *Learning, Media and Technology, 30*(2), 107–130.

Schmid, E. C. (2008). Using a voting system in conjunction with interactive whiteboard technology to enhance learning in the English language classroom. *Computers & Education, 50*(1), 338–356. doi:10.1016/j.compedu.2006.07.001

Schussler, D., Poole, I., Whitlock, T., & Evertson, C. (2007). Layers and links: Learning to juggle 'one more thing' in the classroom. *Teaching and Teacher Education, 23*(5), 572–585. doi:10.1016/j.tate.2007.01.016

Scott, P., Mortimer, E., & Aguiar, O. (2006). The tension between authoritative and dialogic discourse: A fundamental characteristic of meaning making interactions in high school science lessons. *Science Education, 90*(4), 605–631. doi:10.1002/sce.20131

Scrimshaw, P. (2004), *Enabling teachers to make effective use of ICT.* Becta, Coventry, UK. Retrieved January 27, 2009, from: http://www.becta.org.uk/page_documents/research/enablers.pdf

Scrimshaw, P. (2004). *Enabling teachers to make successful use of ICT.* Coventry, UK: Becta.

Selwood, I., & Pilkington, R. (2005). Teacher workload: Using ICT to release time to teach. *Educational Review, 57*(2), 163–174. doi:10.1080/0013191042000308341

Sharma, P., & Barrett, B. (2007). *Blended learning.* London: Macmillan.

Shaw, M. (2006). Board fun fails to raise game. *Times Educational Supplement,* (4673): 5.

Shields, J. (1995). Now appearing on the big screen.... *Technology and Learning, 15*(6), 38–43.

Shulman, L. (1987). Knowledge and teaching: Foundation of the new reform. *Harvard Educational Review, 57*(1), 61–77.

Sillman, S. E., & McWilliams, L. (2004). Observations on benefits/limitations of an audience response system. *Paper presented at the American Society for Engineering Education Annual Conference and Exposition 2004.* Salt Lake City, USA.

Simpson, M., Payne, F., Munro, R., & Lynch, E. (1998). Using information and communication technology as a pedagogical tool: A survey of initial teacher education in Scotland. *Journal of Information Technology for Teacher Education, 7*(3), 431–446.

Simpson, V., & Oliver, M. (2005). *Using electronic voting systems in lectures.* Retrieved January 10, 2007, from http://www.ucl.ac.uk/klecturingtecnology/examples/ElectronicVotingSytems.pdf

Skehan, P. (1998). *A cognitive approach to language learning.* Oxford, UK: Oxford University Press.

Slay, H., Sieborger, I., & Hodgkinson-Williams, C. (2008). Interactive whiteboards: Real beauty or just lipstick? *Computers & Education, 51*(3), 1321–1341. doi:10.1016/j.compedu.2007.12.006

SMART Technologies Inc. (April 2004). *Interactive whiteboards and learning: A review of classroom case studies and research literature.* White Paper. Retrieved June 15, 2009, from http://dewey.uab.es/pmarques/pdigital/es/docs/Research%20White%20Paper.pdf

SMART. (2004). *The History of SMART Technologies Inc.* Retrieved June 15, 2009, from http://www.smarttech.com/company/aboutus/history.asp

Smeets, E., & Mooij, T. (2001). Pupil-centred learning, ICT, and teacher behaviour: Observations in educational practice. *British Journal of Educational Technology, 32*(4), 403–417. doi:10.1111/1467-8535.00210

Smith, A. (1999). *Interactive whiteboard evaluation.* Mirandanet. Retrieved February 22, 2009, from www.mirandanet.ac.uk

Smith, F., Hardman, F., & Higgins, S. (2006). The impact of interactive whiteboards on teacher-pupil interaction in the national literacy and numeracy strategies. *British Educational Research Journal, 32*(2), 443–457. doi:10.1080/01411920600635452

Smith, F., Hardman, F., & Higgins, S. (2007). Gender inequality in the primary classroom: Will interactive whiteboards help? *Gender and Education, 19*(4), 455–469. doi:10.1080/09540250701442658

Smith, F., Hardman, F., Mroz, M., & Wall, K. (2004). Interactive whole class teaching in the National Literacy and Numeracy Strategies. *British Educational Research Journal, 30*(3), 395–411. doi:10.1080/0141192041000168 9706

Smith, F., Higgins, S., & Hardman, F. (2007). Gender inequality in the primary classroom: Will interactive whiteboards help? *Gender and Education, 19*(4), 455–469. doi:10.1080/09540250701442658

Smith, H. (2001). *Smartboard evaluation final report, Kent NgfL.* Retrieved June 15, 2009, from http://www.kented.org.uk/ngfl/whiteboards/report.html

Smith, H. J., Higgins, S., Wall, K., & Miller, J. (2005). Interactive whiteboards: Boon or band-wagon? A critical review of the literature. *Journal of Computer Assisted Learning, 21*, 91–101. doi:10.1111/j.1365-2729.2005.00117.x

Smith, P., Rudd, P., & Coghlan, M. (2008). *Harnessing technology: Schools survey 2008 report 1: Analysis national foundation for educational research September 2008.* Retrieved April 7, 2009, from http://partners.becta.org.uk/upload-dir/downloads/page_documents/research/ht_schools_survey08_analysis.pdf

Somekh, B. (2007). *Pedagogy and learning with ICT: Researching the art of innovation.* London, New York: Routledge.

Somekh, B., & Haldane, M. (2006, June). *How can interactive whiteboards contribute to pedagogic change? Learning from case studies in English primary schools.* Paper presented at Imagining the Future for ICT and Education Conference. Ålesund, Norway. Retrieved

December 10, 2008, from http://ifip35.inf.elte.hu/alesund/?q=node/155

Somekh, B., & Haldane, M. (2007). *Evaluation of the primary schools whiteboard expansion project.* London: Department for Education and Skills.

Somekh, B., Haldane, M., Jones, K., Lewin, C., Steadman, S., Scrimshaw, P., et al. (2007). *Evaluation of the primary schools whiteboard expansion project - Report to the Department for Children, Schools and Families.* Retrieved June 15, 2009, from http://partners.becta.org.uk/upload-dir/downloads/page_documents/research/whiteboards_expansion.pdf

Somekh, B., Lewin, C., Mavers, D., Fisher, T., Harrison, C., Haw, K., & Lunzer, E. (2002). *ImpaCT2: Pupils and teachers' perceptions of ICT in the home, school and community. A report to the DfES. ICT in schools research and evaluation series No 11.* Coventry, UK: Becta.

Sorensen, P. D., Newton, L. R., & Harrison, C. (2006, September 2006). *The professional development of teachers through interaction with digital video.* Paper presented at the Annual Conference of the British Educational Research Association (BERA), University of Warwick.

Stake, R. (2004). *Standards-based and responsive evaluation.* California, USA: Sage.

Stake, R. E. (1995). *The art of case study research.* California, USA: Sage Publications.

Starkman, N. (2006). The wonders of interactive whiteboards. *T.H.E. Journal, 33*(10), 36-38. Retrieved March 14, 2009, from http://www.thejournal.com/articles/18500

Starkman, N. (2006). The wonders of interactive whiteboards. *T.H.E. Journal, 33*(10), 36–38.

Stein, G. (2005). *Pedagogy, practice & ICT.* Canterbury Christ Church University.

Strassmann, W. P. (1974). Technology: A culture trait, a logical category, or virtue itself? *Journal of Economic Issues, 8*(4), 671–687.

Strauss, A., & Corbin, C. (1998). *Basics of qualitative research: Techniques and procedures for developing Grounded theory* (2nd ed.). Thousand Oaks, CA: Sage.

Stuart, S. A. J., Brown, M. I., & Draper, S. W. (2004). Using an electronic voting system in logic lectures: One practitioner's application. *Journal of Computer Assisted Learning, 20,* 95–102. doi:10.1111/j.1365-2729.2004.00075.x

Swan, K., Kratcoski, A., van 't Hooft, M., Campbell, D., & Miller, D. (2007). Technology support for whole group engagement: A pilot study. *International Journal on Advanced Technologies for Learning, 4*(2), 68–73.

Swan, M. (2005). *Improving learning in mathematics: Challenges and strategies.* Nottingham, UK: University of Nottingham, Standards Unit.

Tameside, M. B. C. (2003). *Interim report on practice using interactive whiteboards in Tameside primary schools.* Retrieved June 15, 2009, from http://www.tameside.gov.uk/schools_grid/ict/whiteboards.pdf. Accessed 12th. November 2007

Tanner, H., & Jones, S. (2007). How interactive is your whiteboard? *Mathematics Teaching Incorporating Micromath, 200,* 37–41.

Tanner, H., & Jones, S. (2007). Using video-stimulated reflective dialogue to learn from children about their learning with and without ICT. *Technology, Pedagogy and Education, 16*(3), 321–335. doi:10.1080/14759390701614454

Tanner, H., Jones, S., Kennewell, S., & Beauchamp, G. (2005). Interactive whole class teaching and interactive white boards. In P. Clarkson, A. Downton, D. Gronn, M. Horne, A. McDonough, R. Pierce & A. Roche (Eds.), *Building connections: Research, theory and practice, Proceedings of the 28th annual conference of the Mathematics Education Research Group of Australasia* (pp. 720-727). Melbourne, Australia: MERGA. Retrieved 10 December, 2008, from http://www.merga.net.au/documents/RP832005.pdf

Taylor, P. C. (1996). Mythmaking and mythbreaking in the mathematics classroom. *Educational Studies in Mathematics, 31*(1-2), 151–173. doi:10.1007/BF00143930

Teacher Training Agency. (1999). *The use of information and communications technology in subject teaching. Identification of needs: Secondary modern foreign languages. TTA 13/3/1999.* London: Teacher Training Agency.

Terrell, I., & Capper, S. (2003). *The Hedley Walter High School: Cultural change in learning through the use of new technologies. Research Bursary Reports.* Coventry, UK: BECTA.

Thalheimer, W. (2007). *Learning benefits of classroom Iuestions.* Retrieved July 20, 2007, from http://www.audienceresponselearning.org/question_benefits.htlm

Thalheimer, W. (2007). *Questioning strategies for audience response systems: How to use questions to maximise learning, engagement and satisfaction.* Retrieved July 20, 2007, from http://www.audienceresponselearning.org/the_report.htlm

Tinzmann, M. B., Jones, B. F., Fennimore, T. F., Bakker, J., Fine, C., & Pierce, J. (1990). *What is the collaborative classroom?* Oak Brook, IL: NCREL.

Tobias, S. (1982). When do instructional methods make a difference? *Educational Researcher, 11*(4), 4–9.

Triggs, P., & John, P. (2004). From transaction to transformation: Information and communication technology, professional development and the formation of communities of practice. *Journal of Computer Assisted Learning, 20*(6), 426–439. doi:10.1111/j.1365-2729.2004.00101.x

Twining, P., Evans, D., Cook, D., Ralston, J., Selwood, I., Jones, A., et al. with Heppell, S., Kukulska-Hulme, A., McAndrew, P., & Sheehy, K. (2005). *Tablet PCs in schools: Case study report.* Coventry, UK: Becta. Retrieved June 15, 2009, from http://www.becta.org.uk/corporate/publications/documents/tabletpc_report.pdf

van 't Hooft, M. A. H., & Swan, K. (2007). *Ubiquitous computing in education: Invisible technology, visible impact.* Mahwah, NJ: Lawrence Erlbaum Associates.

van den Berg, R., & Ros, A. (1999). The permanent importance of the subjective reality of teachers during educational innovation: A concerns based approach. *American Educational Research Journal, 36*(4), 879–906.

Van Essen, A. (2002). A historical perspective. In M. Grenfell (Ed.) (2002). Modern languages across the curriculum (pp. 10-25). London & New York: RoutledgeFalmer.

Veen, W. (1993). The role of beliefs in the use of information technology: Implications for teacher education, or teaching the right thing at the right time. *Journal of Information Technology for Teacher Education, 2*(2), 139–153.

Voogt, J., & Knezek, G. (Eds.). (2008). *International handbook of information technology in primary and secondary education.* New York: Springer. doi:10.1007/978-0-387-73315-9

Vygotsky, L. S. (1978). *Mind in society: The development of higher psychological processes.* Cambridge, MA: Harvard University Press.

Walker, D. (2002, November 1). Meet whiteboard Wendy. *Times Educational Supplement.* Retrieved October 13, 2008, from http://www.tes.co.uk/article.aspx?storycode=371268

Walker, D. (2002, September). White enlightening. *Times Educational Supplement, 13*(19).

Walker, R. (2003). Interactive whiteboards in the MFL classroom. *TELL and CALL, 3,* 14–16.

Walker, R. J. (2004). *The review project.* Hull, UK: The University of Hull. Retrieved February 26, 2004, from http://www.thereviewproject.org/

Wall, K., Higgins, S., & Packard, E. (2007). *Talking about learning: Using templates to find out pupils' views.* Devon, UK: Southgate Publishers.

Wall, K., Higgins, S., & Smith, H. (2005). The visual helps me understand the complicated things: pupil views of teaching and learning with interactive whiteboards. *British Journal of Educational Technology, 36*(5), 851–867. doi:10.1111/j.1467-8535.2005.00508.x

Ward, D. L. (2005). *The classroom performance system: The overwhelming research results supporting this teacher tool and methodology.* Retrieved January 25, 2005, from http://www.einstruction.com

Warschauer, M. (1999). *Electronic literacies: Language, culture, and power in online education.* Mahwah, NJ: Lawrence Erlbaum.

Warschauer, M., & Meskill, C. (2000). Technology and second language learning. In Rosenthal, J. (Ed.), *Handbook of undergraduate second language education* (pp. 303–318). Mahwah, NJ: Lawrence Erlbaum.

Warschauer, M., Grant, D., Del Real, G., & Rousseau, M. (2004). Promoting academic literacy with technology: Successful laptop programs in K-12 schools. *System, 32*(4), 525–537. doi:10.1016/j.system.2004.09.010

Warshauer, M. (2002). A developmental perspective on technology in language education. *TESOL Quarterly, 36*(3), 314–328.

Wasteney, J. (2004). *The impact of voting systems in the classroom.* Retrieved September 10, 2006, from http://www.naace.org/attachment.asp?attachmentId=26309&menuItemId=8-270K

Watkins, C., & Mortimer, P. (1999). Pedagogy: What do we know? In Mortimer, P. (Ed.), *Understanding pedagogy and its impact on teaching* (pp. 1–19). London: Chapman.

Watson, A., & Mason, J. (2002). Student-generated examples in the learning of mathematics. *Canadian Journal of Science. Mathematics and Technology Education, 2*(2), 237–249. doi:10.1080/14926150209556516

Wells, G. (1999). *Dialogical inquiry: Towards a sociocultural practice and theory of education.* Cambridge, MA: Cambridge University Press.

Wenger, E. (1998). *Communities of practice: Learning, meaning and identity.* Cambridge, UK: Cambridge University Press.

Wertsch, J. (1991). *Voices of the mind: A sociocultural approach to mediated action.* Hemel Hempstead, UK: Harvester Wheatsheaf.

Whittaker, M. (2004, October). Students are running the show. *Times Educational Supplement,* (4603): 29.

Wiley, D. (2000). *Connecting learning objects to instructional design theory: A definition, a metaphor, and a taxonomy.* Retrieved March 1, 2009, from http://www.reusability.org/read/chapters/wiley.doc

Williamson, B. (2005). What are multimodality, multisemiotics and multiliteracies? A brief guide to some jargon. *Viewpoint article, 49*(1). Retrieved February 22, 2009, from http://www.futurelab.org.uk/resources/publications-reports-articles/web-articles/Web-Article532

Wood, D., Bruner, J., & Ross, G. (1976). The role of tutoring in problem-solving. *Journal of Child Psychology and Psychiatry, and Allied Disciplines, 17*(2), 89–100. doi:10.1111/j.1469-7610.1976.tb00381.x

Wood, R., & Ashfield, J. (2008). The use of the interactive whiteboard for creative teaching and learning in literacy and mathematics: A case study. *British Journal of Educational Technology, 39*(1), 84–96.

BECTA. (2003a). *ICT and pedagogy: A review of the research literature. National Grid for Learning Research & Evaluation Series, Report No. 19.* London: DfES/BECTA. Retrieved January 29, from http://www.becta.org.uk/resarch/reports

BECTA. (2003b). *What the research says about interactive whiteboards.* BECTA. Retrieved January 29, 2004, from http://www.becta.org.uk/research/reports

BECTA. (2004). *Getting the most from your interactive whiteboard: A guide for secondary schools.* Coventry, UK: BECTA.

BECTA. (2007). *Harnessing technology review 2007: Progress and impact of technology in education. Summary report.* Coventry, UK: BECTA. Retrieved February 11, 2008, from http://www.becta.org.uk/research/

Yin, R. (1994). *Case study research: Design and methods.* California, USA: Sage Publications.

Young, M. D. (1999). Multifocal educational policy research: Towards a method for enhancing traditional educational policy studies. *American Educational Research Journal, 36*(4), 677–714.

Zevenbergen, R., & Lerman, S. (2008). Learning environments using interactive whiteboards: New learning spaces or reproduction of old technologies? *Mathematics Education Research Journal, 20*(1), 108–126.

Ziolkowski, R. (2004). Interactive whiteboards: Impacting teaching and learning. *Media & Methods, 40*(4), 44.

Zittle, F. J. (2004). *Enhancing native American mathematics learning: The use of Smartboard-generated virtual manipulatives for conceptual understanding.* Retrieved October 8, 2007, from http://edcompass. smarttech.com/NR/rdonlyres/3E2A063B-6737-400F-BD07-1D239C428729/0/Zittle.pdf

About the Contributors

Michael Thomas is Professor of English Language at Nagoya University of Commerce & Business in Japan. His research interests are in the philosophy of language, ICT and education, and TESOL. He is author of *The Reception of Derrida: Translation and Transformation* (2006), editor of *Handbook of Research on Web 2.0 and Second Language Learning* (2009) and *Web 2.0 and Education: Applying the New Digital Literacies* (forthcoming), and co-editor of *Interactive Whiteboards for Education: Theory, Research and Practice* (2010) and *Task-Based Language Teaching and Technology* (in press). He is editor of the *International Journal of Virtual and Personal Learning Environments* and organizer of an international symposium series on digital technologies and language education (http://wirelessready. nucba.ac.jp).

Euline Cutrim Schmid is an Assistant Professor of English and Applied Linguistics at the University of Education (Pädagogische Hochschule) Heidelberg in Germany. She teaches at undergraduate and postgraduate levels on a variety of topics including: computer assisted language learning (CALL), applied linguistics, and qualitative research methodologies. She is a CALL researcher and her recent academic publications have focused mainly on the use of IWB technology and learner response systems in the English language teaching context. She has a PhD in Linguistics from Lancaster University, UK. Her doctoral research, concluded in 2005, focused on the use of interactive whiteboard technology for the teaching of English as a Foreign Language (EFL). She is the author of *Interactive Whiteboard Technology in the Language Classroom: Exploring New Pedagogical Opportunities* (2009). Her current research investigates English teachers' pedagogical needs and developmental paths, as they integrate IWB technology into the language curriculum.

* * *

Diana Bannister is the Development Director for Learning Technologies at the Midlands Leadership Centre, University of Wolverhampton, UK. Her work in the application of new technologies has placed her at the forefront of current thinking in this area. Diana has worked on two major national projects across the UK and several projects based locally within the West Midlands looking specifically at the use of interactive whiteboards. Prior to leading the REVEAL project (Review and Evaluation of Electronic Voting and its uses within Assessment and Learning) discussed within her chapter, Diana gave substantial input to the University of Hull on the REVIEW Project – REVIEW and Evaluation of Interactive Electronic Whiteboards funded by NESTA, UK. This led to the development of the CD – *The Good Guide to Interactive Whiteboards.*

Stephen Bax holds the post of Reader in the Centre for Research in English Language Learning and Assessment (CRELLA) at the University of Bedfordshire in the United Kingdom, where his research mainly concerns the role of technology in language education, evaluation and assessment, Computer Mediated Discourse Analysis and the analysis of discourse in its social context. His publications encompass research and development in discourse, technology, online education, international education, methodology, teacher development and related areas. He has been invited as plenary speaker to present his research at WorldCALL 2008, English Australia and other major conferences around the world. He has previously worked in Canterbury, Edinburgh and extensively in the Middle East, Latin America and in other settings overseas.

Barbara Bettsworth has been teaching Modern Foreign Languages in UK secondary schools for 18 years, and is currently teaching at Lancaster Girls' Grammar School. She studied French and German at Pembroke College, University of Oxford, and subsequently completed a PGCE at St Martin's College, Lancaster. She has been involved in several European projects and has research interests in European-wide approaches to innovative language teaching. She has developed a keen interest in ICT and frequently delivers training on its use in the classroom. Barbara has had practical experience with the IWB for the past eight years and is particularly enthusiastic about the impact of this technology on pupil motivation and retention of language.

Julie Cogill was awarded the degree of Doctor in Education at King's College, London, for her thesis on pedagogy and interactive whiteboard practice in primary schools in 2008. She initially taught mathematics at a sixth form college and comprehensive schools and latterly became an Assistant Head Teacher. On leaving teaching she was Chief Education Officer for the BBC for 12 years which involved working with TV, radio and online producers on educational programs. Since leaving the BBC she has undertaken consultancy work for many UK government organizations, authored ICT resources for commercial software companies and written several books for teachers to accompany software resources. Julie Cogill has a first class honors degree in mathematics, and an MA in mathematics education focused on problem solving. She is chair of the publications committee for the College of Teachers UK which publishes *Education Today*.

Doris De Almeida Soares has taught English as a Foreign Language in a variety of contexts in Rio de Janeiro, Brazil, for 22 years. From 1991 to 2007, she worked at a renowned English language school as a teacher, teacher trainer, materials designer and consultant. She also developed blogging and podcasting projects using IWB technology with her students. Currently, she is Assistant Professor of English at the Brazilian Naval Academy and a tutor / materials designer in an online English course in the Navy. She holds an MA in Applied Linguistics and a Cambridge RSA COTE. She is also a PhD student in Language Studies at the Pontifical Catholic University of Rio de Janeiro. Her research interests include teaching and learning English for Academic Purposes, teacher training, technology and education and distance learning.

Rosemary Deaney is a Senior Teaching Associate and Research Associate in the Faculty of Education at the University of Cambridge, UK. She has a background in teaching across a wide range of educational settings and was head of an ICT department within the school sector before taking up a research post at Cambridge in 2001. Since then she has been involved in several major funded projects focusing on practitioners' pedagogical use of ICT in secondary school subject areas, mainly science and mathematics. She teaches research methods at master's level, and supervises teachers who are researching their own practice through degree study. Her research interests also include teachers' professional learning and development, particularly within early career years.

Derek Glover was for 20 years head of a large secondary school in Oxfordshire, UK, before moving into higher education and becoming involved in initial teacher training and leadership development. He became a member of the IWB research group at Keele University and has worked charting the introduction of the technology into English secondary schools and their impact on pedagogy. He has published several texts on leadership and over 50 research articles on schools and continues to be associated with research at Keele and Warwick Universities as well as the London Institute of Education.

Carol Gray is Senior Lecturer in Education in the field of Modern Foreign Languages at the University of Birmingham, UK. She teaches mainly on programs of Initial Teacher Education, leading to publications on the themes of mentoring and on teaching tacit knowledge and decision-making. The use of information and communications technology in the languages classroom has been an ongoing theme in her work and publications since 1996 with the beginnings of government directives for trainee and newly qualified teachers. Further publications reflect an interest in equal opportunity in language learning for pupils with special educational needs developed during a career as a language teacher in the compulsory secondary education sector, part of which was spent teaching in a school for pupils with visual impairment.

Maureen Haldane is a Senior Learning and Teaching Fellow at Manchester Metropolitan University and Director of the University's IWB Centre of Excellence which supports IWB research projects across the university. She has been engaged in IWB research since 1997 when she began a 2-year investigation into the impact of IWBs on early-adopter teachers. She was a key member of the research teams that undertook two nationally significant IWB evaluation projects funded by the Scottish Executive (2004) and the Department for Children Schools and Families (2004-2007). Maureen's doctoral research is focused on emerging IWB pedagogies and communities of practice.

Sara Hennessy is a Lecturer in Teacher Development and Pedagogical Innovation in the Faculty of Education at the University of Cambridge, UK. She has a background in Psychology and extensive experience of research into subject teaching and learning using technology, particularly in mathematics and science in secondary schools. Her current work focuses on understanding and developing pedagogy and working collaboratively with teachers. She directed the T-MEDIA project (Teacher Mediation of Subject Learning with ICT: A Multimedia Approach, 2005-2007). She has recently explored the potential of the interactive whiteboard to support classroom learning through dialogue. Sara has taught research methodology at postgraduate level for over a decade and currently teaches on a new distance, blended learning MEd course in Science Education. Before she joined the Faculty at Cambridge in 1999 she worked for the Open University doing research and teaching.

Steven Higgins is Professor of Education at Durham University, UK. Before working in higher education he taught in primary schools in the North East where his interest in children's thinking and learning developed. His research interests lie mainly within the areas of effective use of ICT in schools, understanding how children's thinking and reasoning develops, and how teachers can be supported in developing teaching and learning in their classrooms. He has conducted research into effective pedagogy and ICT for the UK's Teacher Training Agency and the role of technology in personalizing learning for Becta. He was selected by the British Education Research Association to write a review about the impact of ICT on learning and teaching for their series of Professional User Reviews. He is currently investigating the use of multi-touch computer interfaces to support collaboration and interaction in classrooms.

Andrew Hutchinson is an experienced teacher and adviser to schools and specializes in applications of new technologies to support teaching and learning. He works directly with many practitioners implementing the effective use of interactive whiteboards and learner response systems. Andrew undertook the role of REVEAL Project Manager and was responsible for the management and operation of all aspects of the project on a day-to-day basis.

Carey Jewitt is a Reader in Education and Technology and Deputy Director at the London Knowledge Lab, Institute of Education, in the University of London. Her research investigates the relationships between representation, technologies and teaching and learning as well as visual and multimodal research methods and theory. She is a founding editor of the journal *Visual Communication*. Her publications include *The Routledge Handbook of Multimodal Analysis* (2009), *Technology, Literacy, Learning: A Multimodality Approach* (2006), *English in Urban Classrooms* (2005), *Multimodal Literacy* (2003) and *A Handbook of Visual Analysis* (2001).

Miriam Judge is a Lecturer in Multimedia in the School of Communications at Dublin City University (DCU), Ireland. Having been awarded a Government of Ireland Scholar Award in 2001 to complete her PhD on ICT in Education, she has since managed a number of research and evaluation projects in this field on behalf of the National Centre for Technology in Education, the Department of Education and Science and IBM Ireland. These include the Wired for Learning Project (2001/2003), the Dundalk Learning Network (2004) and the Hermes Project (2004-2009), a longitudinal study assessing the pedagogical impact of the installation of a thin client broadband wireless network on a cluster of nine North Dublin schools.

Annette Kratcoski is a researcher in the Research Center for Educational Technology at Kent State University in the United States. Her research examines the effect of various technologies on the authenticity and complexity of student work. She also coordinates evaluations of various state and national technology initiatives and is involved in a teacher mentoring project.

Brenda Lim-Fong is a classroom teacher and has had experience teaching at both the elementary and middle school levels. She is particularly passionate about science education, technology and teaching pedagogy. She is working towards her Masters of Education at the University of British Columbia in Canada and is interested in the unique context of the Livingstone Inquiry Group and its community of elementary teachers that have identified the educational potential of interactive whiteboard technology. Her research project involves investigating the ways teachers make sense of their beliefs, attitudes and practices as a result of the introduction of the interactive whiteboard in the elementary classroom.

Dave Miller is a Senior Lecturer in the School of Public Policy and Professional Practice at Keele University, UK. He has led the Keele University interactive whiteboard research team for the last ten years and successfully produced reports for many UK government agencies including Becta, the National Centre for Excellence in the Teaching of Mathematics, Secondary National Strategies and the Training and Development Agency. He has also undertaken research for the Nuffield Foundation. The research reports and other publications are listed at: http://www.keele.ac.uk/depts/ed/iaw/. He regularly speaks at international events about his research and his innovative mathematics materials for use with interactive whiteboard technology in secondary schools. In addition he delivers professional development sessions in schools and for regional bodies, nationally and internationally. Many of his resources can be found at http://www.iwbmaths.co.uk.

Gemma Moss is a Reader in Education at the Institute of Education, University of London and Director of the Centre for Critical Education Policy Studies. She has written extensively on gender and literacy, children's informal literacy practices, and literacy as a social practice. She has recently completed an ESRC-funded research project on the evolution of literacy policy in England. Her most recent book is *Literacy and Gender: Researching Texts, Contexts and Readers* (2007).

Rebecca Robins is a resource teacher, working with students who have language and academic challenges in Vancouver, Canada. She is interested in a critical literacy curriculum and uses her IWB to design digital units that explore sophisticated topics in a way that her struggling students can access the information. The Interactive Whiteboard Inquiry Project has supported her exploration of how to add multimodal layers to her units such as visuals, auditory components, video clips and student-centered activities. She has recently graduated from the University of British Columbia with a Masters of Education in Language and Literacy.

Byron Russell is the Director of Woodstock Publishing Partnership Ltd. (WPP), a consultancy specializing in providing business development and editorial services for educational publishers. WPP specializes in working with companies involved in the creation of language learning materials. Byron is also a co-director of Eazyspeak Ltd., an educational software company, and Pete Sharma Associates, a teacher training organization providing ICT training for practicing teachers. Byron has over twenty-five years experience in international educational publishing, having held senior management posts in companies such as Pearson and Berlitz before establishing WPP in 2001.

Helen Sargeant was Lead Researcher in the REVEAL Team at the University of Wolverhampton in the UK. Helen has experience in project management, marketing and research and dissemination in both commercial environments and the education sector. Her research projects have focused on a wide range of age phases, initiatives and curriculum areas including qualification comparison, impact of e-learning initiatives and technology, motivation and attitudes to language learning.

Jason Schenker is an Assistant Professor in the Department of Evaluation and Measurement in the College of Education, Health and Human Services at Kent State University in the United States.

Estelle Schimmack is a qualified primary school teacher of English and History. She has an MA in Teaching English as a Foreign Language (TEFL) from the University of Education (Pädagogische Hochschule) Heidelberg, Germany. Her MA dissertation, concluded in 2008, focused on the design of interactive whiteboard training for language teachers. She currently teaches English as a Foreign Language (EFL) at a primary school in Berlin. She is particularly interested in the role of new technologies in language learning at primary school level and plans to undertake action research investigating the potential of IWB technology in the language teaching context.

Karen Swan is the James J. Stukel Distinguished Professor of Educational Leadership at the University of Illinois at Springfield. She has published and presented nationally and internationally on educational technology issues for 25 years. Her current research focuses on online learning and teaching and learning in ubiquitous computing environments.

Chris Tooley has been Deputy Principal at Bottisham Village College in Cambridge, UK, since September 2005. One of his key areas of interest is the use of ICT to enhance teaching and learning across the curriculum. He worked as an Advanced Skills Teacher from 1999-2005, as well as being a Lead Science Teacher for Cambridgeshire during which time he received a commendation in the Innovation category of the National Teaching Awards. Prior to this Chris taught for 15 years at Soham Village College and was central to the introduction of the use of ICT across the curriculum. He also has a particular interest in the development of pedagogy through practitioner research and the development of a knowledge creating school.

Alison Twiner is a research student in the Centre of Research in Education and Educational Technology at the Open University, UK. Her particular research interests focus on teachers' and pupils' uses and understandings of interactive educational technologies, when used alongside other classroom resources. Her current work addresses classroom dialogues, interactions and perceptions around interactive whiteboards and other tool use in English schools.

Mark Van 't Hooft is a researcher and technology specialist in the Research Center for Educational Technology at Kent State University in the United States. His research interests include teaching and learning in mobile and ubiquitous computing environments and data literacy. Mark is a co-founder and current chair of ISTE's Special Interest Group for Handheld Computing (SIGHC).

Index

A

active learning 102, 113, 147
activity theory 127
ad hoc basis 194
adoption 20, 21, 22
Advanced Skills Teacher (AST) 119
analysis of variance (ANOVA) 134

B

BECTA 71, 73, 74, 81, 82, 83
Broadband access 70

C

CALL practitioners 199
CBI project 250
CD-ROM 54, 62, 73
CD-ROM storage 54
Celtic Tiger economy 251
City Learning Centre 80
classroom pedagogy 58
co-construction 44, 45
Cognitive Acceleration in Mathematics Education course (CAME) 125
cognitive development 7, 9
cognitive interaction 170, 175
cognitive learning theory 44
cognitive load theory 45
collaborative classrooms 119
collaborative enquiry 120
collaborative projects 238, 239, 247
commercial content 54, 63
commercially-developed resources 47
complex LRS software 157

Computer Assisted Language Learning 197

Computer Assisted Language Learning 197
Content and Curriculum Knowledge (CCK) 169, 171, 174, 176
Content Knowledge (CK) 162, 163, 164, 165, 168, 171, 172, 176
Continuing Professional Development (CPD) 180
Continuing Professional Development (CPD) provision 180
CPD activity 180
Curriculum Knowledge 162, 163, 164, 166, 168, 169, 171, 174, 175, 176

D

datalogger 43
Department for Children, Schools and Families (DCSF) 70
Department for Education and Employment (DfEE) 69
Department for Education and Skills (DfES) 69, 93
Descriptive data 88
desk activities 124
digital age 55
digital content 54, 57
digitally-recorded 179
digital microscope 104
digital natives 54, 63
digital pen 253
digital publishers 54
digital resources 102, 103, 113
digital technologies 132, 142
digital video recordings 102